COLLECTED POEMS
1996-2010

PETER CHELNIK - HEY GIRL - COLLECTED POEMS

PETER CHELNIK

HEY GIRL

COLLECTED POEMS

1996-2010

LITTLE SKY PRESS

Typeset by
Denise Blatt, Owner
Denni's Typesetting Studio

Library of Congress 2015957663
© Copyright 2015
ISBN: 978-0-692-03157-5

For
My Great
Mom and Dad

———

My Super Nephew
Charles Chelnik

———

A Great Friend
Laura Boss

———

Bob Feldman
A Go Cat Go
Saxophone Jazz
Poetry Mentor

PETER CHELNIK - HEY GIRL - COLLECTED POEMS

Contents

I. EAST COAST LINE *(1994-1998)*

Hey Girl	3
The Bronx and Beyond	5
Schizophrenia	6
Independence Day	7
Party	8
Nowhere	9
Don't Need It	10
Providencetown 1982	11
Thanks Joan	12
Heat Wave	13
Fear	14
Red Hair	15
Solitary Days	16
Overdrive Thoughts	17
Flood Tides	18
Hey Sister	19
Humidity Drops	20
Summer Light	21
Have Mercy	22
Hyacinth Garden	23
Big River	24
Shinnacock Point	26
Hen House Poets	27
Comfortable Victorian Sofa	28
July Rain	29
2 A.M.	30
Words	31
No Cowgirls Around Here	32
Blues Time	33
Revolution Days	34
Miracle Day	35
Manhattan Saturday Night	36
Grace	37
Colorado	38
Abandoned Beatnik Self	39
New York Jive	40
Supreme Court Justice	41
When Will It End?	42

CONTENTS

Demons	43
Uptown	44
Friday Night	45
Byzantine Confusion	46
Kindergarten Diploma	47
This Thing Called Romance	48
Somalia	49
East Coast Line	50

II WILD FLOWER SERENADE *(1997-2003)*

Express Yourself	55
I Smile Hello	57
Wildflower Serenade	59
Celebrate	61
Gender Train	63
Chickens Come Home to Roost	65
No to Apocalypse	67
Two Hearts	69
Magic Heart Tribe	71
No Open Exit	73
Freedom Time	75
Brats	77
Rise and Shine	79
Allen Ginsberg Dies Tonight	81
All is Well	83
I'm Dying	85
Yes New Jersey You Call to Me	87
We Wait for Spring	89
Groove	91
Joe Goes Violent	93
I Dream	95

III HOPSCOTCH HOME *(2002)*

Tell Your Story	99
Blue Moon Magic	101
American Manchild	103
Let It Flow	105
Barn Raise Sanctity	107

CONTENTS

Resurrection Monday Morning	108
Let Freedom Ring	110
Poets Will Soar	113
Straight Line Highway	115
Homespun 2002	117
Stay Hungry	118
Pedal Steel Guitar	120
No Bad Vibes	122
New Jerusalem	124
Stand and Fight	126
Bald Eagle Flies	128
Stop The Bombing Yugoslavia	130
Sing Mockingbird	134
Liberty Highway	136
July Heat Wave	138
Common Sense	140
L.A. You Call Me	142
Woodshed Blues	144
Unplug Daddy-O	146
Gregory Corso Dies Brother	148
Deal	151
Empower Yourself	152
Sweet Devotion	154
Hopscotch Home	156

IV PARADISE HIGHWAY *(2006)*

Rhapsody America	161
Earth Turn	163
Bohemian Howl	165
Break Out	167
Soft Machine	169
Whole Grain Resurrection	171
Spring Break Dogwoods	173
Saturday Rain	175
Howl Friday Afternoon	177
Buckshot Renegade	179
May Lilacs Supreme	181

CONTENTS

Horizon State Line	183
21st Century Excellence	185
Flag Day	188
2005 Move Forward	191
Big Country Poetics	193
Denim Joy	195
Paradise Highway	198
Spirit Dance	200
Have Mercy	202
Blueberry Providence	204
Promised Land Express	206
Checkercloth Transformation	208
Full Moon Aquarius	209
September Epiphany	211
Tapestry Weave	213
Good to Go	215
Pick Up Sticks Wednesday	217
August Dog Days	219
Summer End Game	221
Celestial Dreams	223
Hardscrabble Opportunity	225
Heart America	227
Hope Eternal	230
Freight Train Autumn	232
Workboot Excellence	234
Righteous Night Glide	236
Angel On Shoulder	238
Home Grown Dreams	240
Quicksilver Delight	242
Go Cat Go	244
Let Go Let God	246
Mojo Rising	248
Thanksgiving Grace	250
Rainbow Providence	253
Karmic Keeping On	255
Pork Pie Hat	257
Paisley Joy	259

CONTENTS

Crescent Moon Magic	261
Apple Pie Serenity	263
A Winter's Tale	265

V ETERNITY ROAD *(1996-1998)*

I've Had Enough	269
Nightride Texas Interstate	271
Combine Children	272
You Ever	275
No Buy In	277
American Angels	279
End of Depression	281
Sleepy-Eye Morning	282
Four Days into January	283
Money Boys	284
Spring Pain	286
Stillness of Pink Ballerina	287
MTV Media Dream in Skull	290
Revolution of Spirit	291
2 AM Saturday Night Hold Up	293
Woodstock 94	295
Lover	297
Sanctuary 1970	298
Mad Poets	300
Christmas 1994	301
New Years Rocket	302
Corporate Culture	304
Iron Agenda	305
River Raft	306
Liberation Europe	307
Bad Cards	309
Blew Off	310
Talk to Me Lord	311
Indecision of Brisk Season	313
Noose	314
Spirit Beatitude	315
Highway Spirit	316

CONTENTS

Yahweh	317
November 17	318
Therapy	319
Borderline Personality	320
Thanksgiving Always	321
Bravado	323
Now	324
Night Vortex	326
Youth Wonder	327
April	328
Village Magic	329
Plume Tribe	330
Road Partner	331
Where Are You Girl?	332
Strung Out	333
Battle of Soho	334
Hungry Women	335
On the Table	336
January 23rd	337
Revolution 24	338
Prairie Delight	339
I Sleep into Twilight	340
Homeward Bound	341
Eternity Road	342

VI SPRINGTIME AMERICA *(2000-2003)*

One Day At A Time	345
Fire On The Lake	347
Thousand Comebacks	349
Springtime America	351
Renegade	353
Tell It	354
Calico Changes	356
We're Better	358
Liberty Train	360
Wildflower America	362
High Tech Auch Tung	363

CONTENTS

Catch A Wave	365
Poem Electric	366
Shoot The Moon	367
My Country	369
Open Chalk Circle	371
Soul Transcendence	373
Fifty With Love	375
Mentor Now	377
Come Around Mama	379
Moscow Sky	380
2 A.M. Delight	382
High and Dry	383
Sing	384

VII CINNAMON REBIRTH (2004)

Kite On String	389
18 Wheel Semi Salvation	390
Gospel Train	392
Lean On Me	394
Roll On	396
Bebop August	398
Whole Grain 2004	400
Ticket To Ride	402
Creative Revolution	404
Crosstown Covenant	406
Wildcat Independence Day	408
Real Deal	410
Spiderweb Fog	412
Heartache	414
Pan Fry Love	416
Praise God	418
Dead Souls	420
Oak Wood Dignity	422
Coolsville	424
Silk Glide	426
Babylon Tuesday Morning	428
Cinnamon Rebirth	430

CONTENTS

VIII MILLENNIUM WEAVE *(1998-2002)*

Highway Time	434
Stand Tall	436
Have Faith	438
Catch as Catch Can	440
I Call to You America	442
Time to Heal	444
Open Road	446
God Set Met Free	448
Fly Away	450
Embrace 1	452
My Ship Comes In	454
Can It	456
Blessed	458
East Coast Underground	460
Nation Building	462
Too Early in Morning	464
Pinewood Sanctity	466
Oh Big River	468
Gabriel Blow Your Horn	470
Embrace 2	472
Free	474
Millennium Weave	476
Rooster Crows	478
Straight Shooter	479
Write a Poem	481
Take My Heart Poems	483
Revolutionary Kindness	485
Breezin'	487
Stride Piano	489
American Genius	491
Cut the Pie	493
America Call My Name	495
Do Something Do Anything	498
God Sanctify Soul	500
Wilderness Seekers	502
Long Way Home	504

CONTENTS

Parking Lot Satori	506
Home Grown New York City Poet	508
Laura Boss's Heart	510
Fever Time	512
Sometimes	514
We Are Born	516
Rev Up	518
Flannel Warriors	520
October Cool	522

IX RIDGELINE ETHICS (2007)

Halloween Trick Treat	527
Willow Weep Eros	529
Spirit Humble Pie	531
Chevrolet Dreams	533
Blue Ridge Crossroads	535
Holy Sabbath Lights	537
Heaven's Gate	539
Taurus Sun Glory	541
Cherry Pie Creative Revolution	543
Ridgeline Ethics	545
Satisfied Mind	547
Optimism	549
Hope Eternal	551
Holy Redemption	553
Shining Star	555
Chick Pea Notions	557
Patchwork Quilt Emotions	559
Peace of Mind	561
Flat Out Smooth	564
Travel South	566
Caramel Compassion	568
Woodstock Field	571
Hog Heaven	573
New Beginning	575
February Rain Freeze	577
Friday Sunshine	579

CONTENTS

Daybreak Express	581
Wilderness Redemption	583
Riverrun Wednesday	585

X SLOW RAMBLE *(2008)*

Jack Kerouac Highway Genius	589
Oakwood Democracy	591
Scarsdale High Excellence 1967	593
Harvest Home	596
Corduroy Faith	598
Honey Bee Commotion	600
Night Song Heart	602
Sleeve Roll Aesthetics	604
Gravy Train	606
New Years Rialto	609
Boy Scout Compass	611
Wind at Back Groove	613
Marmalade Tuesday	615
Slow Ramble	617
Needlepoint Joy	619
New Morning	621
Saturday Night Clean and Sober	623
Cash and Carry Aesthetics	625
Glory Promise Land	627
Heart Glow	629
Pecan Pie Poetics	631
Spring Time Glory	633
God's Old Testament Miracles	635
Flash Flood Saturday	637
Glory Train Consciousness	639
Apple Pie Liberty	641
Onion Peel Friday	643
Home Run Jubilee	645
Strawberry Happy	647
Creativity August 1st	649
Soy Bean Futures	651

CONTENTS

XI STRAWBERRY HARMONY (2010)

Joy to the World	655
Winter Solstice	657
Flannel Prayers	659
Candy Cane December Dawn	661
Sassafras New Year	663
Thursday Morning Create	665
Flat Out Heart	667
Camomile Tea Tuesday Night	669
Flannel Peace of Mind	671
Full Moon Women	673
Sweet Sunshine	675
Early Spring Celebrate	677
Saturday Morning Pancakes	679
Prairie Love	681
Iced Green Tea Ecstacy	683
Feeling Good	685
May Wonderland	687
Strawberry Harmony	689
Home Run Crack	691
Always Upbeat	693
Kaleidoscope Wonder	695
Wednesday Morning Sunshine	697
Midnight Sidewalk Grace	699
Friday Night Straight and Narrow	701
Kentucky Yarn Cats Cradle	703
August Joy	705
Red Rose Poetics	707
Green Valley Harmony	709
Found Penny Good Luck	711
Word Harvest	713
New Jerusalem Love	715
Ten Commandment Rock Steady	717
Wilderness Faith	719
Apple Pick Jubilee	721
October Sky Create	723
Pumpkin Pie Notions	725

PETER CHELNIK - HEY GIRL - COLLECTED POEMS

I
EAST
COAST LINE
1996

PETER CHELNIK - HEY GIRL - COLLECTED POEMS

Hey Girl

Hey Girl
Annie Oakley baby boom cowgirl sister
yes to single moms full fridge
Bronx Science high school kids warm hearth
third floor walk up.
Yes to Macy's Thanksgiving Day sale's savvy
Key Food's coupons cheshire love
like Vermont Maple syrup pancakes.
Hey Girl
Bring on magnolia heart
baker's dozen lover
like April Arkansas pasture spring planting
Central Park Bethesda Fountain tulips
sassy Cornelia Street hip sway.
Hey Girl
Green cash independence
like MG roadster mint condition
rock steady career like Darien, Connecticut oak
401K social security down Chicago
railroad line.
Hey Girl
Quest Provence, France August sabbatical like
stretch canvas vagabond passion 1971.
Renew D.H. Lawrence earth hold creativity
touch Taos, New Mexico sky again and again.
Hey Girl
Jack Daniels Texas two step pregnancy 1977.
Female warrior morning Lamaze class
Astor Place tribal rights
8 year old daughter's softball knee scrape tears.
Hey Girl
No to dead beat walk out door men
no to cocaine disciple milquetoast PhDs.
Sisters embrace sweet zen satori
born again Christian heartland ethics
embrace honest flannel shirt love.
Sisters moon lodge heart like Puget Sound
high tide.
Hey Girl
Good men rare like hens teeth
59,000 guys oh Vietnam Memorial Wall

ten thousand Federal Prison
ebony Black men on shelf
walking wounded dudes surface like dandelions
highway crabgrass.
Bring on Pilgrimage to elegant Paris, Berlin,
goat dance Mikonos
male soul mate cherry wood quest.
Always mascara eye out
like top Los Angeles Dodger
major league scout.
Hey Girl
Embrace first Chevrolet kiss
tassel Weegen crush.
Hey Girl
Pinewood woman
I honor gingham courage
fierce mama lion jungle valor
Ann Arbor hopscotch 1980's me decade wounds
a thousand field hockey heroics
Hyannis Massachusetts salt tears.
Bring on February afternoon caress
warm Pennyslvania Quaker quilt whispers
tooth smile rainbow salvation
the road is always yours.

The Bronx and Beyond

Good folks up against
cellophane walls,
mirror LSD distort
Lenox Hill Hospital blood,
red sirloin meat scraps
the Bronx and beyond.
Black crows crash into
Miami Beach white gown high rises,
sun balances
on high wire horizon
the Bronx and beyond.
Two days July fourth
hearts explode
chemicals from
Elizabeth warehouse,
homemade Molotov cocktail.
Chase Bank heist iron submachine guns
wildcats dis media reality
like red clay Nebraska prairie.
the Bronx and beyond,
heat on red neck shoulder slope
downtown park,
wooden chess board commotion
the Bronx and beyond
abandon silk queen beyond
Central Park cut grass, frisbees scarce
fall out of fashion.
One mad cyclist battles
Riverside Drive green artery
Manhattan firecracker limbo
the Bronx and beyond.

Schizophernia

Schizophrenia, long
opaque tunnel
flash demon illumination
like July spider web
demon.
Old Hank Williams cowboy song --
faint F.M. radio frequency.
Schizophrenia.
Quicksilver madness. Dearth of silver trout
alog Neversink Rapids,
schizophrenia
tunnel with a 1000
delicate offshoots
sugar coat brain
synapse, bare knuckle on blackboard
liberation promise, prolonged portage --
schizophrenia, no Rand McNally map --
no roadside watermelon.
No six of Coors in riverbank chill,
no fire hair woman
to pitch canvas tent, leather river comrades.
Schizophrenia.
Odd sneakers line labyrinth shard clothing
surely rodents
equations carried
beyond the power of million.
No pencil in hand.

Independence Day

Independence day
Christ cries like infant --
tears of Johanna,
Santa Cruz menstrual blood.
Too many years
on San Francisco Bay,
granite West Coast rock
America's Independence Day.
Trim sail to leeward,
Renegade guest, tiresome
task for Homeric sailor,
struggle to reclaim
American heart
left handed grab hot biscuits.
Hands like circus freak,
Independence Day
Charlie Parker resonance
patriotic bunting, t-bone steak crescendo
need for cool
I wait for cool Atlantic seabreeze,
nylons on wicker rocker
Independence Day
Bensonhurst straight line parade
six of Coors
I wait for Ft. Hamilton gulls
transcendence's b flat curve.
I cry for son
I never had, for Cheshire
lady beyond fierce Rockies
Independence Day,
quarter tone demon, hand cuff crucifixion.
No promised land cheshire homecoming.

Party

Hey dudes time to party
unravel cellophane noose
put down mythic Jack Daniels
shoot hard for purple sky.
Hey dudettes, drop
Buckingham Palace guard,
place mountain garb on
tough body move out
to crystalline river.
Party time East Coast Line --
Hell we've been manhandling spirit
no reckless iron plow
over Montpelier field,
no psychotic jailhouse coffee jags
stone and pinewood
termite decay.
Party --
time to talk glorious green metaphor
revolution Miles Davis trumpet cool
gingham poetic revolution
Ohio River future --
summer morning perky
carrion fudge Sunday delight.
Party,
break it down, no stiff poses,
canine snarls, I'll keep
in fore deck blues, under
ensign's care.
Party, fire prophecy begins
waters recede like last pitch Yankee Stadium
celebrate our string bass genius essence,
appaloosa heart --
it's about time.

Nowhere

Sneaker people, going nowhere
myriad broken circles,
pieces of egg shell sky
Manhattan turf.
Nowhere people wallow in desolate
Surf City anger, loaded firearm,
hallucinogen short circuit
Nowhere,
too downtown hip for therapy,
12 step cheshire heal
demons, night fears like hemp noose
granola perceptions, insights
twisted like cold Brooklyn corpse
Nowhere.
People too cool
to admit Byzantie computer scramble egg obsession
admit on rose bush thorn
Nebraska field divide.
Nowhere.
Absolut bottle, gold hashish
pipe, train on sleep grade stall
move from cold water ditch
Hollywood fun house dream
people St. Mark's Place D.T.'s,
poverty mud youth vision.
Nowhere people year after rave year
excuses for Santa Fe freight train
clamshell mom and dad hate
Harlem addiction,
Maoist politically correct promises,
Keep nowhere digital anger, polyester suit
university insights
Sesame Street hard drive
skateboard torture rack
embrace October midway.

Don't Need It

Christ beat up highway self
like Mohammed Ali sparring
partner, been drunk
by Turkish taffy shame over long asphalt
stretch of road.
Don't need it.
Take Kansas City snarls
hand soak Yorkshire lambs blood,
your scrawl, pennies
coated in cheap sealing
wax and leave like night vandal.
Don't need it,
I move like
Bermuda afternoon light,
clarity chosen over gin and tonic
self hate grind, cold water
downtown Miami heated sweat shop
Don't need it,
your cinematic audacity, teenage call girl
nerve not welcome
on sweet Kansas prairie,
on Chinese silk loom.
Don't need it.
Do not preach marijuana utopia
Virtual reality horizon slant
No drunked bouts with
Smirnoff and saltines --
don't need law court
gravel pit cross examination
female bonding across
flannel shoulders,
stale Wonder Bread loaf
No upper crust Darien Connecticut
delusions
no stove pipe feminist round house rights
I move to green New Jerusalem
like grey pack mule
Don't flat out need it.

Provincetown 1982

I stride along Provincetown
Beach, dead end winter
freeze cold ice puddle, barnfire embers
stale bread diaspora.
Provincetown 1982.
blue jean days
distant like college maypole dream.
Empty rucksake lay
in Deborah's corner room, Old Rolling Stones,
grilled hot dogs, home made baked beans
narrow western wilderness
Northern Pacific diesel halt
Provincetown 1982 --
Joni Mitchell battles BMW cocaine yuppies
Remy shots fill crystal afternoons
Reagan presidency destroys
Santa Cruz calico dream
no roulette wheel hope
for us antique hipsters, mad oracle
winter Provincetown burnouts
even gays, madmen, guidos
vacate for balmier southern points.
Fire small like matchbook
this tiger cage decade
corporate electric shock
Promised land Israel salvation
Jerusalem bone dream fades like India ink
Provincetown 1982.

Thanks Joan

Joan stays with me,
ten day wildcat demon skid
I am Guernsey cow birthing,
salmon on Shanghai wood dock
cactus criticism --
Tarot card hang man
check list Vietnam blood ambush.
Thanks Joan
Pittsfield easy glide love
Maple syrup resonance
fire crimson and south Berkshire County
Massachusetts cirrus sky dream.
Thanks Joan.
Demons like drunk out of state vagrants
crescent moon darkness, bare feet madness
blues beyond Vermont border.
Thanks Joan.
Pinewood shack four alarm commotion
Southern California brush fire
orbit beyond Burger King, Ivy League Harvard.
Thanks Joan.
Universe's darkness
defunct limestone quarry
velveteen warmth, Zen New England dawn serenity
Demon lift like Mass Pike
highway fumes.

Heat Wave

Heat wave kicks in
like DEA cops
smash down South Bronx
crack house door
cinnamon apple slow bake
heat drains fluids, tuna on rye
spirit out of tender body.
Heat wave,
blue collor hombres steel torture rack
old folks check out like
Westbury Hotel guests
babies bawl in psychotic freak out
no wild card sparrows
100 degree day slow motion celluloid
Heat wave.
Sky fixed image like Remington rifle scope
all along East Coast,
Biloxi southern slowdown.
Canada cool green mint winds
hover like
14th Street drag queen
Mekong Delta in blood carnage.
Heat wave.
Not ready for Broadway state entrance.
EMS howls like lone Wyoming coyote
hydrants emit symphony of
cool water quicksilver relief
Heat wave, no trick bag, no smoke and
mirror show
in New York City heat, tea kettle
on red boil, breath short like pancake stack
everywhere.
Chests heave in mud landslide cave in Aspen.
We wait for ace of diamond break.

Fear

Nighttime fear, around 11 p.m.,
night's black crook,
razor point by bed,
vial of lithium
today's Dewars bottle
measuring cup madness --
fear no end
to demon mule caravan
Binghamton poison letter
quarter tone John Cage maelstrom.
I sink into Manhattan tar pit
like red rubber ball in sewer grid
fear -- end Fellini parade now.
Bring on Arkansas razorback fight
gather mulch bucket
siphon ceiling crack hexagram
scramble Jersey eggs
hop next westbound train --
night dreams separate paper mache fear.

Red Hair

Joan Massachusetts phone call
move on moon splinter
hot damn lady dyes hair red,
carrot red fire like Yosemite
blaze.
Red hair a sensual Parisienne delight.
Heart beat pounds
like jack hammer
beyond Hudson, railroad grid.
Red hair -- love Joan up
hug bones
across Colorado continental divide --
run hand through palomino mane,
no academic nuances, minimal Hyannis sea breeze
messages in morse code
friendship across Robert Frost picket fence.
Red hair -- looking good
like striped bass
on end of line,
Missouri morning lake mist
motel room nuclear bom communiques,
prairie fire home town passion
Red hair -- yeah love you babe,
been long time coming
got that cowboy smile
Elko, Nevada hand on taut leather reins.

Solitary Days

Large Pacific heat wave iron pan fry
no erotic ommuniques
Bloomingdale's gift wrap marble heart
left shoulder diamond back rattler.
Solitary days.
It ain't happening with ladies
two half assed Amoco pitstops in 1980's,
gas up, tank full
more Nevada highway commotion
heat wave like opening
titles on French avant
garde film, closing time prix fix menu.
Solitary days.
Shop around for July chemise serenity
Eureka Springs broad shoulder blond bartender
firework on buttered bagel hold
soul mate search
needle in Kansas haystack
solitary days --
Manhattan Island
Condor on
Madison Avenue lamppost.

Overdrive Thoughts

Fast overdrive quicksilver thoughts
vintage Austin Healy
on straightaway burn
rubber, tire screech.
Overdrive thoughts.
Hard drive brackets
Texas highway dream
Austin to San Antonio
reckless wino commotion.
Overdrive thoughts.
Steeple chase speed -- 11 p.m.
humid night slingshot.
I break sagebrush sweat
like 14 year old Russian gymnast
pinball arcade frenzy.
Overdrive thoughts.
I harness cognitive thrust,
like lower forty Army mule
I brace in front
obese woman's diet dessert
of IBM, spastic tied to wheelchair
Corpus Christ tide on brow.
Overdrive thoughts.
Blackbirds vanish like Reagan jellybeans
bobsled thought hunkers down,
a senior wood study hall --
no insanity along D line,
no Kings County Hospital handcuffs.
Crazy glue -- paisley knee guards,
slow down overdrive
literary structure binds,
like tan corset.
I've turned threadbare terror
into poetry.

Flood Tides

Cornstate flood tides
Davenport straight
out to cobble Des Moines
like faucet jam on wood farmhouse
sink.
Flood tides.
Mississippi, Missouri, Des Moines
even Raccoon River --
a grand overlow, like July porcelain bathtub
hard times for
Buckeye wetland, no electricity
no hamburger meat, dry crisp clothes
overcast skies, demon wetback rain.
Flood tides.
A million acres of corn
soybean, gone like Denver bound
tourist.
No water, rows
and corn row wash out,
homes destroyed in mad blue water torrent.
Flood tides -- river becomes fur beast.
Des Moines' two bridges destroyed like
erector set.
Rock steady Route 80 shut down
like grain elevator,
barns, livestock, family wood farm houses
in ruin.
Flood tide God's sign
need for larger spirit devotion
faith beyond town hall
soon new season
to dry out heirlooms, lazy divans --
a new calio season
to resurrect John Deer tractor
corn plant in heartland faith,
a new beginning
beyond tragic waist
high water.

Hey Sister

Sister we will
make it, drive pinewood
soul and metal fendes
Chevy wagon
through needle's Grand Canyon eye
out to
Pacific Northwest Whitby Island.
Hey sister!
We will set spread for
day glo children, bushel
watch black crows
light out for blue ice Canada points north
yeah sister
take delicate silk wisdom
hands
walks down Cherokee crimson
path, autumn light --
bold medicine drum.
Hey sister, yeah we'll shake off snake coil
light
cigarette bask in
mythic white Key West bone light,
hey sister, place bodies
together like spices on
kitchen rack, note our
broad shoulder passion,
night laughter like mad jackels.
Hey sister, walk down road
soft shoe 2nd Avenue traffic motion,
promise land cinnamon scent,
beyond city limits oasis.

Humidity Drops

Humidity drops like
purple sky carrion
cartwheels now in
Great Lawn display
stews simmer,
napkin rings liberation
from wooden French chest.
Humidity drops,
lunch is served
Haute Cuisine fashion, garden outdoors
Shakespearean celebration
begins.
Humidity drops.
Children's laces furl
watershed small hands
no city grime,
no Hershey's chocolate melt.
Humidity drops.
Eternity school recess,
pink watermelon appear like small sparrow.
Mom's Passover seder recline.
Humidity drops
dice games draw linen sailors along Broadway
call girls place nylons on race horse legs
no taxi driver lilac wilt.
Humidity drops.
Hexagram erotic blue sky vibration
Central Park green garden renewal
a cheshire sabbath rabbi close to
redemption.

Summer Light

Provence summer light, cushion
mescaline, brown tab
jack rabbit to stars
stairways curve.
Summer light rapid
hand movement like
West Virginia coal mine yellow canary
with Auden clairty, concise
logic, 12 step purple serenity
summer light, child spins self
Scarsdale high grass
and sweet youth's library card ecstasy
yeah summer light,
watermelon dripping,
baseball bat Louisville sweet crack
whiffle ball delight.
Feather pillow July magic.
Summer light, youthful daydream,
milk, chocolate cookies
horizon sun skins silver dollar affirmation.
Always dawn's straight back faith.

Have Mercy

Have Mercy on down home hardscrabble
souls up against hard
adobe wall,
Tucumcri bone dry, cracked desert vowels
confused like aimless derelicts
earth no prophetic back road transverse.
Have mercy on overblown chiffon
fools, ballroom ego
bronze bain de soleil package
aimless bewitched
West Side fog.
Have mercy on sit com dudes
Smith and Wesson in hand
John Wayne tough strip steak ego --
crack pipe mini skirted Kool Aid seduction.
Have mercy on brutal folk like
tattersall preppie canines,
primal gift
tossed off
like Plains, Georgia peanut shells
Milky Way wrapper.
No pinewood chop,
no IBM Jack Kerouac typewriter glide.
Have mercy on souls
twisted in tabloid hate
like Kansas tornado
Witchita prairie apocalypse desolation.

Hyacinth Garden

God liberates spirit marvel
hard mythic ride,
Israeli crossroad
cut loaf, hot oven
bread for all divine souls.
Yeah fear knot twist
terror draught gone
the strip searches, car alarms
like madcap kite cut from string.
Move to Jerusalem
ham, eggs over time,
dance hora and celebrate desert stars,
Negev galaxy, sensual tribe delight.
Prophesy surfacs
on bold street corners, bazaars
Jews, Arabs and Christians
unity in bone spirit transcendance's cool breeze.
Sturdy olive tree grace.
2000 year rumble mosaic
ceases, like River Jordan carnage
no steel voices
no blood marks on Jerusalem sidewalks.
Abraham appears
like Eden Express, Jesus' humble sandal grace,
textured angelic illumination
world becomes hyacinth
garden, yes.

Big River

Oh Mississippi
big river runs wild,
mad brown mud fury --
flood takes fertile land and
soul of good
Midwest folk.
Big river.
Out in Indian Grave's Illinois
Levee, fight basic survival,
sanctified life, hold on,
toss another concrete sack
got to hold river rage.
Big river,
thousand sand bags
placed by hand,
rednecks, Midwest daughters,
stocky sheriff has
inmates help out.
On big river your brutl demon
force, got to hold one
more sand bag,
call for iron tractors
50 show up,
work, scoop nasty mud, levee wall build
Big river,
family farms at stake,
survival flat out
work all starless night on
levee, farmland tender link
go home mud caked
clothes detergent, metal washer
big river,
a night's restless damp sleep,
too much rain torrent
and then up again, like jackrabbit
pot of coffee and go --
attack inhuman mud river again, rising
levee of cheshire hope
hold back ungodly river.
Big river,

flood's frenzy
spook fear, Illinois fatigue --
more rain
cinnamon buns, break
catch wind --
big river, pile on more sandbags
American can do
American heartland,
and river raises like inch worm
looks bleak farmland destruction
big river too lunch bucket fierce --
next morning
rain pellets stop and levees hold. Amen.
Hosannah Hosannah
oh big river,
place your wide wrath elsewhere
than these small Illinois,
Iowa towns,
too much hands on terror in heartland --
spare good folk
from darkness and disaster,
turn of the screw.

Shinnacock Point

Whittle down Central Park stick,
perfect Shinnacock point --
go scramble four Jersey eggs --
got to have cholesterol
pump in cardio-vascular
cell block.
Shinnacock point, empty Hefty bag --
sour poems wastebasket cradle
carrot juicer shards -- cigarette butts,
T-bones scraps.
Shinncock point --
two blue tranquilizers in
Course riverbank threat.
spirit pipeline
carnival demon -- nighttime quiescence
quiet like breast feed infant
Shinnacock point,
Manhattan wilderness salvation
Nashville country music
mellows out Montana coyote
soul.
Shinnacock point.

Hen House Poets

Slap together peppermint
poems, bequeath gild frame
reputation to
hen house poets, madmen,
corduroy sycophants
yeah Poets place
SSI checks,
in velvet waistcoat
hen house poets,
passiion like faucet drip
no climb
Wisconsin oak tree,
no magic language craft weave
bloodless staccato poems.
Too much nip and tuck,
no highway big sky risks.
Hen house poets -- conformist
newsprint consciousness in
this singular poetry
quest. Pecking order
like bookie joint,
hen house poets.
Poetry no
junior high school
clique, Little League hierarchy
yes strive for fierce log cabin voice
more river again and again
no hen house politics
small time Ivy university payoff.

Comfortable Victorian Sofa

Crystalline vision focus
vibration smooth
like December ice,
no red felt rage,
no seedlings uproot --
comfortable Victorian sofa,
easy Virigina glide
full mulch tin,
honest American
quest --
comfortable Victorian sofa,
firm Kansas handshake
confidence brims over
like New Rochelle tilt wading pool
calibrated mind slow
like flood traffic
on Interstate 80,
scuplture heart
comfortable Victorian sofa,
love chakra opens
hydrants gush, children sing sweet Mozart
Cherry wood Amagansett beach house,
high tide silk grace
yes dream moves to
a texture reality, cotton candy notion
gull hovers on red horizon
magic silence
between cyprus grove, rideline
crystal Hudson River --
good summer day,
God's signs abound.

July Rain

July summer rain
silk splinters
velvet pin cushion
wet all day
ruby watermelon innards.
July rain.
Chill, sun
beneath hat brim horizon
catch night crawlers --
off to Howard Beach --
yeah Rain, cry on
tapered flannel shoulder,
Kettle of Fish Bar, ice coffee
a smoke,
July rain kaleidoscope
perfection,
Myrna's denim hip sway
behind oak bar.
July rain.
Shake off uban grizzles,
catcalls, green card blues
quarter Macintosh apple, rainbow feast
glass mirror innocence.
July rain.
Sensual breeze moves
throught Tudor paned bar window --
beatnik raps, decades distill
like hard cider
Jack Kerouac picture
hangs in view --
July rain, sort file cabinet
hallow highway search
round world quiescence.
silence in this green garden.

2 A.M.

Serpent coils around
metal oil stick,
few cars hurdle down
avenue, cat screams barb wire
definace,
ears muffle like cupcakes.
2 A.M.
Computer seizures,
Joni Mitchell
on cheap stereo,
Thoreau transcendence
purple American night --
2 A.M.
Tar paper mind like
tool and die shop,
Waterbury, Connecticut brick
factory.
2 A.M.
Poems shuffle along index
finger
refuse phone calls
like undercooked pork shop
I see vast Yosemite
wilderness move through highway
heart, revolution's typewriter
ribbon,
dream's round premise.
2 A.M.

Words

I embrace my words
with luncheonette wonder --
like hurricane
ocean foam,
cotton testament
to season miracle, green flesh,
glass bell jar
words Epson salt tub
dry red towel
late 20th century cheshire road text,
calligraphy like small inch worms
no chicken scratch,
no IBM red rust
I embrace through
catacombed mind,
layered hot ember language emotions
words --
quartered poems like crabapple,
hot blueberry pie
white paper stock, a gypsy dance.
Yes words are
Courvoisier, shooter
Golden Seal capsule
Ice coffee Manhattan reality,
loose stripe pajamas
singular comet,
maple tree fire glow.

No Cowgirls Around Here

Not enough cowgirls
around Jesse James
parts,
too many television
soft flesh day glo
jokesters, city slickers,
no cowgirls around here
no bandanna wrapped around
forehead, no southern drawl
no America maple syrup sisters
no cowgirls around here,
who talk of red clay range cadence.
No hearty Texas laughs,
no prairie bronze thighs,
no gentle rawhide hands
Oh cowgirls, you lovely calico breed
you who pass
over my city, south bound
who move to ho down,
chicken fried steak, Lone Star beer
small town cobble grace
Missouri show me integrity.
No cowgirls around here.
You do not appear in New York City
Greek coffee house,
local tenderloin bar --
Village hard edge
poetry reading
no rumor in Chelsea auto shop.
You board greyhound
out of city vortex
Savannah, Austin, Oklahoma City bound.
No cowgirls around here.
I see you leave city
like startled hand
on hot plate, gone.
No cowgirls around here.

Blues Time

New York blues time
smoke filled caverns
Jack Daniels ice click, Memphis
Gibson guitar wail
BB King calico resonance
tight blue jeans,
round buttoks,
like curve of Central Park
transverse.
Yeah it's blues time.
down and kickback Pall
Mall dirty
Chicago metal blues harmonica
angel dance country road
shuffle.
Blues time.
Urban hot wine celebration
Sonny Boy Williamson infinite
salvation, Muddy Waters
cut apple pie genius
Tennessee hot biscuits,
gravy
Quicksilver highway
delight,
midnight special
prairie deep blue
splendor.
Mississippi delta
hardscrabble delight.
Blues time.

Revolution Days

Revolution days
mythic future
in bold hand
whole cotto tapestry
golden youth --
Revolution days
VW micro bus day glo design
Aquarian sublime consciousness
California dream imagination,
Pachouli blonde woman, Indiana bred
create garden planet now
sweet Mississippi justice
end Vietnam blood carnage.
Revolution days,
hippie rides through marijuana
forest -- Christ
wondrous sequoia redwoods
highway hitchhike delight.
Revolution days,
crashpads like snug home
seize Black Panther time,
America's 1960's
children become
halcyon selfs
again and again.

Miracle Day

Psychos dance marenga,
children slurp tall Cokes --
conga reaches for
blue sky universe,
miracle day,
damn I'm happy today,
got Volvo roadster
hunker down, outside park's edge --
I purr like tabby cat,
no fur demos oak park bench
miracle day
no burnt flesh, -- no lithium vials
no cactus skin pricks
wilderness children's delight
square sandbox, red wheelbarrow
miracle day
calico eye, texture cirrus cloud
touch blue pail essence
I am cowboy poet
free poems, Tarot deck read
Jack Kerouac beatnik rap
Allen Ginsberg highway vision
wide apple pie slice
yellow rose sensual imagination.

Manhattan Saturday Night

Manhattan asphalt flatland
muscle Saturday night
bourgeois blood
bronze limbs.
Manhattan Saturday night,
Bensonhurst lamb's blood sacrifice
Hamptons upper crust dominoes
iron gates down.
Manhattan Saturday night,
short circuit computer tribe
whiskey ramble, Straight Avenue
spirit death
City weave gunshots
China white drug noose
Manhattan Saturday night
Apocalypse beast
middle class goose step --
greed strangles cheshire heart
hard steel sex in rented apartment.
Open purse cherry lipstick --
Manhattan badlands,
desolation kitty litter
night demon terror
86th Street killing fields.
Machine America learn
to rock and roll forget.

Grace

Sunday morning grace,
strawberry jam cadences,
Laura Nyro serene lyrics
child on trainer
wheel bike -- young father
follows like Cree Indian
Great Plains initiation rite.
Grace.
Sunday morning church
East River currents
spires scrape New York yellow sun
sky tame -- no rigid
dogma, no petty squabbles
no erotic power play
Sunday morning grace a glory train.
Across Texas sagebrush
hot coffee, two sugars
illusions scaled down
like Atlantic flounder
Sheepshead Bay
fishing boat catch
karmic wheel
turns, mothers stretch blue jean
limbs take
break from children
wet pampers.
Grace.
I wait for Kassoundra
aesthetic madness
fire glow,
like clean laundry fold
God's hot bagel hope.

Colorado

Colorado silver dollar
Aquarian full moon,
I move
on computer outback, beyond oil tank
narrow turnpike.
Cancerous stiletto town,
greed hi tech mirrors
Colorado
rail lines
points ten gallon hat west.
Paradise like slim jim
miners' shacks,
Rocky Mountain cathedral sublime
one day I whisper
I'll be there.
Colorado, in studded spades.
Leather reins taut.
Ecstasy like worn cowboy boots
horizon eye Gregory Corso
Denver ice blue desire.
Colorado wildflower
dream measure
mountain stream rebirth
low rider puff clouds
promised land Aspen
tree honest beauty.
American highway Chevy
place on shoulders dream coat --
let's go!

Abandoned Beatnik Self

I scoot along wood floorboard
Cincinnati fast, scoop up
metal thumb tacks, odd socks --
nothing else.
abandoned beatnik self.
I push aside green garden, like
steel back dream
lotus emotion fantasy, French kisses
retreat of Confederate
calvary Gettysburg killing field
Abandoned beatnik self.
Years on metal S & M rack
mad poet beggars, hungry carnival clowns
pier party girls.
I am lower Broadway hop scotch
poetics, empty bucket smoky voice.
I am saint prostrate
on pyre,
give up Manhattqan heart,
ham and eggs soul
a jagged redemption
like cheap wine bottle
highway August
somersault dream.
Abandon beatnik self.

New York Jive

New York jive
insane gyroscope,
Broadway dice game
string lanyard
stone out craftsmen.
New York heirloom,
bourbon wiseacre,
hundred dollar bottle
blond showgirls
essence is
Jersey red Cadillac
New York jive.
Finger bowl fandango,
high culture weak tea fraud
lemon meringue illusion
rock and roll cocaine addicts
New York heirloom
big time aficionados
barracuda stretch vision ambition
leather crew cut losers
no parking lot, design studio apprentice
no humble lotus heart
no Cherokee wisdom
no purple horizon spirit
New York jive.

Supreme Court Justice

Judge Ruth Ginsberg
hallow Supreme Court justice,
pays a bushel of dues
along road to high court sanctity.
Like her sisters, 1950's
new toaster oppression
back seat Chevrolet ethics,
hide the cognitive genuis mind
calico talent tuck in
support whiskey rap hubby,
raise chocolate kiddies --
yeah like her sisters
Judge Ginsberg Supreme Court Justice
no law clerk
job after
Columbia Law School 1960
savvy university woman
kick ass skills
in Science, Economics, Law
toss off gift like Wrigley's gum chew.
Raise family. Knowledge
down porcelain sink.
Like Chinese female babies,
snuff opportunity, feet bind
keep minds in tiger cages
jailer patriarchy tweed coat despots
Judge Ruth Bader Ginsberg's
oppression like endless ocean tides,
salt tears
on wife midwest prairie.
Shut iron door,
too many bake
brownie years.

When Will It End?

N.Y. Times picture of 11 year old
boy, Sarajevo, broken Yugoslavia
like porcelain cairn
shrapnel in legs. Street corner blood
The war goes
on like mad hospital gown
psychotic. Two women,
nurse and doctor
pick steel pieces
from boys' arms tender legs.
When will it end?
Legs built for
soccer ball kick
ride bike up hills
surrounding town.
Pain and terror, evil carnage,
demon land mines
another useless shuck and jive war,
Blood battle ethnic memory,
black terror.
Sweet young boy
should be in school
mathematics,
geography book,
first Amerian cigarette
cheshire girlfriend --
battle for
life sanctity and limb. Innocence
destroyed like nighttime mortars.
When will it end?
Serbs, Bosnians, Moslems
all mad in bloodlust,
fitful end to
20th Century barbaric
carnage.
When will it end?

Demons

Delta black Mississippi
soil, twelve-step
group lower forty --
wooden plow, firm hand
I dig up demon, odd
orange pumpkins
quote Pablo Nuruda
soft scarecrow caress
I capture crazed
Hereford brief incarceration.
Demons in wide chest
royal blue anger, mad howls
cowgirl hard sex hits
hammer lock, Navaho leg holds
girlie magazines, gloss fantasy
sawdust pit, auction betrayals
poetry gig cancel.
Demons like Khe Sahn
firefight,
garden bloodletting
over state line flood banks.
Demons.
Hot cauldron overflow
abandonment like garbage
dumpster infant.
No Wyoming meadow notions.
No seed bag delivery
no wondrous violet field.

Uptown

Home uptown silk stocking
Congressional district,
bourgeois critters,
double breasted suits,
designer skirts.
Uptown.
First to Fifth Avenue
flat out, dollar bill
Rolls Royce Montana stampede.
Yeah wealth like golden calf
few poets madmen
few working poor
upscale French bread
summer chrysanthemums
conform like marine platoon.
Uptown creative genuis unnotice
money consciousness like pearl
necklace.
No shanghai chop sticks,
greasy diners
no Allen Ginsberg beatitude.
Uptown tame roller coaster,
silk pajamas, luxury high rise.
Hope uptown spirit
word 86th Street arid landscape
ink on paper clarity
beyond bourgeoisie noose.

Friday Night

I am teenage restless
like lone coyote
in desert sagebrush,
solitary in mild
pain jagged finger paint emotion.
Friday night.
Where is community
herbals, seers, madmen, poets, painters
bodies, shave
seals and
anchors tattoos, pints of
new Amsterdam in
working class hands
Friday night.
Where is mountain woman,
calico skirt Colorado
cool stream gypsy eyes
strong hands
revolution days
Friday night, eagle beneath Ohio
horizon, Iowa pain and
Canadian wind sweeps
down 2nd Avenue, like police dragnet.
I search Quaker
tapestry weave
old copy of the Times,
string lanyard keeps hands
away from cigarettes.
Wilderness baked salmon solitude.
Friday night. Summer still point.
East River tide rises
three quarter moon decay,
city corpse steeps
Friday night.

Byzantine Confusion

Tonight 86th Street vibration
Harlem pimps, jazzy
whores, rock and roll
beefcake.
Byzantine confusion.
Ultimate fix spirit escape
cut tender Yorkville brain synapse
check commotion like Istanbul
dark alley
bondage thrills thirst
cheap beer, tacky advances --
hand on round buttock.
Byzantine confusion
computer screen respite,
jumping bean consciousness
cocaine madness, rat cage release.
Byzantine confusion.
S M eros brute force,
2nd Avenue ripoff
blouse violence.
Rape notions like
black sidewalk piegon hunger
robot spasm jerks.
Byzantine confusion.
Saturday night prep
school circuit.
Empire's seven layer
cake crumble.
Brown gerbil anger
folks moved beyond
picket fence edge.

Kindergarten Diploma

Big time New York aficionados
wannabe territorial claims,
mad alley rats
egos like Chrysler building --
Kindergarten diploma,
tinted glass windows,
metal rivets
hold newspapers
glossy magazines.
New York healers, quick buck
caretaker grasp on
tide, Hudson River current
urban voodoo.
Kindergarten diploma.
Power quest like sleek
Mercedes-Benz, front row
opera seats.
No calico highway break
no rail track hobo compassion.
Kindergarten diploma,
yesterday's stale croissant
rancid milk
Bekins long distance
hauler breakdown.
Anger like July heatwave
spades trump card
wooden shell game children,
no fringe oracles
no black street corner prohecy
no Turkish taffy kindness,
Kindergarten diploma.

This Thing Called Romance

Erotic romance brings
short circuit
like alley cat on rim
roof top.
This thing called romance.
Saw off shot gun,
cobra jungle fear
graffiti long highway commotion.
Losing proposition
like garbage poker hand.
This thing called romance.
Chest sinews tense up
like a metal slinky,
vocal cords snarl
coarse gravel incantations
feet shuffle like ball
and chain convict.
Boogeyman fear
like wilderness kid away
from dad.
No wisdom stick, compass.
I am failed circus clown,
cheap wine pint
on flank,
railing terrace stumble
disabled ramp wheelchair
bumper car.
This thing called romance.
I run like mad marathoner
Broadwy white shoes pickpocket.
I just fold like accordion
late afternoon Om Pa Pa band.

Somalia

Four American boys die
bright African
sunlight -- jeep runs over
landmine. Mogadishu hairpin.
Somalia.
Tears to eyes for
brothers golden sons
American dream.
Somalia.
From Grand Rapids to Ft. Riley grief
military force overseas
stop famine let milk
grain flow like
surf in Indian Ocean.
Somalia.
Damn warlords keep
action like Harlem number runner.
semi automatic Uzi outlaw protection.
Somalia.
Four American boys dead,
Beirut, Sarajevo, now Mogadishu.
Blood. American corpses.
Somalia.
I am sad too much
20th century killing on round
garden planet.
Somalia.

East Coast Line

On East Coast line,
magic gingham highway
Johnny Walker shooter, t-bone splendor
I am Caribou Maine pinewood
haute cuisine china plate
yeah East Coast line, years
stretch like umbrella
Sabrette hot dog stand
Jones Beach bivouac,
flower skirts, orange tank tops
bib overalls on young Black dudes.
East Coast line.
Sleek Cadillacs, Lincolns,
silver spoon high Algonquin tea
sterling silver money clip
wad of green cash credit card cosmology.
On East Coast line poverty --
shaved ice East 125th Street ghetto genuis,
welfare iron noose --
Tough L.S.D. addiction
China white cruel sidetrack
East Coast line.
Yankees kick bottom
up at Bronx stadium.
Phillie soul brothers read Malcolm.
Poet Gil Scott Heron howls
tourist sloops
Camden Maine glide --
man o' wars on white beach
Wright Brothers Kitty Hawk excellence
East Coast line.
Fresh immigrant's quest
for salvation, big city dollar --
Baltimore harbor real estate
booms like iron cannon
New York poet craft
words like journeyman bricklayer.
Artist stretch linen canvas,
mix primary colors.
Salem witches mix pagan potions

East Coast line,
your marble universities,
politically correct goosestep
computer labs rewire electrodes
to young skull. Cherry pie brainwash
Yale, Cornell,
eggshells crack for omelet,
hot morning bagels
East Coast line.
I am rooted like South Jersey oak tree
year after calico year
demon Atlantic shark turf,
spirit weave nightmare
no wilderness salvation in Pittsfield,
no New Mexico salvation, cowboy poets
East Coast line.
Miami coral, million dollar yachts --
Virigina Beach July surf,
cruel streets that cry like
tin loud speakers.
lotus heart chain
mafia muscle, killer aerobic woman --
Lenox Avenue alley dice game
D.C. bag ladies, a derelict's singular grace
truck smoke, taxi fumes, midtown
heat up like steel kettle.
I embrace you East Coast line,
hot minestrone soup, bread and butter
fracture gyroscope madness,
highway years
like Duncan yo-yo
yes deadbeat in local gin mill,
mud wheel spin
tough America road.

PETER CHELNIK - HEY GIRL - COLLECTED POEMS

II
WILDFLOWER SERENADE
1997-2003

PETER CHELNIK - HEY GIRL - COLLECTED POEMS

Express Yourself

Express yourself in funky prophetic ramble
Bleecker Sreet night coffee jags
Adirondack rod and reel cool mountain stream.
Western Kansas prairie, fire words,
straight shot, ninth inning home run.
Express yourself in milk bucket incantations
bold exits through wooden university doors
brewers years, April delight bologna sandwich
the Lord's Prayer wilderness pine chapel.
Express yourself in magnolia serenade
handshake firm like Jefferson City square deal.
Lush silver voice like green Tennessee hallow
thrift shop work shirt button sew.
No to rude brain damage
hipster bartenders.
No to empty legal pads, marijuana poetic haze.
No to lockjaw apocalypse suicide doom
crack house junkie anger.
Express yourself in Converse high top sneakers
Haight Ashbury purple cape 1969,
Coors Light long neck bottle.
Read lilac Walt Whitman
mythic saint Allen Ginsberg
chop Woodstock poplar dead branchs
create crimson poetic rebirth.
Cheer on winless baseball home team
Indiana hoots, backseat Chevrolet caresses.
Bring silk racket boys mystic poems
San Francisco communiqués.
Express yourself in soothsayer beatnik howl
oracle's corn row insight
kitchen table revelations
lunch bucket American dialects
Bensonhurst broad "r" cadence
Chapparal cowboy twang.
Express yourself like Lake George curio shop
free fall skydiver liberation.
Poets House bound books jubilee.
Express yourself in peach cobbler kisses
July Fourth sparkler gleam
Eureka Springs hillbilly thick frozen yogurt freezie.

Express yourself in Huck Finn fierce outlaw quest
late evening IBM typewriter riff
Generation x honeybee skateboard mambo.
Express yourself in garden earth metaphors
Mobil gas jockey teenager excellence
wood varnish Broadway rehearsal room tap shoe strut
Woodlawn Irish breakfast.
Fight police blotter tangerine demon's narrow pain
St. Johnsbury prison letters desolation.
No to emotional barb wire combine knots.
No to ivy vine red brick schoolhouse noose.
Express yourself in white sand
kaleidoscope dream
Yugoslav Mikey's full house poker serenade
Miles Davis bebop trumpet
fourth grader's Abraham Lincoln honesty.
Sabbath rabbi, radiant hands Torah scroll.
Passover hot griddle.
Matzah Brie.
Express yourself like divine poet madman
Soho hopscotch painter.
Dayton, Ohio rainstorm.
rural Black Eye Susan meadow.
Express yourself like Bleecker Street holy
fringe rambler
on fire, always!

I Smile Hello

I smile hello
velvet watershed years
Soho salmon dinners
Columbia University library easy chair quiescence.
I smile hello Zen koan,
patchouli oil scent,
New Canaan commuter train.
spring equinox silk glide
St. Marks Place afteroon sunlight verities
punk short hair mountain woman sashay.
I smile hello American excellence,
coffee jags Avenue A, Torah eternity high
rabbi's square shoulders
holy covenant weave mud lace boots
silver key ring.
I smile hello Flo Kennedy
kick bottom irreverence
mythic Kansas City justice ham hock equality
apple pie ho down
cross-town bus West Side bound.
Columbus Avenue feather bed celebration.
I smile hello Charlie baby, sweet nephew
sports page obessions,
soccer field hustle.
Washington Square Park May fandango,
daffodils, hot dog vendor delight.
I smile hello new IBM typewriter
Caddy convertible Denver bound highway
sunflower seeds coat pocket
Dejarling iced ted
drug free bohemians resurrection
crescent moon Coney Island
tides,
I smile hello sweet librarian's poetic wisdom
desert flame Hopi Tribe
Tucson, Arizona big sky cadence.
Bleach white meditation room incense,
glory train texture mantra.
I smile hello Chinese take out
chop sticks chow down

free wheeling poets pinewood craft
layer April metaphor,
arch simile, meter San Francisco howls.
Beatnik language illumination.
I smile hello holy crystal life force,
Born Again Christians' grace,
microwave pizza.
I smile hello spring planting time
85th Street tulip bed
Santa Cruz magic dawn.
Illinois heartland prairie.
I smile hello round hyacinth garden planet
Huck Finn Mississippi River tall tales,
hot pea soup
fresh whole grain bread
flannel shirt carrion desire
eye on western horizon.
I smile hello.

Wildflower Serenade

Oh 1960's sister
Half Moon Bay eyes,
strong pinewood hands.
Whittle down hundred pinewood cords.
Slow simmer stew after veggie stew.
1960's sister
crow's feet lines
45-year-old texture face.
Long limbs like Kentucky race horse
yes Sufi wisdom
infinite road years,
Tucumcari to New Orleans.
1960's sister
Heart like hydrangeas
Connecticut oak, bold poetry essense.
No to 25 years metal Byzantine rack.
No checker cloth demons.
No bottom swift kicks.
Lover's sidewinder fracture.
1960's sister heal like urban pigeon wing
Iowa corn field freedom fly.
I am flannel sage
on Santa Monica beach
white stallion, erudite Old Testament saint.
I seek you out
New Mexico road houses.
Vermont Green Mountain hike trails.
Yes years stretch out
like flatbed truck
Texas tornado watch patience
Austin City limits soul mate dream.
Love like prairie fire grace.
1960's sister
Bedford Hills State Prison freedom
Manhattan 86th Street brothel
Louisiana highway truck stop
night scurry home
hearth, Navaho tapestry.
1960's sister
affirm flannel spirit.
No lesbian warm body mirror

no Oyster Bay suburban
Lincoln Town Car madness.
I am Massachusetts horizon heal
no tattered barroom,
no gerbil poetry maze.
No Parkinson's hand shakes
California Sequoia voice timber.
Oh 1960's sister
gone ten year sleeping pill addiction
Siamese twin psychiatrist
top drawer lithium dosage.
Now America red clay earth night flights
like 3 am Telluride clarity.
Come to me sister.
No Vietnam war killing field holocaust
backyard clothesline nightmare.
No chest cavity Diaspora
no pagan blood rites.
1960's sister come to me
in Boston, Savannah, desert Albuquerque.
Yes God's mythic gold tent
Black Eye Susan meadow,
a wildflower serenade.

Celebrate

I celebrate
poetic spirit revolution
Memphis blues guitar,
African American ham hock,
collard greens, gospel conscience,
cold Budweiser.
I celebrate
highway serenity Iowa Interstate 80,
Barbasol shave crem.
Side denim pocket green cash
mom's fierce sculptor aesthetic.
Calico sisters,
sweet toddlers' Hershey bar commotion.
I celebrate
construction worker's high rise
metal tool box skill.
12-step fire comrades,
sweet personal inventory,
wicker basket dollar in kitty.
I celebrate
Washington D.C. Cheshire counter culture heroics
veggies, brown rice, full knapsack justice quest.
I celebrate
black crow independence
like high school senior's first paycheck.
Flo Kennedy
chickens come home to roost passion,
I celebrate
John Z's local 32-B doorman savvy,
window box geraniums,
hops, Valarium bottle
urban cool down.
I celebrate
Jesus' red horizon grace,
Lancaster Quaker quilt holy beauty
love's angelic New Orleans weave.
I celebrate
honest Missouri handshake
green planet harmony
like nursey panda bear lullaby

Asheville, North Carolina front porch
home spun tales
Jack Kerouac magic novel
all day marathon read.
I celebrate
Passover liberation theology,
matzo ball soup,
hearty laugh with old man.
Mentally ill fringe hipster
prize fight discipline
commitment to Lithium,
East End Avenue shrink,
New Mexico road resonance.
I celebrate
down and out madmen
broken like bathroom cabinet mirror.
I celebrate
tinker toy
tender knees Christian prayer
Zen satori
William Faulkner fiction
Catskill Mountain Saturday morning
pinewood wind chimes delight.
Yes I celebrate
denim apple core life force,
belief in sweet Moses salvation
shopkeeper's infinite kindness
a city on round green hill, yes!

Gender Train

Gender Train
feminist locomotive 1990's blood war
Salt Lake City, Grand Junction,
Denver, mile high
Gloria Steinem diesels
furnace blasts
wildcat anger red fire ball,
oppresion's home economics metal slot
suffragettes, pack boxcars
hip Colt revolver,
M-15 vintage Vietnam.
Gender train
lilac diesel panhandle retribution
hot apple pie serenity wedge
patriarchy's blood brutality.
Sisters gun ten Budweiser
machismo, Robert Bly brotherhood,
Ford pick up boys.
Gender train
Americn heroes calico quest
women angry caged like spice rack
20 year Diaspora.
Wound festers, warrior howls
beneath canvas tent
over and over.
Feminist sisters
shuck off ancient crimes,
desert barb wire gulag.
Purple grief, obsessive wound.
Gender train
eloquent Quaker weave,
Manhattan heart like subline ruby.
Sisters walk Cheshire highway,
Big Sur coastline
move towards gender free New Jerusalem
cool oasis America.
Gender train
sisters glory train must drop
steel power ego vector
like Vermont stove, hot iron skillet.
Yes embrace liberation,

full moon Eros
hunker down like gingham midnight
special line.
Gender train
lady justice, Goddess' crimson glow
hearts on Flo Kennedy fire
Seneca Falls passion,
yes green garden planet,
equality's steady South Georgia
hand on plow always!

Chickens Come Home to Roost

Chickens come home to roost
mental illness dark tar pit.
Oh Yahwah
too many barbed wire prisons,
electrified brothels,
wicker bedpost S & M rack.
Angels split skull
like July watermelon,
oportunity vanishes like breadcrumbs
pinewood dinner table.
Sleeping pill jones.
Chickens come home to roost
too many years flat out no's.
go away like junkyard dog
strung out like
New Jersey 18-wheeler cinder block.
Thugs dance draw blood
tug shinbone like mad toddler
milk bottle freak out
fractured reality road years.
Chickens come home to roost
too much Missouri tar pit hate
cold revoluionary flashbacks
Parkinson shakes back beat years
show biz poetic two-bit advice
city limits assaults.
Chickens come home to roost
mad dogs' vagrant halllucinations
sinew neck, late night noose
coffee overdose, purple demons,
dirty laundry pile.
Utah diesel's high speed salvation
train wreck
lithium string out.
Chickens come home to roost
Manhattan derailmens, literary sabotage,
lost yellow schedules.
Parking garage underground mornings
blue collar kindness, hot java,
kind word grey clad car jockeys
morning Arkansas phone call.

Chickens come home to roost.
erector set destruct
weak side linebacker tendon pull
head drive thousand hosannas,
flannel resonance,
Santa Cruz green garden grace.
Chickens come home to roost
hard drive combat
semi conductor mental illness battle
sharp jolt brain genius.
No unibomber
no anarchist
no Manhattan tundra Frankenstein
no vagabond rapist round groin blood
no Texas railway psychosis.
Chickens come home to roost
blue highways, Pine Sol urinals,
desert trading posts
red highway quiescence.
Yes the chickens come home to roost.
Battlefield quiet now
gunpowder faint
no corpses.
Peace yes real cool bop
Zen peace.
Chickens come home to roost
Walt Whitman affirmation ferris wheel
Joni Mitchell guitar
hot oatmeal, French napkin rings,
cotton skirt swirl.
Chickens come home to roost
kaleidoscope Eureka Springs wonder
mythic Greenwich Village underground dream
New Mexico eastern dawn.
I rise like grey Lazarus
Massachusetts pine valley
Jones Beach box kite.
I cut apple pie.
Begin, yes.

No To Apocalypse

I am Pacific Grove, California good vibrations
hot coffee
Charles Bukowski celebration down beat vision.
April syrup afternoon red flannel shirt
manuscripts shelf like safe
dry dock sloops.
I am faith in God's pork pie rebirth
grunge angels dance
Hudson River Palisades horizon,
Jesus' whole grain salvation.
No to computer fray death wish.
No to mass suicide
nut job San Diego cult.
No to heroin weekend snort.
I am humble like Bowery panhandler
Colt 45 delight wildcat drunk.
Bleecker Street beatnik creative rap.
No to dark bathroom fears
dull double track razors.
No to apocalyptic stale breath vision
Nike sneaker corpses
New Age whole grain death vortex
Nostradomas's half ass delusional prophecies.
I am Saturday morning dads
stroller in tow
Second Avenue scoot.
I am flannel construction dudes
SUNY students' red hot desire
Cheshire education.
Greenwich Village gin joint Myrna.
No to machine convocations.
No to made dog BMW yuppies
notions like prostitute's lamplight celluloid shadow
no to credit card prophets
pension fund hunger.
I am American road passion
Las Crusces desert quest magic
holy grace like stretch canvas
Jersey City loft sanctity.
Saturday afternoon mountain woman's
moist Santa Fe kisses, wetland communiqués.

No to carny shadow time poets
fast buck psychiatrists
no to TV holy men
cult leaders
bizzare tin cup spirit poverty.
No to Chelsea small time narcissism.
I am cherry blossom soul
Manhattan salvation journey
humble round planet denim spirit
Illinois sky dream vision.
I am a craftsman's toolbox wisdom
Harlequin fool busy cobble rialto.
New Jerusalem wonder
Willa Cather's prairie beauty
hot biscuit breakfast
open wildflower heart.
No bold highway fandango short cuts
easy cereal box answers.
No to spiritual charlatans
spiritual hip pocket cash hustle.
I am God's gingham faith
MacDougal Street pizza
democracy's poetic weave.
I am Cleveland, Ohio blue chops
New Orleans levee Christmas fires.
Texas barbecue ribs outdoor grill
John Coltrane love supreme, yes.
May afternoonh life force ecstasy,
No to apocalypse.

Two Hearts

Two hearts
straight New Mexico highway
cathedral stain glass brilliance
Nuyorican Poets café beatific howl
prairie eyes barn fire.
Two hearts
move beyond highway salvation
Champion spark plugs
Chevy sacred engine hum.
Two hearts
Georgia slow glide
Allman Brothers ascent
Baptist steeple
puff cumulus clouds
warm peach pie
road hunger
New York City gulag overland years.
Two hearts
Colorado winds rock steady
like truck stop waitress,
shrimp curl vibrations
road warm Scarsdale afghan
thin football legs.
Two hearts
Aquarian metaphors beaver dam
personal histories
West 3rd Street
Marlboro smoke.
No Thai stick stone out.
No thorazie night terror.
No paprika measure prison cell.
Two hearts
Connecticut April hilltop
layer sweater, lumberjack coat,
peaked baseball cap tilt.
City corpses like lunch break coroner
1965 Ford Mustang tip-top tune up,
raw eggplant ho-down.

Two hearts
Manhattan highway
well stock bodega bold tarragon mornings
hot oatmeal dialectic
memory like Persian cat.
Two hearts
needlepoint coginitive thought
hyacinth poetic notations
bawdy Texas smile
carnival shoulder caress.
Two hearts
take it home free range sister
penance over like Vietam quagmire
June piano lessons
High Sierra courage
fog-bound ferries
passion flat skimming stones.
Two hearts
wipe salt tears
lush Mississippi delta cheekbones.
No to thousand rapes.
No to thousand buffalo nickel come ons
sealed in Bedford Hills prison cell desolation.
Two hearts
garden like Elizabethan lovers
San Francisco hippie poets
Tompkin Square Park miracle sages
southern California hot rods 1958.
Children of God's infinite glory.
Two hearts
Zazen lotus road partner
loves' cool Virginia reel
steak T-bones July barbecue
lift resonant voices
Methodist Church choir
Aretha Franklin southern gospel
promise land cobble highway
God's gingham grace, yes!

Magic Heart Tribe

We are mythic Lakota
spirit tribe
eastern bay window fireball
Great Jones diner
wreath round elegant neck.
We are poet saints
New York City metaphor
harbor poetry craft
balsam wood sandpaper
Avenue A runaway Ford Bronco.
We are rainbow vision
crisp postage stamps
tales quicksilver homeless
mud ditch hosannas.
We are Virginia Beach magic Eros
West Broadway kisses
midnight passion
break hearts
Colorado free-range mend.
We are beauty's matchbook flame
denim pocket Swiss army knife.
God's desert covenant.
Homeward bound hyacinth imagination
86th Street cross-town bus.
We are underground Zen seers
revolutionary cadre
St. Mark's Place hot falafel
lover's knit socks January freeze.
We are bold resistance
to metal technological machine
grey flannel CBS News vampires.
Repo men black leather crew cut.
We are Cheshire dawn
global mythic campfires,
fourth floor walk-up
rural Michigan back roads
angelic illumination
Los Angeles to sweet Boston.
We are tattoo renegades
grunge oracles

hip-hop baggy pants visionaries
Puerto Rican back beat shaman.
No porcelain cup conformity.
No yuppie cocaine Jeep Cherokee roll over.
No to Hollywood death vipers.
No shuck and jive cold sweat
clinical nightmares.
No fresh Lower East Side corpses
heroine aficionados
internet black hole terror.
No Bleecker Street tire tracks
ham and eggs breakfast special denial.
We say yes to Evander Holifield
cobra discipline
tattersall liniment gym years
corn on cob equality
clover leaf calico love affair
miracle dream like Jones Beach
ocean sea shell breeze.
Yes we are bold New Jerusalem salvation
mythic Harlem wildflowers
hearts on fire like Miguel Pinero
street wise revolution
Easter Sunday glaze ham serenity.
We are garden planet daydream
Rikers Island self-educated poet
pencil, legal pad, sassy woman's
wet kisses.
We are American Promised Land salavation
Albuquerque square deal
Hot Frontier Café sweet rolls
textured daily journal entry quest
Ice high top sneakers
generation x drum circle
calico gift renewal
magic heart tribe!

No Open Exit

February days like slow motion
French cinema basement
Coors keg
fitful sleep, carney dreams,
Irish female barender snarls
rude white apron deli clerk.
Dull dreams mythic brain synapse.
Veggie stew desolation
ham on stale whole wheat.
Winter days, Transylvania demon roller blades,
top hat tough money language breaks
wildflower senses,
young dudes fry brain synapse.
No Jack Kerouac interest in road stories
personal blood history
generation x like
Bible pages Turkish taffy melt.
Chicago midway trick bag
bring on Atlantic Ocean tide
bring on Camden, Maine miracle harbor spring.
No Captain Queeg cat's eyes marbles.
No concrete demon blues.
No media brainwash skim milk days
hard drive underage cigarette smokers.
No shoulder blade caress.
No open exit
German fringe call girl
refrigerator breakdown
Snapper Creek Bar new window panes
Jack Daniel's cocaine haze terror
sheet rock dreams
bob and weave
IBM typewriter word block.
No hot fire apprenticeship groove
George Washington's Valley Forge winter
orange ball caps.
Yes knotted fingers beg
North Dakota high prairie release
like Dannamora prison poet
shut up and consume
die like mine canary.

Mythic word liberation
Prince Street poetic party purge.
February death swoon
God's Alaska tundra silence
I see no open exit.

Freedom Time

Oh freedom time
Tenneesee barn fire
broken railroad watch
lover's knee sock fray
cool Yankee Stadium ale.
Freedom time
God's Ellis Island spirit illumination
Coney Island cornucopia boardwalk knish
thousand passionate whispers.
Freedom time
canned corn, silk blouse lady,
New Haven green eyes,
fire chestnut hair
sweet potato pie poetics.
Freedom time
work Manhattan mother lode
wooden bar banter.
No Vietnam pungi sticks.
No kamikaza attacks.
No West Side outback desolation.
Freedom time
sisters kibitz like Star's Deli waitress
business size envelopes, sealing wax,
Dewars shots.
Detroit City black corner prophets
save country again and again.
Oh freedom time
homeboys rock casbah
eloquent muscle
Hunts Point drag strip serentiy.
Oh sweet Tupac
Biggie Smalls we mourn misguided genius
new breed fire.
Oh freedom time
poets transcent blood feud
sexual puffed pillow betrayal
ball Rego Park jack.
sing like sister Roberta
angel concert choir
sing cathedral Thursdays
transcendent cinnamon weave.

Freedom time
tuna on whole wheat
gentle San Francisco Zen dawn
leather bikers rev mythic Harley
Vancouver bound.
Freedom time
old man's bow tie genius
200 real union jobs
back beat black, sweet Latino workers,
blue collar providence.
Freedom time
Yes Jackie Robinson second base
major league excellence
breaks race barrier
always A plus dignity
Ebbets Field grace.
Bold Saint Valentine love
Astor Place kisses
fringe youth bebop planting time
fertile lower forty.
Freedom time
purple cape sisters
delta New Orleans kick bottom,
proud neck amulet.
Freedom time
red beans and rice, port wine
Denver afternoon breeze
Rocky Mountain quiescence
Joni Mitchell cadence.
Lips sweet Bartlett pear
Niagara Falls daybreak
Freedom time
it's in poker cards, you bet.

Brats

Small chocolate children
run parents hula hoop maze
incessant Nintendo quick fix
obsolete toys closet
constant whine
tantrum whack out
yes children consumer myopic eyes
culoture coup d' etat.
Tykes run America
8-year-old frenzy
cold water ditch vortex.
Video games short circuit
natural ball field.
No innocence
no tanned legs
no Nancy Drew mystery joy.
Brats become metier for twelve-hour workday
credit card quicksand
Tylenol hits.
Yes kids future
Cincinnati sunlight silver
Virginia Wolf novel
next calico century future.
Too much 1990's short circuit antics.
Whack on bottom
goes long way
psychological Navy mind control place
Christian straight back chair discipline
young mush brains
tinderbox bodies
cinder track regress.
No Hilary Clinton children's rights hustle
virtual reality prophecy, S & M chamber.
Anarchy new curriculum
mediocre 3rd grade indoctrination.
Yes teach tykes American history
George Washington, Nat Turner,
American honeybee civics.
teach old time science kits,
bunsen burner, battery doo hickeys.
remove computer small sticky hand

yes to green neighborhood wonder
yes to Massachusetts woods delight
Cherokee camp fires marshmallows
cool pink watermelon evenings.
Yes to multiplication tables genuis,
yes hot chocolate reading passion
Cub Scout achievement.
Tykes our Cheshire future, yes!

Rise and Shine

I am Hong Kong harbor junk
rise and shine cowboy
cat's eye marble
glass ashtray paper clip
denim hip pocket greenbacks
free wheeling lace curtain dream,
Santa Fee dawn like calico cat.
I am breadbasket mandala
take-out Tandoori chicken
mom's suburban hacienda attic rafters.
I am Saturday night
Polish polka
Kansas bleach flour
round skull Rembrant slide show.
I am American highway poet
Manhattan East River dawn.
I am acoustic singer songwriter
guitar pick excellence
parquet rialto cool.
I am Baggot Inn prophet
night watch ethics lone downtown outpost
Jesus' gospel like Tennessee hot biscuits.
I sing interstate diesels
Kansas City hobo jungles
butterscotch rail link,
hot Boston beans, Hershey bars.
I sing American genuis
raw bone optimism
Joni Mitchell fierce independence.
No careerist assistant editors.
No quick talk hoodoo boys.
No casting couch hustlers.
No shuck and jive shadow culture
creativity internet shred.
I am early morning Dave Herman
WNEW harbor joy
wake up Bruce Springsteen juice.
I am valarium herb chill out
March afternoon radiator warmth.
I am red neck layer metaphor

five pound brown rice sack
fresh cauliflower on sale.
I am night ride upstate Woodstock bound
Steely Dan texture resonance quest
JC Penney seamstress skill
green revolutionary eyes
soft prairie thighs.
I sing to angels
Albuquerque, Seattle, sweet Eureka Spring.
I sing wild blossom honey rural outback
70-year-old Bleecker Street beatnik
poetry salad days
Jack Kerouac photographic memory.
I am midnight special line
well worn spade, hoe,
Greenwich Village tundra.
I am wide open
west bound Houston Street
Friday night freedom roll.
President Bill Clinton's knee surgeon
Leonardo di Vinci hands.
I am windshield wipers double time
full gas tank three steps ahead of posse
I am Oklahoma red clay vision
Santa Cruz eucalyptus resonance
big sky desert grace
rise and shine poetics
Ice coffee salvation.
I am baby boom generation can do
Mississippi delta excellence.
Amen.

Allen Ginsberg Dies Tonight

Allen Ginsberg dies tonight
karmic wheel check out
crimson beatific glory
round Buddhist smile
Cathetdral ear end.
Oh poet saint, howl
Colorado horizon, Bowery gin joints.
Allen Ginsberg dies tonight
American fringe angel
kick bottom oracle
Paterson short stroke beatnik text
common word fandango heart
yes 1956 Gallery Six, San Francisco.
Howl poetic beatitude
generation's frailty
hispter's rainbow providence.
Allen Ginsberg dies tonight
13th Street loft
friends lay man to rest
halcyon consciousness
prairie fire Kansas magic vortex
transcendent road marker
purple spirit harmonium Washington Square Park.
Nations master fire poet packs
large velvet halls, Avenue A ramble.
Yes *Howl, Planet News, Reality Sandwich*
sir your fierce voice
moves young poets
New York City to Seattle
like checker home spun tablecloth
miracle Vedic scriptures.
Allen Ginsberg dies tonight
fifty years poetic highway,
angelic grace, voice cord wood commotion.
Always Denver bound
Peter Orlofsky, Jack Kerouac. Gregory Corso,
Neil Cassidy, imagination's
wildflower essence.
Allen Ginsberg dies tonight
dream high Sierras, Indus Valley,

Morocco casbah.
Modern crazy quilt language
typewriter affirmations
William Carlos Williams invention
like Model T Ford.
Bold lotus blossom mantra.
Allen Ginsberg dies tonight
black bebop passions
Hebraic compassion
eros red heat sublime,
man on man.
Walt Whitman yea saying,
poetics shatter Ivy League noose
19th century straight jacket
meter rhyme.
Yes Allen Ginsberg dies tonight
poetry road explodes like spontaneous nova
generation after mythic generation
lush garden resonance
Lower East Side Holy Spirit revolution.
I will miss you Mr.Ginsberg
6th Street vegetable curry
mythic highway literacy risks
April sweet hyacinth cool.
I will miss your Bleecker Street
scuffle dream Maya eyes
home spun miracle raps.
Yes Allen bring on a planet quiescence
rare promise land peace
nirvana like cosmic river run, always.

All is Well

All is well
Saturday morning paper
mache rialto
quarter note hot Cream of Wheat on simmer.
Village hipsters dream Texas wildflowers
thick vanilla shakes.
All is well
New York City Saturday morning ho-down.
Bring on rye bread hope,
strawberry preserves,
bring on mythic Massachusetts
ridge line spirit.
All is well
after hours joints cool down
like blueberry muffins
street whores pocket cash
New York Post prophecy
hot bathtub transcendence.
All is well
street smiles like hip pocket
subway tokens
computer combine second gear down shift
taxi sage
blood warrior chill out.
All is well
kids baseball opening day excite
Derek Jeter short stop glory
mustard hot dog
funky tweed dad.
All is well
flannel early spring morning
weekend threadbare poets
nail texture word
sweet IBM typewriters
purr like tabby cat.
All is well
large canvas stretch
Greene Street acrylic vision
Matisse imagination outrage.
Gone are midtown gasoline fumes,

gone Friday three martini lunch
get down,
boss' bottom line raves,
headstrong commuter trains.
Gone single moms hot wire
rent bill psychosis
kids' third grade homework rebellion.
All is well
Albert Owen Washington Square Park
comic rap excellence
Bette is Pacific Northwest
bone and grain driftwood dream
cats' eye marbles
Ray turns on couch
heart open
highway freedom ride
chocolate donuts in fridge.
All is well
God's carrion vibration
red brick heart chakra
steady Philadelphia hand.
TV cool San Diego suicide
mind control madness fades,
Second Avenue like liberated zone
green Vermont truck farm
creativity's tablecloth grace.
Yes, round sun does rise.
All is well.

I'm Dying

I'm dying
New York City cruel barb wire gulag.
Brain synapse Scorpio moon shred
crops plow under.
Ball and jack winter.
Black crow desolation
starch shirt avenues.
I'm dying
blood shot Thursday,
wrinkled neck butcher's cleaver
rumors of chariots faint,
Jesus' salvation faint like distant freight train.
Septic tank raps consume
Santa Cruz passion,
broken vase, cast off tomatoes,
shallow riverbed language cadence.
I'm dying
like outhouse metaphor.
No Ohio horizon while stallions.
No telephone ring.
Old time Jackson Browne
keeps torso alive.
Grey ash spirit.
No phoenix rise.
Hollywood legs embalming fluid
orange dawn pine coffein.
I'm dying
few words on cherry lips
bedroom floor dirty laundry
funeral wake line forms to right
no takers.
Aficionados show no interest
redwood poems
wildcat western quest
Vermont Green Mountai dream.
I'm dying
like Abraham Lincoln Ford's Theater
assassin stalks me, Yorkville barrooms
downtown poetry hideout
cross town bus lines.

No checker pain herbal medicine
sooth out.
Downtown romantic betrayal.
Blood flows
between wrist, East River, barroom.
I'm dying
like Second Avenue gasoline fumes
Budweiser bottle break.
New Jerusalem distant notion.

Yes New Jersey You Call To Me

Oh New Jersey you call to me
green Garden State
wonderous blend cobble weave
miracle ocean texture
blue collar heart.
New Jersey you run strong
in this poet's mythic corned beef blood,
December 1969 turnpike paranoia
road terror.
Oh New Jersey you call to me
red brick tribe
on surburban spiked roads Ford Econoline
Bruce Springsteen back beat resonance
paisley hard drive.
Yes Jane R. first lover
out of seaside Deal,
back seat wrestle, bulls eye score,
Bradley Beach hardscrabble reconnaissance
girls rare orbit, Kupie Doll boardwalk fandango.
Oh the money like Giants
Phil Simms touchdown strike
Joe Morris backfield kick bottom power thrust.
New Jersey you call to me.
No chi chi New York City
wannabe shuck.
No reinvention barroom identity.
No literary cowards
yes to sons and daughters streetwise savvy
handshae integrity
yes to classy Frank Sinatra baritone croon.
New Jersey you call to me
eye on Garden State back road
cumulus sky
Sunday whole grain pancakes.
No I do not mind Linden
chemical plants
kamikazes headed for Delaware
line frenzy Toyota
jazzy Cadillac
18-wheel Teamster muscle.

New Jersey you call to me
Blairstown diner March afternoon
dream Ohio and west
eggs over easy vortex.
April Jack Daniel's soiree
Bernardsville carriage houe.
Yes New Jersey you cut the pie
Governor Christie Todd Whitman
firm statehouse renaissance
roll pine green work shirt.
I embrace you nylon Princeton co-eds
Rutgers leather crowd
Trenton State grunge fandango.
Yes your mythic poets
Atlantic City muscle,
lilac neon, ocean salt dream.
Erotic seashore
string bikinis, tank tops.
New Jersey you call to me
Delaware Water Gap marker Manhattan home
close at hand
long haul New Mexico run.
East Coast home fires.
Straight back Amercican dream
small town quiescence
William Carlos Williams Rutherford invention
Allen Ginsberg Paterson pine wood passion
Camden down home grit.
New Jersey you call to me
this humble New York boy
wildflower green eyes
arch horizon embrace,
flannel shirt poetics.
Your easy Woodbridge tooth smile
your Newark Ironbound District paella
Point Pleasant boardwalk cotton candy.
February dawn, highway revelation.
New Jersey you call to me, yes!

We Wait For Spring

We wait for spring
green down parkas
almond 21st century fire eyes
American wheel, steady hand
Cynthia's burning bush cobble Harlem.
We wait for spring
miracle thaw Manhattan liberation
buds emerge like dental assistant's
noontime appointment.
Magnolia crescendo hearts.
No desolate literary hijinks.
No fast food cheeseburger hallucinations.
No cherry lipstick East Side party girl snarls.
We wait for spring
God's white light joy
Jesus' salvation texture city on a hill.
Bay Ridge transcendent hope
Central Park affirmations eloquent bloom
a Zen kite overhead.
We wait for spring
Cheyenne, Wyoming ho-down
table top erotic dancers,
narrow G-string, whole grain delight
frontier spirit Interstate 40
Hopi Desert,
holy ground rebirth,
celebration of cumulus sky.
We wait for spring
like cakewalk madmen
work shirt parking lot car jockey
Greenwich Village West 3rd Street
basketball ramble,
No fracture marble winter death.
No Madison Avenue gasoline fumes.
No wool mittens
Steroid gangster muscle.
No narcissistic old girl bonding
Saint Monica's Church crazy commotion.
We wait for spring
black's Bedford-Styvesant jubilee
rebirth like metal Teamster lunch bucket,

open mic poetics,
Dionysian rambles, cool lemonade,
Hale-Bopp comet vibration.
Holy Iowa corn field,
Alabama magnolia miracle.
We wait for spring
box lunch fried chicken,
fresh potato salad,
oatmeal cookie.
Endless staccato Jack Kerouac highway
Sunday March morning slumber
Jerrado's surreal Latino eye
drug free bohemians
Gypsy revelry joy.
No computer combine city noose.
No hunger kindergarten kid's belly.
No cabin fever blues.
We wait for spring
East End Avenue dawn
Toledo, Ohio truck stop sanctuary
ham and eggs over easy,
hot java.
America's freedom time promise.
Yes we wait for spring's
sweet youthful breeze
flesh on flesh
Manhattan's angels' wide smile
grey hair ladies yellow orchids
Walt Whitman's lilac fire.
Pagan May ecstasy green earth
magic rebirth
Laura Boss's Hudson River faith
Joni Mitchell sweet guitar resonance
God's covenant shoestring faith
American dream rebirth
garden beatitude
We wait for spring, yes!

Groove

I groove
liberation Saturday easy roller blade cha cha.
Whole grain pancakes
crisp bacon
Vermont maple syrup.
No New York City buzz saw credit card hold.
No nine to five cell phones.
No black Lincoln Town Car ego.
No quest for double mutual fund bonanza.
I groove terrace pigeons
cirrus miracle redemption sky
Charlie hustle downtown soccer mix-a-lot.
I groove
Utah promise land spirit
Baggot Inn poetry read commotion
bebop Allen Ginsberg download
I groove
mythic Laura Boss
New Jersey rainbow eyes
china tea cup aesthetics
hot rod Saab.
Yes to Yorkville dads
small Star Trek tykes' gentle tow.
Yes to mom's day off stroller weekday push.
I groove
milk train dream
Pennsylvania Quarker horizon
Alabama magnolia kisses
Second Avenue hot pastrami, coke.
I groove
Susan's easy flanks
soft cotton shoulders
wildflower meadow upstate Livington Manor.
Texture words bleach white paper
Teamster semis southbound Interstate 95.
I groove
Sheepshead Bay fishing quest
Atlantic spring salt air
Dave's New Orleans voodoo poetics.
Bring on Central Park noontime

au pair girls' finesse.
Bring on slow roll down lox and bagel
Manhattan straight line avenues
frisky secretary's grunge Saturday flannels
April sunlight caress.
No virgins wooden stake burn.
No hip hop gangster gangland rub out.
No taxi driver snarls.
I groove
pagan lunch mushroom omelets, red wine,
slow Louisville simmer.
I groove
oak tree buds cobbled side street
geometric parks
D.H. Lawrence's erotic promise.
No multiple conference calls.
No literary editors' cruel psychosis.
No garbage hauler weight room chest
tight lasso.
I groove
Jackie Robinson excellence
Alvin Ailey down home
weeping willow choreograph
bebob saxophone salvation
sweet Sullivan Street sexy mountain women
layer long skirt sashay.
I groove yes
young folk's visual quick cut dream
eye deep into garden planet aesthetics.
Yes I groove
like falcon backwater power lines
Woodstock back road morning deer
beatific silver trout poem
magic easy beat glide.
I groove, yes.

Joe Goes Violent

Joe goes violent
red fire breaks whiskey glass
straight out
Fitzpatricks wooden bar.
One loud thud.
Indian Joe part Muscalara tribe
part Sicilian mythic seeker
feather warrior spirit on
holy ridge line.
Joe goes violent
too many barroom screw offs
aerobic class ladies nose up in ar
cold shoulders
no holy urban grace.
Joe goes violant
tatter pariah
fly fishing gal broken heart
five years string out
five years marriage dream
tear apart like AK-47 blasts
down Second Avenue.
Joe goes violent
desolution ramble three months
Queens apartment rent unpaid
Los Angeles drug bust
too many yuppie light weights
frat boy beers
hairless nautilus chests,
playboy fantasy
too many Perry Ellis back turn
oh Native American holy spirit.
Joe goes violent
whiskey drunks, cheap corner whores
cold Dublin bartenders
off banana boat
too many plastic surgery pretty girls
BMW prince charming quest
too many years party crowds
stucco wall brutal push
get lost psycho

get with corporate white bread program.
Joe goes violent
high rise window cleaner
magician spirit like Adirondack woods.
Joe goes violent
criminal law book like bible
thick loadstone
fight billy club cops,
California highway patrol, anyone.
Los Angeles court date
moves to jailhouse
hard prison time.
Three squares, no broken wheel gospel.
Makeshift home.
Joe goes violent last night
shatters whiskey glass
barroom hard drive mess
shatters American dream
I feel very sad.

I Dream

I dream
righteous garden planet
cool Rocky Mountain
Amsterdam Avenue air
hip hop boys
pop medicinal herbs
take on Shakespeare
sweet butter heart consciousness.
I dream
Little Rock hot apple pie
poverty ghetto opportunity
trim lawn suburbs
Queens Richmond Hill row houses
city purple Zen students, serene Islamic holy men
eye on sidewalk cracks
Buddha belly brown rice
truck garden veggies content
I dream
lunch bucket jobs
honest days' work greenbacks
January steam radiators
subway ear Dizzy Gillespie jubilee
end of down beat ball and chain blues
end of cro magnon anger
I dream
Diane's mythic toothed smiles
silk Bangkok kimono
Cherokee highway ramble
thumb out like mythic Roman candle
Appaloosa hitchike quest.
I dream
clean striped sheets
warm Quarter quilt
hot oatmeal breakfast
Greyhouse Bus Denver vortex bound
Iowa cornfield like golden beatific aura
funky truck stop ham and eggs
Omaha 30 miles
green cash motel
T-bone get down
I dream

sweet vision hipster
American highway redemption
texture blue ocean eyes
mythic California horizon
trucker's t.v. room snooze,
shower, trucker's fuel ticket
Jack Kerouac road magic, Gregory Corso
funky back beat.
I dream
God's corduroy spirit,
sourdough word, grace,
boded paper, ink
long overland apprenticeship
I dream beef stew simmer
corner thrift shop tweed coat
sexy neighborhood sweetie sashay
I dream
lumberjack salvation
drug free bohemians
American creative renaissance
spring arboretum easy glide
I dream
holy Mohegan Island cliffs
southern Colorado chaparral deliverance
ten-gallon Stetson hats.
pine green work shirt excellence
upstate mud work boots
I dream
poetic hearts open like cupcake box
God's cathedral grace.
Milk train passion for blueberry craft
wildflower perfection
I dream.

III
HOPSCOTCH HOME
2002

PETER CHELNIK - HEY GIRL - COLLECTED POEMS

Tell Your Story

Tell Your Story
In Illinois pine grove
New England Walden Pond camp fire
bus station shirt pocket Winston cigarette pack.
Tell Your Story
In calico poets' room
like Key West macho shark high gauge line
downtown Lexington Avenue subway run.
Tell Your Story
To tweed coat psychiatrist
911 NYPD steep cliff rescues
howl down Sullivan street shout out wild west
lasso passions
house arrest in barb wire Wyoming corral.
Tell Your Story
Broken heart blue jean jacket gambits
dead end Westchester back roads
Washington D.C. one toke over the line
desolation blues.
Tell Your Story
In mental hospital padded seclusion room
occupational therapy hot coffee break
Mobil gas station New Jersey side
Holland Tunnel,
Lopez Island December New Age wood shack.
Tell Your Story
Savoy Lounge Rolling Rock howls
steamfitter bold beat prosody
no piano scale lies
no ecstasy tab brain fracture.
Tell Your Story
From Kuztown, Pennsylvania Main Street
Pikes Market Seattle soho salmon fresh catch.
Tell Your Story
On flatbed truck Salinas bound
bright eyes Mexican migrant workers
Monterrey Penninsular puff cloud vibrations
Second Avenue stone park bench
David Carle's cool bop painter's groove.
Tell Your Story
On Samaritan 24 hour hot line

to Bette Portsmouth miracle rooted
closing time barroom comrades
last call bourbon poetics.
Tell Your Story
To gingham God
prairie fire three county glow
lady liberty's open arms
a greyhound bus ticket west, Yes.

Blue Moon Magic

Blue Moon Magic
Navajo crossroad mercurial wood nymphs
like wildcat kaleidoscopes
30 year Diaspora stone cold finish
Green Woodstock garden magnolia delight
brother Marc's July maple tree cathedral
holy San Francisco Mission District cool.
Blue Moon Magic
Second crazy full moon
in lanyard month Mamaroneck harbor
dingy adrift
steamers Heineken green bottles
purple felt book marker.
Blue Moon Magic
Keith Jarrett piano excite
camisole clad lover Red French Bordeaux wine
Thompson Street corner kisses
t-bone steak medium rare.
Blue Moon Magic
Coyotes howl Sante Fe outback
corn flake cereal bowl
cobra snake insane passion.
Poetry craft brick by brick
hopscotch Emily Dickinson American
excellence.
Blue Moon Magic
Western Massachusetts wilderness
white birch delight Mt. Greylock summit
vision clarity
new morning highway renaissance.
Blue Moon Magic
comic strip lunch bucket notions
red Marlboro smokes frozen Milky Way bar
no Bellevue canvas straight jacket
no street corner high-tech cell phone
no literary bizarre tool and die hierarchy.
Blue Moon Magic
Wicca pagans hunker down
green salamander woods

God's halcyon redemption
fireflies front porch groove
fresh strawberry preserves
candles like small calico metaphors.
Blue Moon Magic
Pacific ocean heart high tide
West Point Hudson River beauty
freedom like downtown number 6 subway car
easy glide.
Big old blue Moon
steady Chevrolet steering wheel
straight shot silver quarter night sky quiescence.

American Manchild

I am American Manchild
New York City tuber roots run hard
wildcat heart prairie fire beatnik poems
three Budweiser vibration Jones Beach sand
dune mad oracle.
I am American Manchild
Two years psycho ward soft boiled egg lock up
Lithium green eyes like Jewish sour pickles.
I am American Manchild
Highway flannel providence
San Francisco Mission district halibut
baked potato
faith like sweet Mississippi river
Hannibal, St. Louis sweet Natchez
I am American Manchild
Demons obsess back room cedar closet
downtown parking lot.
Long skirt blond Santa Cruz lover
jack hammer pine tree emotion.
I am American Manchild
Central Park ridgeline wilderness serenity.
Motel 6 desert vortex
baby boom John F. Kennedy excellence
yes to Jack Kerouac today wine rialto
yes to James Baldwin Black man's
eloquent fire.
I am American Manchild
Bar room ice coffee laughs like June
cumulus clouds
Wednesday Thompson Square Park
afternoon serendipity
Cape Cod clambake corn on cob beatitude.
I am American Manchild
Eureka Springs July hillbilly redneck cool
Monarch butterfly calico sisters
Bob Feldman's saxophone cathedral delight
earth hold harvest true grit.
I am American Manchild
Mom's no frill pot roast aesthetics
Always think think think.

Butterscotch idealism
Hegelian sugar beet dialectics
frozen Milky Way bars, 7-11 slurpy
Zen Mentor shoulder whack
Greenwich Village skate board
hard drive celebration.
I am American Manchild
Upstate blue highway quest green truck garden
harvest quiescence
bring on gingham Manhattan kisses
bring on late night Miami raps with
mythic Myrna
move iron Susquehanna and Ohio railroad rig
down mythic kick bottom track.
Yes I am American Manchild coming home.

Let It Flow

Let It Flow
American maple syrup excellence
opportunity like grilled
t-bone home fries
good paying rock steady union job.
Let It Flow
Equality like homespun gold yarn even full tilt
playing field
Brown versus Board of Education 1954
bring it home for black folk.
Let It flow
Work feather tail off chop quarry limestone
twelve hour day
sweat labor
rise strawberry children
no spirit break move down checker cloth table
full blown achievement.
Let It flow
Thurgood Marshall Supreme Court passion
pork chop Harvard University eating club
no Jim Crow soul highjack.
Let It flow
All across millennium American put aside
hundred year tar pit hate
women's old time throw away trash minds
bound Chinese feet
top notch child care vortex.
Let It Flow
Over New Mexico engine hum
holy orange arroyos steadfast desert buttes
jalapeno chili pepper five alarm delight
New Mexican bandito faith.
Let It Flow
Mentally ill cats sidewinder chicks leather
satchel medication
Gallo wine West Coast surf's up notions.
Embrace leather cobra snake
climb Adirondack Rock Mountain
thousands times.
Let It Flow

Gay cats New York City sanctuary
Oscar Wilde velvet dream
kick deadbolt AIDS virus howl in Broadway
theater wood stage
walk purple riverfront rialto.
Let It Flow
Bring home God's covenant Bob Feldman
saxophone
holy Hebraic letters on yellow
Red Sea parchment.
Yes, Let It Flow
Broad grins from Memphis up river to St Louis
Davenport, Iowa
firm handshake Gracie's diner counter
integrity kindness like Washington, D.C.
cherry blossom jubilee.
Let It Flow
Good people
Let It flow.

Barn Raise Sanctity

Barn Raise Sanctity
Sweet love's rainbow sky essence
Carmine Street chalk poems
generation X pat on fringe back.
Community together like main street
Baptist church.
Barn Raise Sanctity
Clean cinnamon body like cool Canada wind
encyclopedia mind Pacific Grove wind chimes
God's wheat field wonder
bronze hands reach out
West 3rd Street Baggot Inn ho down
12 step dollar in kitty heal.
Barn Raise Sanctity
Matchbook Joe Camel primrose analytics
rainbow hopscotch road journey.
Barn Raise Sanctity
Live clean like 20 Mule Team Borax
drug free bohemians
fresh Kleenex tissue box
Tennessee I-40 interstate tears.
Barn Raise Sanctity
Central Park footloose cosmic red kite
vision stretch to straight line syrup
Ohio horizon
East Coast Jazz Poetry Explosion
buy back groove
fierce poetry fireball.
Belief in crimson self like 7 year old shortshop
new rubber spikes aluminum Modell's
baseball bat.
Barn Raise Sanctity
8 hour sleep cool sheet slumber
Thoreau Walden Pond self-reliance
individual Oregon Trail quest
grandfather clock bold strokes.
Wyoming firm handshake
more from raven death to Quaker quilt
halcyon life
Holy Lenox Massachusetts Christmas
Zen quicksilver satori
Barn Raise Sanctity yeah.

Resurrection Monday Morning

Resurrection Monday Morning
Heat wave like burnt toast
tail end July fourth crap shoot weekend
hot wire string out hipsters.
Resurrection Monday Morning
Oh, Jesus we call for grace
Avenue A holistic heal humble home fries
New Jersey eggs over easy.
When will straight jacket madness cease?
Resurrection Monday Morning
Young dudes spirit shut down like weekend
Chase Manhattan bank vault
too much red coal anger
too much high school fracture
too much back seat Mercedes Benz psychosis.
Resurrection Monday Morning
Rise like Phoenix in Bronx empty sand lot
rise like Elizabeth Dole
New Hampshire Sunday hot dog picnic
Oh, Jesus, we wait for cayenne resurrection
end dark pickle barrel commotion
bare bone racist hate.
Resurrection Monday Morning
Too many years on poetic iron rack
too many pork chop years
in coal furnace diaspora
ace of hearts poets
Vicki Hudspith
Angelo Verga
sweet Laura Boss
cry to be heard beyond computer gulag
chat room
rancid poetry network
beyond Atlantic sea breeze.
Resurrection Monday Morning
Doorman Yugoslav Mikey overnight double
dreams clean sheets cool lemonade
union meat and potato raise.
Oh, Resurrection Monday Morning
Too many years on Calgary wood cross

ignored like candy wrapper litter
homeless Belleview psychotic.
Resurrection Monday Morning
Gregory Corso drunk cool cat incantations
Allen Ginsberg holy spirit saint poetics.
Bring it home sweet Jesus, Steve Stills
kick bottom 30 year old melody in head
flannel warrier fierce rolling thunder
Arizona desert rose in calico
work shirt front pocket.
Colorado mountain stream crescendo
Yes!

Let Freedom Ring

Let Freedom Ring
No to September 11 Black Tuesday
terroist blood lust
no to 6000 cherry pie
American World Trade Center murders.
Let Freedom Ring
James Madison Federalist Papers
liberty Ames Iowa cornfield
hoe down
Baton Rouge quick lunch stand
Manhattan rice and beans parking lot.
Let Freedom Ring
President George W. Bush
get tough joint Congress
mythic call to arms.
57 year June 6th 1944 D-Day
Omaha Beach
Camp Le Jeune marines tough
leatherneck savvy
Navy seal kick bottom valor.
Let Freedom Ring
Sweet Mohammed Ali takes out
Sonny Liston 1964 American hero
always quicksilver poet
Bob Dylan Washington Square Park genuis
end Mississippi Jim Crow Black man's
crucifixion.
Let Freedom Ring
Governor George Pataki eloquent
Hudson River courage
mythic Mayor Rudy Giuliani
gotham excellence
Rosy the riveter Detroit assembly
American 'can do.'
Let Freedom Ring
Vietnam combat soldiers
girlfriend's sleepless Nebraska nights
always cheshire prayers
yellow ribbons overseas
rose petal letters

too many cotton pillow tears.
Let Freedom Ring
No World Trade Center Taliban
gravestone black hole evil
no Osama Bin Laden New York
Pentagon horror chamber
no American corpse butcher
cleaver frature.
Bring on brother Americorps volunteers
in Chicago, Bostonm, sweet St. Louis
true grit neighborhoods
crystalline corduroy youth.
Always pine tree faith,
chainsaw hard work
grass roots American dream.
yes to St. Vincent Hospital EMS
September 11th stethoscope doctors
no nonsense nurses.
Let Freedom Ring
Yes to little league dads
aluminum bats in tow
yes to ball cap sons and daughters
baseball diamond sanctity
autumn Abner Doubleday ritual.
Yes to Boy Scout moms
merit badge sew in
good oakwood citiznes
personal responsibility
Ralph Waldo Emerson Massachusetts
self reliance.
Let Freedom Ring
Old man's Anzio Beachhead
mortar platoon courage.
1945 Dachau liberation
Yes to grunge youth San Francisco
touch sky like holy Quaker weave
Let Freedom Ring
United We Stand
like sweet Bensonhurst American flags
one nation under God.
Let Freedom Ring
Bring on Thomas Jefferson political genuis
bring on Ben Franklin Philadelphia Renaissance

Elizabeth Cady Stanton Seneca Falls
suffragette savvy
John Coltrane ghetto fire.
Let Freedom Ring
From New Hampshire church towers
Washington D.C. southeast
street corners
tough east coast Los Angeles barrios
Long Island suburban shopping malls
President and Laura Bush's Midland
big sky west Texas.
Let Freedom Ring
Yes to flannel prayer salvation
blue collar excellence
New York Fire Department valor
NYPD rescue hard hat ground zero muscle
corn on cob National Guard.
Let Freedom Ring
Yes to overland constitutional optimism
tough raw bone justice
yes to American liberty beacon
Save the Republic
Save the Republic
Let Freedom Ring.

Poets Will Soar

Poets Will Soar
Spread feather wings
Massachusetts blue jay howl
light out for golden heavens.
Poet Will Soar
Rise over Manhattan parking lot
Corner Pakistani deli
Midtown glass steel high rise.
Poets Will Soar
Colorado wildflower dream again and again
like Sierra Club trail hike
Guggenheim Museum Frank Lloyd Wright
wonder.
Poets Will Soar
Robert Frost Vermont magic
Cannonball Adderly jazz genuis
Cornelia Street sparrows
God's up front holy pink pigeons markers
feather spirit revolution
Poets Will Soar
Move to cumulus cloud Ohio horizon
Atlantic Ocean wide open salt serenity
move to Nebraska prairie grace America.
Poets Will Soar
No to apocalypse short order paranoia
no to white ruffle shirt Pulitzer prize politics
no to snake oil hand in pocket oracles
no rooted spirit break heart.
Poets Will Soar
Freedom's June dusk scurry home
highway iced coffee Gregory Corso
beatnik dream sublime.
Poets Will Soar
Like National Pubic Radio
crystalline morning riff
Flo Kennedy bold move on gender garden
monarch butterfly justice.
Poets Will Soar
Embrace Missouri soy bean fields
Arkansas green whiskey hallows
Boston Tea Party harbor sanctity.

Poets Will Soar
Become dream like Salinas, California
artichoke layer peel
bold Bronx strong foreams
always maple syrup sky on fire passion.
Poets Will Soar!

Straight Line Highway

Straight Line Highway
Cut hot wire macadam swath
1992 cherry red Volvo
wind at flannel back full Mobil gasoline tank.
Straight Line Highway
Hosanna ice coffee 6 lane run
bologna sandwiches on ice
back seat Marlboro carton
fire heart like wilderness noontime glow.
Straight Line Highway
tape deck Joni Mitchell, Rand McNally antique
road map denim lap.
Straight Line Highway
Wray, Colorado small town gulch
western dream
Kansas wheat bale September dead sunflowers
quest calico mountain woman.
Straight Line Highway
Ball cap zen movement rearview mirror
truck stop transcendence
cowboys line Lander, Wyoming
five and dime streets.
Straight Line Highway
Far right lane slow poke 55 miles per hour
no short bolt hurry
seatbelt across broad Manhattan chest.
Straight Line Highway
American beatitude mythic journey
night ride across rain soak Nebraska prairie.
Vending machines Hershey bars, diet Coke
American heartland slingshot drive.
Straight Line Highway
engine purrs line tabby cat brakes
like Wrigley Gum
roof of mouth
bring on spirit road salvation
bring on wide open hot coffee fill up
bring on pink clad waitress kindness
cocky high school gas jock
bring on Louisville, Kentucky

Black overall river men
W.C. Handy Memphis trumpet cool.
Oh, Straight Line Highway
Always lone Grateful Dead hitchhiker
always eye on next steel tool booth
state line rainbow serenade
Yes.

Homespun 2002

Homespun 2002
Bring on calico
North Star thythm
gazpacho soup cool lemonade
whole grain seers community
like Amish barnraise.
Homespun 2002
Open First Avenue bay windows loose shirts
print dresses
t-shirt fringe vest
Hyannis Harbor mooring serenity.
Homespun 2002
Quicksilve broad grins firm West Coast
handshakes
sleeping bag roll upstate cornfield celebration.
Homespun 2002
30 year pinewood stories day glo road trip
Santa Cruz lentil stew
cross country Arkansas bohemian rhapsody.
Homespun 2002
Brothers and sisters cobble highway
crimson vision
break bread devotion Vermont loom
weave tapestry.
Vietnam Harley Davidson vets brain pick
rolling thunder quiescence.
Cool bop minimalist ladies
Yorkville loan sharks twenty dollar
aqueduct bookies.
Beehive hairdo numbers runner.
Homespun 2002
Joni Mitchell Tapanga Canyon cool vibrations
David Amram overland mythic
phone testament.
Laura Boss velvet incantations.
Homespun 2002
Preserve bone memory
dream like crystalline dawn
storm clouds scoot out to Atlantic
faith like baked blue fish
soft shell crabs
pigeon father in work shirt pocket
Ames, Iowa corn on cob grace
Homespun 2002.

Stay Hungry

Stay Hungry
Like burly Texas oil rig wildcat roughnecks
Bronx middle weight fight contender
Mexican seamstress in 12 hour day sew
machine roll.
Stay Hungry
Like old man's 1942 basic training
hard grind liberation
Dick Tracey hat bow tie 50 year kick bottom
midtown Manhattan parking lot quest.
Stay Hungry
Like Fort Lee 24 year old waitress tough heart
single mom
Fern's singular Zen quest
faith like California eucalyptus.
Stay Hungry
Manhattanville College Catholic salvation
heroin addict barn fire sobriety
hard work pelican desire
2 year psycho ward lock up mentally ill
calico hard drive
for salt ocean serenity.
Stay Hungry
Choir boy's immense New Mexico
sky devotion
JFK Jr.'s Camelot humanity
Manhattan pork chop potato fry
blue collar checkercloth dinner
Daily New hardscrabble politics
Lotto Pick 6 dollar and dream.
Stay Hungry
For New Testament South Carolina
Baptist salvation,
Jewish Holy Torah read redemption.
Islamic Ramadan gentle desert fast.
Stay Hungry
Burger King high school part time job
send kids to New Jerrsey computer school
ham and eggs City College
Cornell Medical School.
Stay Hungry

For Walt Whitman Brooklyn Ferry
velvet jubilee
George Washingon American Revolution's
bold Valley Forge winter
blood exile courage.
Stay Hungry
Like Vietnam vets 30 year mid summer's
night dream
Georgette's security guard cash and crry
work gig.
Stay Hungry
For holy providence ham hock Montgomery,
Alabama opportunity
parking lot car jock five dollar outlaw tip.
Stay Hungry
For American don't trend on me musket load
holy cowboy sage eyes on wilderness horizon
always!

Pedal Steel Guitar

I am Pedal Steel Guitar Navaho moccasins
Tooth pick in after diner hot meat loaf mouth
front porch American flag.
Bomber over Al Qaeda Afghanistan
high-tech computer rev all night
Allen Ginsberg read.
I am dump truck down Second Avenue pipeline
Soda machine Coca Cola corduroy messiah
mythic tears.
15 year old black Pulsar watch
moist hydrangea chest.
I am full grocery bag Queens
Grand Central Parkway easy glide.
Grandma Bessie's 30 year yogurt culture.
I am Marion Prison maximum security lock up
Dreams like street corner kick can beatitude
dreams like killer red hair gold chain
sweetheart.
I am July Katmandu
Himalayan mountains like hypodermic needles
sweet and sour soup
chopsticks in cartoon ears
Brooklyn chocolate egg cream.
I am New Mexico promise land
Like postcard in square metal Federal mail slot
Vermont April maple sap.
Diane Feinstein U.S. Senate California
excellence.
I am Broad Street Newark soul brother hip hop
fandango.
Prairie fire rage like Arizona
hot jalapeno peppers.
I am Avenue A hot wire Chevrolet
easy shimmy
cool Budweiser buy back.
Yellowstone clockwork Old Faithful geyser.
Mom's cool antique tape measure collection.
I am America magic land
Bangor to Los Angeles.
Iowa field straw scarecrow

86th Street found copper penny 30 year cotton
candy good luck.
Wide smile on uptown number 6 train.
I am Mayflower providence God's new world
Covenant
Magna Carta wool texture weave.
I am 1958 Cold War air raid drill
Marshal Filler's doo wop radio
New Rochelle June running bases.
I am rock and roll salt air cadence
Edge city wet kisses brassiere unclasped
Friday nights
kind Turkish taffy works for highway
road warrior.
Local librarian tabby cat Austin, Texas sublime
Waylon Jennings outlaw fire.
I am Pedal Steel Guitar always!

No Bad Vibes

No Bad Vibes
Wolverine scowls
jackhammer anger assault 38 magnum in fat
cheek face.
No Bad Vibes
No wide bottom egomania no leather round
flannel shoulder whip crack.
No Bad Vibes
No Jersey City heroin whamping
third rate saxophone boys
corduroy delusion
no abortion's embryo murder.
No Bad Vibes
New Hampshire can't get straight in
wilderness haze
30 years on iron rack.
No tight tan short shorts
hooker high heels, nose up in air pose
no Sarah Lawrence poets
yellow press clippings bravado.
No Bad Vibes
Whacked out chunky Bronx doormen
No paranoid stroller moms spoil brat Gap kids
no golf bag on Lacoste shoulder
no cocaine glide jeep Cherokees
no trust fund ecstasy tab radicals
no girl talk five star eating holes
Friday night end of month rent hustle
Bloomingdale's revolutionary cadre.
No Bad Vibes
No grizzly senior citizens jerks at 40 years
still gray hair mutants at 80
no Irish woman bartender with bumble bee
up bottom
No Bad Vibes
Leave full urine bottle at doctor's office
leave dead flowers by Paterson Falls
Mercedes Benz in Scarsdale circular driveway.
No Bad Vibes
Bring on God's velvet ham and eggs grace
revolutionary smiles

kindness like content tabby cat
eloquent gade school librarian.
No Bad Vibes
Bring on straight shot lunch bucket
pinewood talk
Laura's 100% bonded sweetness
I-78 Easton, Pennsylvania toll booth
heart women.
Mary Jo's out of state Arkansas
Ozark telephoe calls.
No Bad Vibes
Bring on Louisiana Dave's RC cola
moon pie beatnik sandal
beatific words
velvet Frank Sinatra high dice roll voice chops
bring on Sagittarius full moon quiescence
South Jersey log cabin morning tea
maple syrup incantations
Navaho holy drum circle.
No Bad Vibes now!

New Jersusalem

I am William Blake
New Jerusalem ripe Connecticut
cucumber jubilee
well stocked wood toll shed Susan's brown hair
singular daisies
I am harmony's crescendo angel
Holy Redemption
like cork board thumb tacks
bologna slice tin foil.
Thomas Jefferson Declaration of Independence
genuis.
I am amazing grace Crosby Steet cobble alley
Forget me not soul sister search
Marlboro pack January repentance.
Mexican wool blanket around square shoulders
sweet Jesus whole grain salvation.
I am Arkansas green hallow whiskey still
Hillbilly gentle twang
salt cashews porcelain bowl
Dad's Anzio beach combat G.I. crimson valor.
I am cognitive thought blue sky ramble
Three quick hazelnut coffees highway bound
Rand McNally map in tow
FDNY, Police Rescue, EMS World Trade
mass murder gotham heroics
President George W. Bush west Texas
big sky grace.
I am New Jerusalem cool
No aerobic cell phone zombies
no internet brainwash upper class baby boom
fat cats
no cat 'o nine tail poetics
no Bahamas oil down vacation.
I am clean cotton sheet providence
Martin Luther King letter from
a Birmingham jail.
I am 85th Street fire station American
Flag unfurl.
I am promised land rhubarb stalk
Compassion like Boy Scout masters easy smile
constitutional freedom time America

First Lady Laura Bush simple eloquence
I am flannet warrior
sen-sen flannel shirt pocket
New Mexico low humidity delight
holy Greenwich Village Waverly Place
purple daybreak
1-40 Oklahoma highway groove
Yes, I am kick bottom New Jerusalem
12 gate city on April hill
heaven's cinnamon eternal life promise yes!

Stand And Fight

Stand and Fight
Corporate brain fracture
madcap 20 year old kids credit card buy spree.
Stand and Fight
Crazy quilt crack pipe
district attorney greasy pole questions
quick talk interent cad carry
Calvin Klein losers.
Stand and Fight
Goose step allegiance to high school
cut throat friends
Ritalin snort pushers Ecstasy tab death wish.
Stand and Fight
Half baked 1960's granola holocaust ideas
communal sidewinder mediocrity
Columbine High School ice mountain clinques.
Aryan Nation gun tote thugs.
Stand and Fight
Big deal stock market millionaires
nose in air like Paris bound Concorde.
Aeorbics body mirror freaks
New Canaan, Connecticut chandelier lies.
Stand and Fight
Kamikaze sleeping bag narcissistic get down
glossy magazine feminists raw power play
Jim Crow racism
clam shell hate.
Stand and Fight
Wannabe poets black turtle neck Italian shades
milquetoast text.
Stand and Fight
Upper class Mercedes cut throat dream.
Lexington Avenue cell phone aficionados
Hollywood skinner box rat T.V. sitcoms.
Stand and Fight
Baby boom cocaine addiction french fry
brain short bolt
women on speed freak diet pills
hand in pocket prescripton pad psychiatrists.
Stand and Fight
Yes to corn on cob senior citizens

mythic blood stories
yes to 50 year old dudes' pinewood wisdom
yes to Lady Liberty's open arm embrace
yes to common man's red white blue valor
patriots keep powder dry vigil.
Holy Jewish mystic Kyoto Zen monk
California new age saint.
Toledo, Ohio trucker
beatific Fort Bragg Army staff sergeant.
Stand and Fight
Black folks Harlem street corner justice
teamster local 272 honest day wage
U.S. constitution move to cherry pie union
corduroy human dignity yes.

Bald Eagle Flies

Bald Eagle Flies
Over Yosemite National Park
California Redwoods
over sparse Mohave desert magic Utah arroyos.
No longer endangered species
no longer extinct like Emily Dickinson
sealing wax
Bald Eagle Flies
Over green Arkansas Ozarks
thank you President Clinton your passion for
green wilderness wildlife
American gingham democracy.
Thank you Interior Secretary Bruce Babbit
DDT ban earth hold beauty.
Thank you Conservation Corps steady hand
hundreds diamond eagle eggs
Bald Eagle Flies
Over majestic Teton Mountain, Yellowstone
holy ground.
Yes Bald Eagle Flies
Over Washington D.C. Anaconda River
American green garden ecology.
Teddy Roosevelt bold vision
conservation pine tree beauty.
Yes, Bill Clinton wildflower heart.
Bald Eagle flies in 50 states
No longer endanger species.
America's July fourth magic bird.
Bald Eagle Flies
For our Hershey bar sons
our Girl Scout daughters fierce "can do"
independence.
Bald Eagle Flies
Bring home American convenant
God's promised land grace
blue Massachusetts sky optimism.
Bring home hardscrabble opportunity
homerun faith
wetlnds glory environmental Greenpeace vigil.
Yes, Bald Eagle Flies
Over my cherished Manhattan Island

Bald Eagle Flies
Above my city
Lincoln Center ballet grace
Teamster union hall horse trade
over sweet Duke Ellinton Harlem
over holy World Trade ground zero.
yes, Bald Eagle Flies again
God Bless America.

Stop The Bombing Yugoslavia

Stop The Bombing Yugoslavia
NATO B-52 Yugoslavia carpet bomb
blood litany
America you boy scout merit badge saint
foreign policy morality
like attic spider web.
Serbia countryside moon crater
corpses line mountain towns.
Stop The Bombing
Too much fire cracker violence
Revlon lipstick snarls
quick score stock market greed.
Too much white picket fence delusion
media side show denial death march
high-tech blood sacrament.
Ecstasy tab in soft mouth.
Stop The Bombing
Cruise missiles like made fandango over cobble
Balkan villages
Bill Clinton hearts and flowers sensitivity
training ideology
foreign policy desolation row.
Stop The Bombing
Oh America business as usual
roll bone dice
push diaper infants down corpse lined Second
Avenue millennium steel on black steel
media Tai Bo sweat workout
too many Oprah Winfrey powder puff oracles,
plastic surgery aficionados.
Stop The Bombing
A million tattered refugees,
bread, fresh water thirst delirium,
F-15's strafe Belgrade again and again like
punch-drunk middle weight club boxer.
Milosovic death wish,
mass graves,
cat 'o nine tails violence upon violence.
Stop The Bombing Yugoslavia
Ten thousand Yale Skull and Bones cults line

American highways,
poets dream computer chip power plays,
marijuana Machiavellian big-time Pulitzer Prize
orgasm.
Stop The Bombing
50,000 union cats yell more green cash
front burner health care.
Littleton, Colorado blood red carnage
13 corpses in white bread Denver suburb
black clad Goths
MTV propaganda
O.K. City Nostradamus holocaust tornado.
Pioneer ethic dies like September Kansas
wild flowers.
Stop The Bombing
Hard earned Federal budget surplus down metal
drain in schizophrenia Yugoslavia blow out.
Bronx County food stamps cut like hemp rope.
Snake oil salesmen replace San Francisco
oracles
holy madmen
calico prophets.
Generation X dreams Zen heroin score
thousand dollars a month East Village squat.
Stop The Bombing
Boom town Wall Street stock market
five star Madison Avenue haute cuisine lunches
Jeep Cherokees off Michigan assembly lines
Antigua top shelf vacation junkets.
Too much copper glass wildcat anger.
Stop The Bombing
Serbs, Croats, Kosovars
all in 500 year hillbilly Klan feud.
Refugees fill Montenegro
hardscrabble Albania
cluster bomb liberation
wood 2 by 4 crack on Milosovic's round skull.
Stop The Bombing Yugoslavia
Internet illiterates worship computer chip God
old folks' pharmaceutical pills string out each
ozone day
televisions addiction like cherry cheese cake.
Stop The Bombing

Oh America your soul like dawn
Nebraska prairie
small town Iowa barn raise
heroic G.I.s on Omaha Beach.
Stop The Bombing
Ethnic diversity
divide and conquer like apple pie thin slice.
No faith in God's Rocky Mountain glory.
No faith in Constitutional quiescence.
Stop The Bombing
Oh America your literary junior high hardball
cliques
barb wire town fathers and mothers
workacholic baby boom crimson sisters in
Dexedrine string out.
Clever district attorney aesthetics.
Stop The Bombing
Oh America
come home to Harry Truman plain talk
Abraham Lincoln common sense
texture weave ethics.
Stop demon black trench coat vortex
Stealth bomber Star Wars attack.
America, move to God's holy white light prairie
dawn sanctity.
Sharecropper overall kindness
blue collar excellence
Black Street corner miracle bebop Cannonball
Adderley saxophone.
Stop cold cash money rosary
Boardroom power play computer shimmy
Hollywood flash bulb fame delusion.
Stop The Bombing
No more rude Yuppie decay
Ritalin addict fourth graders.
Stop The Bombing
Oh America,
you are too Thomas Jefferson good for clinical
drive by paranoia
too good for carpet bomb blood violence as
pinewood salvation
too good for Bowie knife on two year old
toddler's throat.

Too good for Manhattan blood wound fashion
show tango.
Stop The Bombing
End the war
End the war
bring wildcard Russians to oak diplomacy table.
Bring Madeleine Albright,
State Department savvy to blood work.
America, let Utah wild flowers bloom like
eloquent Dizzy Gillespie bebop cool.
Let hometown Massachusetts cherry pop
wilderness excellence surface
let Detroit City ghetto streets bring on gospel
eloquence.
Negotiate peace like lace doily.
Enough is flat out enough
bring on green garden planet serentiy
Yugoslavian hearth fires
God have cathedral mercy
Stop The Bombing Yugoslavia Now.

Sing Mockingbird

Sing Mockingbird
Take it to empty July football grid
drive in movie Coca Cola caress
cheshire heart parents round
cotton shoulder angels.
Sing Mockingbird
Sweet like August Maine blueberries
Mr. Ladensack senior English James Joyce
excellence
miniature golf first summer date
Jennifer's old man's maroon Chevy Caprice
Singer Johnny Mathis velvet cool.
Sing Mockingbird
Howl for Bobby Kennedy blood on L.A. Hilton
ballroom
Martin Luther King
Memphis Shirley Motel bloodbath
White Plains bowling alley long neck
Budweisers
Jones Beach West End 2 miracle day trips
ocean tide quiescence.
Sing Mockingbird
Vietnam unwelcome guest in cosmic
butterfly skull
Khe Sahn, Da Nang, Mekong Delta,
broken promise like AEPi fraternity
blood rite cult.
Sing Mockingbird
After dinner trips to Manor Park
Long Island Sound
easy cha cha Hilltop Bar roadhouse virtue.
Sing Mockingbird
Jane R. virginity loss in 3D August coming of
age.
George Washington University
sophomore English
Mr. Claysenes American lit wildcat
firecracker genius
Thoreau Walden Pond wilderness glide.
Sing Mockingbird
Literature wildflower addiction like cheshire

sorority girl shack up
Kentucky bourbon and soda.
Sing Mockingbird
Youth's eight cylinder hard drive
April Washington D.c. cherry blossom delight.
Triumph TR-250 sports car fourth gear
highway overdrive.
Youth's sweetcake essence.
Sing to me, mockingbird.

Liberty Highway

Liberty Highway
White line kaleidoscope Oklahoma sanctity
God's carpet ride bing cherry metaphor delight
mom's October baked apples
heavy sweet cream.
Liberty Highway
Boulder, Colorado cayenne groove
J.C. Penney magic sewing machine
pine green down vest
Missouri mud work boots.
Liberty Highway
Acoustic bass resonance
Brooklyn Atlantic sea breeze
Mary's Long Island rosary bead hot rod faith
Camden, Maine harbor lights
like prophetic fireflies.
Liberty Highway
Mary Jo and Dale's calico Eureka Springs
Arkansas small town quiescence
12 step meeting higher power
dollar in the kitty providence.
Liberty Highway
3 A.M. lilac night prayers
Albuquerque desert typewriter rides
maroon prairie comforter pinewood
wisdom stick
New Jersey eggs over easy.
April Washington Square Park
Jack Daniels jubilee.
Liberty Highway
Rare Nigerian incense
Methodist Sunday bell toll
Livingston Manor easy July kisses
with Susan 1970
Zen notions like California beach
white stallions
South Carolina slow motion Ferris wheel.
Little Amanda's library read passion.
Liberty Highway
8th grade young dudes unlock gray
pit bull dream

skateboard serendipity vision
like railyard hobo fires
cheap sneaker bravado.
Wisconsin maple tree craft
red hair denim poet Goddess.
Liberty Highway
Brigid Murnaghan poetry read
down beat delight
hot apple pie always chocolate ice cream scoop.
American Spirit Cigarettes outback smokes.
Liberty Highway
God's Lincoln Tunnel grace
firm East Coast handshake
tabby cat smiles
walnut brownies on slow bake
Oh Liberty Highway Yes.

July Heat Wave

I am cool Michigan wind heat wave break
First Bruce Springsteen album
New Jersey interstate fire lyrics
Manhattan 10th Avenue mirage,
Jones Beach body surf celebration
I am Delphonics New York Hospital July
Psycho ward 1970
gymnasium soap shower.
Stelazine vial White Plains day pass.
Samantha's formal garden kisses hot flesh
like Indiana highway tar firecracker passion.
Moses Ten Commandment holy law on fire.
I am Jackson Hole, Wyoming summer Stetson
American flag t-shirt
West 23rd Street Chelsea Catholic angels.
Black can man work a day heat up
I am brother Marc's ham and cheddar
Phone calls
Manhattan July heat wave evening
100 degrees flat out.
Cool Maxwell House iced coffee.
Clem Norelli Rockland County grace
straw hat serenity.
I am noontime Budweiser beer
Mad commotion like erratic
Coney Island sea breeze
cotton candy loop the loop.
Flo Kennedy's cool bop lemonade country
legal advice
Harlem open fire hydrant
Remy Martin classy black sister hustle
1969 Volkswagen van ice chest lumberjack
Jack Kerouac typewriter ride
sidewalk egg fry Jesus have mercy salvation.
I am cool cimplex movie theater
Popcorn crunch hot butter
Coca Cola sweet like Georgia nectar.
Hawaii rubber flip flops number 30 sunblock.
Harley Davidson I-87 Canada bound
I am Con Edison mahhole heat wave
Like Astoria bakery oven
worker 3 A.M. sweat overtime

Marlboro carton in early morning downshift.
New York Post sports page serendipity
mythic grandparents toddler rescue
public swim pool celebration.
I am NYPD detectives Batman
Short bolt assignment.
Little Italy white undershirt racket boys
grappa, mozzarella, al dente pasta
mythic cool shade quest.
Baby boom sassy sisters looking real good
Washington Heights electricity black out
sidewalk dominoes
I am God's infinite paisley vest grace
Virginia trucker ball cap
highway faith like Episcopal grace
holy American liberty sweat on brow
Wildcat true grit.
July Heat Wave.

Common Sense

I am Tom Paine common sense
Belt Parkway cattails
test tube blood Depakote levels
Life Free or Die
American revolution's bold credo.
I am clear head red neck mouth lollipop
John Deere tractor lower 40 pea patch.
I am June sweet Georgia peaches
High school guns zero tolerance
yes to gym coach basic sweat hard drive
yes to flannel English teacher poetry groove.
I am library maple leaf celebration like Roman
Candle read
cowboy fence ride essence
tin mess kit bacon and beans dinner.
I am Ellis Island sweet immigrants
Grandpa Charlie
3 year old third class wood hull steerage.
American promise like Conastoga wagon
homesteaders
Black men, women tough underground
railroad heroics 1856.
I am billionth grain of sand
Humble like Albuquerque bus station
pretzel tin can homeless
old time gymnasium dance floor shing-a-ling
Bronx break dance rapture.
I am Black doo wop boys
Harlem four-part harmony.
Sunday glazed ham Flo Kennedy angelic vision.
I am Amtrak diesel, Chicago to New Orleans
Bar car iced coffee.
Illinois heartland easy roll notions.
Don't Tread On Me.
I am Manhattan June afternoon overcast gray
Blanket sky
subway number 4 train 14th street bound.
Pony Express like Nevada horizon lightning
good luck copper penny dream
push comes to shove
Roy Rodgers, Dale Evans rodeo swirl

lock and load liberty.
I am unemployed steel worker Gary, Indiana
Like Bob Dylan desolation row
cheap market Russian steel
soup kitchen spaghetti lunch.
North Dakoka depression prices wheat farmer
3rd generation farm foreclose.
I am funky nephew Charlie
Litlle league catcher glove shin guard valor.
I am Tom Paine common sense
No to legal cardboard interrogation
no to voodoo university slick talk
no to cell phone communiqués.
I am God's cherry tomato faith
Full cupboard whole grain flour
cardamon, cayenne.
I am Santa Cruz Pacific Ocean salt sea breeze.
Jack Kerouac typewriter ride
dawn New Mexico desert highway
rock stead westbound.

L.A. You Call To Me

L.A. You Call To Me
Cool Tapanga Canyon earth vibrations
white Chalis dream
dawn Pacific Ocean fog coast
highway quiescence.
L.A. You Call To Me
Purple cape sisters, Sheryl Crow
Santa Monica Boulevard
Budweiser buy back casting call steel glass
high-tech cat pen.
L.A. You Call To Me
Joni Mitchell silk glide
July fourth West Coast kisses
lavender sheets, Mexican sweat gardeners.
Congresswoman Maxine Waters East Central
L.A. hardscrabble ghetto passion
Ventura Freeway Tuesday afternoon riot act.
L.A. You Call To Me
Pound cake, cool lemonade
always mythic reefer
sweet Michelle Phillips classy City of Angels
bikini yin yang.
L.A. You Call To Me
Nathaniel West bourbon bottle *Day of Locust*
shady side apocalypse drag race
muscle bodies always the number 30 sun block.
Maria Shriver cheshire cat cool.
L.A. You Call To Me
This East Coast flannel warrior
chop sticks in left hand
Dionysian Mercedes Benz desire.
L.A. You Call To Me
Movie studios executive office China White
charge account Chanel mistress.
Oh, L.A. You Call To Me
Yes, City of Angels, Ronald Reagan American
spring garden optimism
Sunset Strip 20 dollars a night
West Coast neon.
Come to me L.A.

you raw wild west dream city
full saddle bags like infant's water wings
California crescent moon Zen incantations.
L.A. You Call To Me!

Woodshed Blues

Woodshed Blues
Hide out from New York City madcap
speed freak power hondo egomania.
Woodshed Blues
No Louisiana sweetheart double bed hip grind
cool July moist Delta kisses betrayal.
Woodshed Blues
Years of floor board walk
howls down Santa Fe Trail
Charlie Parker's burly lunch bucket saxophone.
Woodshed Blues
Too many cold turkey whampings
pie in mustache round face
slander like raw oysters.
Woodshed Blues
22 year old fashion model prostitutes line
Madison Avenue
like made gray pigeons.
Oh, Woodshed Blues
Gold bag gangsters growl
like Michigan wolverines
hard nose Bronx leather punk illiterates.
Woodshed Blues
Philadelphia to mythic Portland
strip down high-tech steel ball paranoia.
Woodshed Blues
Blood draw too many wildcat violent moments
politically correct like Brown University
professor
dark marijuana cynicism.
Woodshed Blues
Victims abound like Coney Island kewpie dolls
early morning Lafayette Street taxi
after hours joint voodoo.
Woodshed Blues
No to ten year friendship
walk away
no to Kurt Vonnegut ice nine exchanges
bring it home pine green work shirt roll
Northern California Mendicino dream
funky folks quest for birch beer serenity

wildcat redemption
Jesus' maple syrup love New Jerusalem
gingham holiness.
Woodshed Blues
Fly to bald eagle fierce Tidewater independence
honest Utah handshake
faith in July's blue sky grace.

Unplug Daddy-O

Unplug Daddy-O
High-tech doo hickies Information Age
dice and cut.
Computer brainwash digital chips
mercenary T.V. sitcoms
quick cut commercials.
Unplug Daddy-O
Compact disc laser ice pond security web
SONY walkman headphones
pierce sanctified ear drum sanctity.
Unplug Daddy-O
Keep movie theater subliminal messages from
kaleidoscope eye.
Unplug Daddy-O
Internet drainage ditch illusion
useless hound dog information.
Unplug Daddy-O
Read top shelf Classics
Henry James, Sweet Shakespeare,
exile James Joyce.
Keep book on lap hour upon hour like orange
tabby cat.
Unplug Daddy-O
Pick older cats highway brains like Georgia
church Sunday turkey dinner.
Listen to flannel vagabond sages
corn on cob mythic stories.
Unplug Daddy-O
Embrace C-Span, Weather Channel
read hallow New York Times
Reader's Digest homespun apple pie
tend own Cherokee mind
embrace Hegelian dialectics
Declaration of Independence genius.
Yes to chicken in every pot politics
Congress district grass roots canvas.
Unplug Daddy-O
Think beyond patent leather shoe stereotypes
designer anorexic fashion credit card eyes.
Hollywood screenplay quick fix delusions.
Unplug Daddy-O

High-tech cognitive desolation row
Western vision long way home.
Yes to New Mexico horizon blue highway faith
yes to old bald eagle flight.
God's Holy Bible revelation.
No to computer brain addiction
no to black magic Marilyn Manson music
no to 5 dollar popcorn Star Wars fantasy.
Unplug Daddy-O
No to Wall Street Enron money payoff
no to fifth grade trinket materialism
no to market place firing squad.
Unplug Daddy-O
Like mad bohemian shuck digital life support
ecstasy tab fascination, T.V. blood violence
sleazy red light sex
walk mythic Appalachian trail journey's
teacup Zen satori
plow pasture with crystalline vision
strong flannel shirt back.
Bring on National Parks Service
oakwood ecstasy
Colorado wildflower wonder
Maine cozy harbor salt air heart.
April Appalachian Trail mythic hike
pristine New Jersey wetlands
Green Planet holy green vibration now.

Gregory Corso Dies Brother

Gregory Corso Dies Brother
Beatnik poet manchild
Minnesota morning late January
crimson saint Greenwich Village
madcap oracle halcyon soul.
Gregory Corso Dies Brother
Desolation row rawbone childhood
hardscrabble youth
early jailtime.
Gregory Corso Dies Brother
Bring on wildcat poetics
dead serious passion
for word like fires
down on Hudson piers
Denver August nights.
Gregory Corso Dies Brother
Hooks up with sweet
Jack Kerouac, Lowell angel
Allen Ginsberg kick bottom
cut the pie visionary
sunny side up David Amram.
Break down academic walls
starched shirt velvet
poets room.
Gregory Corso Dies Brother
quintessential beat
straight shot spirit
American literary
ground zero genuis
Seventh Avenue early dawn satori.
Gregory Corso Dies Brother
Harvard self educate
drop in books
Gasoline, Happy Birthday Death –
13 magic volumes
poems like freight train
Canada bound.
Gregory Corso Dies Brother
Poetry bad boy
fire eye log Tequila shots

late into Carmine Street night
always gray hair mane
always top notch craftsman.
Oh Gregory I spend three
Greenwich Village March afternoons
1995 brain pick
Kettle of Fish Bar bartender
buddy Myrna rap
cherry pie full aces poetry
rap black leopard
wildflower beatnit women
rap Riviera Café mad cap rave
always writing tips
beatific prosody.
Gregory I pick brain like North Beach
Sunday turkey.
Your kindness to this young
cat beautiful like Tuscany pasta
red wine outdoor manga.
Gregory Corso Dies Brother
You talk Homer, Zeus
tough hide Prometheus
Tokay wine Dionysus.
Bring Allen Ginsberg
third street digs scoot
check out my embryo poems.
Gregory Corso Dies Brother
Always hip checker board outrage
outlaw wildcat sublime
Washington Square Park
night saxophone.
Gregory Corso Dies Brother
1995 yes we move through mythic village
t-bone optimism steel girder clarity
Gregory tour guide honcho
Old joints café Figaro, Back Fence Bar.
We hook up Brigit Murnaghan
Bleeker Street beatnik riff
déjà vu 1958
hand wave like alabast doves
cut to rainbow essence
no small time poetry con
fat bottom pretense

no shuck and jive nose in air.
Sweet beat liberation.
Gregory Corso Dies Brother
Democracy's sweet MacDougal air
eye on urban abyss Dharma Bums
western sky
American literary cool bop beatitude
poetry chops like Florentine
magic fresco always ruby heart
on denim sleeve.
Gregory Corso Dies Brother
Bring on Lester Young
saxophone cool Charlie Parker
on the road sublime spontaneous poetic riff.
Gregory you die in Minnesota.
Three mythic afternoons you take this
young buck under feather wing
radical kindess beat hip
buy buy cool, go cat go.
Yes Gregory Corso Dies Brother
We will miss you
always cash and carry integrity
highway firecracker witness
outlaw anarchy word on paper excellence.
Yes Gregory at Kettle of Fish
You bless my poetic quest
bless Yorkville two head demons
bless Colorado quest for promised land
salvation.
Thank you sir
go in cool bop peace, Godspeed.

Deal

Deal Bronx outlaw carrots in garden sanctity
Minnesota sugar beats, bootleg JFK Airport
Wild turkey whiskey.
Deal sweet Muddy Waters Delta Blues like
Bottle cap collection
straw broom sweep over Memphis porch.
Deal aces wild on green poker table
Bronx sandlot dream. Louisville Slugger
Saturday afternoon homerun crack.
Deal Kosovo peace communiqués
Fort Lee wet Memorial Day kisses
passion like Times Square neon.
Deal poetry lids metaphor twigs and stems
Howl beyond New Mexico contraband
nickel dime
down beat Greenwich Village juke joint.
Deal fried chicken, pink lemonade meander
Early morning Marlboros
holy word on white cotton page.
Deal God's full wicker basket passion
Late night Bar 55 Dale Hardman Guiness pints.
Deal cat bird seat analytics
Courtroom black Bible justice
hungry Cleveland women
mini skirt smoke mirror high heels.
Deal orange Navajo blanket Duke Ellington
American genuis
kitchen table hot biscuit politics Laura Boss's
New Jersey highway quest
Joe Davancens West Coast acoustic bass magic.
Deal Nebraska road passion like prairie fire hay
bale glory.
Willa Cather red clay novels.
Take is home big cat like corn on cob
gospel choir
Jimi Hendrix left hand guitar genuis.
Deal in mythic black
Low rider Latino Nuyorican cadence
full rucksack, firm hand on Chevrolet wheel
cash and carry cool.

Empower Yourself

Empower Yourself
Eat hot dog sauerkraut Nags Hed,
North Carolina
April renegade surf wonder.
Albuquerque open sky sanctity
Vicki Hudspith I-40 Gallop bound
turqouise sky quest
Move from cold water highway ditch
morning heroin jones
ball and chain cattle herd dysfunction.
Empower Yourself
In codependent anonymous 12 step
baked apple heal
one day at a time.
Empower Yourself
In Chesapeake Bay Bridge salt breeze wonder
Camden, Maine July harbor magic
North Carolina Outer Banks immense beauty.
Empower Yourself
Pick outlaws Silverado brains
brown bag Budweiser
run bronze hand up sweetheart's nylon leg.
No to queen of spades
blood arrogance.
No to corporate shell game.
Empower Yourself
Wait for Ohio rainstorm like monthly rent bill
wait for Boston dawn break.
Empower Yourself
Move down mythic brown rice Lao Tzu
spiritual path
30 year trellis roses, Woodstock oak trees,
Nirvana like Oklahoma prairie fire.
Empower Yourself
Dance tango like wild white witch
Dionysian maple syrup incantations
Fillmore West hippie happening 1969.
Empower Yourself
Talk to Go flannel morning prayer
down comforter Bible read

apartment sweep out fry two eggs over easy
hot sauce.
Empower Yourself
Embrace Russell, Kansas prairie ethics
Beethoven cognitive rambles
can man hip hustle
Park Avenue yellow tulips
Southern State Parkway
hard drive like World War Two
Red Ball express.
Empower Yourself
Daily hot shower shave hallow spiral
notebook journal
buckle down to flowered hat welder's
high rise craft.
Move from high-tech addiction
computer Skinner Box digital gulag.
Empower Yourself
Self esteem like Niagara Falls torrent
liberation's quilting bee excellence
Love's Rainbow essence.
Move to calico dream like California Monterrey
Bay dawn majesty.
Dream on brothers and calico sisters, yes!

Sweet Devotion

Sweet Devotion
God's flannel shoulders nylon stocking on
straight backed wicker chair
shouts down Cherokee firecracker
Second Avenue.
Sweet Devotion
Grandfather clock tick-tock
attic room cirrus sky
paisley dream back seat Fort Mustang
honey bear hugs
holy glow redemption.
Sweet Devotion
Providence like North Carolina fried oysters
forth morning coffee
Erika Springs Dale Bramhall piano glide.
Sweet Devotion
Like lower forty spring plow honesty
Central Park radio cool bop.
Sweet Devotion
Interstate 40 O.K. City two step
New Mexico hip hot java coffee house hustle.
No funhouse mirrors
no junior high school madcap vanity
no M.F.A. sidewinder poets
Sweet Devotion
Bring on George Washington Bridge
mythic Manhattan panorama.
Fort Lee lace curtain serentiy
Miles Davis cut the pie trumpet sublime
Sweet Devotion
Late night floor board ramble
commotion electric North Star light essence
Norman Riley percussion cool
soft boiled egg beat prosody.
Sweet Devotion
No Hampton's white linen tequila wheel spin
no two year old fracture milk bottle
mad scream.
Bring on Sweet Devotion
Joint jumps like grasshopper cake walk

Jack Daniels shooters.
New York City urban Black dudes
Bleeker Street June night get down prophecy.
Sweet Devotion, yes!

Hopscotch Home

Hopscotch Home
Through Pennsylvania green valley
Hudson River gingerbread house Pony Express
lightning speed excellence.
New Rochelle running bases trim backyard.
Hopscotch Home
Fifth grade girls' soccer team
June strawberry afternoons
Conastoga wagon California bound
Good Humor bells
like Episcopal cathedral.
Hopscotch Home
Oven bake peanut buter cookies
cool milk gallon jug
13 year old cat skateboard genuis
toothpaste tube half squeeze.
New York Times Sports page flat out obsession.
Hopscotch Home
Sweet Scarsdale high school kisses
unclasped brassiere
maroon knee socks hug.
Hopscotch Home
Chalk hieroglyphics hopscotch box pirouettes
maze like mythic Isadora Duncan
Chesapeake and Ohio northbound like mad
crimson demon.
Nighttime ghost stories to hot wire
brother Marc.
Hopscotch Home
To Manhattan tough hide ho down
hot corner Fifth Avenue pretzels
number 1 subway train downtown roll
Christopher Street bound
stain glass Marc Chagall holy synagogue.
Heroic American farmers breadbasket harvest
George W. Bush Crawford, Texas honest heart.
Poets room holy ground cinnamon craft.
Hopscotch Home
American transcendence like peach cobbler
Henry David Thoreau's Walden Pond

wilderness salvation.
Home fries like East River pearl necklace
JFK airport London flight return
patriot's salt tears 1973.
Davis School crossing guard silver badge.
Hopscotch Home
Newark Jazz radio sublime
Dizz, Miles, Ella Fitzgerald excellence,
clean sky blue sheets tide laundry load.
Hopscotch Home
30 long road years, closet medals 5 A.M.
morning corduroy prayer
too many sidewinder missiles
too many Second Avenue rabid dogs
too many Brooklyn wildcats at tender throat.
fly by cheeseburger dinners.
Hopscotch Home
Manhattan orange sun illumination texture
Zen roundhouse satori
medium-rare Kansas City t-bone home fries
parking lot down and dirty Red Volvo
easy drive
high school choir girl soprano crush
next hairpin turn optimism.
Holy bebop tool box redemption
Catskill Mountain rainbow glow
love's hip swing beatitude.
Hopscotch Home, yes.

PETER CHELNIK - HEY GIRL - COLLECTED POEMS

IV
PARADISE HIGHWAY
2006

PETER CHELNIK - HEY GIRL - COLLECTED POEMS

Rhapsody America

Rhapsody America
Freedom planying time grace
South Michigan farmland, wheat, corn
quiescence,
long haul Greyhound bus driver
ultimate cool.

Rhapsody America
Baltimore harbor crabcake delight,
Lady Liberty's cotton arm oracle
like Davis School librarian sage.

Rhapsody America
Cannonball Adderly broad shoulder
saxophone excellence,
Kansas City stay at home mom's
enterpreneur pay bills, invention.
Local truck driver Puerto Rican
Second Avenue delivery ballet.

Rhapsody America
Bank teller Chase Manhattan
mathematics quick step brain
social security hot oven bread senior
citizen lifeline.

Rhapsody America
Myrna Van der Linden immense Christian faith,
Dallas Texas choir angels
Baptist church barbecue faith hoe-down.

Rhapsody America
Southbound Richmond, Virginia
quiet magnolia salvation,
January morning Greensboro
breakfast all you can eat buffet
three coffees Florida Panhandle
mythic bound.

Rhapsody America
Ella Fitzgerald scat sublime,
Metropolitan Opera Joan Sutherland
voice chops like cool August green tea.

Rhapsody America
St. Cloud, Minnesota spring thaw
puff cumulus cloud poetics.
Yes to Home Depot Saturday
morning holy errands.
Yes to Anthony's Wagner Junior
High School basketball
point guard dream.
Yes to Beethoven edge city piano
sonatas.

Rhapsody America
Dogwood Madison Avenue bloom
like Big Apple Circus cotton candy,
Salt Lake City arched back Mormon ethics,
working men and woman pine tree
genius, Ingrid's Baldwin Piano lightning hands
ruby heart horizon excellence, always.

Earth Turn

Spring early Sunday morning spring
equinox, 7:34 A.M., wind chime Georgia bound glory
Cherokee tribe walk land
like purple holy men.

Earth Turn
Planting time
calico promises like door to door
knife salesman,
telephone line Indiana grace
Tuskeegee, Alabama black soul train delight.

Earth Turn
Fire on lake poetics
muscle forearm narrow waist
gingham cowgirl,
highway like Arizona sagebrush melody.

Earth Turn
Verrazano Bridge nine dollar toll
New Jersey to sweetheart Brooklyn
Williamsburg hot java
Woodstock Phillip Levine chop wood
easy does it poetic salvation.

Earth Turn
No to demons in round ball cap skull
No to manic gryoscope baby boomers
No to nasty Madison Avenue gin drunks.
Bring on God's spring spirit heal,
black railroad men touch sky wisdom
bring on toddler first rocky road steps.

Earth Turn
Back door kisses like butterscotch
Sunday, cameo hearts firebrand eros
ridgeline ethics.

Earth Turn
Boy Scouts merit badge Be Prepared
penny candy Hillsdale Michigan delight,
2006 baseball card flip.

Earth Turn
Large whole wheat dream,
Skidmore dance major sophomore,
morning paprika stretch exercise, three hour
ballet delight.
Truck stop pink clad waitress,
faith like Manhattan sunrise six A.M. halcyon
glory, Youngstown, Ohio sugarland bound.
Always mustard seed growth,
lake trout Missouri serenity,
poetic magnolia craft, wilderness freedom, yes.

Bohemian Howl

Bohemian Howl
Fringe cats like gyroscope spin
Memphis blues guitar pickers
grace like sweet Austin, Texas
outback January pasture.

Bohemian Howl
touch sky clean and sober
flannel dream,
wide poets Cincinnati smiles,
Newark, New Jersey
stretch canvas, acrylic
multicolor paradise,
Tuesday afternoon silver rain.
Miles Davis be-bop trumpet genuis.

Bohemian Howl
Change calico America
Harlem after school purple
mythic tutors,
National Public Radio
morning Burlington, Vermont
black coffee crescendo,
Joan's Drum tobacco roll, Santa Fe cool bop.

Bohemian Howl
Maple syrup social justice,
straight back cod fish opportunity
Pakistani taxi drivers Manhattan
food on table heroics.

Bohemian Howl
Allen Ginsberg Golden Gate Park
Buddhist sandlewood grace,
Monterey Peninsular
morning persian cat fog,
New Paltz long skirt Wicca rainbow hearts.

Bohemian Howl
Yes to Fern Filner's San Francisco
mythic Bay Area drum circle,
tribal zen vibrations.
Yes to Lopez Island Big Dipper
bring it home night sky. Crescendo.
Yes to orange ball Panama City Beach
January sunsets.
Egg scramble, bacon, southern grits.

Bohemian Howl
Massachusetts hammer dulcimer
literary outlaw all day
Charles Bukowski read.
Flesh on flesh chamomile tea
April afternoon sidewinder eros.

Bohemian Howl
Beethoven on road ruby passion
fresh Martin guitar strings like
yellow forsythia glory,
groove down.
Cinnamon creativity apple pie delight.
Flannel poets touch sky pasion.
Bohemian Howl, dig it.

Break Out

Break out
Winter bleach white straight jacket,
Greenhaven Prison hard time jail term,
steel NYPD handcuffs.

Break out
No to poets marijuana craft throw
words on paper
No to martini long leg Bloomingdale's ladies'
 snarls.
No to Lexington Avenue New York State Lotto
 dream aficionados.
No to corporate cheap suit ego boys.

Break out
Yes to spring gentle Manhattan
harbor breeze, Mo's snickers bar aesthetic,
La Guardia High School Friday afternoon liberty
 time.
Yes to late night iced tea IBM typewriter
ceative poetry jags.
Walt Whitman Brooklyn May lilacs.
Yes to Woodstock night ride New York
State Thruwy freedom north bound.
Yes to Tinker Street morning fandango.

Break out
Embrace Utah big sky epiphany
flannel howls Monterey Bay magic
sunset, John Steinbeck's Mexican migrant grace.
Embrace salt tides like Maurice ravel classic
 French cool out.
Provence moist kisses.

Break out
Yes to red down parker shed
like hibernate yellow caterpillar,
St. Patrick's Day afternoon
Robin red breast melody chirp.

Yes to Chevy pick-up Robert Moses Beach
bound, wrap-around sunglasses
iced coffee thermos,
thousand calico hosannahs.

Break out
No nine to five Times Square computer
digital noose.
No ball and chain hard core Wellsley College
feminist girl friend.
No ten Absolut Vodka drunks, morning wrm
Budweisers, get straight.

Break out
Bring on Johann Sebastian Bach birthday
miracle fugue.
American Spirit morning tobacco smoke,
WQXR Vivaldi greet day.
Bring on Palm Sunday ham glaze serenity.
Bring on Jesus, blue jean knees rainbow heal.

Break out
Yes to America's Illinois heartland spring planting
time, wheat, soy beans, corn.
Yes to bread basket jubilee.
Yes to Park Avenue tulip grace, Central Park March
mud earth imagination.
Yes to cheshire hearts on orange fire,
youths San Francisco back-beat promise,
a thousand dreams, yes.

Soft Machine

Jack Daniels kama sutra buy back
shady Friday night crinoline ladies
thousand wilderness kisses,
nighttime cherry pie rock steady
reefer heads.

Soft Machine
Jim Morrison America edge poet 1969
needle and thread carrion aesthetic,
clown face business suits cats,
Lexington Avenue Grand Central Station
rock homestead suburban scoot.

Soft Machine
Greek Peter's blue collar 86th Street
chicken shack,
Fox News lock and load,
rainbow steady North Carolina bootleg dream.

Soft Machine
Rosary bead Boston John Kerry
lilac President election quest,
damp morning mist
New Jersey Turnpike 18 wheel Kenmare trucks
overglide New York City diesel
glory bound.

Soft Machine
Poets' midnight howls,
Union Square cigarette smoke deliverance.
Quiescence like red sky night Libra full moon.
Coffee jag, King James Bible revelation
overland Appalachian Trail markers,
Second coming like William Butler Yeats
maple syrup prophecy.

Soft Machine
Rent hustle women's long, high heel nylon legs
Madison Avenue martini cocaine
hard drive neon light corpses.
Pat Methany jazz guitar genius
Greenwich Village 1978, honeybee rainbow caresses
youths feather bed dream on
like tulip bloom Katmandu radical hope.

Soft Machine
Jewish Passover transcendence pick up sticks,
matzo brie, sweet wine holy revelation,
black thread liberty vortex.
Two day weekend freedom time dice roll,
poetry create like madcap tango.
American's rolling thunder
red rose kick back delight.
Redneck gun rack heartlnad hope.
Soft Machine, dig it!

Whole Grain Resurrection

Whole Grain Resurrection
Tucumcari, New Mexico desert highway
cirrus cloud epiphany,
Jesus' raise from dead like
tin can kick Indiana back gravel roads.

Whole Grain Ressurection
Baby boom hippie ladies Sufi swirl
patchouli oil aesthetics
calico cat quiescence.

Whole Grain Ressurection
Western omelet, bagel toast
hot coffee Tuesday morning Paul Sondheim's
  oak tree essence.
Poetic craft like mythic Mississippi River flow.
New Orleans Delta sublime.
No to Minnesota high school gun violence.
No to fun house mirror lies.
No to boardroom blood fist to cuffs.

Whole Grain Ressurection
Wood cross purple sin
like woodshed fantasy fracture
Woodstock maple syrup afternoon March delight
hot lentil stew, deaf Joe's Haight Ashbury 1967
mythic San Francisco cosmic delight.

Whole Grain Ressurection
Bobby Short Carlyle Hotel piano class,
Harlem Duke Ellington composition
genius,
Billie Holiday cigarette voice
blues chops, take no prisoners.
Whole Grain Resurrection
Wilderness 20 year olds' America

quest, dream time like hot muffin
North Carolina mornings.
Hot rod back to wind.
No to penny ante hip-hop anger.
No to Texas Hold 'Em wimp poker game.
No to sophomore pot smoke throw
rainbow talent away.

Whole Grain Resurrection
Mary Magdalene white light Jesus love
late night bran flakes, Tony Montana's
Mexican Cuervo Gold passion, counterman
cobalt blue cool
La Jolla, California spring afternoon 1974
sixties over like movie theater inferno.
Flannel poet touch sky, Manhattan
prairie calico notions,
leather coat New York Yankee fans
Derek Jeter short stop excellence,
Bronx rice, beans, pork. Yes!

Whole Grain Resurrection
Prayers on knees, shirt pocket
rosary beads,
mud workboot aesthetics, blue collar
  pinewood can do.
Local 1199 Health Hospital workers
rock steady union pension fund,
highway wildflowers grace like
Arizona Grand Canyon God's miracles,
resurrection real deal, whole grain. Yes!

Spring Break Dogwoods

Spring Break Dogwoods
86th Street holy square window box,
daffodil redemption
earth birth like Atlantic City salt
water taffy,
karmic sandlewood incense new beginnings
maply syrup East River crystalline air.

Spring Break Dogwoods
Number six train Washington Square
Park, cayenne poetry read, NYU cinnamon girls
hip sway bare midriff saltine magic
long racehorse legs.
Sharecropper long hair mythic dudes.
Guitar picker dream time hosannahs.

Spring Break Dogwoods
Yellow forsythia, Bleecker Steet West Village
paint palate pansies,
Good Council church
holy communion,
Jimmy's Yorkville renegade mad dog parade.
Waverly Place sicilian pizza slice jubilee.
Serenade April sugarland cool.

Spring Break Dogwoods
Terri Schiavo fallen angel
life fight 15 years touch sky
heaven like pearl gate city on hill.

Spring Break Dogwoods
Myrna's Ford Bronco Christian wildcat faith
mythic highway woman.

Spring Break Dogwoods
Pope John Paul 2 dies like
holy saint, two thousand years Vatican salt tears,
Polish pariot free
eastern Europe iron fist
communist terror.
Velveteen rainbow Jesus soul.

Spring Break Dogwoods
89th Street soup kitchen bare bone ethics,
can man dollar bill hard grind,
Rikers Island prison morning cornflakes
like Passover Seder.
Holy jailhouse ashram.

Spring Break Dogwoods
Mary's Cold Spring Harbor rock
steady Catholic faith, beats mental illness
 cardboard box
madness, fun-house mirror reality warp,
multiple sclerosis wheel chair ball and chain.

Spring Break Dogwoods
Hot wire New York Mets Shea Stadium
field of dreams you gotta believe,
cold Budweisers, Willie Randolph manager
Queens excellence.

Spring Break Dogwoods
April 21st poem in pocket day like
caramel candy, hot ember
prairie fire metaphors
Jack Kerouac Mexico City tokay wine horizon genius
winter over like Chicky's Tuesday night
restaurant close, clean grills,
floor mop
garden earth paradise express New England
lobster shack holy providence,
cameo hearts on fire again.

Saturday Rain

Saturday Rain
promised land stay at home
morning coffee vortex,
Leonard Bernstein West Side Story
genius 1957, teeth floss
thousand comebacks like
middle weight club boxer.
Spring rain
Second Avenue dads tykes in tow
like wooden dinghies,
West coast San Fancisco
rainbow quiescence,
blue jays Central Park
garden green spring.

Saturday Rain
Calico lovers sleep in like
apple turnovers,
slow hand fandango,
bourbon mouths, highway
American freedom time.
Love's hairpin curve.
No to manic jitterbug poets.
No to botox fountain of youth
wolverines.
No to red brick high school cliques.

Saturday Rain
Woodstock wood burn fire storm,
Tinker Street wind chime wake-up call
black umbrella paradise, Allen Ginsberg
cut pie poetics like Kentucky
short order grill.

Saturday Rain
Yes to clean and sober
12-step dollar in kitty excellence.
Yes to high school junior SAT hard work
heroic brain glide.
Yes to down home corduroy
aesthetics.

Saturday Rain
Holy Passover night
Red Sea liberation.
Rost chicken, matzo ball soup sublime.
grandparents keep wooden schooner
afloat.

Saturday Rain
No to family saltine cracker break up.
No to bar room jimson weed work out issues fracture.
No to credit card red debt upper class mirage.

Saturday Rain
Coney Island grey battle ship sky
easy beat, violin etudes
Ingrid's small upper west side
piano sweeties, Chopin Manhattan fingers.

Saturday Rain
Pick up lines like trout
fish bait, Witchita tick tack house suburban flirtations
week-end grey gratitude, rest bones
sugar shack essence.
Stretch canvas Elmhurst, Queens
underground painters
creativity's homestead magic,
Saturday Rain, dig it.

Howl Friday Afternoon

Howl Friday Afternoon
Late March spring, emerge
fandango, daffodil bloom
like yellow like pads, IBM typewriter
Montana white stallion charge
Archer's Bar log neck Budweiser's.

Howl Friday Afternoon
Reefer Second Avenue afternoon scurry,
blood artery eucalyptus create
Harry's crossword quest,
social security cash string out,
pork chop flashback 1961
thousand New York City calico
country girls dreams.

Howl Friday Afternoon
High heel denim Westchester County
women, oh so fine,
cheshire cat siles, five star maple syrup class.
Mercedes Benz Pandora's Box glory.
Green planet A plus groove
like 30 year Pacific Coast Highway
Big Sur mythic vibrations.
Washington Square Park journal entry sublime,
ham and swiss picnic.

Howl Friday Afternoon
Jack Kerouac American highway cadences,
St. Marks Place ramble
rainbow sky like sweet Van Gogh's
magic paint palette genuis.

Midtown computer liberation,
like hi-tech promised land vortex.
Jeff packs S.U.V. kids, holy wife
Catskill Mountain weekend maple tree trail hike.

Howl Friday Afternoon
New York emerald city turn trick
like three card monte pro,

paradise engagement ring, salt tears, joy.
Gristedes parmalat milk,
jumbo New Jersey eggs,
86th Street Tal's hot everything bagels.
Trojan condoms get lucky
Chelsea eros bourbon laughs
mini-skirt thigh caress.

Howl Friday Afternoon
WQXR classical Stravinsky
iced coffee typewriter
geranium flowerbed, spring sugarland beauty.
Corn on cob poetic rebirth,
middle age broad North Moore Street Tribeca smiles,
downbeat Charles Mingus
acoustic bass, sunset shake bake Hindu saffron cool.
God's born again, Christian wood cross resurrection.

Howl Friday Afternoon
Two day weekend cobble eternity road
sleep in Saturday, clean sheet morning.
4th grader little league short stop field of dreams.
Zen sugarland Buddism like westbound glory train.

Howl Friday Afternoon
84th Street barber Joseph snip snip haircut
supreme.
Turn on dime.
Martina McBride country western patriot passion.
Guggenheim Museum sidewinder
kiss on sly.

Howl Friday Afternoon
Bring home Wisconsin bacon,
go to limit roses, white picket fence
Huck Finn delight,
prairie essence, like Joanna laid back baby-sitter
Cornell dream grace.
Hudson Riverflow New York harbor freedom
fish fry Harlem soul kitchen jubilee,
March Madness U. Conn basketball hi-jinx.
New York City slow motion weekend redemption.
Howl Friday Afternoon, yes.

Buckshot Renegade

I am Buckshot Renegade
Left hip poem tote hombre,
Colorado sky puff cloud
rainbow vision,
lasso like needle thred,
metaphor spool.

I am white palomino kick up
holy land American dust.
No to cob wet quitting time.
No to cattle rustle easy con.
No to circle conestoga wagon
bacon and beans group thought.

I am wild west big dipper individual
like stand tall gold star bounty hunters,
broad shoulder sheriff,
law and order highway slim jims.
Willa Cather red clay Nebraska pioneer courage.

I am Hopi Indian mescalito tribal
rites, horse blanket serenade,
desert calico poetics, Oklahoma
territories glory train freedom.
No to eastern city slickers
starched shirt vocabulary.
No to silk refined airs.
No to poetry academic thin wrist
turn corner deceit.

Yes to Ponderosa big country rapture
ranch hands whiskey bottle Saturday
night t-bone overtures.
Yes to velvet brothel wildcat pleasure.

I am prairie schooner voice like
gravel ditch roll your own smoke,
bald eagle American grace,
western gingham sidewinder dream.
I am Go West like Jack Kerouac
Beat poets, San Francisco North
Beach cool.

I am Miles Davis Live at Black Hawk
down beat soul riff, Allen Ginsberg Gallery
Six *Howl* Redondo.
Bay Bridge, Telegraph Hill, Mission district
finger snap, black cotton leotards,
mythic brown hair beat woman.

I am resonance like fresh water Montana trout stream
big sky open denim embrace.
Preachers Sunday Missouri territories
hell fire sermon.
I am coyote on heartland prowl,
poetic excellence, dig it.

May Lilacs Supreme

May Lilacs Supreme
Purple roundhouse fragrance
Maypole creative revolution
like Pacific coast morning fog,
cinco de mayo Corona and lime,
Mexico City Chipultepec Park
free range ramble 1969.
Marijuana etudes.

May Lilacs Supreme
New Orleans Mississippi River magic
Kentucky Derby mint julep metaphors,
hot streak New York Mets
Carlos Beltran center field big cat excellence,
rice and beans home run crack.

May Lilacs Supreme
No to dead beat Archers Bars afternoon
alcoholics.
No to twenty something technology short
bolt lobotomies.
No to tight buttock Aryan gym morning
treadmill machine narcissists.

Yes to 1st Armored Cavalry Iraq
can-do discipline, Mom's apple pie heroics.
Yes to morning Miami calls to
mythyic spitfire Myrna.
Yes to cuchifrito overland
Mexican workers.
Greenwich Village Washington Square Park
  beatnik souls.

May Lilacs Supreme
Walt Whitman Brooklyn ferry cross,
spring pomise like second graders
open world library card scurry,
New Jerusalem steady hand

brownie bake, resurrection.
May Lilacs Supreme
Embrace Ray Charles blues time
southland black eye peas essence
embrace Oxford, Mississippi small town
rainbow quiescence,
embrace Maureen Holm rest in peace
River Seine poetry excellence.

May Lilacs Supreme
Santa Cruz youths
counter culture cartwheels,
kisses like northern California eucalyptus.
Mom and Dad Manhattan rock steady
bring it home dignity, American dream Godiva
   Chocolates.

Canvas stretch Upper West Side 122nd Street
acrylic paint jubilee,
Manhattan School of Music Channel's tuba
Bartok flat out delight,
May day Massachusetts Wrigley gum chew,
renewal like silver key chain
cirrus sky pinewood revolution.
May Lilacs Supreme always!

Horizon State Line

Horizon State Line
Corn on cob Sunday Ohio afternoons,
trout fish worm hook easy beat,
morning Manhattan prayers like
Swiss timepiece.
Saint Ignatius church bell toll.

Horizon State Line
Nebraska Interstate 70 Goodland
foothill paradise, red clay redondos,
beat poets silver essence memories like
cafe finger snap 1956.
Gallo wine Gregory Corso howl.

Horizon State Line
Zen meditations, cobalt blue
Quarker quilt, Wicca Pagans
dream time white witch spells,
Catholic angels Tribeca rooftops,
sweet kisses afternoon baby oil eros
Renaissance.

Horizon State Line
Amarillo, Texas baby back ribs,
Austin Sixth Street pedal steel guitar
Lone Star beer, Stetson hat jubilee.
America freedom time excellence.

Horizon State Line
Opportunity like truck stop Florida
oranges, Orlando Disney World small
tyke excite,
Miami bound no habla español, Myrna's broad smiles
Mom Carmen's senior citizen life zest,
McDonald's Wednesday specials 49 cents cheeseburgers
bring it home cheap home hearth eats.

Horizon State Line
Wal-Mart sneakers rock steady promise
heartland tympany, gold St. Louis trumpet wail
John Philip Sousa July fourth Independence
Day glory train.
Memorial Day Arlington Cemetery
pay ultimate price heroics.
Midwest Illinois oak grove honest
like Abraham Lincoln self-taught red write.

Horizon State Line
18 wheel semis Denver bound,
self reliance like wild west Oklahoma
cowboy, drifters wildcat
tall tale hustle, caravan westbound
like Salt Lake City Mormom ethics.

Horizon State Line
Black man's sharecropper cool river bed
　freedom drive.
Condoleeze Rice's American dream quest,
rise like phoenix hardscrabble Jim Crow
Alabama, Secretary of State pine tree
excellence.

Horizon State Line
God's Wyoming Grand Teton Valley, immense beauty
promise oh wildflower promise,
rainbow, high school sophomore liberty
next halcyon highway turn
next Arizona psychedelic mirage.

Horizon State Line
Harvest cornucopia full bellies
innovation like Bill Gates Microsoft
computer screen genius
New Orleans magnolia rain
knit one purl two scarf
create quicksilver beginning.
State Line Horizon, yes.

21st Century Excellence

21st Century Excellence
Albuquerque fire poems
canvas stretch fertile ground
Williamsburg, Brooklyn,
Joffrey Ballet wind at back cool.
Pine tree craft bark canoe
Lake Hoosetonic morning serenity.

21st Century Excellence
Raise rainbow bar like Bach fugue
Phillip Glass rococo avant garde
wildcat music,
sobriety's cool mama jama Central
Park dusk.

21st Century Excellence
Redemption like lack curtain
metaphor, half shell clams
Long Island Mary's aries halcyon fire.
Horizon quest, Saturday morning
be-bop serenade,
Colorado wildflower grace.
No cry-baby teenager Second
Avenue vodka drunks.
No baby boom sisters top shelf credit
card hopscotch delusion.
No Big Kahuna cocaine Cadillac Escalade
gangster gun battles.

21st Century Excellence
Hungry New York Mets Shea Stadium sweetness,
101st Airborne can-do Iraq, band of
camouflage brothers true gri.
Marlboro smoke Tucson desert morning
quiescence.

Laura Boss poetic Hudson River passion.
Firm Boise, Idaho handshake.
No shuck and jive Kansas City con game.
No Rutgers University six pack
oil down orgies.
No Burlington, Vermont candy cane
Che Guevara radical prozac pill pop.

21st Century Excellence
Touch crescent moon Woodstock sky,
dream like third grader summer vacation
ruby red watermelon,
soft backyard green grass hullabaloo.
Bring on cats cradle Whitney Museum Biennial.
Bring on Lincoln Center New York Philharmonic
like apple pie oven bake French croissant.
Bring on America's big sky ingenuity,
Elko, Nevada noon time solitude,
Gatorade thirst quench.

21st Century Excellence
Pillow prayers, ethics like
Macon, Georgia Baptist grey hair pastor
one day at time easy does it,
cheshire heart slow motion cadence
veranda honeysuckle kisses like
South Carolina June lemonade dusk.

21st Century Excellence
Dads little league aluminum bat
glory train,
Sophia's needlepoint genius,
Mom's hammer chisel sculpture delight,
Georgia O'Keefe Abique, New Mexico
desert flower painters magic.
No to semi-conductor digital
fracture, i-pod machine psychosis.
No to Darth Vader black cloak demon
college freshman.
No to white powder heroin aficionados.

21st Century Excellence
God's rose trellis graden grace
Sunday morning Methodist prayer book magic
hymns, Steinway piano lesson Tuesday
afternoon peanut butter and jelly aesthetics.

21st Century Excellence
Figh war on terror homeland security
valor, California Interstate optimism
faith like t-bone medium rare, fries hoe-down
self discipline like Belmont Raceway
jockey, Wal-Mart asisstant manager
Hillsdale, Michigan savvy.
Peach basket family calico friends.
21st Century excellence always.

Flag Day

June fourteenth Betsy Ross mythic
red white blue needle and thread
flag sew.
Philadelphia steady hands,
nation liberty birth.
Ripe California peaches 99 cents,
butterscoth humidity dreams like Second
Avenue taxi scoot, Nebraska
late prairie silver rain.

Flag Day
Monday morning paprika heart romance
U.S. Marines can do Iraq uncommon valor,
Ronald Wilson Reagan rests Simi Valley,
California holy California sunset,
cellphone wizardry Columbus Avenue
heroin score.

Flag Day
Pledge of Allegiance One Nation under God
stand Supreme Court tall,
eight to nothing round house verdict.
South Glens Falls, New York
wildcat vodka rap, USA cheapo cigarettes
25 dollar money order, medium rare
roast beef dinner, rap it out
college kid's magnolia youth.

Flag Day
Portrait hang ceremony Bill Hillary Clinton
White House Pennsylvania Avenue shrine
Eureka Springs, Arkansas strawberry smoothies,
San Francisco velvet red brothel.

Flag Day
Sunday Puerto Rican Day Parade
Catholic high school science whiz Joanna,
Mayor Bloomberg step-by-step in stallion lead
celebration like San Juan afternoon,
Bacardi and coke salsa delight,
Yugoslav Mikey's big heart
American dream.

Flag Day
No to 35-year old corporate frat boy
Coors light beer bash.
No to groin-on-groin sex partner
roll dice exchange.
No to gymnasium muscle thigh
work-out trainer gigolo on sly 500 trick.

Flag Day
Elisa's Portugal 747 big bird returns,
castanet cadence like Algarve
rainbow serenity dawn,
Hershey Bars Duane Reade drug store
fly by delight, dollar sixty nine easy glide.

Flag Day
George Washington Commander in Chief heroics.
Yes to Monday blue sky afternoon,
Massachusetts bald eagle self-reliance.
Yes to Gideon Bible read, quilt comforter
iced coffee Rocky Mountain revelation.
Yes to Freedom time rock casbah,
Williamsburg master painter,
Van Gogh revolutionary aesthetics.

Flag Day
Francis Scott Key Nation Anthem
Fort McHenry bring it home,
'O say can you see', yes!
Carrion grace like half sour pickle barrel,
Mega Million long odds quick score,
embrace Dad's bring bacon home
parking lot quest, weekend pinochle groove,
Radcliffe University Random House square
shoulder poetry editors.

Flag Day
Weekend 50,000 Americade Harley Davidson
Lake George low riders, highway black leather
Easy Rider essence.
Gristedes late night grocery dream time
shelf stock like Jacob's ladder.

Flag Day
Cinnamon kindergarten diploma scroll graduation
Savannah, Georgia crayon achievement,
low heel moms, honey bear smile, denim dads
pecan pie little tykes fudge Sunday joy.

Flag Day
America's City on Hill blue jean blessings,
Burly muscle longshoremen hard sweat,
Old Glory's Bosto Harbor salt air equality, yes.

2005 Move Forward

2005 Move Forward
Oklahoma prairie miracle blue highways
cobble back street Park Slope, Brooklyn
flannel shirt serendipity,
mythic Pacific Coast Highway
begin again.
5-card stud dawn.
Curlicue pinewood optimism.

2005 Move Forward
Highway's crescendo
like feather Mohawk warrior,
mystic black hood big smile
Franciscan monk,
Zoot Simms gold tenor saxophone
excellence, monarch butterfly
diamond dance Santa Cruz, California
easy beat.

2005 Move Forward
No to tin can blues time depression.
No to prozac pop glory days memory fade.
No to leather ecstasy tab
S & M hate crowd delusion.
No to blind man's tin cup quarter moon
boot strap nostalgia.

2005 Move Forward
Bring on Columbia, Georgia Coca Cola
planetarium night star jubilee,
God's Orion belt crystalline wonder.
Bring on Disney World nine year old's
bumper car cheshire delight.

Bring on chocolate ice cream cone
innocence like Washington Square Park
toddler's rainbow metal slides,
Bronx cumulus clouds touch
future like grade school reading score ascent.

2005 Move Forward
Telluride, Colorado cool mountain stream
ice chamomile tea consciousness,
t-bone steak medium rare metaphors,
full tank Conoco; Reno, Nevada,
high sierras pine tree cathedral San Francisco
   bound like
carrion mad dash.

2005 Move Forward
Howl American peppermint optimism.
Yes to Alex 'A Rod' Rodriguez Yankee Stadium
   excellence.
Yes to long hauled 18 wheel Peterbilt trucker.
Yes to Eugene, Oregon eggs over easy.
Drop load like feeral mail box slot letter.

2005 Move Forward
No to dollar bill juke box aesthetics.
No to stop freight train Georgia
and Pacific paisley eternity break down.
No to bar room Jack Daniels shooters.
Blues time long nect Budweisers.

2005 Move Forward
Barrel house Mississippi River dream.
New Orleans metal guitar twang, jumbalaya chow
   down.
Henry Miller book on lap excellence,
broad shoulder Chicagom, God legal pad creation
always eye on June horizon. Yes.

Big Country Poetics

I am Big Country Poetics
Wyoming wild stallion break heart
salt shaker down Union Pacific
rail line, mulligan stew
hobo's singular sensibility.

I am L.L. Bean city slicker bedroll,
porterhouse steak metaphors
Texas plains broad smile hoe down,
Manhattan flannel good old boy.

I am rainbow fingers IBM typewriter
86th Street Yorkville easy beat,
chamomile iced tea freedoms magic
wind song.
Paprika heart like pine green
work shirt aesthetics.

I am black wallet on punk rock silver chain
Liberty's American SUV Illinois prairie
noon time westward quest,
crystalline Adirondack watershed,
skinny dip water wheel similes,
ethics like Presbyterian rock solid minister.
Zen blue eyed monk round house joy.
Zendo meditation bell quiescence.

I am Declaration of Independence
Life, liberty, pursuit of happiness
West Virginia banjo quest, underground railroad 1857
end to slavery cruel hanging noose.
Scarsdale High School concert choir, buy back
  excellence.

I am Manhattan Central Park jazz vocalist
Frisbee toss, ham and swiss picnic
moist pound cake kisses Wrightville
Beach parked car delight 1972.
Peppermit number 6 train melody.

I am chicory dream cadence like
Navajo stone tip arrows, Albuquerque cumulus
cloud desert vision.
Jones Bech surfs up lifeguard
body tan chicks galore like honey bees.
Wonder Bread middle class
Chevrolet cotton caresses.

I am American Constitutional Bill of Rights
Bring it home horizon opportunity,
Pioneer Kansas windmill pride,
Hunter College July summer school excellence
cool martinis Pierre Hotel,
limos like black bullet Lincoln Center bound.

I am bacon and bean Appalachian Trail virtue,
Honey Abraham Lincoln self taught
education brilliance.
Wildcat beatnik howl
Horatio Street be-bob cool.
Bold experience's cobalt blue tango.

I am Jewish Torah scroll bar mitzvah knowledge,
Quaker meeting house infinite
cinnamon silence, Islesboro, Maine
rock beach steamers bucket.

I am cheshire cowboy, beet read soul
Like Big Sur sunset, sweat lodge
break down cleanse.
Highway sanctity yellow brick road tin man desire,
Mamaroneck Harbor high tide
Canadian geese like God's miracle sign,
thousand hosannahs.

I am humble like 42dn Street panhandler,
Salvation Army thirft shop extra large sweater,
Hudson River Line values always.

Denim Joy

Denim Joy
Tennessee summer solstice
twilight green forest delight,
ramble like robins egg hatch,
cool Dr. Pepperm pick-up truck
rainbow aesthetic.

Denim Joy
Texas cowgirls hearty laughs,
long legs Dallas dance floor narrow hips two step
pedal steel guitar twang
July fourth big city barbecue,
baby back ribs like melt in mouth
chocolate ice cream.

Denim Joy
Green tea highway poetics,
America's flag day red white blue
don't tread on me pride.
Buffalo, New York to sweet home Chicago.
Muddy Waters down and dirty
blues time.
Argentina Martine's blues
guitar genuis like Delta good old boy.
New breed pinewood mythic dude.

Denim Joy
Yes to three year old tyke's denim
cowboy jacket.
Yes to six shooter justice, gold badge
sheriff keep calico peace.
Yes to South Carolina back road
Georgia state line whiskey runs.

Denim Joy
Bring on sovereign Alabama shotgun shack dignity.
Bring on Baptist born again trellis rose rapture.
Bring on Waukeegan, Illinois Exxon fill up
Lake Michigan miracle dawn.
Bring on cameo hearts on fire like
Manhattan big ball sunset.

Denim Joy
Full moon Capricorn
roof top red wine jug quiescence
playground jungle gym soft steel
kids universe.
Cool bop silver slide
devotion like sufi dervish.
Sand box rococo easy does it eternity.

Denim Joy
Chevrolet green traffic light dreams,
Lake George canoe odyssey, picnic tuna and
　sandwiches
cool coca sugar rush.
Fort Ticonderoga tourist paddle wheel heaven
like white light Bible angel.
James Joyce's *Ulysses* genuis.

Denim Joy
No to Riverside Drive hard core mad dog radical
　eminists.
No to nose in air Berkeley, California
heroin snort young bucks.
No to flag burn aficionados hate
America crowd, grow up brother.

Denim Joy
Bowling Green, Kentucky blue grass
wide open beauty double rainbow
Hillsdale, Michigan God's marker.
Silver spurs ranch hand
cattle drive, Lawrence, Kansas soft back
seat kisses, cotton hugs
unclasped brassiere like Friday
night paycheck devotion.

Denim Joy
Fort Smith, Arkansad truckers motel
eight hours easy sleep, Brooklyn Flatbush Avenue
cherry cheesecake.
Grace like House of Representatives morning prayer.

Denim Joy
No New Mexico high altitude
delirium 1992.
No new age gingham fabric tear yoga cult work out.
No to marijuana brain synapse burn out.
No to throw creative gift down Colorado
porcelain drain.

Denim Joy
Embrace 85th Street Rohr's coffee house
iced coffee creativity, embrace Kona coffee
10% discount like Target store mid-week sale.
Embrace Second Avenue American
Spirit cigarette smoke, liberty's magnolia promise.
Embrace providences cumulus cloud
summer's cool lemonade poetics.
Denim Joy yes.

Paradise Highway

New Mexico holy night ride
Wing purple angel like
cool vanilla ice cream cone
heavens 12 gate city
white line macadam excellence.

Paradise Highway
Amoco gas fill up
Independence Day patriots
cotton old glory flag wave passion,
Cheyenne, Wyoming wide open
Saturday night hoe-down,
two step like Viennese waltz.

Paradise Highway
America's move to a more perfect
union, Interstate 44 Missouri
engine hum, truck stop zen satori.

Paradise Highway
Summer camp softball complete,
Jewish prayers like Robert Frost
miracle poem, Walt Whitman American genius.
Woodshed Vermont cool July morning,
green garden zen satori.

Paradise Highway
No to radical Islam London underground
bomb terror.
No to Iraq Al Qaeda suicide bomb cowards.
No to holy war retrograde blood
red torn body parts.

Paradise Highway
Embrace morning upstate trout
stream quiescence.
Embrace Jen and Rudy's senior citizen
Rohrs' Cafe gentle carrion grace.
Embrace Gracie's corner restaurant
Mexican glory hondo boys,
easy smiles like Mexico City afternoon
siesta.
Cool Corona's American dream
hard work muscle quest.

Paradise Highway
Yes to Karie Ehrlich's soft
shoe NYU professor excellence.
Yes to Dee Anne's jazz vocal classy voice chops.
Yes to Kansas sunflower salvation.

Paradise Highway
Clean and sober Saturday night
vortex, blue jean aesthetics
like Texas Monday morning hard grind
work week first coffee Marlboro smoke.

Paradise Highway
LeAnn Rimes country music silk
voice supreme, humility like
Brooklyn old time seltzer delivery man,
R train easy glide conductor
rush hour cool daddy iron track scoot,
Big Apple heat wave promise
Aaron Copeland *Rodeo* big sky
essence, hymn book rialto, soup kitchen rainbow dialects.

Paradise Highway
New Jerusalem soda pop
eternal Monterey, California
back streets steady hand on Chevy wheel.
Paradise Highway, yes.

Spirit Dance

Spirit Dance
Sassafras tea, cotton patchouli
lady, afternoon queen Anne lace kisses.
Central Park Saturday dusk
drum circle, honey bee get down,
African cats explode like
Mali magic savannah, tribal ritual.

Spirit Dance
95 degree New York City
heat wave fandango.
Terrorist code orange subway whirlwind,
Rhode Island Rhodes 19 spinnaker
glide.
Block Island mythic bound.

Spirit Dance
Miles Davis trumpet genius
Charles Bukowski
Los Angeles word on paper passion,
Hollywood Boulevard cash and carry
Gallo wine cheap high vortex.

Spirit Dance
Denim drifter's halcyon midnight prayers,
open Harlem fire hydrant, cool down
doo-rag garbage haulers, 86th Street
potato chips, orange soda
easy time 3 A.. break.
Yugoslav Mikey calamari feast sublime.

Spirit Dance
Fourth grade girls ballet class,
karate kings small tykes white
belt being long martial arts
soul journey.
Yellow return school camp buses,
Second Avenue rainbow unload,
long skirt rock steady moms, t-shirt dads night
  time July
full nest.

Spirit Dance
Yes to NYPD bullet proof vest heroes.
Yes to red neck easy does it love
wife up, calico kids like Knoxville,
Tennessee bedtime stories delight.
Yes to high school buddy downtown
four leaf clover family.

Spirit Dance
Yes to Waldorf Astoria fox-trot wedding celebration.
Yes to Bolshoi Ballet Moscow cinnamon
grace like hearty cabbage winter soup.
Yes to Greenwich Village Bridgit Murnaghan poet
  beat cool.
Spirit Dance. Yes.

Have Mercy

Have Mercy
On zig-zag pot smoke sidewinders,
corporate big time cheat on wife hondo boys.
Down and out Jack Daniels racket boys, dudes.
New Jersey Route 22 cocaine runs,
green cash paper greed quest.

Have Mercy
On stroller mom's social climb, credit card
Palm Beach delusion,
youths hate hard grind workaday old man,
Catholic priest one toke over line litany.
Yes to wildflower Colorado ethics.
Yes to George Washington father of country
rock steady, humility.
Yes to flannel good old boys Interstate 80 overland
 truckers,
heart.

Have Mercy on tattoo ecstacy tab Marxists,
Holland Tunnel toll takers, San Francisco crimson
 dream,
Super 8 motel aid swindle.

Have Mercy on slow float botox narcissistic
Long leg style girls,
500 dollar Argentina midtown call girls,
six-pack Heineken king size bed
funky NYU sophomore orgies.
Yes to Saturday night poetry beat riffs
IBM typewriter excellence.
Yes to Red Cross Hurricane Frances overtime
cherry pie relief.

Have Mercy
On last call 14th Street Cellar Bar,
Budweiser fog, desolation
Garden City trim lawn sheep herd conformity,
broadside lies, white shroud demon heroin junkies.
Yes to Lisbon, Portugal mythic Eliza
wood stage Manhattan drama dream.

Yes to New Milford, Connecticut
Sunday afternoon fried chicken
potato salad picnic.
Yes to West 11st Street moist
pound cake kisses, narrow waist Hudson River caress.
Yes to broad tooth smile like cheshire cat,
dignity like white California beach stallions.

Have Mercy on jack of diamond
Astoria, Queens poker playing early morning riff,
three card monte 34th Street hustlers,
satan's black cloak cobra religious cults.
Plato's damp cave dull edge aesthetics.
Have Mercy.
Have Mercy, brother.

Blueberry Providence

I am blueberry providence
God's blue highway delicate down quilt,
Missouri sunrise.
Promise like open French's mustard jar
bologna pound, white bread,
cool metal diet Pepsi can.

I am sugarland express
Half shell clam poetry,
be-bop jazz Max Roach percussion invention.
Brooks Brothers button-down shirts,
taxis scoot FDR Drive Saturday night
downtown mix a lot.
Greg Richard's CBGB's guitar excellence.

I am Beethoven crescendo
Cool September afternoon lanyard grace
thousand cardamon beef stew daydreams,
broad smile like orange upstate New York
calico cat.
Woodstock deaf Joe's miracle painter's vision.
Judy Whitfield blue flame ethics.

No to dead-beat corpse Broadway theater.
No to hangman black cloak psychiatrist couch muse.
No to runaway minds halfway house,
mud delusion.

I am Islamic five times a day
Allah prayers,
fifth grader Spanish second language
delight,
Snickers bar sweet tooth bring it
home after school reward.

I am starched white shirt
Sunday school Christian bible teach,
ham glaze sweet potatoes,
trainer wheel bicycle little tyke
open prairie explore.

I am Laura Boss Paterson, New Jersey
Touch sky poetry dream,
full laundry load, long black skirt hip sway.
Frances Hurricane reek havoc holy land,
Florida peninsula 150 mile break down winds.
Tea time elegant Plaza Hotel,
hot scones, British vanilla wafers,
long leg Manhattan honey blond vibrations.

I am singer Nora Jones Louisiana
Boudoir, eros sugar joy
vocal chops like Jack Daniels,
club soda,
cherry pie laughter, flesh on flesh,
love's straight back Delta hope.

I am corned beef and cabbage metaphor sanctity,
New York Giant Eli Manning quarterback
bring it home play-off promise,
Jewish one God desert holy tabernacle wisdom,
Glory train rhapsody westbound.

Promised Land Express

Promised Land Express
Hip cats Horatio Street bourbon
down beat,
Dizzy Gillespie trumpet blow genius,
July heat wave like thick yellow
butterscotch.

Promised Land Express
Garden grove, Tree of Knowledge
holy fandango, Adam and Eve purple temptation
Bangor, Maine cool breeze like
cotton sheet afternoon kisses,
Columbia University jazz radio sublime
Horace Silver morning daybreak.

Promised Land Express
Heavens rainbow sanctity,
coffee jags like sidewinder vodka drunk,
Cairo, New York skinny dip,
sweet Moses sidewinder 40-year desert diaspora
reefer aesthetic noon day holy
rialto, Italian wine Florence cafe
frescos paint genius.

Promised Land Express
Zen satori Oregon Gary Snyder trail
hike, granola bars, cool bottle
water, mountain boots double socks,
horizon twilight delight.

Promised Lane Express
Montana big sky cool mama
jamboree, boots spurs
Saturday night two step
cattle graze like JFK airport taxi line up.

Promised Land Express
Miles Davis Fillmore East Jazz Fusion,
Dog days poetry cadence.

No to comedians prozac nihilism.
No to rock and roll blow ear drums
out New Jersey slugs.
No to whiskey rap cardboard atheist.

Bring on Skidmore College ballet disciple.
Bring on senior citizens humble paisley delight.
Bring on good old girls stand by
man mythic quiescence.

Promised Land Express
Billie Holiday vocal genius
like Sugar Hill Harlem step out,
Baptist church fish fry,
collard greens, sweet potato pie
John Coltrane alto saxophone 1950's cool
bop genius.

Heat wave Manhattan lemonade big band Artie Shaw,
Sedona, Arizona orange canyons,
green valley Pennsylvania rain clouds
optimism like high school clean cut senior.
Wesleyan College bound world on half shell
eye on Promised Land Express yes.

Checkercloth Transformation

Checkercloth Transformation
Change like late September paisley sky swoop,
gray squirrels Central Park
acorn nut hide and seek,
scurry like mad-hatter.
Bring on Austin, Texas cowboy boots.
Bring on Ford pick-up truck Colorado state line.
Freedom time Willie Nelson mythic guitar pick.

Checkercloth Transformation
Atlantic City, New Jersey red roulette
like madcap Bacardi and cokes.
Hire wire act, red maple tree autumn changes,
boogaloo Boston Red Sox World Series double play
Cooperstown Baseball Hall of Fame
holy ground.
Highway Exxon Mobil full gas tank promise.

Checkercloth Transformation
Cheeseburger full bellies,
kindergarten first day salt tears.
Daily double Budweiser delight,
Yonkers Raceway five dollar wager.
Jesus' holy conception, ridgeline
butterscotch melody, bald eagle salvation.
Johnny Cash Folsom Prison Blues excellence.

Checkercloth Transformation
American flag wave liberty beacon
magic peanut and butter and jelly sandwiches,
cool farmland milk,
fresh Woolworth spiral notebook,
Jack Kerouac beat prosody.

Calico changes, spare parts jubilee,
First aid kit river run rialto.
Change gears like 18 wheel
Interstate 80 semi's.
baby-boom sweetheart
Seattle bound tapestry quest.
Change always in wind, yes!

Full Moon Aquarius

Full Moon Aquarius
U.C. Berkeley Telegraph Avenue
grunge hippie jubilee,
Persian cat window ledge
sandlewood incense like
purple spirit miracle,
vibration cherry pie revolution.

Full Moon Aquarius
Bud Powell piano glide 1955
be-bop jazz cats July heat wave
Chicago 100 degrees melt down.
Argentine blues man Martine Pavan
young buck long hair cake walk.
Guitar pick sublime.

Full Moon Aquarius
East Hampton chi chi supra nova,
Vermont trail hike
blue sky cumulus cloud quiescence.

No to World Trade Center September 11th murder.
No to London radical Al Qaeda
underground bombers.
No to manic wind chute baby boom
sisters made money quest.
No to thirty five year old
Archer's bar known nothing
empty bucket alcohol ignorance.

Full Moon Aquarius
Surf's up Santa Cruz cats chicks hang five
like eucalyptus warriors,
Oren and lady More's
Israeli Negev passion

Full Moon Aquarius
No to body beauty German 1930's Aryan
gymnasiums.
No to New York Sports Club
taut muscle sweat like short order grill.
No to i-pod music clones.
No to computer comatose illiterates.

Bring on William Faulkner's Mississippi fiction.
Bring on Samuel Beckett Waiting for Godot
theater nuance Left Bank cafe red wine twilight.
Bring on crooner Joe Williams black man's
hip vocals, supreme.

Full Moon Aquarius
Sweet Cleveland, handscrabble
Toledo Chicago bound, hell bent midwest
excellence.
Carl Sandburg heart poetics.
T-bone steak, home fries
get down.
Integrity like front porch Carbondale, Illinois
morning sweep.
Antique ceiling fans parlor cool down.

Full Moon Aquarius
Dad's 85 years old tough GI hard grind
Atlantic City dice roll like pigeon feathers,
blue jay Central Park flight
touch night sky, big dipper upstate
New York freedom time,
freight train night glide American excellence.
Full Moon Aquarius always.

September Epiphany

I am September's
Israeli holy Wailing Wall,
New York Post patriots musket river-run dream.
A thousand Lafayette Street strawberry
re-inventions.
Electricity like Ben Franklin
kite flight.

I am hot-cross buns
Sunrise like 4th graders
soccer goal high tide glory
Franklin D. Roosevelt World War II
iron commander-in-chief courage,
Manhattan, Kansas halcyon yellow sunflowers.

I am Far Rockaway Beach,
Hurricane Ivan demon rip-tides,
new moon mud Dutchess County
backroads, spice rack metaphor celebration.
Charles McDonalds vintage 1959 mint
Jaguar, Northhampton bound,
blue-plate meat loaf, mashed potatoes
corn special, spiral notebook cobalt blue vision.

Yes to mythic Temple Emanuel Synagogue
choir excellence.
Holy paprika freedom time word.
Yes to Ecuador delivery truck dude
onion sack, carrots, green spinach
lightning break sweat.
Yes to neighborhood funky Jimmy's
1960's hippie marijuana stick flashback.

I am Louisville slugger, Gary Sheffield Yankee
Stadium home-run crack,
WQXR Johann Sebastian Bach
silk thread fugue genius.
Eggs over easy, Woodstock morning
dawn like Bible psalm magic revelation.
Hunter College, denim senior grace
like Union Pacific freight train
Utah bound.

I am American cheeseburger, fries
3 A.M. late Saturday night virtue,
Jack Kerouac zen satori, Battery Park Whitehall
parking lot flannel groove,
Harlem Duke Ellington big band excellence
delicate prairie serenade
firm 86th Street handshakes, yes!

Tapestry Weave

October sugar daddy comic book
Manhattan Columbus Avenue street vortex,
thousand Big Sur mythic Pacific Ocean dream times
fruit in basket Hebrew Redemption,
election day cinnamon democracy
Tennessee ham smoke delight.

Tapestry Weave
Portugal Eliza's sign of cancer
touch 86th Street cobalt sky like
Rembrandt excellence, Twyla Tharp dance cool.
Yes to Dutch egg noodles, Mexican red
peppers 99 cents a pound, street
corner broccoli head.
Yes to Brother Marc's Shadow Light
cinema overland vision.
Yes to American entrepreneurs can-do
genius. New jobs like Hudson Valley yellow apples.

Tapestry Weave
Cloisters' medieval uptown renaissance
ebb and flow, WNYC week-end baroque quiescence
Budweiser Friday afternoon denim thigh caress,
Sabbath Jewish candle light 5:55 P.M.
yellow desert Yaweh glow.
Deep dish apple pie aesthetic litany
Jay Chollack bring it home carrion,
desire Saturn poetry read, Monday
night east village halcyon craft.

Tapestry Weave
Washington Square Park jazz be-bop
firecracker break dance down
beat.

Yes to salt pretzels, Poland Spring water.
Yes to Jack Kerouac highway ease like
Tennessee November Interstate 1977,
Marlboro morning smoke.
Yes to Islamic prayer mat lemon
meringue easy glide.
Yes to small newborn God's
holy spirit soft shoe promise.

Tapestry Weave
10 dollar dozer rose jubilee,
French kisses Crosby Street
back alley like tabby cat magic,
God's flannel nightride redemption,
SSD disability rent scramble
broad dervish swirls,
beatnik Neal Cassidy road warriors.

Tapestry Weave
Chelsea 23rd Street big mama hip sway
Colorado calf-length rocket ride
skirt, Star of David chicken soup redemption.
Eggs over easy, desire like upstate New York
trout fishermen
prairie fire gold passion, old school red brick ethics.
Tapestry Weave always.

Good to Go

Good to Go
Manhattan mustang Friday night
Oliver Lake avant garde jazz 1978
flesh on flesh Greenwich Village
holy vortex, wide angle camera
retina, memory like calico cat.

Good to Go
Gin and tonics East Hampton beach house
zone out, Long Island Expressway
cocaine speedway like NASCAR
straight-away.
Amagansett beach house sandlewood quiescence.

Good to Go
Tenor saxophone George Kelley Miami
ham hock roots, Big Apple always sublime, 1945.
New Jersey peaches 99 cents a pound,
Rohrs' Cafe iced Moroccan mint tea
come back baby come back.

No to Monday morning August 1st comatose
  broken wing
warriors.
No to Summit, New Jersey hob-nob
Mercedes Benz third wife aficionados.
No to Israeli filmmaker small time
nickel ante shadow delusion.

Good to Go
Embrace foggy mountain Blue Ridge Virginia
jamboree.
Embrace country fiddle like
morning Tennessee biscuits and gravy.
Embrace Dolly Parton humble good old girl
sweet voice groove.

Embrace Bill Monroe bluegrass foot stomp delight,
Joan Carney western Massachusetts sheep herder like
Jesus New Testament miracle,
thousand August fireflies, clean sleep
bag, Coleman lantern, t-bone steaks,
cool mountain stream Cokes
camp-out wilderness crescendo.

Good to Go
South Carolina summer highway quest,
Interstate 95 Charleston bound, guitarist Amy Hills
grandfathers shrimp company salt air rough
necks.
Plantation homes like Audrey Hepburn's
elegant grace.
Veranda lemonade, sexy flower
cotton dress, bare porcelain arms
like China tea cup.

Good to Go
Alka-Seltzer long haul afternoons,
Greg Velez's parking lot checkerboard genius,
kindness like Saint Joseph's priest,
God's creation holy vibration,
Theolonius Monk piano revolution Harlem 1941,
full pocket green cash Dizzy Gillespie trumpet
providence.
Cool big hip mama.
Good to Go, that's what I say!

Pick Up Sticks Wednesday

Pick up sticks Wednesday
God's red and white checkercloth
kitchen table straight shoot integrity
forty acres and mule rialto
silk camisole afternoon air condition
caresses downtown subway scoot like
cobra snake.

Pick up sticks Wednesday
Good old grils hump day weekend
vision, Hudson river crimson sunset
like shitsu dog scurry.
Motel 6 Greeley, Colorado six pack
party time, highway dead end
Colorado black hole vortex 1995.

Pick up sticks Wednesday
San Diego, California desolation blues 1975
Torah scroll Saturday suede shoe
Sabbath, Bar Mitzvah Brooks Brothers
suit 13 year old easy glide.

Pick up sticks Wednesday
Denim desperados like cigar store Indians,
space shuttle Discovery
high tech American genius
86th Street Robert's Red Lobster
filet mignon, lobster tail big old
king crab dream,
Joseph Brodsky crystalline poems
like Saint Petersburg mid summers
night dream,
Atlantic Beach, North Carolina
soft sand easy down beat
beach houses like wood matchbook, charm
ceiling fans August beatitude.

Pick up sticks Wednesday
93 degree Manhattan heat wave,
Second Avenue corner fruit stand,
fresh green grapes, watermelon
$2.50 each bing cherries always fresh
like Georgia river run.

Pick up sticks Wednesday
Illinois farmland drought,
Denver wildcat heat wave.
Weekend calls out to brothers sisters
like side-show carney barker,
patience like Rugby Mikes corporate
mid-town kick bottom quest.
Weekend oh weekend.
Freedom time like Connecticut
white water raft ride,
upstate New York dawn tennis match,
Manhattanville College lawn mower hum.

Pick up sticks Wednesday
Side street hand hold love doves,
liberty's white light glow
Walt Whitman Brooklyn hopscotch poetic excellence.
Pick up sticks Wednesday, dig it!

August Dog Days

August dog days
Manhattan heat wave like
short order crisp bacon,
sweat Equinox gym aesthetics,
Tasty Delight ice cream
cone cool down.
Chelsea outdoor cafe salvation.

August dog days
New York Mets lose afternoon
hallowed ballgame, Shea Stadium split season
like ripe Florida watermelon.
Rabbi's cloistered prayer like
oven-baked apple,
Emily Dickinson Amherst, Massachusetts poetic genius.
85th Street shoe repair rock
steady heels and new soles,
fresh brown shine like quarter moon
rialto.

August dog days
Sweet Dallas, Texas Cadillac
air condition slow motion,
brother Marc's Kingston, New York
wood floor renovation genius,
iced Moroccan mint tea
cool down.
NYPD 86th Street
crime incident, beat cop hard
breath hustle, squad car siren fracture.

August dog days
Penn Station knapsack search
like first grade grab ga,
Gracie's Diner cool Greek salads, vinaigrette
dressing, Tony Montana easy Mexican taco vibration.
Morning Thunder tea notions, yoga class
rainbow tighten up.

August dog days
Thursday morning beatific
WZXR Vivaldi optimism,
Louis Armstrong New Orleans
birthday, trumpet excellence
wildcat solo riffs, chitlin
voice raps like cornbread
West Bank Paris side-streets.
Wind chime 14th Street jubilee.

August dog days
Iced green tea like silk Geisha girl
honey blossom rub down,
Greenwich Village quiescence,
Back Fence bartender Charlie hip gop-heavy
hand cocktails,
orange mythic sunsets
ham and swiss dinner time picnics,
early to bed like pajama infant,
eye on cold front Alberta, Canada breeze
rain shower like needle point pillow cover
Muddy Waters' blues time Chicago down beat.
August dog days, keep on.

Summer End Game

Summer End Game
Jones Beach crimson Labor Day
lifeguard body build last chance
oil down,
Fort Worth, Texas baby back rib barbecue.
Belfast, Maine two-pound lobster dinner delight.

Summer End Game
Russian blood grade school holocaust
iron evil Al Qaeda terrorists,
children death-like delicate
Moscow red roses wilt.

Summer End Game
Union Square peace now candlelight
protest, kaleidoscope imagination turn concrete corner,
rock steady New York P.D. iced tea cool
70 hours overtime.
New York finest protect t-bone steak peace,
dream Orange County kids pajama hugs.

Summer End Game
Magic Long Island Sound Mamaroneck harbor
salt air quiescence.
Cyrille Romer's water color painter excellence,
robin eggs senior citizen eyes
on cumulus Saturday afternoon sky.

Summer End game
Pinewood Pound Ridge Reservation
lean-tom, snugly early September
overnight revelry.
Morning chicory coffee,
fire embers like debutantes diamond Tiffany
earring.

Summer End Game
Frank Sinatra WNYC radio cool swing, 1962.
Dewars and soda perfection, ripe cantaloupe melons,
hearty New Jersey bring it home tomatoes,
3 A.M. night hang-out at Mo's cool bop 86th Street
  tobacco stand.
Penthouse Magazine teen-age browse.

Summer End Game
President George W. Bush, John Kerry
Ohio kiss Buckeye State pink baby
vote quest.
Conventions over like Barnum and Bailey mythic circus.
Red, white, blue
round balloon serendipity.
Democracy lives on like New York harbor, lady liberty.
Coney Island magic bleach white ocean sea gulls.

Summer End Game
Kentucky moonshine country woman
yellow ribbon dream.
Brunswick, Georgia truck stop, country western faith.
Martina McBride hot muffin excellence.
Miles Davis Detroit city jazz groove.
Charlie Parker gold saxophone be-bop revolution.

Summer End Game
Strawberry 4th graders ready return
magic brick, New Rochelle Davis School.
Composition book lilac beginning
read read read.
Educate kids
Tulsa, Oklahoma Red Bronx, red clay
math potential, Brooklyn charter school excellence.
Science whiz high school, Joplin, Missouri bunsen
  burner
chemistry lab.
A thousand summertime dreams, yes.

Celestial Dreams

Celestial dreams
Sidewinder Oklahoma red clay Will Rogers vision
oil rig deep drill metaphors
paisley hearts on fire like
East Village lit match.

Celestial dreams
85th Street camisole honey
women, long legs like race horse
fillies,
humid skin stick August night
Hurricane Katrina Gulf Port,
mythic Biloxi, sweet jubilant New Orleans
holocaust destruct.
Death toll sky high.

Celestial dreams
Charlie Parker saxophone
Snapple in Apple be-bop hey day.
Genius like Harlem dawn.
Martin Luther King I Have a Dream
end Jim Crow hate twist.

Celestial dreams
New age touch sky psychological therapy
break down brick wall yellow fear,
tame Wichita cattle herd spook
like night light pajama toddler.

Celestial dreams
Jewish sabbath candle light,
God's oneness like eastern
Portland, Maine dawn
wide open calico promise
whole grain fresh bread bake
afternoon caress,
hobby horse smiles
clothesline string out like
Kansas prairie back 40 sunflower quiescence.

Celestial dreams
Army fatigue knee-length shorts,
muscle shirts, flip-flops
like big Mike's incandescent
rugby quest.
Greenwich, Connecticut Nutmeg State La Coste cool.

Celestial dreams
Kabala purple angels
Eastern Europe ghetto
turn of 20th century Jewish diaspora.
Red wine Harvard freshman
writer Vladimir Nabokov Genius, youths
ink on paper wide Ohio redemption.

Celestial dreams
Corn on cob 26th Street Sunday
night blues jam, Big Ed hominey
back-beat.
Blues cats humble like
honeycomb bumble bee
sweet potato pie guitar chops.

Celestial dreams
Bring it home America's
front porch night glide, West Virginia dulcimer pick
pillow talk like bleach white
love doves.
Celestial dreams that's what I say!

Hardscrabble Opportunity

I am hardscrabble opportunity
Good pay white collar bring
home bacon jobs, corporate women's high heel
managers wheel turn.
Tom's 83rd Street auto mechanic
genius, entrepreneur can-do.

I am cash and carry Gristedes
Supermarket barbeque chicken,
potato salad, cole slaw delight,
Latina check-out girls straight back discipline.
New Hampshire ready Sunday
morning smiles, back road flea market jubilee.
Dad's G.I. Bill NYU real estate knowledge
hard drive 1946.

I am late August end of summer
Vacation scoots, SUV kids pack
Jeff's Virginia Beach surf quest.

I am mega-million lottery
Dollar and dream on like
Rhinebeck short-order grill man,
four star eatery desire
Lenox Hill muscle paramedic
coffee break.
ABC talk radio Sean Hannity college interns
t-bone steak ambition.

I am Vassar Clement country
Fiddle supreme, Hunter S. Thompson
Aspen, Colorado gonzo journalism.
Eye in Rocky Mountain big sky, Jack Daniels
word on paper American desperado hip cool.
Work typewriter like Las Vegas one-arm bandit.
Fear and loathing, yes!

I am Bangladesh Bunyut's corner fruit man
Hustle like Dakar marketplace,
August cherries $1.99 a pound
ripe avocados like quilt bean bags.
IBM computer salesman over land long distance haul.
Own white picket house Syossett dream Long Island.

I am welfare check stock
Refrigerator chicken, porch chops,
two Catholic school scholarship kids.
Metaphors like Sprig Street Soho
Mercedes Benz city grand tour.
Logan, Utah Sunday little league afternoon baseball
   game,
tennis match Roosevelt Island
sweat work out, twohand back hand buy back skill.
Sky, the limit wildcat west Texas secret recipe
barbeque sauce.

I am three morning coffee
Rohrs' Cafe poetry read like
outlaw Waylon Jennings country guitar
pick, New York Tech computer school
black apple pie ambition.
Red neck Missouri lake bass quiescence
fly fishing craft like old time 14th Street
Swiss watch repair.

I am Friday night sabbath candle light,
Jewish prayers Second Avenue holy
sky vision, redemption like
freight train Topeka, Kansas bound.
Edgemont High School principal red rose excellence.
Montana cattle rancher's straight back pride.

I am Sally Milgrim Hunter College professor
excellence, bring it home like
sweet Massachusetts wildflowers, porcelain vase
   beauty.
Yes to wicker basket opportunity
a thousand August day dreams, yes.

Heart America

Heart America
New Orleans Hurricane Katrina
125 mile wind break heart
flood destruct.
Local state feds asleep
at switch like Hattiesberg, Mississippi
night watchman
black folks white southerners life force scramble
Basin Street corpses toxic sewer waste.

Heart America
September Manhattan
liberty goblet Thursday afternoon
blue skies, school open like
fresh water trout stream,
Second Avenue fire hearts
Jenny's white bread pigeon feed
homecoming.
Labor Day weekend rialto over
like Jones Beach bikini.
Blessed God's bone dry homes
air conditioning, Con Edison electricity
New York City peach of mind
salt peanut crib infants.

Heart America
New Orleans, Gulf Coast dies
like 4 A.M. cheap Night Train drunk
60 year old St. Peter's Square vagrant
Louis Armstrong trumpet hey-days silent
Tennessee Williams Streetcar Named Desire de-rail.

17th Street levee breaks like New York balloon
National Guard keep peace
poet Dave Brinks Metarie cool out
Jefferson Parish, French Quarter
Goldmine Bar flood waters natural disaster America
voo-doo saints destruct.
Blue jeans Gap store looting.

Heart America
Yugoslav Mikey A-plus daughter
St. John's Law School cherry pie excellence
Charles Chelnik's St. Anne's senior year
crack books highway quest
88th Street Elm Health Food carrot juice squeeze,
veggie burger chow-down like Santa Cruz,
California reefer desperado.

Heart America
Houston, Texas Astro Dome
warm blanket Red Cross heal
pecan pie rooted home jumbalaya
Creole cooking
families begin long journey heal like hot baguette
Louisiana chicory coffee.
Neville Brothers Harry Connick National T.V.
fund raise.

Heart America
Clean cut straight lace Yorkville ladies
grey hair senior citizen greatest
generation quiet dignity, red brick strength
Secure bone-dry New York apartments
checkercloth kitchen table aesthetic.

Heart America
New Orleans floor water dead souls,
hunger, dank water thirst, glass break
family fracture
Charity Hospital doctors white shoe nurses
battery power heroics
Red Cross Salvation Army life raft rescue.

Heart America
Bring back Lack Ponchetrain July afternoon caresses.
Bring back brown bag Budweiser.
Bring back French Quarter bourbon laughter.
Bring back Biloxi veranda grace.
Bring back thousands Big Easy dreams.
Bring back Bourbon Street Fats Waller stride piano.
Bring back levee Christmas fires.
Bring back Mardi Gras rainbow parade jubilee.
Time to re-build mythic crescent jazz city,
re-build Gulf Coast southern beach charm,
re-build Mississippi River delta,
Heart America, yes!

Hope Eternal

Hope Eternal
Jack Daniels' Sunday afternoon
whiskey raps, wide eye metal strollers kids
cotton afghan miracle knit
lasso love like Wyoming
cowgirl, cattle range bedrolls.

Hope Eternal
Jewish sabbath roast kosher chicken left overs.
Synagogue prayer book river run redemption
fire angels taxi scoot Lexington
Avenue 51st Street subway station
homeward bound like carrier pigeons.

Hope Eternal
No to body beauty small hip
narcissists peach fuzz ladies.
No to tight pants i-pod revolutionaries.
No to spaghetti top lingerie
hundred dollar bill feminists.
No to Hunter High School oral sex orgy fracture.
poets, Jamaican June's raise great honeybee kids genius.
Bring on Madison Avenue black woman
uptown bus driver, cotton candy smile.
Bring on Yankee Stadium fourth grader
tweed dad double play delight.

Hope Eternal
DeeAnne Gorman's cash and carry jazz vocals
southern velvet charm, old man's NYU Hospital
  pneumonia
come back like Joe Lewis prize fight true gotham grit.
September easy does it breeze
BMW cocaine blues time
Chicago cats, mythic nightride
Lake Michigan top down quiescence.

Hope Eternal
New Orleans gospel revival
French Quarter cool Budweiser
electricity on American can-do,
Davis School bake sale
cotton clad librarians
freight train deliverance,
ethics like Betsy Ross flag sew.
Big Sur immense wildcat beauty
Gristedes mum plants 2 for 10 dollars.

Hope Eternal
Garden planet like Ryans Daughters
Bar green felt pool table
green eye Atlantic City boardwalk
toddler,
Central Park late summer maple trees.

Hope Eternal
Yes to magnolia Wal-Mart manager optimism.
Yes to American pioneer spirit.
Yes to straight back rainbow excellence.
Yes to God's eternal life pinewood
salvation.

Hope Eternal
Madison, Wisconsin junior high school
book crack, memory
like Polaroid camera 1981
Interstate 80 dream time,
Davenport, Iowa late night love letters.
Bring it home like Steuben Day bratwurst.
Bring it home heavens calico heart country
new day funky New Balance sneaker ramble.
Hope Eternal dig it!

Freight Train Autumn

Freight Train Autumn
Erie Lackawanna 30 car train
mythic heartland roll,
fire leaves like gin joint
pool table,
fall equinox easy ride South Bend rail yard
serendipity.
Work boot aesthetics, New England Patriots
meat and potato Pittsburgh Steelers pro football
 rumble.

Freight Train Autumn
No to Hurricane Rita Louisiana
Noahs flood gates.
No to Ryans Daughters Bar meathead
Irish bartender, whiskey soak brain.
No to Manhattan late September cool
Sunday afternoon clinical black tar depression.

Freight Train Autumn
Paprika optimism like American 1940's can-do,
thousand leather saddle Gene Autry
western horizon dreams,
Salvation Army compassion
rid addiction like bubonic plague,
demon leg brace polio.

Freight Train Autumn
U.S. Army Second Lieutenant Nick Gerace
Alabama helicopter training regiment,
large Albany, New York forearms,
Mohawk Indian tattoo, freedom time
heroics Middle East bound.

Freight Train Autumn
English Breakfast tea loose by pound,
Morocco mint tea dialectics, hobo jungles
Chicago to Microsoft Seattle, rolling
thunder.

Mulligan stew open campfire jubilee.
Freight Train Autumn
Self reliance chop wood
like Vermont homesteaders,
pot belly stove two quilt
early morning rise, warm Burlington cardamon kisses
cuddly leg twine like
knit wool scarf.
Maple syrup God's creation sweet tooth.

Freight train Autumn
North Platte, Nebraska red clay Willa
Cather pioneer dream, iron clankety-clank wheels
wildcat west bound hard drive, track crossing
locomotive green light.

Freight Train Autumn
No to Manhattan jack up price Sunday brunch.
No to marijuana smoke illusion dwellers.
No to New York Times Style section
light weights.
No to fashion model King Kong card
carry intellectuals.

Yes to 4 year old whiffle ball dad
bat swing over and over like
Chopin piano etudes.
Yes to apple juice school yard kids
Paterson, New Jersey immigrant
5th graders opportunity dreams.
Yes to Laura Boss Lips Magazine poetic excellence,
Nevada cumulus cloud big sky resonance.

Freight Train Autumn
Parking garage blue collar
flannel shirt, hard sweat, concrete floor
checkerboard Mercedes Benz set up.
Henry David Thoreau transcendence like late
  September
Springfield, Missouri trout stream
Eureka Springs, Arkansas Raggedy Anne dolls,
Ozark silver trinkets
eternity caboose cat nap supreme.
Freight Train Autumn always!

Workboot Excellence

Workboot Excellence
October Massachusetts dawn valley like
crimson pin cushion, Abraham Lincoln preserve
  Union ethics
camcorders Sunday daydream video shoot
Morgantown, West Virginia half pound
smoked ham, mayonnaise
bring it home apple turnover.

Workboot Excellence
Central Park brown sparrow hip-hop
Gods immense Georgia state line
promise.
Ray Charles soul brother blues supreme
Manhattanville College straight back
chair English department excellence, 1973.
3 A.M. Dizzy Gillespie trumpet riff
flannel shirt hugs like Arkansas
Ozark trout.
Big heart country mama hip groove.

Workboot Excellence
Jewish Rosh Hoshonah, Manhattan, Park Avenue
glory train.
Harvest time New Hampshire cornucopia,
Hudson River blueberry mythic trail hike.
Nylon backpack, hike shoes, cool water bottle
mythic oyster shuck, Panama City Beach
salt air serenade, key-lime pie birthday celebration.
Teddy Roosevelt National Part revolution,
pine tree crescendo, Yellowstone touch sky immense
  beauty.

Workboot Excellence
Calico memory like Monterey, California
sandpiper, morning fog caffeine jags,
American Rocky Mountain front porch
dream, U.S. Constitution rock steady justice.
Scarsdale High School sophomore dance, clean black
  levies
shirt starch, Rolling Stones, London
East End groove, self-discipline like Turkish taffy,
  nightride.

Workboot Excellence
Horizon epiphany like Deborah's
kick bottom drama quest 1972,
Ford Mustang backseat kisses,
wind chime Riverdale zen sublime, brown rice
  veggie dice.
Poetry craft like 55 year old
journeyman bricklayer, flannel river-run warrior,
Ohio grandmother's take-charge
family fracture.
Teenage skateboard scrape knees valor.

Workboot Excellence
Personal history like sagebrush wide
eye holy man, 1950's soft shoe
two-step, suburban schoolyard serenade.
July Cherry Lawn Farm homegrown tomatoes,
Islamic prayer mat 5 times
daily God's holy praise,
wisdom like garlic clove
born-again christian white light faith,
open highway dawn Indiana engine hum
ethics, Nashville to Madison, Wisconsin
15 hour hard drive.
Workboot Excellence, always.

Righteous Night Glide

Righteous Night Glide
2004 election over like mad dash
New York City marathon finish,
blue collar whiskey howl Brooklyn waterfront
heartland sweet Jesus heroics.

Righteous Night Glide
Red Volvo breakdown
psychiatrists full wait rooms,
pill pop blue state short end of
stick hondo girls.

Righteous Night Glide
Yassir Arafat dead small Israeli children
breathe deep Jerusalem sigh.
No to red blood terror nightmare.
No to suicide bombs sabbath purple blood.
No to iron edge Palestine hate twist.

Righteous Night Glide
Heart America like gold Nebraska
prairie, Yellowstone National Park immense beauty
delta Louisiana miracle wetlands,
Lafayette local cafe gumbo,
jumbalaya, hot baguettes.
American Republic's Texas plains virtue
Midland sky's-the-limit grade school dream.

Righteous Night Glide
U.S. Marine Fallujah semper fi
breakthrough, liberty on move
mideast halcyon freedom train.

Righteous Night Glide
Good old girls Homosassa Springs, Florida
four day Manhattan vacation get down,
easy Coors lights, wheel luggage
skyscraper dream, gotham honeycomb delight.
Yes to corduroy Jewish compassion.
Yes to Harlem Pentecostal Sunday stained glass
    hosannahs.
Yes to Zen Buddhism tip-toe serenity.
Yes to Islamic Ramadan meditations fast.

Righteous Night Glide
Let freedom ring
singer Martina McBride Kansas country
western Cheshire heart, God's will,
like hot cherry pie,
Halloween pumpkin delight.
Kris Kristofferson hard ramble 40 year
hoot joint howls,
two-step Nashville nights.

Righteous Night Glide
Eye on California cosmic red ball sunset,
Big Sur wave crash holy crescendo
highway open like clams casino
honest denim notions.
Righteous Night Glide, always.

Angel on Shoulder

I am Macon, Georgia flag wave
Patriot, beef jerky
back seat Ford Mustang kisses,
Shakespeare's Juliet search Manhattan Island
crimson wilderness blaze.

I am prairie fire revolutionary
Justice's salt tears, warm
wood stove coffee,
ridgeline poetry, Oregon seacoast
November daybreak ramble.

I am Christian saint, parkinson hands
Mediation satchel like Johnny Appleseed,
Appalachian Trail hike Augusta, Georgia
to snow lace Maine.
Hot chocolate National Public Radio
Juan Williams urban northern lights politics.
Late night typewriter groove time,
Walt Whitman flapjack create.
Photographic holy Utah highway memory.

I am redneck Roanoke, Virginia
Country bluegrass, ham smoke
liberty like Andrew Jackson
common an country moonshine.
Missouri genius, hunt season
Chevy gun rack pick-up back road
muscle rambles.

I am easy smile calico cat
Glory American notions, coffee ball jack
sidewinder aesthetics,
Manhattanville College 1973
Hamlet to be or not
to be, ace of heart vibration.
New York Hospital psyche ward quiet February
lock-up butterscotch jailhouse
sunlight, devil's roundhouse noose.
Folks Greatest Generation rainbow wisdom.

I am flannel warrior like Billy the Kid
Bank robber outlaw burn down.
Peace on earth contra dance.
Jesus' Salvation Army hot minestrone
soup compassion, down-beat New Jerusalem poet,
Bleecker Street touch sky howls,
shirt pocket rosary bead faith.
Angel on round plaid shoulder, yes.

Home Grown Dreams

November morning time
Warm quilt cotton candy fire glow,
radiator hot rod aesthetics,
hot coffee, cigarette smoke,
Greensboro, North Carolina bound
like day trip road warrior.

Home Grown Dreams
Manhattan Island silverado 86th Street
broad grins, grey beard Harry milk crate saint
two year Cornell drop-out, move company veteran
pick up sticks, butterscotch sky, raps.

Home Grown Dreams
Panama City Beach Gulf of Mexico
sunset quiescence, sand in sneakers slow float
fried chicken, sweet potato red-neck
all you can flat-out eat
New Orleans sugarland jazz radio.

Home Grow Dreams
Greg Velez straight shoot Union, New Jersey
parking garage hondo dude, V.O. whiskey glide
Frankie Vallie Four Seasons,
Newark teenage ramble.
John Z's rock steady Bronx genius.
Yes to flower stand
ten rose ten dollar square deal.
Yes to SAT hard study high school seniors.

Home Grown Dreams
Fireplace sweetcake kisses
Eastern Colorado whispers like winter bison,
Canada wind, love's Manitoba easy does it, wind
  at back.
Gristedes grocery shop
peanut butter and grape jelly milk jug
fill stomach like Pennsylvania fur beaver.

Home Grown Dreams
God's infinite kaleidoscope heal
open Michigan field, Jewish prayers
Chicago blues time horn section excellence,
hopscotch poetics, Union Pacific freight train
theology, black bible ethics like
Connecticut oak tree.
Pumpkin pie white light revelations.

Home Grown Dreams
Freedom time earth turn
Sara Evans country western velvet voice
sexy hip sway Nashville groove,
Veteran Day t-bone, french fries, coca-cola delight.
Dr. Jason's Memphis Children's Hospital
mythic residency blueberry patch heal.
Yes to belly fire like Navaho Indian
tribal pow-wow.
Yes to 35 year workboot literary quest.
Yes to cat's eye marble cool,
garden green Macadam Highway road essence.
Home Grown Dreams, all right.

Quicksilver Delight

Quicksilver Delight
Los Angeles sugar coat easy glide
surf's up, nylon stockings
doorstep French kisses,
cotton caresses like November warm spell.

Quicksilver Delight
Prairie fire poetry riffs, sidewinder
big time laughs, hardscrabble calico cats
Manhattan Thursday afternoon
Gristedes supermarket trips,
cameo dreams like Virginia truck stop trinkets.

Quicksilver Delight
90-year old Chinese dancer Ming's classy
tea ceremony, morning oatmeal
always impeccable lady day,
Charlie Parker crescent moon howls,
Allen Ginsberg poetry dream time
Hudson River flow, noon-time Volvo
scoot like iced tea lemon slice.

Quicksilver Delight
Corporate girls hard drive brief case
honeycomb bring bacon home reality,
Chelsea computer graphic cats, high wire
digital groove out
midtown receptionist ruby red nail coat,
slice whole wheat break savvy.

Quicksilver Delight
No to cardboard zombie trains.
No to cocaine Antigua Beach riff holidays.
No to Kansas City critic finger point bourbon
aesthetics.

Quicksilver Delight
Glory train bring on Thanksgiving
like White House's gobble gobble turkey
pardon, highway bowling pin ramble
hot tomato bisque soup, buttered bagel
dream on, like high school senior
University of Massachusetts new world
prize fight ring bound.

Quicksilver Delight
Second Avenue truck route iron horse
rambles, stroller moms' mini muffins,
little Emma and Sophie butterscotch twins
year-old sweet pies.

Quicksilver Delight
Apple crisp saxophone buy-back
poetry in motion calico craft,
lotto pick-six pocket cash, like
lettuce leaf,
Metro North rail lines wide open
Grand Central Station bound
thousand city promises, yes.

Go Cat Go

Go Cat Go
Fresno west coast passport side pocket
stamp, revolutionary Colorado
River raft fandango,
Astoria, Queens 2 A.M. poker chip
dark water ditch.

Go Cat Go
Steve Lacey avant garde soprano
saxophone shake and bake
like side pocket billiards,
October Indian summer wait on
jack front Thursday morning, cool down.

Go Cat Go
Cornbread aesthetic, Miles Davis,
mythic John Coltrane silk riff
Los Angeles 1955, Kama Sutra metaphors
eggplant delight like Mulberry Street
tratoria, Tribeca acid lounges,
Lsd killing fields, New York Yankee
IQ fracture fascination.

Go Cat Go
Oliver Lake free jazz zone out
liberation, oatmeal raisin cookies
Lotto 2 dollars a shot Yorkville rip off.
Blues lady's Sonoma, Arizona sweat lodge sashay.

Go Cat Go
Underworld finance like Park Avenue
internet computers, brown bag Coors Light
Ryans Blockbuster Video
cash and carry dollar bill rialto job.
Charles Mingue be-bop lazy day
New Hampshire fire leaves, Nashua
coffee house broad r's, spiral notebook
memory like cotton candy delight.

Go Cat Go
God's Tennessee calico redemption
CBS News rack and pinion information
straight shot,
Channel Thirteen Bob Dylan eggs over
easy magnolia highway stint, American red clay saint.
Tumbleweed smiles, grace like
late night Broadway Theater dinner,
pick up sticks Jackson, Mississippi veranda joy.
Go Cat Go. Yes.

Let Go Let God

Let Go Let God
God's rainbow chalk circle
providence, oven hot meal loaf
red checker cloth family meals
calico wife earth hold rooted
in Kansas prairie heart.

Let Go Let God
Dollar in twelve step wicker
kitty, testify like fire angel
Mohammed's mountain top sky sermon,
85th Street seamstress steady hands
Brealey Schook sassy clique highway
girls November valley Thanksgiving hope.

Let Go Let God
Yawehs rose trellis bring it home
sabbath bush burn white light
high school sophomore chemistry
periodic table hopscotch magic,
Rosa Parks Montgomery, Alabama
bus boycott year of lord 1955.
No to Jim Crow south demon racist evil.
No to Jack Daniels brain fracture
bullock cosmology.

Let Go Let God
Vermont back roads hot chocolate
afternoon kisses,
tenor saxophone serendipity.
Saturday night big mama down beat
hustle, two step like
Mississippi River boat casino
roll dice,
Attic Allams' tobacco shack Indian
cool daddy computer beatific gate swing,
C-Span overnight plywood
House of Representatives democracy
mix a lot.

Yes to NYU film student Hollywood
dream time small 20 minute diamond celluloid.
Yes to U.S Marines
black hole Iraq accordion heroics.
Yes to life liberty pursuit of
peppermint happiness holy vine America.

Let Go Let God
Surrender like Albuquerque hot air
balloon desert pageant,
holy evangelical spirit South Carolina
Sunday church pew bible read,
rapture like Cincinnati hot fudge sundae
a thousand upstate New York green garden
apples, freedom trail like
Davey Crockett Lone Star State barbeque
revolution.
God's straight back chair prayers, always.

Mojo Rising

Mojo Rising
Sunday morning licorice
Beethoven Berkshire Mountain
trail hike essence,
wide panda smiles
like fur bear November down parka
bundle up.

Mojo Rising
Jim Morrison edge city Los Angeles
acid tab aesthetics, Vietnam jungle
gyroscope blood, 1967.
Iraq five U.S. Marines dead
car bomb, heartland parents
yellow ribbon Kentucky denim
wives grieve.

Mojo Rising
Sunday stroller push Second Avenue
multi-color fandango, cheddar and bacon
omelets, guitar twang
Lower East Side miracle sunlight
daddy-o music scene, grab bag
midnight guitar gigs.

Mojo Rising
Six-pack orgies, peppermint snaps
Park Slope lesbian easy glide
chamomile tea hide out,
Doors' Ray Manzarek keyboard genius,
America's rough edge youth high
wire act, addicts like Margaret Yard's
125th Street methadone clinic 1976.

Cheap hike boots K-Mart
rolling stone specials
Thanksgiving on way like
Lake George Fort Ticonderoga
paddle boat.
Pony Express leather St. Joseph, Missouri satchel.
God's Ten Commandment grace,
Alabama holy water baptism like
Muscle Shoals Allman Brothers
velvet recording studio.

Mojo Rising
Joan Carney's calico Santa Fe, New Mexico
bring it home phone call,
touch cirrus cloud eros contra dance,
drum cigarette roll
gallery curate excellence.

Mojo Rising
House of Representatives sidewinder
war on terror stray dog shouts,
Amman, Jordan wedding bell
Al Qaeda bombs.
Paprika American sophomore high school thanks.
Manhattan Island steel girders
like Rube Goldberg inventive emotions
computer death wish, turkey stuff jubilee.
Jonelle's family chill-out Co-Op City
big harvest dream cornucopia crescendo.
Mojo Rising, it's worth a try!

Thanksgiving Grace

Thanksgiving Grace
Atlantic City red roulette
bicycle wheel slot machine,
cut turkey quiescence.
4th floor union steamfitter
holy spirit South Carolina Baptist
bible study,
prayer like Aaron Copeland Appalachian Spring
pinewood excellence.

Thanksgiving Grace
Mom dad Fifth Avenue heart passion
ethics like Manhattan Central Park
appaloosa, always morals like
4 star Second Avenue veal scallopini.

Thanksgiving Grace
Dr. Martin G. five year pharmacological
tapestry weave magic, Depakote pill pop
steady like Caribbean bound schooner.
No to pagan devil masks.
No to circus sidewinder smiles.
No to sugarland elitist
New York Times Italian loafer aficionados.

Thanksgiving Grace
Bring it home like state of Maine
November harbor mooring,
brother Marc's two Johnny Walker Red
Woodstock highway bound magic,
Jewish sabbath candle light, holy Friday night dusk.

American dream mustang alive
beacon like Bangladesh corner
fruit stand man, winter hard drive
dollar a pound tomatoes,
cheap five tangerines, $2.50 pineapples
Jackson Heights saffron rice, lamb
family get down.

Thanksgiving Grace
101 Airborne Iraq freedom fight
Islam fascism jihad defeat like Topanga Canyon
fire snuff out.
Bring on White House turkey pardon
garlic powder integrity,
fresh cranberry sauce
nephew Charles straight and narrow
top notch college quest.

Thanksgiving Grace
America's rainbow providence,
Plymouth rock wilderness optimism,
talk radio lock and load Salt Lake City truth,
down-home calico cat families.
fourth grader Andrew guitar pick
passion, gold saxophone beginners chops.

Thanksgiving Grace
Cafe coffee girl Sonya's
flamenco fire, Paraguay 18 year old
always the lady day cool,
Zen Buddhism morning meditation,
Kundalini shake and shimmy chakra
fandango, Theodore's dread-lock outlaw cool.

Thanksgiving Grace
Central Park West Macy's parade jubilee.
Yes to Betty Boop, purple
Barney, Humpty Dumpty wood scarf like Episcopal
minister holy vestments.
Rainbow ski parkas, hot coffee roundhouse
river run joy.

Thanksgiving Grace
Mythic John Z Dallas Cowboy
football blood skirmish wager
John Fitzgerald Kennedy optimism 1961
baker's dozen dream kisses,
hippie ladies wide skirt, cowboy boots
two-step swirl like sufi dervish.

Thanksgiving Grace
Heartland thanks New Orleans break
bread promised land jumbalaya hope.
Always redemption like hot pumpkin
pie delight.
Thanksgiving Grace, yes.

Rainbow Providence

Christmas time short haul
Local bread truck delivery jubilee,
Park Avenue white light pine tree
America heartland pearl handle
essence like December crescent moon,
gravel road.

Rainbow Providence
Gillette Good News razor shave,
bake soda teeth floss
mythic Colorado ladies Quaker quilt
weave, hot flap jacks thick maples
syrup like Steamboat Springs metaphors.

Rainbow Providence
Jesus' white light gleam, virgin birth
hopscotch miracle, 37-cent postage stamps
evening phone calls, Brooklyn and beyond.

Rainbow Providence
Homeless Harry 86th Street dreams
1958 doo-wop Garden City, Long Island
salad days,
Scott Peterson Redwood City death charge,
Steely Dan mythic lyric, like
Los Angeles surf up high tide
reefer hustle.
Ham and swiss sandwich, senior citizens
93rd Street Isaacs Center hot meal easy glide.

Rainbow Providence
No to yuppie short-circuit Bloomingdale's shop spree.
No to social climb 55-year old
charge card blue cobalt delusion.
No to ecstacy land throw creative
gift away generation x.

Rainbow Providence
Laura Ludwig Cairo, New York wood burn
stove homestead, oak tree aesthetics,
Green Party fire eyes.
Coach Lenny Wilkens whips New York Knicks
into 5 game win streak, honest sweat groove,
Madison Square Garden electric
excite like 1971 Willis Reed cinnamon
glory days.

Rainbow Providence
Yes to mythic Steve's Woodstock Hardware Taoist
ramble,
deaf Joe's Haight Ashbury purple vibration.
Yes to Bread Alone counter ladies, cheshire smiles.
Yes to upstate December cool daddy small town
Saugerties quiescence.

Rainbow Providence
Holy June's Jamaica fruit cake,
vodka rants down Madison Avenue,
Tallahassee, Florida State cameo hearts,
Panama City Beach mythic red ball sunrise,
birthday key lime pie essence.
Rainbow Providence, that's right.

Karmic Keeping On

Karmic Keeping On
Saturday night gin drunks
scat beat, Lenox Avenue chitlins
collard green gospel,
ledge calico cat.

Karmic Keeping On
Winter solstice two days
butterscotch afternoon hugs,
Absa Ivory Coast mama hip sway
Mo's tobacco shack shake and bake
Dakar, South Africa cool down.

Karmic Keeping On
Poetry rambles, five and dime
sweet serenade, Latino hoop earring
take no guff sisters,
gypsy cab Bronx bound,
New York City chill-out, like
Merce Cunningham Dance Company ballet slipper
excellence.

Karmic Keeping On
Yes to nephew Charlie Saint Ann's junior
year read on excellence.
Yes to Metropolitan Museum
Gilbert Stuart George Washington mythic
paint portrait jubilee.

Karmic Keeping On
Clean and sober Alcohol Anonymous
flannel easy beat cats,
stretch cotton canvas, Williamsburg
working artist loft,
paint palette quiescence,
veggie stew, Volvo oil change
New York Thruway City bound Monday
night cake walk.

Karmic Keeping On
Pick self up like senior citizen
sidewalk December ice stumble,
stock wood pantry food stamp card,
tuna, baked beans, can of corn
urban cobalt blue survival.

Karmic Keeping On
Christmas choral Saint Ignatius Church
epiphany,
Moira's Chatham, New York Ford Escort
homeland corduroy dream.
Karmic Keeping On, always!

Pork Pie Hat

I am Memphis black felt
Pork pie hat,
Cheerio box cool milk
breakfast table checkercloth rapture.
Promised land New York Post
redneck editorials.

I am prairie fire poetry
Cut pie, like South Carolina
textile assembly-line worker,
cross-town 5 A.M. black sister
bus driver, sunrise cool.

I am USC Trojans Orange Bowl
Muscle romp,
limo driver's cigarette sneak,
thousand January prayers like
silver Bay Ridge raindrops.

I am 23rd Street New Year's Eve
Vodka hullabaloo, Interstate 5
California snow blizzard sleigh ride.
Grand Street linguini white sauce garlic bread
bring home delight.

I am WQXR Bartok white light
Revolution, shoestring workboot
poetry howl,
Bleecker Street rainbow grey beats
flannel prairie metaphors, like
pork rinds, cherry soda.

I am highway aesthetics,
Cape May ocean dream,
winter horizon like holy Catholic
angels, communion wafer
straight back faith.

I am Baldwin piano, 7-year-old
Mozart kick-back finger joy.

I am desert Nevada brothel,
Red velvet eros, jacuzzi
baked Alaska desire,
Lake Tahoe snow drift miracle
essence, self-reliance, like
straight leg pine tree.

I am bran muffin cadence,
Su Polo's Christmas pork and beans,
Saturn poetry read,
Albuquerque outpost solitude,
Motel 6 clean sheet dream,
grace like God's 76 truck stop
sugarland buffet table,
winter caterpillar vision always.

Paisley Joy

God's big tent Paisley Joy
Notions like porterhouse steak
electric trains, horizon barn fire move.
Utica Avenue street congas,
chitlins, Jamaican white rum.

Paisley Joy
Steady 55-year old hands, Marlboro
smoke, like Arizona cirrus cloud
sky markers,
jubilee broad laughs.

Paisley Joy
No to 30-year old soul search yarn tangle
obsession.
No to head case Latino counterman
cocaine late night delusion.
No to angry-at-world grey hair upper east side
non-believers.

Paisley Joy
Hudson River flow, January fog
West Side Highway ratatouille
rush hour easy glide,
Beethoven sonata Reisling wine
quiescence.

Paisley Joy
Yes to 2005 Grateful Dead come-back
baby west coast celebration.
Yes to junkie Sean's dollar bill
panhandle quest, return home
clean and sober, Ellenville, New York,
grand mom, love.
Yes to Woodstock incense
mountain ashram, serenity
like fallow earth sunrise.

Paisley Joy
Jesus' savior back-beat
eternity road, fresh bagels
iced coffee Manhattan sugarland daybreak.

Paisley Joy
Folks Artie Shaw up-tempo
open hearts, highway Cadillac,
senior citizen's cool
Carnegie Deli corned beef and rye.

Paisley Joy
Bring on Tannersville, Pennsylvania
cross-country wilderness morning satori,
Martin Luther King
freedom time justice,
Selma to Montgomery march,
black man's touch sky liberation.

Paisley Joy
World peace like Central Park
winter sparrow, brothers and calico sisters
big dipper love.
Joffrey Ballet epiphany delight,
a thousand crimson night moves, dig it.

Crescent Moon Magic

Crescent Moon Magic
Early December crystalline
Manhattan air, snow forecast like
black crow telephone wire,
Westchester County draft resistance 1970
frankenscence and myrrh
holy Jesus Christmas birth.

Crescent Moon Magic
Electric Second Avenue cashmere
top-coat scurry home, Merlou wine
brie cheese, lovers eyes like
Hannukah candle incandescence.

Crescent Moon Magic
Pearl Harbor attack 64 years ago
Day of Infamy December 7, 1941
stroller kids God Bless America
cherry pie providence.
John Lennon dead 25 years ago
Strawberry Fields Central Park
rainbow jubilee, denim grey hair
saints, young folks like baked Alaska,
Jack Kerouac dharma bums.

Crescent Moon Magic
Chicago blizzard, midwest turkey
scramble, white shroud Missouri
to sweet Ohio.
Senior citizens snow bird
Florida dream, West Palm Beach movie theater
paprika joy.

Crescent Moon Magic
Brooklyn salt and pepper pork chop grill,
home fries like New Haven, Connecticut
sexy red head.
Taos, New Mexico stretch canvas
winter flesh on flesh, piñon cordwood
pot-belly stove aesthetics.

Crescent Moon Magic
Poets howl like Hudson Bay, Canada wind,
City Harvest soup can Ladder 13 fire house drop off,
Bruce and Joanne Weber miracle freight train
Sunnyside, Queens excellence,
Shakespeare hearts, yes!
New Year's Day poetry hoe-down sugar plum
  marathon read.

Crescent Moon Magic
Pinewood wisdom like black Huntsville,
Alabama local sharp scissors barber,
New Orleans Christmas re-birth.
No to nose in air baby-boom diamond ring aficionados.
No to trust fund art scene crazy glue artists.
No to San Diego Congressman on defense contractors
money take.
Bring on George Washington Valley Forge
Continental Army courage.
Bring on sixth graders back pack homework self-discipline.
Bring on Miles Davis trumpet American invention.

Crescent Moon Magi
Wicca religion herbal white magic spells,
faith like Macon, Georgia stone
Baptist church, Navaho Indian tribal peace pipe rialto,
Laura Ludwig's Emily Dickinson
poetic passion, steady hands like
Cairo, New York big dipper night sky pine tree genius.
Winter quiescence radiator heat bring it home.
Down J.C. Penney lovers quilt.
Prairie fire December passion.
Crescent Moon Magic, dig it.

Apple Pie Serenity

Sandlewood incense burn
Zendo brown rice veggie sublime,
heart songs like Paul McCartney
maple syrup pop musci excellence,
calico cat soft-shoe leap.

Apple Pie Serenity
America green garden providence
cobalt blue liberty train
Boston to hot Latino Miami,
kick can salsa, South Carolina
immense Baptist faith.

Apple Pie Serenity
No to ecstasy tab cob-web brains,
No to black cloak sidewinder
Saugerties waitresses.

Apple Pie Serenity
Bring on Ella Fitzgerald torch
song jazz sublime.
Bring on western Kentucky January fallow pasture
heartland grace.
Bring on U.S. Navy tsunami compassion
desolation Sir Lanka, Phuket, Thailand
hungry brown children.

Apple Pie Serenity
San Francisco, Tuesday afternoon
Tokay wine literary glow, like
Bay Bridge golden salvation, Oakland bound.
Freedom 86th Street red rose notions,
wilderness moist 2005 kisses.

No to Westchester country black ice
back roads.
No to computer robots whiskey drunks
like high school sophomores.
No to yuppie elevator radio music brain wash.

Apple Pie Serenity
Seven layer cake corduroy Toledo, Ohio
metaphor stack,
Vermont whole wheat aesthetics, wood burn
pot belly stove essence.
Memory like Bronx Zoo Zimbabwe
elephant
January late afternoon Red Zinger tea quiescence.

Apple Pie Serenity
Yes to Hershey bar rehabilitation
wine bottle homeless.
Yes to Sweet HIV AIDS sidewinders, daily
pill cocktail, 21st century dream
beyond demon grave stone,
grey chalk ashes.

Apple Pie Serenity
Peace train calico groove
Jones Beach empty beauty like ornate metal
butter cookie tins,
denim cool daddy mental patient
ready Canal Street smile,
God's eternity road rainbow love, dig it.

A Winter's Tale

A Winter's Tale
Bone cold Canada arctic air
mad swirl, wind tunnel straight line
Madison Avenue, downtown
Tribeca Hudson River
glass ice freeze.

A Winter's Tale
Shakespeare's wide-eye tundra freeze
small calico tykes bundle,
like out of season strawberries,
L.L. Bean lace boots, scotch plain scarves
January frigid cold.

A Winter's Tale
White shroud blizzard
New York City 14-in nor'easter
snow bolts like wedding
lace, birthday gig warm
3-foot Italian hero
California Merlot bottle groove,
Miles Davis Columbia University
radio,
nephew Charlie baby t.v., New England
Patriot blow-out.

A Winter's Tale
Hot porcelain bathtub
soak, Mimi's Puerto Rican 20-year
old cheshire smile,
14th Street pizza time howls,
be-bop Roxanne Hoffman's Back Fence
poetry read.
Taxi scoot downtown like
FDR highway open rainbow road.

A Winter's Tale
Miracle glow, planet earth fallow stillpoint
rock steady radiator heat,
double J.C. Penney honeybee
comforter,
red Volvo Harrison, New York
highway quest.
Dad's square post office box,
laid-back Anita Baker soul sister elegant chops,
truck convey New England Thruway
I-95 city bound,
black clad party girls, shop cart senior citizens.

A Winter's Tale
Holy C train derail breakdown
mythic Duke Ellington A train
slows down like wildcat
Teamster's strike,
Mad Jimmy three day lock-up
100 Centre Street, pharmaceutical
cool-out round blue tranquilizers
blood pressure pills, always Budweiser
riff out.

A Winter's Tale
Bring home spring promise
pigeon's immense hunger,
snow shovel aesthetic,
late night between white sheet
caresses,
dream Bisbee, Arizona desert warmth,
wait cobalt blue sky weather break.
A Winter's Tale, yes.

V
ETERNITY ROAD
1996-1998

PETER CHELNIK - HEY GIRL - COLLECTED POEMS

I've Had Enough

I've had enough, hard scrabble
finger point hate
sleek words evade spice rack
fur encased demon slam dance
on skull and beyond.
Too much politically correct oil sludge
take off week old bedclothes
Birkenstock sandals
waves that crash assertive jetty
in South Carolina storm.
I've had enough darkness,
ethnic diverse serpent
gin joint yellow fog lights switch
on, FDR rush hour traffic
blood wounds do not heal heart snarl
dream hallucination
elevator plastic jazz
I've had enough.
Darkness on darkness
coffee cup retribution
September leg vice,
band-aids on knife wound.
I've had enough
move me away from
nocturnal terror, truncated mirror
descent, corporate state gulag
click of silverware.
Let Jewish redemption
corral counter culture wildflower spirit
bring on illumination like
Mendocino glory,
American July 4th
fried chicken excellence.
No more pit bull deaths,
no San Francisco cut cable car wire,
no cell phone poets,

no cognitive seizures at noon.
Let spiders, scorpions
Sarah Lawrence College
wash off into Gilgo Beach undertow,
away from mad hatter feminists,
jarry curl disco girls
minimalist deranged aesthetics hypocrisy --
I've had enough.

Nightride Texas Interstate

Texas Interstate 40, mythic
straight shot quest
sugar daddy to wet lips,
cerebral marbles in Levis jacket
enough cash for McDonald's,
Exxon, pack of Dentine.
Texas Interstate 40
we moved quicksilver to Amarillo --
panhandle glee.
American T-bone clarity
like overripe pomegranate,
harvest moon cowgirl quiescence
Lone Star bravado.
Texas Interstate 40
no cracker barrel compromise, low ride
on bourgeois Harley,
no half Eastern measures,
no elastic regrets, no place
for timid response
oh Armadillo pride,
silver chimeras. Stetson chapeaus
we ride wildcat sidewinder.
Texas Interstate 40
blood like purple heart
caked on cowhide denims
dream on in mythic night ride.
Yes Texas Interstate 40
wild range stallions
move hard through golden November prairie
wildcat rib joints, curio shops,
Motel 6 sanctuary.
Oh Texas Interstate 40,
we move towards big time salvation,
K-Mart sneakers, public radio
bowls of Quaker oats, highway excellence
no used Chevy salesman,
no tornado watch
yes a rose in narrow white desert hand.

Combine Children

Slick national combine children we
give you flat out nothing --
green thumbtacks, fax messages
bar East Village squat.
Cattle prongs pace on
leather hips, computers
to pay homage, goose step worship,
Star Wars is Einstein physics of era,
National Enquirer holy grail
children we give you little
as earring head, flannel shirts emerge
in green onioned street, universities --
television soap opera replaces
Shakespeare, Jack Kerouac
no cast iron standards, rules
bend like circus rubber man.
No touchstones on outer reaches
of Riverhead potato field.
Children we give you sitcom fascination
with electric Christmas lights, Ninja Turtles --
Park Avenue plastic surgery,
cruel Coors habit. Babylon
grimace staccato dream. Hollywood violence
reeks on skull as emotions
end in 38 magnum O.K. corral.
Children we give you nothing,
hole of doughnut, one sheet
of Yellow Pages, New York
City sky, narrow slice
battleship grey nautical.
Swoops through air conditioned mall
rust shut iron door that no
Bohemian soul enters.
No hippie road passion,
where is prairie flame,
Rocky Mountain need to
preserve lilac essence, shoot crescent moon
you turn back on
old time prankster bluesman --
miracle silver poetry, senior
citizen tin can wisdom craft

no cognitive rambling, no sheet music
a blue ink blotter, crazed hunger
to read each book
no Miles Davis down home bebop
on Scarsdale Library shelf.
No Stephan Dedulas quest, impossible
Don Quixote dream
no keen eye on Santa Monica
Surf, no Yosemite horizon.
Children you embrace
South Dakota crossroads,
no traffic light,
sombreroed state trooper path.
Seven Eleven convenience store
mythic signs not
deciphered, pigeons feed on stale Cherrios
too much concrete, 5 and dime reality
too much Apex Technical School aesthetic.
Where is textured dreamweave, consciousness
mythic poem Bach fugue,
Ford Taurus genius tune-up --
street corner excellence,
Charlie Mingus sting bass delight
souls fall away like Dachau inmates.
Children forgive our lies kerosene
outdoor grills, Mercedes Benz
fancy Antigua vacation
our consumer obsession, computer leg irons --
no to your long diatribes on St. Mark's Place,
2nd Floor rave ins, heroin addiction.
Yes we give you AIDS plague,
hospital I.V.'s, hospices without ribbed logic --
we give you L.S.D., crack,
cheap marijuana to ease pain
of starless Portland night.
Anorexics on torrid lam
from game show fisticuffs.
Children we give you nothing,
broken families who reek in
psychotic down shift, Ritilan behavior
modification, the pattern thrift shop plate
empty like American dream
a nameless prison term

combine offers cheap t.v.'s, VCR,
record clique CD's. Computers
that store information
like rotted beef.
American providence on short bolt --
parents who push kids for Law or
Medical degree. Black demin Prozac zombies.
Children we give you nothing,
a university bold lie --
sweatsuit granite legs, torsos
on weight program bodies
yes dreams evaporate like
Elko, Nevada mirage. Western civilization
beheaded like Louis 16th
criminal as mythic hero, gangster ethics.
Ignorance courted like prom
queen beyond brick schoolyard, violent kisses.
Chop suey passes for sirloin.
Oh children we give you nothing
in round cary America,
yes out of dustbin ashes,
neon Jiffy Lube main street Colorado
you must rise, like falcon, highway passion
fierce freedom wildflower spirit perfection
Children ride Chisholm trail month upon
crescent moon month.
Children raise heads, apprentice self
to poet madmen, bebop tenor sax man.
Learn cajun fiddle, learn red clay pottery
and read, read, red
Children make way our of combine's
mouse trap, Manhattan tar pit
Information Age tiger cage
gulag, to higher mountain ground.
Seize magic lunch pail ethics --
sing miracle salvation,
children preserve wing angels, genius
roadhouse cadence, walk Appalachian trail --
ride milk train to global green glory.
Bohemian rhythmic salvation,
return to magic garden,
Children, the time is now.

You Ever

You ever ball peppermint jack in
a hundred quarter tones
on the high rialto.
You ever put narrow hand through
girlfriend's golden hair
touch of palomino mane.
Jump start a 68 T-bird,
You ever place cockatoo in metal
cage without hinge or lock.
You ever drink three Bacardi
shots in slingshot half hour and talk poetry
with fringed madman.
Crawl on bedroom floor
in search of eyeglasses
Playboy magazine.
You ever move through Guggenheim
Museum painting a vessel of magic
form and kaleidoscope color,
you ever sit in popcorn movie theater
during december blizzard awed by
Jack Nicholson's receding hairline,
Kim Bassinger's sultry shoulders --
you ever drive Pontiac from Eureka Springs
through sparse Kansas prairie land,
jug of iced coffee
clutch of Egg McMuffin.
You ever declare adolescent crush on
college sweetheart
groove to 3 A.M. John Coltrane,
you ever walk Times Square
killing fields geared for
calico angel quintessential fire poem,
Caribbean carnivale,
with precise farmland sighs,
green eyed recognition --
a frozen yogurt milkshake,

wicker basket wisdom weave
down on Carmine Street.
You ever dream of wildflowers
in November Sunday morning,
almost icebound, Allen Ginsberg
text in grasp, prairie notions
in green eye carousel
7 A.M. Missouri eggs
down right over easy.

No Buy In

No buy-in to American
porterhouse steak
corporate philosophy.
Upper class computer (cacophony),
polyester dream time
no buy-in desire for fashion
model waif, the danger
of Missouri railroad crossing.
Third week haircut,
taut Texas competition
like new moon sugar embrace,
spaghetti el dente caught
in fork prong.
No buy-in to Kansas dry cleaner's bill,
bell bottom chic, sculptured buttocks.
Yes to camp out in
geodesic dome icon,
February Berkshires daydream
away from suburban dollhouse.
Yes to black Bible underneath toggle coat.
Bring on oneness of unnameable purple spirit
I dream of eastern
Colorado prairie --
power lines move to eternity
two Chevy hot rods wired in tandem,
Yes to rock steady defiance hard nose
quest for Albuquerque truth.
No buy-in to poetry like cold milquetoast
feminist blood wars,
burly cocaine barroom bouncers.
No buy-in Madison Avenue
cologne set, a starched sleek Mercedes
Brooks Brothers' shirt, green money God
no buy-in mini skirt poseurs,
suburban trim law warriors
impotent like shampoo commercial,
86th Street aerobics,
Mexican jumping bean aesthetics.
Howl poem out to crystal horizon,

day breaks like earth celebration
wide Boston promise -- Navaho spirit,
Yes to children mittened
affirmation, cup of hot chocolate.
A push up rock candy mountain.
No buy-in walk singular road apart
from metal harness and crazy glue
newspaper clipping sewn into
overcoat. Key West winter gin and tonic haze.
No buy-in, I travel own meridian,
fierce like Montana Rodeo,
appalachian wilderness trail
love's textured essence,
cotton Manhattan embraces
western horizon like hot apple pie dream
New England grace,
April spring dawn providence
eye on salvation's soft shoe prize.
No buy-in, brother.

American Angels

American webbed angel, hoop
earrings, Bloomingdale's
makeup counter sheen --
Fitzpatrick's bar and grill
half hour before close,
3:30 A.M. checkerboard vortex
lust iron clad delusion.
American angel, toothpick
in wire mouth, rucksack
down by sneakered ankles. Pants roll
choose your toxic poison,
gin rummy hand, diet Coke, China white,
American angel, sensual notion on massage
table, Johnson's baby oil
American angel, hands on flat buttocks.
Road twists in ebony
darkness, 10th Avenue
paranoia, a chamber maid
in hock to leather clad loan shark
LaGuardia Airport traffic
snarl, a cravat knot, midtown sun play.
American Angels bring it home --
suicidal electric spasms
quarter for homeless oracles,
tap shoes Westside rehearsal room.
American angels move in nighttime desolation
Ray's generation X boogaloo
Christmas red wrapping paper,
bar sawdust sweep aside -- closing
like lit cheroot after meat loaf,
side counter hand job.
American Angels, I am
Big Sur fierceness delight
Youngstown blue collar integrity
a rare steak sandwich,
ice tea on the run.
American dream held like newborn
infinite possibility --
no to desolation row Coors
Light, no switch off mind like

square Radio Shack clock radio,
no to corporate vacant Internet
stares, no dating game hearts
I move to eastern Washington sweet salvation
hot chestnuts, hot coffee thermos
cheshire phone calls
Flo Kennedy Kansas City eloquence
I talk of poet's passion,
March's early springtime promise,
ascent of genius
a long ride home enough killing fields
Ohio barbed wire commotion.

End of Depression

End of depression blues
Lincoln Tunnel lifts like
crates of Tyson chicken
wide Peterbilt load
dead weight toss off on
open Missouri soybean field.
Demo tautness gone.
End of depression
Victorian frivolity moves in
like intoxicated dice game,
Kingston Jamaica carnivale.
Captain of tramp steamer
on wooden deck, helm in
revolutionary grasp.
End of depression
clean shave, visionary like
Hyannis high tide, gone like
traveling carney show
hit and run blues.
End of depression
midnight prairie fire
delight of china silk angels
freedom from New Jersey turnpike demons,
Black Panther soul kitchen liberation,
brain synapse free from
cul de sac logic.
End of depression night rides west
concrete handball court delight
Ansel Adams calendar,
breeze along curve spine,
Catskill redemption
clarity of IBM typewriter
grade school motion.
End of depression'
yes freedom from serpent, demonic guilt,
hanging judge's verdict.
No cobra beneath
fluff pillow, gone the end of
angular torment, holy flannel crucifixion
weeks without leather shoes.

Sleepy-Eye Morning

Sleepy-eye morning, Tuesday
5 A.M., groggy like drunk sailor
Lithium in warrior blood,
medieval ax on grinding wheel,
wildcat jolt Vermont pancake notions
maple syrup, rococo mood swings.
Sleepy-eye morning nocturnal
swamp second avenue, rain
clouds ride hard from Carolinas.
Silver beaked pigeons, Cole Porter gossip
dark street corner Mexicans,
nylon jackets,
square delivery trucks --
first stop, fresh Brooklyn bread.
Sleepy-eye morning, taxi meters flick
on like slot machine handles, shoe horns --
suited doormen cat nap
New York you flex silicon breasts
French etiquette,
breakfast table morning paper
place panties on curved bottom --
sleepy-eye morning
April nuclear flashes
no hot bubble bath.
No Chick Corea piano groove
homeless without proper bed.
Jersey bridges and tunnels
fume like English tea kettles,
down Park Avenue vortex.
Sleepy-eye morning, 5 A.M.
Broadway curtain time
no cut rate innocence
patent leather ballroom glide
steel New York City day begins.

Four Days Into January

Four days into January
garden dense
years of metal hoe
red neck shovel
topnotch fertilizer,
no sleepless night
2nd Avenue catacomb
serene like calico cat.
Four days into January
Ft. Dix convoy line up
pool room combination shot.
Four days into January
garden planet sweet surrender
bootleg genius, sweet potato pie deluxe
no trick bag tonight,
no orange plastic wildflowers
no dial a psychic cardboard delusion.
Four days into January
Horace Silver quintet sublime
road thirst moist like
lemon ice tea
no bloodshot Bukowski eyes.
Four days into January
drive hard on flat out Oklahoma
possibility, full Ford pickup gas tank
a winter field
minimal like tribal whiskey bar
rainbow bold winter
liberated by mythic Godhead, sky spirit
Rye Beach high tide
lunch bucket passion, always.

Money Boys

Money bare bone greed
bedrock lies, wannabes immobile
like 19th century hutch,
ruse of paper wealth.
Defrocked knight on wanton
baseball diamond.
Truncated personal histories
deceit, accordion curl-i-cue
watered down Chivas.
Money boys wedding band hidden
from Madison Avenue mascara eyes.
Condo wildcat sublet
where are honest folk,
craftsmen, yellow pencil
behind ear? Poets like Manhattan glazers.
Firm handshakes on
34th Street sidewalk,
straight Missouri talk.
Stone mask, Perry Ellis shirt,
money boys, bold faced lies.
Reality reinvented
Brooks Brothers money suit --
Jeep Cherokee cocaine drive
big shots in black athletic sweats.
Yes money boys, no cheshire heart,
Colorado passion, monogrammed attache
stacks of yellow Wall Street Journals --
NASDAQ holy grail.
Money power status in chainsaw litany
manicured nails, London haircut
reinvention of all disguised notions.
Money boys self love a Broadway burlesque
take corporate tinsel dream
personality like prefab quonset hut
take two dollar shoe shine,
take china white ramble, ego like

ETERNITY ROAD

a squadron of black alley
rats, half eaten baked Alaska.
On money boys you leave me
broken highway spirit
rewire corporate brain synapses
move on cheshire eternity road
become mythic bebop self
again and again.

Spring Pain

Spring pain cruel season
racks rainbow emotion
like overripe jelly beans,
too many sugars in coffee,
twisted limbs like
hot wire catacomb.
Oh spring pain you talk of eros,
maypoles, skirts in swirl --
mixture of saliva, bandannas
around neck, French kiss hot devotion.
Spring pain cut and paste poems
North Carolina tall tales
St. Cloud brotherhood
ecstatic buffalo herds,
last rites of Jewish rabbi.
Spring pain false sophomore starts
short bolt, small joys of unwrapped
Hershey bars. I sit,
minuscule in dark hutch,
the sun in charcoal eclipse,
hope like tethered pitbull
spring no season
Texas panhandle spirit arid fields
poetic whiskey shack lies,
carbon paper recycle
no candy coated Mississippi
jamboree, canvas circuit tent --
do not move towards red horizon,
drum circle rebirth
do not move towards red horizon,
fertile dream days faint,
lilies in early wilt
spring pain.

Stillness of Pink Ballerina

I desire to be heard
like rooster sunrise --
sweep of Oklahoma wind
over oil field.
Hoot Cafe along I-40.
Silence an ill fated
diary lock.
Rikers Island jail cell.
It is winter, a sparse
swirl like frozen
yogurt combo. North Dakota
winter wheat.
Wind on shoulder blade.
A Harlem painter stretches canvas --
no time for mythic planting,
no time to drag iron
plow through topsoil rich Kansas field.
Steady patience.
I speak out like Lithium psychotic --
Stillness of pink ballerina,
pause between Virginia reel,
woman in turquoise cowboy boots --
traffic light hesitation
on Public Theater Lafayette Street --
Yes I desire to howl
to bandit and university coed,
to soda can men who comb trash bins
for perfect Dr. Pepper, $100 bill.
I turn from gagged mouth,
hostile hot prejudice
out of orbit yuppies --
egomaniacs in flowered tights --
I turn from stock brokers who believe
large amounts of marijuana
will cure bottomed out Delta moods --
take my calloused hand,
lace up duck boots,
Robert Bly mythic analytics --
cast a plaid scarf over
red neck and shoulder and

follow me down Iroquois trail.
Move with this fracture
poet along the leafless
Pennsylvania valleys,
always with baseball cap
magic rivers locked in mirror ice.
Past Ohio, Missouri, Mississippi Rivers
into the winter sun
unbounded harbor hope
yes I place harness on
electric brain, roam from
East Harlem hovel to
overnight Greek café.
Purchased uncountable cartons
of Marlboros. Cut the pecan pie
with steady hand.
Maybe some white cloud whip cream.
I desire no movies, no
Hollywood wholesale vanity --
tumble down distortion.
It is 2 A.M. I see cellophane
sarcasm, dark mounts of
cro-magnum hate, bus driver anger.
I desire to be heard like Black Panthers
eon upon eons ago.
I speak out in crystal clarity, cirrus horizon
yes I see subway cars shoot
beneath city street like mad pinballs.
Yes guns abound, lessons not
learned, spiral notebooks left
on green park benches.
Half empty wire trash bins
week old ham sandwich
yes I desire Puerto Rican
hobos beatitude over
trash can fire --
rain pelts this urban electronic box
like William the Conqueror.
Too many cults,
Satan's blood rights.
Hear me America, hear my
green eyes as they fix

on gravestone and paisley horizon.
I will not quit quest for garden
hear my heart, like Diz on gold trumpet
I yearn for holy completion.
Burning bush on MacDougal Street --
salutation of miracle planet -- erotic
thighs in search of mountain woman
woman with ocean grace and
memory beyond stock answers.
I desire on Columbus Circle,
125th Street embrace
Flatbush Avenue.
Where eager eyes do meet,
recognition of Hobi tribe,
where poetic fragments
liberate East Side 11 year olds,
hope in AZT plastic vial
hear me combine, I am your child,
American dream, fire's oakwood spirit
horizon at New York red dusk
baseball glove under New Rochelle mattress
I embrace meat and potato family
like stone wall --
a belief in God's spirit, acoustic Martin guitar --
benevolence, midway wonder
essence of poetic redemption, highway aesthetics
possibilities of spring illumination
brilliant East River light,
hope of loaded wooden cupboard.
Road fascination in ocean bone and scope.

MTV Media Dream in Skull

I am a fractured cats eye marble
thrown against tough plastic angular
sideboard,
streamlined hot wire commotion
casual like leather street whore.
I am cheap flounder fillet
baked in Chardonnay
and basil,
a runaway crosstown bus
headed to Coney Island, Denver
points between.
I am Black man in Port-au-Prince --
Miami cha cha dream
hot barrio angst.
I am 23 year old in grunge flannel
MTV media dream in tender skull,
Metallica T-shirt, used Firebird --
I am sacred white light
consciousness
reams of Canadian newsprint
bound for *News* Building.
Orange afghan toss rugs,
hand me down notions,
thrift shop Columbus discovery.
Trigger man at Tiffany's --
I am lonesome Bosnia dove
in quest of ancient Israeli sprint
singular Hebraic passion
close to charred skull.
I am a designer garbage can lid,
american gopher, sometimes
Whitney museum in studded tuxedo
lookin' good.

Revolution of Spirit

May Day passed like North Shore lilacs
Whitman's expansive poetics --
scruffy kid hunkered on tricycle.
Yeah May Day passed,
no wildflower revolution, destruction
of media short bolt, CBS News.
America still full of
sideshow fire eaters,
snake charmer, painted fat ladies --
yes I yearn for revolution
of beleaguered spirit,
sawdust on Youngstown
workbench. Good paying jobs for all,
the ascent of prairie genius.
Now sky is crystalline
like pimple free face
of narrow carney barker,
doubts remain an educated Cornell tongue
an empty queen sized bed
waits me, demon slot machine.
Tiger cage remains locked, like poet's cabal.
Life sentence for casual misdemeanor.
Bread and dark water.
May Day brought no celebration --
in Union Square commotion,
no Dizzy Gillespie trumpet wails.
In high gear
along 8th Avenue. No tethered Maypole,
America you kill your children,
place them in computer chips,
psychedelic skateboards rolling nowhere like
deck of rudderless transport
no Mt. Desert Island wildflower and paisley
dream. Chips Ahoy Cookies,
zen glow.
A fierce revolution of spirit
calls me like tracks from Memphis to Chicago,
an unplugged media consciousness --
come to me, hispters proud bohemians,
spirits on rare golden road, seekers,

bold cherry outsiders --
no to folk who dream
of Mamaroneck condos
and peach sorbet vacations.
Wither with Sony Walkman --
get it on through
Pacific surf risks,
a miracle personal history,
memory's short stop perception
another metal dead
bolt picked.
Like Mao's long march
I wait for prairie schooner
Topeka bound,
a Willa Cather redemption
red clay ready to ramble voice.

2 A.M. Saturday Night Hold Up

Small fractured Israeli dream tones
2 A.M. night twisted gangland turf.
Square dominos fall like
Tennessee land slide,
dual air bags in Chrysler,
puffed whipped cream
on homemade Greek
rice pudding.
Callouses picked
with surgical precision
death divides terrace rail,
upstate Taconic Highway.
Oh 2 A.M. no sleep surrender,
Hindu cosmology,
no dried black eyed susans
in clay vase. Mark Twain spun yarns --
Dave down in Louisiana
fencing Tulane bandits,
Cuevo Gold warriors.
2 A.M. hands steady
like QE 2 captain,
starched dress whites --
half picked over buffet,
Lady Clairol in action,
Delta Charlie asleep in
red brick projects,
Mike the bouncer hustles prepped up winos
out into New York night.
I sit with bull whip placed
aside, American dream astounds
mud drainage ditch
Capricorn sun moves
in like gymnasium sweat, Spandex lurches
fruit cake devoured by stooped
delusional homeless.
Yeah brother 2 A.M.,
wooden ruler measures
Blakean brain and Hegelian reason,
cruelty of Proposition 187 --
dominos fall as afghan lay on bedroom floor,

Lite F.M. dulls Saturday
night senses.
Providence envisioned in storm coat pocket
Space Shuttle's tiptoe glide above marble planet,
a tenor voice noted in
rippled cheesecake imagination,
hallucinations emerge --
freedom sometimes close at poet's hand --
2 A.M. hold up and incense stacked
like cord of pine wood.
Desk cluttered with electric bills,
the night seethes
a demon torture rack in Bucharest --
Christmas expectation
within grasp.

Woodstock 94

Oh Woodstock you bitch goddess,
sanguine dame --
raise head i bizarre swirl, bracketed
by too much marble delusion,
youth anger rap and jest.
Generation X down
porcelain sink, bungie suicide --
slashed psychedelic jugular
as condors fall from cirrus sky.
Illusion layered like
used Salvation Army mattresses,
Berlin Luftwaffe cut-offs
cauterized prophets --
kills the pain with surgical cool.
Chemical short bolt oh Woodstock
tears flow in August dawn.
Open veranda to rugged beast --
crack, L.S.D. and music industry
Mafia short bolt --
nickel and dime tripping
Woodstock 94, iron noose around
brain, mud and empty brown paper bags,
sanitary napkins, exposed breasts --
salvation in marijuana
lifeboats no longer observed.
A storm watch noted.
Another lieutenant commands
fractured horizon.
Quick fix lobotomy --
you Woodstock distressed child genius --
marbles beyond chalk circle.
Big wheel turns in truncated
turf, death appears in
Saugerties field of black crosses,
ecstasy's hour glass pain.
Discarded cans of Bud. Kids you dug hole
this weekend in August, towards earth center,
Dante's 7th level of hell,
hallow resonance, numerous serpents
a hallway of mirrors --

through mud and Etruscan tundra.
You opened Pandora's box, no escape hatch,
death of creative brain --
no MTV fix. Chemical plant liberation.
Heavies on curb, backstage Hoot boys.
rock and roll hoochicoo, Crimson flashback,
upstate distortion --
wounded abound.
Blood has been drawn.
Death of magic liberation spirit --
fringed casualties accrue,
like passing Amtrak diesels.
Woodstock 94 you drive me
away from hyacinth
cognitive purple creation and promise --
with no wildflower wonder, road rhythm --
dark Byzantine horror,
another generation's holocaust.
Oh children touch the sky,
not corporate garbage dumpster,
LSD shuck and jive promise --
nihilistic dead tulips --
yes move to blue skied salvation,
hard work, Kerouac creativity,
embrace golden sunlight,
of New Jerusalem,
the potential of genius, a new world.

Lover

Lover's sweet river current
flow across
chiseled Manhattan
table top. Faded denims fold
gold ring in soap box --
oh magic love
essence in dollar laundromat
among undershorts, brassieres
ladies' muscular waxed legs.
Lover come to me you rare Shanghai
tonic, shadow and
wilderness mushroom hallucination
a vase of beached lilies. Godiva chocolates.
Lover talk to me sweetness
in clipped Quebecois dialect
a lasso on leather saddle horn, frisky palomino
fringed cowgirl get up yeah
caress me -- imagination ad Monopoly madness
clean green striped sheets,
Joni Mitchell's fierce poetics
sardonic limbs,
lover no more lonesome river valleys
runaway critters,
lady love me in vertical corn silos
carpet psycho wards, Dean Moriority
parking lots, snake subway
underground. Lover belief in plain talk
spirit, heated nova that drives me
coast to coast like
runaway diesel out of East Hartford
no Rwandan corpses,
o blood caked wounded,
no dank bearded derelicts, empty Nighttrain bottle --
large penny ante crowd --
place bodies outside demon barb wire fear
light West Coast purple candle
and let's get it on.
Clean the damn Victorian house
bring in the Georgia gospel choir
hear me lover.

Sanctuary 1970

Sanctuary wonderful moist geranium seeds
planted in private psycho ward 1970
time to zen expand
over and over again
like ragged right fielder, weighted bad in hand
in steel batting cage.
No gulag prison ward ball and chain.
Sanctuary 1970, twenty year young buck
without poetic language, muted
in a song. Sight lines
settled in Four Men
New York Hospital ward --
innumerable cut throat
pool games, three squares
with boys. Orange Thorizine on schedule --
Will, Louis, Mike, Tom.
We transform iron psycho ward
gulag into literary prairie.
Better than U.C. Berkeley
LSD killing fields.
Boiler plate sanctuary 1970.
We plant mythic seeds like Viet Cong
pointed spade, metal hoe, gardener's gloves --
miracle dreams no hearts and minds
spirit holocaust.
Sanctuary 1970 two tours 15 months total --
learned prairie barbed wire limits
grace of hot coffee
cold shower, fried chicken dinner,
solitary black-eyed pea,
inner voice howl,
Gregory Corso dream hospital library
I pick up Marlboro habit,
rescued soul out of psychedelic
American killing fields,
striped circus tent --
smoke mirror pine green freak out.
Sanctuary 1970
15 months removed from
LSD 25, cut marijuana, Vietnam hydra glide

I am clean like 20 Mule Team Borax
generations nihilistic jackknife
into empty tiled pool, cut brain synapse
no suicide in cluttered suburban basement --
no Vietnam cold oatmeal frenzy.
Golden seeds in 20 year old hand
April planting time, green earth
California garden dream,
a thousand etudes, Marlboros
sweet North Carolina kisses,
highway like cheshire wonder.

Mad Poets

Round up all mad poet psychos
scoot out to Carnaby Street
mirror closet. Set wooden
clothespin to nose, feast on
Plath, Whitman, sweet Allen Ginsberg.
Mad poets cool down Indianapolis 500 jets,
root out looking glass delusions,
weak chuck meat craft
embrace magic herbs, jug of ice coffee
embrace garden mulch pit.
Oh you mad poets too cool for tweed mentor,
Minneapolis apprenticeship
reinvent Albuquerque desert
heart, move from
narcissism to high North Dakota prairie.
Mad poets nail wooden wall with
supermarket coupon economy
no briefcases full
of Communique hate mail.
Mad poet rid self of Hollywood big time
ego desire, a reserved table
at Sardi's. NEA quick draw hallucination.
Mad poets take on ancient
muse, observe tides at Jones Beach
month after month.
Embrace flannel metaphor
move like a feather Cherokee,
belief in holy spirit, ther fertile land,
Wrigley's chew gum
get straight like Northern Pacific
Diesel. Rehab crack head pop cherry Coke,
remove self from high school cliques
hen house poets
like metal gyroscope,
endless crosstown bus.
Mad poets no JFK airport commotion
a narrow slant on university English muffins
move toward Red Zinger tea liberation's
textured rainbow cadence.
Now.

Christmas 1994

Oh Scotch plaid Christmas 1994, like
clown garbed hanged
man, Fruit Loops
in pocket, resolve
to settle all blood feuds, birth of Christ.
Blood lust priest's bamboo chambers.
Oh Christmas 1994, aluminum electrodes chest,
a trout hook in poet mouth
toss off short circuit whine
desolation's tough gingerbread highway
frontal lobe lobotomy.
Christmas 1994, sacred morning under
Canadian pine tree --
sort mended socks, Arizona desert coat,
moon lodge Seattle mythic fire
Jesus bring it home
in wild barnfire vision,
Jack Daniel quest with mythic Hank.
Christmas 1994 no broken children oracles
no computer brutality.
Greed's round shoulder, computer
wide eye hoax.
Oh angle fly
like Iowa 4 and 20 blackbirds.
Oh Christmas 1994 I reel like Brooklyn
grandpa, green whiskey eyes,
chariot in melon skull
Christmas 1994, cardamom and wonder
quiescence of avenues devoid of
Chevrolet and metered taxi.
Fresh Butterball turkey, mince pie,
no iron medieval chastity belt.
No hemp noose on flannel neck,
eye on boxed angel prize.

New Years Rocket

New Years rocket like mesh cannibal
night, angular females scream up
2nd Avenue -- 50 dollar barroom joints,
click of high heels,
bag of Northern California reefer --
New Years rocket untangle string ball,
chest pocket Marlboros
cantina's promise adobe,
Yorkville hardscrabble slow burn
East Village stairway kisses, poet's cabal.
Branding iron like goose step
culture prep crowd.
Chop a layered onion.
New Years rocket --
I watch hipsters age another
sapphire year, turn
screws on picture frame,
ignite Lincoln Town Car,
howl on Indiana I-70.
New Years rocket, Chinese firecracker
poetics, Roman candle
Swiss watch delight.
Jane in wool stocking, warrior bronze torso
cold water loft drive by --
T-bone steaks, garden salad.
New Years rockets, anarchy's mad rumble
Austin five alarm chili imagination
bring on work shirt rebirth,
back pack wilderness ethics
no chiseled misunderstandings,
delicate 3 A.M. pillow talk.
New Years rocket take off to territories,
beyond orange pollution and scream,
Fairbanks bound --
free dead bolt clinical nightmare
free monkey suit, Venus fly trap.

Yes to magic taxi rides along
1st Avenue.
Yes to linen paper, funky hairbrush,
Jane's wildcat sculpture passion.
New Years rocket stow away for
another cheshire year texture
wild fire dream --
railroad heart words.

Corporate Culture

Corporate culture slashes tender artists,
bandits beyond rehabilitation, iron city limits.
No large porterhouse steaks,
peppermint whores in
high heels and Chanel.
Frankenstein reoccurs in
silver lifeboats and sturdy
television scenes.
Corporate culture carny side show,
corrupt fun house without exit, sitcom rerun
motherlode propaganda quick fix
cable T.V. monopoly.
Corporate culture foot soldier dream of
glitter Oyster Bay wealth,
striped Italian cut suit, gold Oscars
technological shuck and jive,
no truck stop dream, no wildflower liberation
remove cognitive chops
let computer cut swath
along highway meridian,
ignore oracles, fringe madmen outlaw poets
too many banks, insurance outfits,
big business gin consciousness
Dodge City noose, shut up and consume.
Corporate culture bottom line obsession
TV central authority
mechanical time warp
by Internet, E mail brain death
a disdain for New York City poet,
bold wrangler on East Colorado range
Harlem prophets, fire in brown eyes.
Corporate culture, American kills delicate
spirit. Ritilan children
hip hop death wish.
No silver passion, cathedral choir voices,
genius shattered like plate glass window.

Iron Agenda

Iron agenda inner miracle quest vanquish
like hood knight on
eastbound crusades.
Oklahoma wind storm marbles
too much realty principle,
law court ping pong
heavy millstone weight,
iron agenda, fabric softener
brainwash evident to few oracles madmen
no quicksilver imagination, no condor ascent
no box kite language
crime scene yellow tape.
Iron agenda like school marm psychosis
straight jacket, spoon fed
cut down like California sequoia,
another soul sideswiped, another reputation
slandered in football field mud
upper class insanity reigns like
rush hour F train --
borderline personality quick shuffle,
30 second interrogations, paranoia
common like urban pigeons.
Scalpels flash like terrorist
black leathered conformists.
Iron agenda, no inner journey rainbow reality
of magic cobbled wonder sweet
Hindu karma, wildflower
splendor. Imagination's Cerrillos New Mexico glow
no five and dime smile --
computers hijack spirit,
digital power glide -- no cognitive
Jean Paul Sartre freedom quest.
A propaganda short bolt,
fear drives tribe, like doctor's wait room,
a late 20th century corpse fix.
Iron agenda.

River Raft
For Mark Twain

I am river raft hard oak wood
silver quick scoot
along Mississippi
arteries.
Snake oil salesmen
breed on cobra hysteria
bounty men abound --
I am mythic river.
Yes it's raft time --
a smooth quartz stone,
by 45 ridge years.
I am river raft
Huck and Jim in American quest,
sweet salvation
carny folk still abound
in Hannibal, Cairo, pearl handle
derringers, obscenities
emerge from ghost rider night.
I am river raft
down by high yellow grass,
Moses again and again
wildcat breeze to arch back,
no to Tom Sawyer conformity
no to tough school marms
I am river raft take me to
warm wisteria kitchens
muffin smells, hot
meat loaf, mash potatoes.
I am river raft
like Huck Finn outlaw passion
oh river currents
holy, holy, holy Mississippi
bread dream.

Liberation Europe

Liberation Europe D Day
50 years ago today Normandy
lick bottom invasion, Omaha Beach,
blood red 29th Infantry division --
American true grit
cut down, German artillery
strong -- concrete bunkers
yet wave after wave of G.I.'s
storm beach, Brits over at
Juno and Sword catch hell.
Liberation Europe
21, 22 year old dudes from
Oklahoma, Louisville, Kentucky,
New York City.
Kickin' ass. Ranger division
mere milk fed kids
scale Normandy cliff.
Blood everywhere, like butcher shop
End Hilter's Nazi
madness, end Auschwitz steel demons.
Liberation Europe navy ships
Texas, Arkansas shell hell out of Krauts.
British, American planes
drop 82nd, 101st airborne
behind German barb wire lines
rough go American fight over and over
B-17's pound German bridges,
Eisenhower, Montgomery
in command. Root out Nazi black evil.
Liberation Europe "Let's go" and Yanks moved
bodies beyond recognition
blood stain English Channel
G.I. excellence medic beyond the heroics.
Yes, kids tough as hell
oh these brave fierce American boys,
"can do" guys yankee doodle
stood firm
cut the pie June 6, 1944,
courage muscle heroism
beyond khaki compare.

Liberation Europe many no homecoming
lay to rest in cemeteries
along French coast,
marble white crosses, star of David
supreme promised land American heroism
50 years later I say thank you sirs.
Our generation's mythic fathers --
I son of a G.I. who cut teeth
on Anzio beachhead down in Italy.
I say thanks for cherished freedom,
uncommon drive, you put lives on
high wire line again and again valor courage.
Thank you gentlemen.
Let Freedom Ring.

Bad Cards

Eight years bad garbage cards
deuce of spades, three of diamonds
killer poker, too many university con men
leather card sharks
subtle thin arm whores.
Eight years nothing,
hooked straight jacket sleeping pill
iron leg shackle thumb screw,
blood red crucifixion
no cool rocky Mountain cadence,
no Kansas calico women
gentle cowgirl hands on round nose
tackle shoulder, no Missoula kisses
poker chips dwindle like Marlboro carton
heavy breath, fringe mental patient
mouth drool.
Road faith still abounds,
yes to Sante Fe dawn,
mashed potatoes pile high, New Jerusalem
yes to calico heart, creases corduroys,
flannel warrior colors.
Queen of hearts, full house salvation,
sturdy jacks and ten,
winning pinewood hand faith.

Blew Off

Blew off poetry reading
deep in Brooklyn Dodger night,
no show in traffic knot,
combine madness.
Blew off poetry reading
oh New York rush hour vortex,
beyond bone humanity
beyond sanctified poem measure
blew off Roslyn's outstretched
hands, in chop
staccato river breeze.
Blew off poetry reading
too many starched shirt
camphor hallway closet,
New Jersey turnpike demons,
the click of glass face stopwatch.
No claim of professionalism,
rock tundra consistency
a no-show far from Brooklyn
wildflower grandeur.
Tonight no big dipper
tonight no cool sea breeze irrelevant
tonight no I-70 Colorado words
tonight no Harlem patchwork quilt
no I do not take Volvo
Brooklyn bridge stampede
no F train caterpiller thrust.
Blew off poetry reading
Roslyn forgive purple two head demon
thousand eye serpent curl.

Talk To Me Lord

Talk to me Lord
I am thick Sunday Times
macadam crack sidewalks,
pile level to
eye and stray doberman.
I am square coffee rolls,
hot out of Canarsie oven,
sugar coated,
dervish swirls like Cape Cod snail
mom's capped Maxwell House.
Talk to me Lord, you place me
through iron hoops,
spirit faith emerges out of
long reach and flannel shirt,
liberation theology --
wooden pick up sticks do not suffice,
ears in multiples pierce.
Talk to me Lord
I am holistic Jewish chicken soup,
a warm Amish patchwork quilt
snug against chin beard.
No shadow university ignorance,
no mirror disco floor.
Talk to me Lord
with Boulder, Colorado resonance --
spunky Eddie over at Gracie's Coffee Shop.
I am easy smile afternoon quiescence
rare cats eye marble
rented saxophone in flowered alley
God take me away from
derelict carousel, no broken furnace,
plastic kupie dolls who line
velvet Second Avenue
feminist shot gun load.
Talk to me Lord, notions run
through red neck skull
father's five battler stars G.I. pragmatism
third gear of Austin Healy 3000
coffee at Mohammed's tobacco stand.
Don's warmth over taut
telephone lines,
out in moonshine Arkansas.

Talk to me Lord,
quarter tones will suffice,
John Coltrane saxophone genius.
Manhattan Wild West frontier --
high tide in Davenport Neck --
I am stand up string bass,
poetry read in mythic Woodstock,
fried egg sandwich.
Talk to me Lord
like Houdini escape genus in steel box,
an antique match book --
bring home vats of five alarm Mexican chili
to crafted poet and cascade madman.
Talk to me Lord,
like laid back three year old
with fresh baseball cards,
clean Oshkosh get up --
tilted black cowboy hat, six shooter --
Talk to me Lord, I unfurl like flag
on fried chicken Fourth,
southbound to Baton Rouge --
fireworks along placid
East River, Myrna's cowgirl two-step.
I come to you cherished Yahweh,
a teeming spice rack,
tarragon and ginger, cinnamon time --
bring on Iowa fiddle ho-down,
Scarsdale milk-fed knee sock sweetie.
Talk to me Lord
I am fresh crimson autumn in motion,
soap box derby rig, pick up baseball game
Talk to me Lord, touch horizon in Oklahoma
hope, dream.
Talk to me Lord
expand beyond frontier California sunset --
reveal mythic sign,
burning bush communique.
Talk to me Lord
I am round planet,
of infinite highway providence,
a hard rubber ball in traffic
in search of watershed liberation
promised land serenity.

Indecision of Brisk Season

I'm not IBM driven
power glide, cream puff
longitude.
Too many soft somatic days
barefoot, harness
on wall peg.
I'm not driven to
Telluride incandescent wonder
November morning's
indecision of brisk season.
Slow motion free fall
like Jersey parachutist.
Prophetic burn
placed in closet
worn New Balance sneakers
leather suicide belt.
Too many fail notches
door no longer opens
key ring metal jangle
coffee banter.
Imagine sleigh rides, rye toast
taxi in search of suited fare
on timid Lafayette Street,
barroom Marlboro afternoons
no, I'm not driven
like Ford pick-up in
Western Kansas
roadside wheatfield daydream.

Noose

Oh New York tender throat noose
hangman's quiet skill
Persian cat from isosceles
ledge jump, no guarantees,
sleeping pill slow motion
kick in. University crowd controls
motor driven wheelchairs
scoot along 86th Street
cripples drive Mercedes
soul death Ricki Lake
prairie fire culture
Mix-A-Lot, salt peanuts.
Poets stumble in cold shower
night dream, New York
like shutter down tobacco shack,
infantile raves, tough guy stances,
aficionado's small grasp of subway token
bring on thesaurus.
Subversive dreamer, Duke Ellington genius
tin cans kindness
wide Hudson text precise
Swiss watch edit,
river dream Jersey possibilities.
New York. Bonzai tree,
bring on cactus serenity
no American Express card flash
hierarchical Italian veal chop
no Macintosh WordPerfect. No
bizarre cat's cradle.
Take 50 year old denim lover,
warrior calico sister
swig Burgundy bottle, Bonnie Raitt blues
Yorkville afternoon kisses
ham and cheese lunch bucket
bronze inner thigh caress
silver highway beatitude.

Spirit Beatitude

Spirit beatitude
smooth glide on Kansas
Interstate, denim lap road map
straight jacket deceit redemption,
Sonny Rollins log jam vanity.
No, no mob black
leather jacket Gallaudet University
sign language poems, highway saxophone
spirit beatitude deaf
warrior brother, sister --
downtown bus Greenwich Village bound
tender Chapel Hill emotion lines,
broad strokes on cotton
note pad. Allen Ginsberg American angels.
Spirit beatitude, February's
broad sculptor hands
Lopez Island ferry, hot chocolate
large marshmallow
Jersey city paella, Staten Island
looms like Lotto Pick 6 freedom fantasy.
Spirit beatitude, East River quarter moon
like bronze subway token.
Language soars like prairie fire illumination
Brigid Murnaghan uptown beat jazz rap
Tokay wine, Woolworth's
five and dime delight.
Spirit beatitude
Denver 3 crimson interstate hours
cathedral beatnik groove
Miles Davis tenderloin district cool bop
promised land highway time.

Highway Spirit

Shovel coal black South Dakota earth
pick up sidewalk penny
spend cool clean cash roll
embrace velvet piano lessons,
pistachio nuts,
lace work boots, read
downtown Number 6 train poem
take a sexy date for
Coney roller coaster ride
surrender to fierce Big Sur surf
Canadian bull moose wind.
Teach Senegal man subway map --
move towards bohemian Thanksgiving
roast turkey delight.
Ask one question like rainbow Zen student
massage brain with Jackson Browne
desert diaspora
calibrate sky in dream
outback perception,
embrace Paul's bone dice collection --
carry pinewood cord armful
'Katonah dried flowers,
delight in New York City silver pigeons
Alvin Ailey choreography
nourish soul like synagogue soup kitchen
hot whole wheat bread, veggie shop
expand mythic Colorado memory, personal
history, apple pie intuition
take action in 3 AM night underbelly
embrace Abe Lincoln log cabin honesty,
choose overland highway spirit, always.

Yahweh

Yahweh, your tumbleweed mythic
revelation, calico weave
fires along Mediterranean beach
prophetic biblical white light,
road passes through
Jerusalem, Tel Aviv,
desert marker, milk and honey fandango.
God's ferris wheel sky bound
pita bread hard stone bake
oasis cool fresh water revival.
Oh Yahweh, cherish revelation
sacred Israel prayer
wildflower garden beauty,
desert violets holy sign
Ten Commandment rock steady.
One God passion
again and again
oh Israel Red Sea logjam, free
no water soaked corpses,
no West Bank blood riot
save round world,
ancient soul Wailing Wall Messiah
dream caravan, Jewish holy God covenant
Yahweh, your Israel spirit
cultivated desert prayer shawl
Kabbala purple mask.
Golan Heights pine trees --
Star of David road, night fires
salvation like sweet honey
underground Messiah
redeem spirit seek wooden
shelter from dust, bullet, steel hate
faith in God, humble like
desert lily in glass jar.

November 17

November 17 a thousand questions
in O.J. courtroom
dust cover bookshelf
Jim's theater dress rehearsal
honky tonk red cushion
brothels, hipsters turn on
thin dime, sharpen fang
python barroom drama.
November 17 Pecos mountain delight
dollar bills like chicken bones,
wood dock, Shell oil can
people line ATM money machines
cash and carry two step,
sweat hand subway token,
deli take out ham and swiss, mayonnaise
poet's three card monte game
7th Street silver fringe cowboy
Wyoming leather boot, spurs.
November 17, southern mirror
smooth infant's buttocks
language cadence, New York
safety deposit vaults, stock options.
Text is irrelevant, like assassin's AK-47,.
Network surveillance
Hershey's wrapper discard
Park Avenue Mercedes headlight --
five fold in poet's room,
large S&M rack
cultural sweetness dried out
like Santo Domingo sun,
machine fur coat money vortex
concrete rialto,
cherry stone clams not consumed,
back cedar closet genius
spirit break like hard taffy
Stradivarius remains in violin case.

Therapy

Mor therapy in corduroy
hip pocket Clockwork Orange
institutional gulag.
Bring on Skinner box,
metal electrodes snap
like Wrigley's gum fresh wire mouth.
Walk wood floorboards like
Wild Turkey drunk, sincere New Mexico
deliverance, desert
hand, green eye.
Been shrinked from Missoula
to Peoria, Chinese firecrackers
resound in tinsel town
skull. Astound
humble pie psyche.
Velvet Santa Cruz fantasy
Red River spring torrent
45 minute spirit
no Aristotle clarity
voter registration drive.
Doctor Stuart you tear me
from urine smoke shack,
pry me from stack of
Maoist leaflet, bag of sensimilia.
Hand deep in money pocket,
East Side January arrest madness
no prairie liberation, highway salvation
just square pill box
hide Balkan emotions.
No slender highway points west.
No harvest moon barnfires.
No cheshire fire leaf October.

Borderline Personality

Clinical borderline personality
mental illness fire bomb
folk untie Nike laces --
food fight outrage -- flying
pumpkin pie garbage bin, asparagus.
Wide mouth taffy smear,
lower Broadway lies --
metal shovel toss
through bay window.
Borderline psychosis
Chinese checkers mad swirl
craze Madison Avenue canter
extra large tweed overcoat,
lack of Georgia responsibility,
inch worm denial
authority sniper attack
no respect for hush puppy
teacher --
terrible two's tantrum
cognitive synapses explode
like bread truck backfire.
Borderline quest to
control tattersall world like
Viennese duchess stone grasp,
narcissistic hot ember core.
Destroy tweed coat shrink
turn on thousand dimes --
theatrical pin ball
high jinx multiple personality
yes leather biker jacket lies,
false jailhouse claims, a
fun house reinvention
personality and harvest moon.
A trumpet on earlobe --
kids take it home, stop
no Hollywood Boulevard ramble,
no Oprah Winfrey center stage
layer Sherlock Holmes disguise.
Keep costumes in steamer trunk --
bring on April top
soil common sense
emotional Navaho healing.

Thanksgiving Always

Thanksgiving always
Scarsdale turkey baste
blood red cranberry sauce, honey up yams,
blue judgement notions
small caliber arms place
on T.V. room
wooden Mayflower Plymouth rock resonance
Indian corn magic harvest.
Thanksgiving always
Columbus Avenue Betty Boop
Central Park
Victorian angels. Give much thanks
to jade souls poetic faith
again and again God's fire revelation
Beethoven sonata, a ten speed bicycle
on hydraglide. Thanksgiving always to
Quitman, Georgia rehab warrior women
late night southern calls,
long summer Manhattan ramble
level Sheep Meadow fried chicken
Miles Davis bebop illumination
thanks to Avalon Bar ladies'
search for yuppie money boys,
least strong lay.
Thanksgiving always to old man
proverbial chops, bust high speed rev up
always with Cadillac love.
Thanksgiving always
my mom glides through green garden
lotus love,
sculpture tool in grasp.
Thanksgiving always to
corn on cob year, April geraniums,
kind Manhattan smiles
Bob Dylan
like vintage red Bordeaux wine,

American renaissance like still
Bowling Green Kentucky
moonshine vat.
Thanksgiving always to quest
down to Arkansas vortex,
Volvo madness, Days Inn and
beyond, highway passion.
Give thanks to funky brother Marc
no to quick shot artists, poetry
no to obscenities craftless ego --
dark obsession like crazy glue
yes to desert prayer Yahweh
in lily pad skull.
Thanksgiving always to bark canoe
on steady Penobscot Bay course,
between seaweed, mooring -- a steady wind
to back westbound always.
Thanks.

Bravado

Cash and carry, pop
can of diet Coke
bloated waist strip down
do Virginia reel
with sexy blonde cinnamon lady
hop Union Pacific freight train
steel gray New Jersey rail link.
No more boasts tabloid rumor,
law court bravado
poets' room silver excellence.
Jump 59th Street subway turnstile --
avoid winter flu like midtown traffic
children read, read, read
cash and carry, Scarsdale train station
6 p.m. Wednesday, hot roast beef dinner.
Commit life on planet to
chocolate syrup
a button overcoat
a San Francisco hug, painter's palate
wilderness tabasco mix
powder keg intuition, like 10 year old
sports page obsession
yes to cash register red fingernails
always packing' calico metaphor.
Cherry tomato bravado like
overland freight train, Denver bound
providence dream stride up bald mountain
highway time, green Lexington
Avenue traffic light.
Bravado.

Now

America fat tabby cat,
large feline belly
marijuana hipster, black leather --
trek to Paramus shopping mall,
remake eggshell image
American total devotion
to crisp dollar bill, Visa card
charge to Lotto hilt and beyond,
Embrace crimson poetic craft.
Let mythic Oregon wonder emerge,
like new born wrens
too much Coast Guard fatigue,
hysterical purple flower
kids, toys and junk fill closets
yes to Dr. Seuss
move from greed, stock market sell out
embrace lost blue collar ethic,
no Washington D.C. quick talk,
no Italian leather shoes
salvation on interstate,
America downtown clique
wrecking ball demolition.
America broken down blues lady,
high school kid's LSD addiction
Estèe Lauder make up mad swirl,
stove pipe legs, anorexic heroin chic.
Teach children Abe Lincoln history,
Thomas Edison wonder,
Rosa Parks courage
Constitution's common sense
founding fathers' genius, a paisley
dream, a thousand morning coffees.
No T.V. image short circuit shootout,
global gulag technology.
Late morning computer spasms --
no watered down ice tea,

no stale tea biscuit.
No Sony Walkman, embrace moral
quaker weave, cowgirl heart
embrace neighbor's blues
coach soccer team,
discard hi tech Nikes,
cell phone psychosis
corporate whores, white collar
Cadillac elitists.
Embrace Walden Pond simple spirit
American covenant
always home spun equality. Now.

Night Vortex

Righteous America night vortex
hallow echoes like spook movie
Amazing Grace mad vagrants
whiskey folk on Second Avenue,
night vortex nation's kaleidoscope
beast surfaces over
burger and fries, trust fund
rent unpaid, like bald bookie
good New York people asleep, toil
computer machine place aside like
black olive pits
children's dream large butterfly meadow
Asbury Park horizon boardwalk --
sweet feminists dream
Susan B. Anthony equality
a small calico cat freedom
night vortex.
Down vest and topsiders,
lay on wicker rocker
Yorkville 2 A.M. flowerbed serenity
gentle Goddess's arms,
all night grocery on 83rd,
Bronx hot Jeep Cherokees
Marlboro insomnia
idle like street whores
wander out for rainbow completion.
America night vortex, NYPD sirens
chop silence, like
Japanese sushi chef
crimson dawn
at long Manhattan distance.

Youth Wonder

On hot wire youth
like tender nested
robins, horizon road excite
blue jeans tight on
narrow legs fire eyes
large Gandhian ideas
spring Iowa cornfield dream
youth circus wonder, world
like oyster, red clay vase
on stone ceramic wheel.
Rock and roll tar shack
A plus potential.
Lotus wonder sweet youth
Haight Asbury flowerbed,
lower Eastside miracle.
Red spade MTV liberation
video supreme essence
no old fold hypocrisy,
no generational lies,
money demon --
South Dakota granite excuses.
Change smoke world,
reinvent skateboard wheel
oh youth tender first love
run out to San Francisco
exquisite kicks. Avenue A
marijuana buzz, navel oranges
new world dream
warm satori soul mate
oh youth wonder become
spoken word excellence
softshoe apprenticeship
herbal remedies
electric guitar brilliance
youth oh youth keep on open highway
be bold like Maine wilderness
in round green world.
Pick self up again and again,
embrace prize fight discipline
always prairie dream.

April

Sleek April basketball slam dunks
Madison Square Garden glass backboards,
false starts Indianapolis 500
a piccolo tuck in work shirt
like white handkerchief
wood bureau copper pennies,
week old local newspapers
April you jump start Chevrolet
hot wire promise
industrial park jimson weed,
green Pennsylvania valley,
universe corner like dense
hyacinth garden
transvestites turn on dime
bulemic's chocolate cake binge,
on delicate stilt, beach cottage.
Oh Spring you crocus rebirth
air sweet like salt water taffy.
Rocky Mountain wildflowers
lifers' exercise room cruelty
wet Amsterdam Avenue kisses
lower forty planting time.
Silk scarf sweet breeze.
April.

Village Magic

Greenwich Village Sunday cobalt
sky overhead like
bluebell orchards Rock Hill
South Carolina garden.
Tight knit circle Hackensack
earring pierce small rebellion rainbows --
Riviera Cafe upscale scatter
sight drunks in.
Rico mythic rap, magic fantasy
artist, saw horse full of
rolled miracle posters
calico guitar saints
Carolina rugby team
howls at Myrna's Charlotte Hornet t-shirt.
Laura Ludwig gets Bleecker Street
blackjacked, Village fandango.
May afternoon delight pinewood serenity
Washington Square park magic beatitude.
Militant Black due pile of African
incense, aroma down to
Waverly Theater. Mozambique dream.
Amplifier ban in park
civil disobedience.
And yes red 57 Caddy convertible
sleek like upstate trout.
Oh Greenwich Village, your
20 year old skirted mountain women sooth
eye and clench fist, homeless dudes dream
Beatnik cool essence
saxophone blue street corner excellence
spring village beatific magic.

Plume Tribe

High Sierra plume tribe, wide
open cirrus sky magic
Sandy Hook sea breeze,
tarragon poetic revolution
trade school excellence
blue collar zen screwdriver genius.
Plume tribe grows like
Virginia winter oak tree,
sparse late night highway commotion.
flannel heart embrace
Myrna's heightened faith.
Hip pocket Red Hots, Bonnie Raitt
on FM radio
40 acres and Army mule
American quiescence
cut hot apple pie.
Vibrations swirl like
Bleecker Street, bohemian
back fence cafe steel string guitar.
Like fudge topping,
wood wind chimes nestle
7th floor high rise.
Birthing cedar take hold like
Macy's salesgirl.
Plume tribe heart folk,
Arkansan back roads
God's tin can grace
green earth fringe oracles
typewriter rides beyond horizon.

Road Partner

We seek lyrical end to jailhouse pain
curved road
wooden 2 x 4's bracket, metal nails
pesky mile markers.
Freedom down beat
limbs entwined limbs, Sunday pancake notions
kite string tangle,
Soho Poet's House excellence
no forearm blood metals
woman silk back trick bag come on.
Angular metaphor language,
we seek Louisiana kisses like
cool lemon ice tea
cherry breast, red Paris beret
bohemian all night Jack Kerouac read
we seek Albuquerque Motel 6 shack up
no diaspora celibacy
no shopping lists
a Marlboro road partner
hands on round wheel
New Mexico honest horizon.

Where Are You Girl?

Where are you girl, you
blond aquarius lady. Indiana bred, 1969
where is bountiful plume soul,
gentle cherrywood hands
Santa Cruz ocean cloud vibration
heart break again and again.
Where are you patchouli girl?
Norman, Oklahoma to
Fort Smith, Arkansas,
Six hours of night ride quest,
tender fatigue, calico soul mate
Hopi Southwest, memory terror,
escape grey demon
seven eleven road dusk
rainbow woman search like
obscure four leaf clover like
metal dumpster, year
after tumble year.
I remain alone
as grey road strangers pass
eyes glaze, tight tank tops.
Norman to Fort Smith
God let me sleep away dust red pain,
Albuquerque desert noose
let me forget 20 singular years
without soul mate, angular table top,
no chess pieces
quicksilver bell bottom diaspora
shatter salt and pepper shaker
mythic lady you move me beyond
beatific vision,
reincarnate nirvana passion,
hot oatmeal delight
where are you girl.

Strung Out

Strung out lightning quick
on pharmaceutical drug
lithium, tranquilizer.
Joe's Plaza drugstore stash
vials line night stand --
25 years pill pop
slow motion shut down
I am horse fly in Skinner box.
Zombies line December street corner,
demon kick round bottom
plastic electrical brain wire
encase Woodstock analytics, dayglo riff
oh modern medicine
salvation's diced up bargain --
like green onions, flank steak.
Dr. Stuart's prescription pad,
straight jacket Kool Aid
strung out like rural clothesline.
No barnfire poetics, craze upstate ramble
yes sleeping pill like iron barbell
sometimes winter tubers, cold pasta
freedom sometimes in chicken coop lock up.
Strung out.

Battle of Soho

South of Houston -- Battle of Soho
1970 -- artists homestead
ramshackle factories,
loft space stiff paint brush
stretch canvas.
Quest for Picasso aesthetic spirit.
Cheap space, light superior
to Provence, Seville.
Small galleries honored
mythic artists struggle
Soho thrives, grass roots,
down home.
1975 Real Estate quick shot boys,
killer gallery owners
eye on paper bag dollar no artistic
passion move in.
Painters, sculptors, bohemians
push out rustic lofts like
unwilling parachutists. Buy
out for ten grand promise
of Hoboken or beyond. Some fight -- heroic
rent strikes, alternative space
Whitney Counter weight
fierce opposition --
most honest artists disband.
Scatter like birdseed
unlike, Berlin artists
who fight police
militant bottles and rocks,
New York artists place crumbs
in satchel, flee like grey mice.
Today Soho expensive glitz boutiques
chic Italian eat joints --
loft space suit stockbrokers
and heiresses can afford.
The revolution is gone,
gone like the bodega
on Prince, West Broadway,
renegade storefronts
gone like wildcat desire.
Cheshire garden
gone to steel greed money art vortex.

Hungry Women

Hungry women shape
like peach schnapps bottle,
tight mini's, sensual overtones
all Black motif -- kiss my bottom,
I sit on Fitzpatrick's bar stool,
Texas dream explodes like
incendiary bomb, New Delco spark plugs,
Chinese firecrackers.
Highway hobo and drool cake poet.
Wet snow cognitive ice coffee.
Oh hungry woman, bare chest
for polaroid, seek thrill like
Second Avenue traffic
no hook up iron ladder to fringe
outlaw dream.
I hop train a thousand times,
1990's cruel diaspora
harlequin blood let
bar stool Colorado wildflower dream.
Hungry woman divine grief,
budweiser, shooter,
no cathedral romance on straight
line night horizon.
I sit on bar stool green wilderness
heart, desolation's corduroy quest
too many hungry want it all women.

On The Table

Place harlequin poems
Tibetan silk bolts
out on table.
Get demon boogey man
out from Hell's Kitchen
hallway corner brain synapse.
Breath truth that
honest Maryland 18 wheel notion.
Brother put poker cards on
red checkercloth table,
embrace Miles Davis trumpet
Colorado Rocky Mountain delight
talk mythic angelic metaphors
call out Jack Kerouac cadence.
Liberate heart from computer
brainwash. Promise electric
typewriter beatific ribbon ride.
Get emotional baggage from cold storage
howl like panther
on African savannah, one day at time
God's winter tumbleweed glory now.

January 23rd

8 singular days before January 23rd
birthday cats cradle.
Dream of American freight train,
a crawfish dinner
Bourbon Street vortex.
Birthday time I grow year older
like redwood too
chain saw fierce.
Another year, highway open
gingham road.
Timberlands tread New York avenues,
too many jump starts,
tears of rage like neighborhood thugs.
American tincan dream,
sparse winter sleigh ride.
Birthday time, Cannonball Adderley,
Lennox, Mass. snow fields
friends pacify mad ramblings,
desire to set wooden match
to Exxon gas can.
East River rides high, I wait for
opportunity with Yankees, anybody.
January 23rd, pigeon on jailhouse rail,
language economy
45 years on marble planet.
Happy cupcake birthday, sort of.

Revolution 24

Revolution 24 hardscrabble
quick cut tenderloin spirit,
dry chrysanthemums
Nescafe jar --
August prairie fire, Nebraska red clay.
Prairie fire glow,
big wheel. One eyes jacks, Texas twister --
tell it sister,
let Woodstock
freak flag dance
cathedral wilderness.
Fill lilac glass vase --
green-eyed sister bring home
cheshire revolution
early morning kisses
Omaha hands
on lathe, build second ark,
pine cabin
Grandpa's miniature doll's house --
revolution 24, small ember poems,
God's hyacinth providence
Emily Dickinson Amherst wonder
Kansas City hobo jungles
Drug Free Colorado night rides,
black shoeshine hamhock wisdom.
Revolution 24
long way home.

Prairie Delight

Prairie delight
brother, place cowboy boots
on calloused fence feet,
beaver line gloves,
calf length great coat, bright orange
move into prairie.
Dream, brother move hard on Dakota plains
study red barn, weather vane.
Mend fence with Cadillac
sensibility, rodeo hardscabble craft
Top Rolling tobacco.
Prairie delight God's simple haystack essence.
Take small holster child in hand,
day glo parka, Cree imagination
narrow deer trail wonder.
Ride crimson prairie two step grace
grain elevator symphony
renew American land in grand birthing.
Wide angle blue sky.

I Sleep Into Twilight

I sleep on butterscotch
February afternoon,
soft purple yarn, sapphire
dream scope, a handy man's
special.
I sleep no more bloody
crystalline blossoms,
black fry pans --
oh beauty come to me in afternoon
slumber, sock feet,
dream Geisha red kimono,
I sleep
Georgia O'Keefe bone and sky.
I sleep wall Canaan field,
dream delight.
Beauty inspires howl poem
highway white line essence
sky appaloosa.
I sleep like Vietnam peace
Chicago blues down beat,
I sleep like peg leg hobo --
navel orange on cotton pillow.
Swig out of ice coffee urn,
no R.D. Laing psycho ward vortex.
I sleep into ruby twilight,
two pillows, mainsail is fasten.

Homeward Bound

Thanksgiving homeward bound
steep Appalachian trail
grade, suburban
Scarsdale back roads.
Montauk chowder stand
sweet I-80 moving hard on
Kearney Nebraska,
glass windshield rain
eastbound like ex convict.
Yeah homeward bound
New York, steel on steel
hardscrabble urban tundra
creamcheese bagel.
Open cumulus sky,
large Illinois prairie
delight American spirit,
Beatnik grace, highway Allen Ginsberg
midwest full wicker basket dry flowers
Days Inn clean sheets.
No Thanksgiving blizzard
Pennsylvania miracle gorge.
Homeward bound Joycean language
weave, crossword puzzle
Joliet Afro-American waitress.
Homeward bound top hat dream again and
again in Pittsburgh quirky texture
frazzle American rain,
bold stars big dipper
move to Manhattan emerald city
avenues, Laura Boss' streetcorner embrace
calico Thanksgiving home.

Eternity Road

Drive heard to Arizona desert charm
hot tar road, risk round emotions
in calico cloth fringe
eloquence. Hopi trade post.
Take to highway in plume
wonder, Episcopal grace.
hammock taut serene dawn
infant dream sleep.
Walk eternity road beyond
seaboard horizon's wide girth
flowerbed Georgia O'Keefe hope.
Poetic words move rainbow spirit.
Yes eternity road long, like free cobra.
road cuts through Hudson River towns --
Tarrytown, Garrison, Catskill,
always Chevron pumps,
midnight traffic, big East Coast push,
eternity road, a line along bronze
thigh, red Rand McNally mark.
American journey like Walt Whitman's poems.
Oh eternity road you call me, like transcendent
glory diesel train, Utah wildflower grace.
Four cylinder engine hum.
Eternity road oneness, bohemian devotion
learn old folks stories
Snickers bars energy burst.
Ohio dawn fog lift.
Always American dream horizon excellence.

VI
SPRINGTIME AMERICA
1999

PETER CHELNIK - HEY GIRL - COLLECTED POEMS

One Day At A Time

One day at a time
God's red checker cloth providence
Yorkville dawn square bread truck notions
pine wood road rules,
Texas tumbleweed delight.
One day at a time
Pull L.L. Bean tan socks across football ankles
delight light Colombian Dunkin doughnut ice coffee jag.
One day at a time
Embrace Louisiana gospel grace
green work shirt roll
Embrace computer hacker nerd ingenuity
Embrace $1.99 Maine blueberries.
One day at a time
Yes to Manhattan Saturday afternoon sobriety
Yes to Shostikovitch mad Russian symphony
Yes to Canal Street Chinese ice fish market.
One day at a time
Call on Springfield Missouri straight shooters
No bait and switch quick talk
No White House pot smoke spin-doctors
No anorexic East Hampton
down and out BMW cocaine snobs.
One day at a time
Place fresh dollar in 12-step wicker kitty
wildcat direct like Georgia Pacific freight train.
One day at a time
No to firecracker demons
No to round skull nightmares
teenage years backseat heart drive.
One day at a time
Yes to bran muffin honesty like Saint Joseph's
oak confessional booth
Yes to I-81 Virginia highway Peterbilt prayer
Yes to crimson God's spirit glide.

One day at a time
Big Sur cirrus sky rainbow celebration
wheelchair folk's jubilee spirit
San Francisco North Beach
poetry howl.
One day at a time
Embrace Oklahoma highway
flannel back to Canadian wind
Embrace Dizzy Gillespie bebop cool,
Jesus' Hudson River deliverance
thousand hosannas hardscrabble gingham faith
small town America Cheshire heal, yes.

Fire On The Lake

Fire on the lake
Techno robot computer quick fix addiction
Heroin sidewinder shoot-up,
peace now foot soldier double deal.
Fire on the lake
Trust fund supernova radicals
daddy rent pay off
laptop stone cold illusion dwellers
top shelf Johnny Walker Red 9 AM hangover.
Fire on the lake
Nose up in air like Manhattan surely rain cloud
SUV's gas guzzle,
brat search and destroy children
Bart Simpson paranoid methamphetamine cats.
Fire on the lake
Yes to earth hold apprentice weave
Yes to holy senior citizen brain pick
Yes to New York Philharmonic Mozart excellence,
John Coltrane bebop cool riff genius.
Fire on the lake
No gender sex like Heineken six pack,
No media cool aid brain fry.
No Grand Central Station Babylon
three Martini rush hour fracture.
Fire on the lake
Cobalt blue illiterates, marijuana road house stone out
Yes to Cheshire love of country,
Brooklyn patriots quiet Sept. 11th courage
Yes to tweed parents,
12-hour workday heroics
Yes to John Lee Hooker's blues
fandango providence.
Fire on the lake
Baggy pants fracture like ecstasy stampede
quiet cult death, again and again
purple kaleidoscope brain holocaust.
Fire on the lake
Lazy granola notions,
counterculture quick take
nostalgia replay

SPRINGTIME AMERICA

35-year toxic flashback.
Fire on the lake
Yes, young folks seize time like Paul Revere
Massachusett's minutemen
revolutionary Flow Kennedy cool lemonade
Columbia Law School savvy,
Mary Jo Rose Eureka Springs Lane House
alternative school brilliance
rebirth like roll work shirt,
Aaron Copeland Appalachian Spring.
Fire on the lake
Yes to Abraham Lincoln's Gettysburg address,
Save holy republic
NYPD keep the Gotham peace.
Stop shuck and jive,
smart aleck 3rd graders yelps,
flat tire laments
Yes to Texas sweat on brow discipline,
Yes to Peppermint bible honesty like Harlem
  Baptist minister
Yes to freedom's silk thread salvation
Oh, fire on the lake, you hear!

Thousand Comebacks

Thousand Comebacks
Down and out rainbow
prize fight canvas
day-glow Santa Cruz demons
peck brain like pick ax 1969
Bellevue checkerboard straight jacket melt down.
Thousand Comebacks
Pick self up again and again
Jesus' resurrection, poetic magnolia liberation
barn fire mythic muscle.
Thousand Comebacks
Too much high wire brain fracture
tokay cheap jug wine, Marlboro outback chain smoke
mental illness like wild card Chelsea soup kitchen rat.
Thousand Comebacks
Greenfield Massachusetts police bust
No sidewinder Wrigley's gum chew
No black-eye susan eros
No Catskill Mountain stream
flesh on flesh.
Thousand Comebacks
Parkinson's shimmy shake
Ambien sleeping pill holocaust
round shoulder serpents like hangman's hemp noose,
rubber cherokee Indian body melt down.
Thousand Comebacks
Manhattanville College calico freedom quest
cheap Napa Valley wine
hope like Jones Beach eastern dawn.
pick self up, walk Vermont crimson road,
Saint Patrick's cathedral steps,
harbor heart woman vision.
Thousand Comebacks
Dante's nine-level rickshaw hell
sleepless nights oyster half-shell
boxcar tweed coat shrink
LSD, cardboard prairie mind
marijuana frenzy like fringe mad hatter poet
Thousand Comebacks
Headless Santa Monica Beach white stallions

gasoline demon blood,
unopened graham cracker,s
IBM typewriter punch,
revolutionary prairie faith.
Thousand comebacks
blue jean patch holy arboretum revelation
Old Testament proverbs
Jesus circus sky grace
wisdom like hot oatmeal America
April Southern Michigan farmland grace.
Thousand Comebacks
Oklahoma roadhouse salvation
No gray monkey on flannel back,
No mad brain Satan twist
bring on corduroy Monday skies like hot butterscotch
pork bean plastic spoon,
Wrightsville Beach, North Carolina wet kisses.
Thousand Comebacks
God's Turkish taffy rebirth,
prayer book lap
fresh ragweed Montana rodeo excellence,
Bolder Colorado hot September coffee,
Cherokee wide tooth smile
Redemption like New York State Thruway
night ride,
Kingston, New Paltz, Suffern comeback, comeback
Renaissance lilac dream,
Rialto hip sway,
friday night rainbow caress,
lotus heart vibration
Renoir soft thighs
rainbow spirit Manhattan celebration.
Thousand calico Comebacks, Yes.

Springtime America

Prairie springtime America
crocus bloom
high heel sashay Madison Avenue
blue blood eatery-hot corned beef promise
knishes, Cel-Ray's soda.
Springtime America
President George W. Bush, Texas plain talk
hominy grits Alabama, outback highway.
Springtime America
Constitutional oak wood like steady
Missouri kitchen table
James Lefkowitz generation X
cinematic bring it home
winter's stubborn end.
Springtime America
Yes to baby boom,
three Bordeaux wine
revolutionary flashback
Yes to gray-haired senior citizens
muffin coffee afternoon snack.
Springtime America
Junior high skateboard cats,
Internet easy glides
Afghanistan kick bottom
U.S. Army savvy, Delta force excellence.
Susan's Mohawk Indian magic eyes.
Springtime America
Glass vase purple lilacs
like Walt Whitman bookmark
second amendment gun tote sisters
calico passion third grade cotton skirt
pine tree warmth
mythic read and write, bring on Hardy Boys, Nancy Drew
landmark history butcher-block civics.
Springtime America
Calls Rebirth like Stony Lodge psycho ward weekend
pass.
Deborah's moon and tide passion 1973
Grover Washington alto saxophone genius,
barroom buyback sassy blues lady satin leg twin

SPRINGTIME AMERICA

Red Oak diner coffee jags
sweetheart Laura Boss.
Springtime America
Wide girth land calls this flannel poet
Massachusetts to garden green Oregon
city on hill cowboys
Austin to Missoula, Montana
Thousand fry pan notions.
Springtime America
Firm pearl handshake
like Missouri truck stop prophets
in God We Trust nightime prayers.
7-year-old blue jean roll
holy multiplication tables.
May afternoon American flag glory
love of country syrup air angels
like old railroad hobos,
black Mississippi sharecroppers,
mental illness Prozac saints.
Springtime America
Youngstown, Ohio steel mill blue-collar genius,
stroller moms Pampers, hand wipe milk bottle.
Springtime America
Yes to Chinatown year of dragon
Yes to New Paltz, black-eyed susan meadow
Queen Anne lace delight.
Springtime America
John McCain five years North Vietnam gulag
Navy fighter pilot heroics, Arizona sagebrush
   straight-talk,
Joni Mitchell silk sarong genius
wild poetic grace
Yes to highway cheeseburger holy primrose
mom and dad grace.
Springtime America
Rocky Mountain snowmelt, flapjacks cool milk
wednesday silk dawn like Dow Jones
stock market ticker tape.
Yes to American noble experiment
green horizon eyes, white Lily open gospel heart
Yes to more perfect union
we the people God's straight back redemption
the Republic holy challenge
Yes, springtime America!

Renegade

I am renegade, Cuevo Gold quiescence
oversize porcelain coffee cup
movie theater butter popcorn.
I am upstate New York garter snake
Geoffrey Chaucer wife of bath cuckold
I am fruit loop box hangman
kick the can hobo
Chevy night right along Virginia Blue Ridge Mountains.
I am 3AM Mozard renegade
No buy in to herringbone corporate culture
shopping mall plastic designer arcade.
No buy in to master slave hot wire brain synapse
I am freedom trail Gilgo Beach high surf outsider
like Billy the Kid outlaw tear
Willie Sutton Bank robber hijinks.
I am manchild in high tech digital vortex
poet beyond white picket fence.
I am kaleidoscope renegade
flannel warrior like Paul Bunyon Minnesota heroics,
U.S. Navy crimson flyboys
I-81 Maryland truck driver's sublime
75 miles per hour cool.
I am white wing Manhattan pigeon
Navel oranges 3 for 99 cents
black cross-town bus driver cool
I am Supreme Court full docket
foggy bottom April afternoons 1968
cherry blossom delight.
No to consumer straightjacket orbit
No to glossy magazine hipper than thou aesthetics
No to poets spiral notebook chicken scratch
I am American rebirth Dublin, Virginia railroad line
small town crosscut
Andrew Wyeth Christina's dream
Victorian prairie mansion.
warm soup on slow simmer
First Lady Laura Bush's prairie cotton grace
I am cactus heart, posse in tough pursuit
left hip six-gun pocket Bible faith
in God's rainbow providence.

Tell It

Tell it to big-time European racket boys
pagan purple Salem witches
Fitzpatrick tavern down and dirty alkies.
Tell it to generation X Hondo cat skateboard freaks
downtown wide hip mamas
grade school girls like pink ballerina.
Tell it to Dayton Ohio horizon
hot walnut brownies
Denver bound halcyon dream,
pledge of allegiance sanctity.
Tell it to Catholic church choir angels,
Varick street short order cook
parking garage overnight dudes,
sage senior citizens like hot February chestnuts.
Tell it to deadbeat chicken scrawl poets
September 11th blood terrorists
free skies over bin Laden Afghanistan
cruise missile freedom strike.
Yes to saxophone hip cats,
Yes to Village Vanguard Kenny Garrett, t-bone gig
Tell it to mentally ill sweetwater psychotics
hard saddle prophets, hard push
high-heel style girls
midnight quiescence garbage haulers.
Tell it to homeless soda can man, overnight kick bottom quest
San Francisco madcap oracles
Jones Beach July baby oil lifeguards,
satori black robe Zen monks like red orchids.
Tell it to 69th Street corner hotdog man
milk bottle bundled up toddlers
Columbia University graduate school
high tea aficionados
publishing minimalist sensible shoes cool bop ladies.
Greenhaven prisoner jailhouse lawyers
Wall Street roll dice stock market crapshoot hustlers.
Tell it to baby boom pension fund revolutionaries
New York Post sport page illumination freaks
Tell it to New Jersey Turnpike madcap short bolt rocket ride.
DTUT coffee house, honey blond Israeli girls.

N.Y. Police 19th precinct, keep the peace chill out.
Tell it in B flat blues riff
Courvoisier afternoon hard drive shots
Congressman John Kasich
Fox T.V. baby boom magic tapestry.
Tell it to young folk video game hypnotic funk
psychedelic west side Rabbi.
Tell it brother with fireball heart
steady American hand
straight shot along Hudson River edge.
Tell it, you hear.

Calico Changes

Calico changes
Manhattan prairie overland
two-step quicksilver freight train.
Denver bound coffee jags
Paul's Bowery guitar twang
bebop skull Columbus Avenue
blood artery smiles.
Calico changes
Blues harp like T-bone steak get down
J&B and coke Cheshire heart Virginia reel.
Calico changes
30-year road fandango
Laura Boss popcorn, snowy night Movie Theater
No to laser beam aesthetics
No computer strip search morality
No deadbeat 32 Atlantic City red desire.
Calico changes
Oh sweet Chicago you call me
big hip soul sister sashay
Midwest architecture sublime
Chicago you call me like stockyards January freeze,
Jesus holy maple syrup joy.
Calico changes
Mississippi river raft slow float
Huck Finn meander
Bob Dole World War 2 combat heroics
Yes to 50-year birthday cake delight
chopped bermuda onion tears
yes to FDR drive Volvo scoot
Pink Pony Friday night cool daddy,
poetry read.
Oh calico changes
Leather marker King James Bible
roast beef on whole wheat deluxe
Hudson river line, firm handshakes.
Calico changes
Yes to Charlie Mingus bebop hopscotch genius
Yes to west coast telephone rambles
higher ground consciousness

Yes to Narragansett pinewood howls.
Calico changes
cumulus Wyoming cloud salvation
desolation quicksand
sharecropper Oklahoma red clay cowboy grace
Mississippi Delta jubilee,
green planet butterscotch serenity.
Calico changes!

We're Better

We're better than psychedelic melt down narcissism
white ass generational bug up bottom
computer game short bolt digital lobotomy.
We're better than breast pocket digital cameos
pagan rites bizarre demon blood sacrifice.
We're better than dead bolt heroin addiction
Internet concentration camps
mildew night Budweiser beer revels.
We're better than group sex, roman orgy outrage
thousand needles in muscle arm
We're better than no faith Maoist group
plastic surgery aficionados
mad swirl Dexedrine commotion.
Bring on cherry coke sobriety
like Phoenix house kick bottom can do.
Bring on poetic hot coffee metaphor excellence
Bring on stadium Irish sweater caress
Pinewood honest, January cold spell cleanse
Bring on river flow in texture skull
like Andrew Wyeth, paint palette.
Yes to Elvis Presley Memphis, young buck delight
celebrate mom's home cooked pot roast dinner
  providence
like flannel Broadway angels.
We're better than tar pit self-hate
dime bag Mexican marijuana caper.
We're better than computer techno throwaway
brain goose step.
Yes to Virginia Woolf calico novels,
Yes to John Steinbeck Cannery row compassion
Yes to Marion maximum-security prison poetic passion.
Yes to cognitive thought down
Mississippi Delta River basin magic
Yes to sunrise Oklahoma freedom dream.
We're better than Vietnam era recycled deadbeat
hippie new-age vortex.

We're better than frayed bellbottom horror movies
clinical paranoia, newborn kids in Austin Texas metal
  trash bins.
We're better than purple youth cult American throw
  genius away
like Hershey bar wrapper, empty tissue box nihilism.
We're better than addicts on three dimensional round
  house tear
dead weight 1968 counter culture ideas
broken like ecstasy tab psychosis, dark cave shadow.
We're better!

Liberty Train

Oh liberty train
shout America's excellence,
pine green work shirt genius
drive 18 wheel Peterbilt across Ohio state line
late night conservative red neck talk radio.
Oh liberty train
Sailors home thanksgiving family hoe down
High School sweetheart moist pound cake kisses.
Oh liberty train
bring on kick tin can humility
Philadelphia independence short bolt
lucky heart ace in Las Vegas blackjack hand
root out brown bag heartbreak corruption.
Oh liberty train
No to tribal tattoos
ego trip trust fund sophomores
though police like Wesley college satin ivy tower rain
  of terror.
Oh liberty train
boom box delight, black ghetto neo bebop hip
rib eye excellence
Dad's entrepreneur hard drive muscle.
Oh liberty train
Des Moines, Iowa cornfield harvest ripe
Miami Cuban American hot jazz
bring on Élan Gonzalez wide-angle smile
Christ's open hand joy, clean sleep bag.
Oh liberty train
Los Angeles to sweet Atlanta
Gregory Corso desolation row cool
No teenage whelps in disco night,
No Wednesday evening hate parents' rage.
Oh liberty train
keep radical coup d'etat off shelf
keep Maoist black window censor train from skull
Yes to justice William O. Douglas Warren court
  freedom train.
Oh liberty train
Yes to Tom Paine, kick bottom common sense
high tide Nags Head beach
August dog day ripe plums, cool chicken salad

SPRINGTIME AMERICA

No to crack pipe poverty addiction
No to peace now 50-year-old reefer heads.
Yes to cherry pie dignity
Yes to ham hock serenity; bring on late night bible read.
Oh liberty train!
Take fireplug touch 101st Airborne Iraq victory
Spring Canadian geese
hot muffin New Hampshire jubilee
dad's car keys, first November kiss excite.
take home Camp LeJeune basic training
leatherneck discipline
in God we trust,
three crisp twenties and yes
a rose bouquet.
Liberty train, dig it!

Wildflower America

I am wildflower America
Greenwich state line
rice and beans, Jack Kerouac, Tokay wine,
spontaneous typewriter, roller coaster excite.
I am Colin Powell, secretary of state can do.
I am downtown M-15 Second Avenue bus
42nd Street, Houston Street
south ferry providence bound.
I am World War II greatest generation ever
Norman Duberstein's cash and carry
Navy flier excellence, battler of Midway valor
grilled turkey burgers, May Massachusetts,
Emily Dickinson lilacs,
black lawyer's Supreme Court brief.
I am Woodstock town limits madmen
fire eyes like January blood red embers
Yes to bartender Tara's cool LaBatts beer
God's singular magnolia vision
Yes to Danbury, Connecticut
Vietnamese rice noodles, frozen carp.
I am nephew Charles Chelnik
Cargo pants computer hip
1st baseman easy grace,
Marlboro outback smoke
ABC talk radio lock and load
Boston to promised land Seattle.
I am Dick Cheney Wyoming
rock steady wisdom
like Oklahoma truck stop, cool seven-up
Yes to Zoot Simms, tenor saxophone bebop
Yes to Canal Street pink five-dollar salmon.
I am rock steady poets room tan forearm muscle
language like fierce appaloosas New York City prairie
Bring it home like bacon cheddar omelet
WQXR classical Handel overnight.
I am North Carolina plaid love seat French kisses
A thousand hammer and nail beginnings, yes.

High Tech Auch Tung

High tech Auch Tung
Youth computer brain seizure
digital holocaust, new breed cadre
strip search video games brainwash.
Yes to cool Vermont breeze
ridgeline ethics
patriotic Chevrolet yellow ribbon apple pie.
High tech Auch Tung
Yes to right and wrong morality.
Yes to cool blue personal responsibility
calico weave home schools
respect for tweed coat dad
muffin bake mom.
High tech Auch Tung
No to junior high school cheap wine stone out
No to parking lot reefer downbeat madness
No to 14 year old sexual
dig down and dirty sexual intercourse.
High tech Auch Tung
Bring on maple tree discipline
metal lunch bucket read and write skills
Yes to Cheshire values, honeysuckle tradition.
No shuck and jive jail house hip-hop excuses
elegant 1 AM lies.
High tech Auch Tung
Keep away socialist group higher power noose
No to laser print mediocrity
keep ice nine Columbine clichés
off lunchroom tabletop.
High tech Auch Tung
Embrace mythic Thomas Jefferson
Declaration of independence American covenant
Embrace high school football team true grit muscle
Embrace girls soccer spider web can do.

High tech Auch Tung
No to fourth grade computers
No to politically correct corrugated box cynicism
Maoist group consciousness indoctrination.
High tech Auch Tung
Bring on freight train Toledo Ohio hard drive
fire like Martin Luther King,
Selma, Alabama justice fight,
freedoms white light beacon,
No to drug addiction fracture
No to youth culture secret con
Yes to highway touch sky excellence.

Catch A Wave

Malibu Beach surf's up, hand ten
California mythic scat fog
bring on irony innocence
French bikini chicks, golden palomino mane hair.
Catch a wave
Body surf Huntington Beach
Gilgo wheel and deal
surf challenge
up against wall, oakwood beach house
fierce wind like Nags Head hurricane tin roof rain.
Catch a wave
Year 2000 mini cotton thong
erotic cakewalk like
lemon meringue jubilee
sun block number 30,
sand castle conquistador dealing
Acapulco madcap surf, Tequila Sunrise.
Catch a wave
Bring on Brian Wilson's cameo heart Beach Boys
1963 woodie surfboard in tow.
Catch a wave
Sweet Virginia Beach
summer fried chicken cool lemonade jubilee
bare breast Costa del Sol mythic women
Mediterranean come back baby.
Catch a wave
Palm Beach mad dog stingrays
coconut crack open Maui mystery
Key West end of America
Baccardi coke underground
elegant sunset celebration
crisp American flag
Ernest Hemingway outpost house.
Catch a wave
Yes to sweet potato risk, midnight Mr. Tambourine beach
Yes to sweetheart Truro sand dune like Persian kitten
Yes to mythic wave
independent like North Carolina redneck
Yes to wave curl hurdle down wet wild canyon.
Always the wave, catch it

Poem Electric

I am pie in sky poem electric
fire words like Massachusetts' barn burn
Battery Park sidewinder seagulls
East Harlem Latino rice and bean delight
I am God's bluegrass sanctity
Indiana pine forest
July fourth quintessential t-bone barbecue
I am Gregorian chant Manhattan wildcat metaphor
like downtown FDR easy glide,
Webster's Dictionary delight
Vietnamese Tribeca stir-fried veggies
Robin Hood longbow chest
I am New Age music tidal flow, Tibetan innocence
number six-train eternity easy glide.
I am poem electric
steady tobacco stain hands
Cassava melon head ball cap glee
afternoon WABC talk radio riffs
Second Avenue sweet serendipity,
Born again Christian repentance.
I am sweet potato pie
languid Woodstock, cherry pie September afternoon
pork pie aesthetics
Joni Mitchell road goddess faith.
I am chest high curve ball, Yankee stadium excellence
freedoms Navy Intrepid swabby bold heroism.
I am mythic June dandelions
baby boom woman's toothed smile
fridge doughnuts like universe stars.
I am wilderness ramble
Army canteen red Swiss knife
thick ham sandwich
next forest ranger station desire.
I am heroic onion peel
God's providence like potato latkes
midnight cool breeze
ocean salt air, dig it!

Shoot The Moon

Shoot the moon
Constitution rock steady freedom
Hudson River squat tugboat dream
Kyoto paper flower delight snug wash denims
Navaho wisdom circle wide-angle dream
like Saturday afternoon Shea Stadium Goodyear blimp.
Shoot the moon
June schoolyard kisses
Yes to sourdough excellence
Yes to log cabin quilt wave
Jewish matzo ball soup redemption
Yes to Georgia redneck flannel compassion
Yes to Mayflower Plymouth's Rock covenant
God's cardamom grace.
Shoot the moon
Embrace cherry wood teamster local ethics
Embrace Omaha Beach can-do GI's
new Massachusetts silver quarters
July fourth flag wave incandescence
t-bone grill kickback, Georgia Saturday afternoon.
Shoot the moon
Typewriter ribbon ride
New Mexico desert tumbleweed revelation
West Third Street Greenwich Village bravado
Wright brothers Kitty Hawk big dream fly away
   cathedral genius.
Shoot the moon
Yes to scotch plaid Cincinnati holy saints
Yes to Jamaican Bobby, 84th Street Mercedes Benz
car mechanic
Yes to third grade math whiz like green mad hatter.
Shoot the moon
Yes to late night Myrna's telephone call back magic
Yes to Gracie Post Office federal quiescence
Yes to George Washington American
down-home patriots courage

SPRINGTIME AMERICA

Montana fence mend, big sky grace.
Shoot the moon
Benjamin Britain late night classical glide
surf's up Bible's 23rd Psalm, Jesus' pinewood salvation
Jack Kerouac freight train bebop American quest
Supreme Court justice, Thurgood Marshall eye on
   prize true grit.
Shoot the moon
Air Forces Colorado springs
F-16 fighter
pilot top gun skill
East village guitar twang, Muddy waters moonshine
buy back Illinois prairie hoedown
green eye cinnamon dream.
Shoot the moon

My Country

My country
media hot wire brainwash
Manhattan square box television short bolt.
My country
Breeds Vladimir Lenin railcar politicos
sensible shoe Eva Peron's
tobacco program, culture blood wars.
My country
Damps Walt Whitman prairie fire
Third grade hallow chests
tin can pine tree ecology notions
granola bar politically correct justice.
My country
Breeds German 1930's Aryan gymnasiums
body eucalyptus oil
No to baby boom straight leg goose step
No to master slave aesthetic, four star eat joint fandango
No to Socialist yoga cells
No to Columbine High school marijuana stick freeze out.
My country
Dies with junior high school baby time oral sex
cucumber condoms sex classes.
My country
Dies with stock market shoot
fish in barrel, brown bag cash
Park Avenue one phone call heroin Colombian transport.
My country
Reels with senior citizens invisible like Cape Cod chimera
Second Avenue purse clutch to chest heart
silent calico stories.
My country
Reels like 1950's do-wop back seat generation
cast aside crow's feet wife, younger model time.
Oh my sweet America,
Yes to steamfitter union twelfth floor savvy
Yes to constitutional James Madison excellence
like Missouri trout stream
Yes to plain talk North Dakota farmers hog price radio
Yes to black Brooklyn garage worker,

Freddy Johnson church go
Alabama apple orchard heart.
Yes, we are America's golden harvest
full moon over Northern Michigan hills
fairground cotton candy
Shenandoah valley revolution full load musket
Yes, we are one nation under God, holy city on hill.
Brownsville, Texas, Mexican immigrants opportunity
  quest
Notre Dame South Bend football excellence
Mayflower covenant Plymouth Rock holy revolution
Saint Ignatius second grade history wonder
Yes to sugar can Catholic angels
like Saturday night drive in low-cut movie date.
Yes to all inclusive picnic box lunch, ham Swiss,
  pumpernickel
small Hershey bar delight.
Yes to GI rations, dry combat boots, 1st Armor Division
  Iraq courage
hope like hot Christmas dinner
Sterling, Colorado dawn
God's Sabbath grace Baptist fire brimstone sermon,
Woodstock November soup kitchen redemption.
Yes, yes my country
Come home, I am yours.

Open Chalk Circle

Open chalk circle
Midnight Avenue A kisses
fringe bohemian soft show rapture
Sandalwood incense, Cornelia street wind chimes.
Open chalk circle
Death row innocent
DNA gray clad convict, 20-year hard time lock up free.
National Public Radio
Andre Condrescu Louisiana fire politics.
Open chalk circle
Medicare for scruffy poverty genius kids,
burger and fries hot school lunch program
Bill Bradley Crystal City, Missouri compassion,
green earth garden satori quest.
Open chalk circle
Zigzag rolling papers, 1970 baby boom women
 calico heroic.
Gloria Steinman feminist consciousness raise crescendo
minimum wage leapfrog, St. Ides 40 ounce beers.
Open chalk circle
Embrace Idaho wilderness conservation
oil slick free Santa Barbara beach
Navaho warrior deerskin grace
Colorado highway hitchhikers dusk prayer.
Open chalk circle
America's Delta dream like Bronx Botanical garden
 symphony,
Jay Schulman's rock and roll cello,
fried chicken box lunch, cool fresh lemonade.
Open chalk circle
Al Gore Democratic party can do
Social Security rock steady benefits
grade school hardwood rebuilds
Arlo Guthrie draft resistance courage.
handgun computer check.
Open chalk circle

SPRINGTIME AMERICA

East Village Pink Pony Café firebrand poets
young bucks like eternity road sidewinders,
John Lennon world peace be in.
Open chalk circle
23-year-old calico woman independent heart quest
grace like Adirondack deer.
California red wine quiescence.
Open chalk circle
No to corrupt city councilmen
No to Greenwich, Connecticut Mercedes Benz fat cats
No to south Texas bizarre hate crimes
No to black folks barbed wire injustice, Jim Crow
　racism.
Open chalk circle
Yes to cool Washington State Cascades
Yes to hot whole grain bread, fresh strawberry jam,
Martin Luther King fire on the American renaissance,
sweet, sweet peace and freedom.
Make it right!

Soul Transcendence

Youth's hot Campbell soup serenity
denim lap, white napkin dreams like
Kentucky Derby holy horse race
Whitney Houston elegant grace
candy cane hope.
Soul transcendence
Youth's neon dignity like T-bone grill muscle
ace of spades bebop quest
blonde hair pull back, yellow ribbon.
Soul transcendence
Youth's adobe desert quiescence
mom's kitchen shrimp marinara
hard sweat T-shirt Eros,
Alabama print skirt hips
June brick schoolyard passion.
Soul transcendence
Hand hold high school diploma
Southbound Georgia Chevrolet
Jack Daniels wildcat notions.
Soul transcendence
Youths work shirt pocket Lucky strikes
James Baldwin marathon read.
Soul transcendence
Higher ground like cool Mamaroneck harbor breeze
leather wristband, pocket twenty-dollar bill
secrets like cinnamon universe
saturday cobble dusk,
Macomb, Mississippi Civil rights justice.
Soul transcendence
Bob Dylan open tulip lyrics,
Big Sur Pacific coast magic
true grit like Fort Bragg basic training regimen
maroon and white football practice,

mud holy ritual.
Soul transcendence
Cheap Gallo wine daydream
Yes to leather shave kit
Stevie Wonder golden lady dream.
Soul transcendence
World waits like Irish handmaiden
Parisian orange hair radical 1968
LSD shuffle cards joke
youth fire ember road like black typewriter ribbon
deep calico breath, Aretha Franklin gospel groove.
always, soul transcendence.

Fifty With Love

Fifty with love
Bold renegade birthday, January 23, 1950
Doctor's hospital kick can
native son of hearts
half-century beatniks ramble.
Fifty with love
Mohawk deer trail meander
Singer sewing machine excellence
sign out prairie fire dialectics
Fifty with love
I embrace serenity like
New Hampshire steel snow shovel
I embrace L.L. Bean work boots
mile high Boulder, Colorado
January miracle dawn.
Fifty with love
Sidewinder outlaw denim heart
God's pinwheel Manhattan delight
cityscape Jewish prayers
Harlem market kick bottom sausages.
Fifty with love
Maple syrup cool daddy physical and mental health
Duke Ellington ear savvy
eyes like US Army Vietnam platoon scout
full Clorox bleach jug
Yes to faith like upstate Ford mechanic
calico slim wrist local librarian.
Fifty with love
Downtown subway number 4 train
folks alive like Central Park elegant oak
Corduroy friends
family like fortune cookie surprise
Yes to Ludlow Street funky ethics
Yes to Colt 45 on wide hip girth
Yes to passion for homeless desolation hipster.
Fifty with love
NASCAR hairpin curve like pared Macintosh apple
Nestlé's hot chocolate
tomorrow's cornfield Iowa caucus
No to glossy magazines corporate credit card nirvana

No to Hollywood Turkish taffy call girl kisses
No to Siamese cat windowsill deceit.
Fifty with love
Yes to American Cheshire blue-collar virtue
Yes to equality ike teenage ice cream parlor first date
Yes to literary fire in belly over and over
85th Street broad toothed smile.
Fifty with love
Brother Marc, nephew Charlie baby
mythic stride for stride
jubilee words on paper bond
cognitive ice fishing huts
Vermont winter ridgeline
flannel layers like prophetic derelict
noontime stir-fry poems
word jams with New Orleans Dave Brinks.
Fifty with love
Birthday don't tread on me
long way from Scarsdale
digs school diploma scroll
long way from Stony Lodge Hospital day-glow lock-up
Greenwich Village Converse sneaker earth scorch
  hipster
  moves.
Fifty with love
Weather channel Michigan, blanket snow forecast
Panorama Café birthday chow down
cowboy hats and hooters
mental patients knit watch cap
hope like Ft. Lauderdale main drag
Jeannie and Paul's downtown marathon friendship
Laura Boss' hip swing sashay
roll over sweet Beethoven.
Fifty with love
Yes to open angelic southbound highway
Yes Roanoke, Virginia by nightfall
Yes, morning grits, smoked ham egg scramble vision
like Alabama promised land barn raise
Yes to hardscrabble birthday faith
Bring on God's rainbow providence, hot biscuit sanctity
Bring on home fire morning kisses
Bring on fifty with love, yes!

Mentor Now

Mentor now
Take young black leather buck under wing
thousand hosanna incantations
plow under lower forty fallow field quiescence.
Mentor now
Heroic senior citizens tell hardscrabble stories
like front porch southwest Virginia sage.
Mentor now
Keep go-cart on straight-line highway
youth's miracle renegade rapture
Manhattanville College Dan Isaac penchant for
   calico peace
Granola justice, Hamlet's cruel dilemma
Jim Jennings theater heartbeat aficionado
daily phone raps like roller coaster jam
sweet Flo Kennedy Columbia University
streetwise kick ass
Collard green aesthetics.
Mentor now
Always kick bottom belief
road sanctity maple syrup vision
third coffee American dream.
Yes, mentor now
Take young kids to kitchen warm hearth logic
clean common sense mind
body drug-free Vermont pasture.
Mentor now
Place John McCain Vietnam Veterans
ecstasy tab kids together like ham on rye
Yes to boot camp combat ready logic
freedom's Rocky Mountain brilliance
steady hand on Chevy wheel
bring on mythic Zen thirty year stories
cool bop Berlin lover

Westchester County roadhouse heroics.
Mentor now
Punk rocker Ryan Pickering
World War 2 fascination
natural light beer, Marlboro pack
living room hours steady kick back rap
Metallica silver passion
chip and dip streetwise logic.
Oh, mentor now
John Deere jump-start
teach road rules like high school senior health class
teenage love affair overdrive.
Mentor now
Save new breed texture soul
give roulette chance for magic road straight shot
Mentor now, you hear.

Come Around Mama

Big leg Delta lady
Southern comfort rock steady Friday night buzz
shoulder chestnut hair curl
fire eyes like Los Alamos burn down.
Come around mama
Round shoulder like New Jersey Devil's goaltender
firm west Texas handshake
Wrigley's gum sidewinder laugh.
Come around mama
No more river road lament
No 2 A.M. ball the jack
No desolation black crow string out
No floorboard singular waltz.
Come around mama
Yes to prairie Kansas republican ethics
Yes to truck stop coffee miracle refill grace
Yes to Erika Springs cherry pie home bake.
Come around mama
Howl forty railroad years like outback barn
Howl wet calico cat kisses
Howl stallion years pony express tumble.
Come around mama
Cradle this New York City flannel homeboy
cast aside Manhattan Island blood wounds
Bring on hip swing like snake eyes dice.
Come around mama
Yes to marshmallow Santa Cruz dream
Yes to brown eye earth-rock steady heart
like Conestoga wagon Nebraska red clay prairie.
Come around mama
I am yours like 7-11 slurpie
Emily Dickinson Amherst small poems
Jack Kerouac road passion Denver 1951
Bring it home sister
Yes to gingerbread house homestead kisses
southern jubilee smile
Yes to Cheshire calico embrace now.
Come around mama, Yes!

Moscow Sky

Moscow sky cold war over
like B movie horror flick
Ronald Reagan ends war
American muscle, German silk weave unity
Russian bear sucks hot biscuits
Budweiser beer
Gorbachev's Kremlin back down.
Moscow sky
Nuclear arsenal dismantle
like steel erector set
Korea pork chop hill memory fades
John Kennedy Cuban missile crisis
Prague flowers spring bloom.
Moscow sky
No American basement fallout shelters
No hooded Leningrad vodka nightmares
flash point Berlin Wall
edge like mad blind man's bluff.
Moscow sky
Night fracture years
cold war stopped
Reagan America military build up
cuts Russians short like metal doorstop
No to Russian missiles point at
 cherry blossom Washington DC
No to Chinese dragnets show time
Mekong Delta blood killing field GI corpses
No to John McCain cruel North Vietnam torture rack.
Oh Moscow sky
American children sleep like sweet potatoes
red tanks in Afghanistan guerrilla roll back
Yes President Reagan's one for
Gipper hard line supreme
America cuts muscle legs from
Communist mad dog aggression
eastern Bloc unravels yarn spool on short circuit.

Moscow sky
Promise dawn freedom quest
fifty years Lenin, Stalin failed social experiment
dead horse politics, iron fist grade schools
eastern Europe jailhouse brutality
Bring on Western market genius
constitutional cherry pie freedom
calico garden children
Lech Welensa shipyard Gdansk courage
No to black boot secret police
No to Joseph Brodsky velvet curtain gulag lock-up
No to Vladivostok bugging devices
No to Siberian barbwire camps cold war fisticuffs.
Oh Moscow sky
Cobalt blue sky clear like April first spring days
Clear in glorious freedom road
America's liberty beacon
Ronald Reagan city on hill.
Oh Moscow sky
Freeze over like fresh red square magnolias
babushka women liberty
green eyes on western horizon
peace like red square jazz saxophone
Freedom sweet freedom
Yes, at last.

2 A.M. Delight

2 A.M. delight
CBS-FM oldies throw back rhythms
chain smoke beyond Canada gray goose freeze
empty taxi gas tank Second Avenue scoot.
2 A.M. delight
No to skull cobwebs
January Aquarian hometown vibration
radiator heat full throttle.
2 A.M. delight
Yellow sweatpants, gym short fray
promise land Jesus vision
No to granite heart holocaust
No to upper class sell-out delusions
2 A.M. Bill Clinton butterscotch
State of Union holiday daydream
parking garage tough, no night shift
2 A.M. soul boys sleep like calico cats
racked next day business suits
mom wake to kids warm bottle pamper serenity
radio mythic Smokey Robinson
2 A.M. count sheep blue oyster fandango
punker Ryan dreams weekend at Las Vegas blackjack
   table
overnight Dominican security guard
American covenant hot thermos soup
2 A.M. delight
Mississippi freak snow blizzard
Phoenix, Arizona desert night cool down.
2 A.M. delight
Two poems write like skillet French toast
Little Anthony and Imperials cool genius
deep kiss Scarsdale living room muse.
2 A.M. delight
rooster crow hours away
midtown computer nightshift
homeward bound aerobics ladies in stretch pants tug.
Oh 2 A.M. delight
clarity beyond half moon yin yang night
beyond paper bag scuffle desolation
I am yours like bow tie old man
wide Franklin Roosevelt teeth grin
warm Bleeker Street good morning, yes!

High And Dry

High and dry
New York City wilderness turquoise serenity
WQXR-FM classical Vivaldi
kitchen liberation clean.
High and dry
Ibadu Diallo not guilty
jury fix ignites ghetto red pain
like wildcat prairie fire
41 bullets, no gun, cowboy hell
breaks loose firestorm.
High and dry
Iced coffee rocket ride
sweet New Orleans phone communiqué
crackerjack romance cool Manhattan air
word week fracture end
Lafayette Street Tokay wine Delta dream
green eye quicksilver flash
buttocks round imagination
Second Avenue quiet like well-fed mama lion
elegant Kenya giraffes.
High and dry
Cold pasta, Coca Cola, green salad
nighttime late night mantra
incense burn universe breaths like crib infant
red cheek small Chopin hands.
High and dry
No to wet feather wild turkey game shoot
No to Avenue A, Hollywood fame fantasy
No to cold yesterday blueberry muffins.
High and dry
American dream half-shell typewriter jubilee
wide open Kentucky interstate.
High and dry
Two months springtime, washing machine loads
mop Pine Sol floors, Jesus rainbow salvation.
High and dry
Demons quiet voice like peppermint candies
Whitman sampler quiescence cool bop
long time coming!

Sing

Sing America's apple pie covenant grace
South Carolina small town honeysuckle hospitality
12 step fire rehabilitation.
Sing sobriety like eternity road devotion Zen master
Korean seamstress tapestry skill
Southern Utah back roads Chevrolet glide.
Sing to Constitution rock steady freedom
black Newark New Jersey church gospel,
Jesus butterscotch love,
January white pigeon wing spread.
Sing third grader green garden inch worm passion
magic caterpillar monarch butterfly
revelation's Southside Chicago glow.
Sing security guard Walter's hucklebuck
late Saturday night cool
Metro north railroad Hudson River glide
Ossining glory bound
Rikers island Big Mac daydream.
Sing holistic mental health care
Hackettstown Marjorie mythic Anais Nin
literary phone calls
California dream like 3 hour Holland Tunnel E-Z pass.
Sing homespun Bronx rhythm and blues groove
Fresh Firestone tires
Garbage workers' late night elegant ballet
Brother Marc's funky Village grace.
Sing Sabbath synagogue bebop
Like matzo brie, hot coffee
Twala Tharpe American dance genius
New York philharmonic Lincoln Center delight.
Sing cowboy poets prairie dog lament
bacon and beans hard saddle aesthetic
Sing William Shakespeare silk thread love
Friday night cool Budweiser's, Marlboro cigarettes
sweetheart's breast curve
Anthony's DTUT café cherry wood serenity
Tuesday morning low rider sublime
key lime pie sugar rush.

SPRINGTIME AMERICA

Sing America's apple core justice thrust
Supreme court Clarence Thomas pine tree wisdom
Washington Dupont Circle baby carriage moms
Capital Hill April cherry blossom grace.
Sing freedom like cat's eye marble
Rock Island Manhattan wilderness steel grinder beauty
hope's broad shoulder embrace.

PETER CHELNIK - HEY GIRL - COLLECTED POEMS

VII
CINNAMON REBIRTH
2004

PETER CHELNIK - HEY GIRL - COLLECTED POEMS

Kite On String

Kite on String
Central Park paprika wilderness
Manhattan sky swoop
thousand beatnik howls
dreamtime like overtime hot dog vendor.
Kite on String
Cumulus cloud June afternoon
pot dealer Louis cool daddy shuck and jive
Holy roller blade chicks style time, wild legs
carrion desire.
Kite on String
Bring it home green oasis cumin desire
No cell phone big time madness
No top shelf Madison Avenue botox scowls
No circus big top egos.
Kite on String
Boathouse iced coffee highway jag
green garden Adam and eve oregano resurrection
skateboard crack rib ethics.
Kite on String
Salvation like tight buttock cyclists
hip jogger chicks half-back legs, Nike sneaker notions
eye on Bethesda fountain Shakespeare sky.
Quick draw black saxophone cat
Charlie Parker genius rhythm
salt and pepper broad Oak tree smiles
thousand wildcat vignettes
Always, Kite on String!

18-Wheel Semi Salvation

18-Wheel Semi Salvation
Sweet long haul overland trucks
river run Interstate 80
George Washington Bridge easy scoot
San Francisco halibut bound
full diesel tank Cheshire thunder roll.
18-Wheel Semi Salvation
America's heartland prairie schooners
ham on rye white line gear shift truth.
State line purple freedom
like Ohio morning black crows,
biscuits and gravy.
Truckers' red neck heartland integrity
CB Radio late night cadences.
18-Wheel Semi Salvation
Big smile Indiana toll road
weight station short order truck line up
like U.S. Marine boot camp
Chi town shaky side
Charlie Daniels magic fiddle radio, sublime.
18-Wheel Semi Salvation
Local shady time ladies,
side pocket reefer,
turn on U.S. mint silver dime
country girls tight Levi's, July tank tops
back door southern kisses.
18-Wheel Semi Salvation
Davenport Iowa Mississippi
Huck Finn mythic wetlands river cross
Christian Baptist fire brimstone sermon
Hank Williams late night vortex serenade
steady wheel hand,
white robes center lane angels
75 miles per hour engine hum
Holy, holy truck cinnamon roll faith.
18-Wheel Semi Salvation
Denver points shotgun west
like Reno, Nevada blue sky
desert mirage cirrus cloud
November pine tree beauty.

West Coast High Sierras purple sky
baby back ribs home made mashed potatoes
hot coffee sanctity.
18-Wheel Semi Salvation
Hayward California loading dock
on time, like San Francisco back bay miracle dawn
old lady's cotton sleeve welcome home hugs
American white line quiescence.
18-Wheel Semi Salvation Yes!

Gospel Train

Jesus maple syrup heal,
cool South Carolina Sunday summer breeze
ham blaze, buttermilk muffins
magnolia Dixie dreams.
Gospel Train
Baltimore and Ohio freight train
black Bible epiphany
Luther Van Dross soul singer supreme
cargo container sky blue heaven
roadhouse McDonalds, Big Mac
American easy beat chow down.
Gospel Train
No Manhattan black hole Babylon desolation
No coffee mug red devil shatter
No Bowery heroin quick score
No Matrix movie hang noose death wish.
Gospel Train
Apostle Paul's evergreen faith
Wednesday evening cedar room Bible study
holy rainbow serenade
Mississippi Delta Baptist crescendo.
Gospel Train
Born again paprika grace,
flannel shirt Pentecost,
ethics like South Michigan corn fields,
Hillsdale County flea market
Saturday morning peace.
Gospel Train
Cherry pie grace
city on hill, Jesus' 12 gate, Kansas prairie heaven
God's lilac glory
holy spirit planet Mars August night sky brilliance
Hyannis Harbor noontime corduroy promise.
Gospel Train, yes!
Myrna's Cuban Miami rice and beans faith
November Methodist church sale,
thousand Midwest flatland hot rod night rides.
Gospel Train
Eternal life city on Arkansas Hill,

Ozarks green hallow serenade.
Oak grove like Galilee salvation
sweet New Orleans pinewood redemption
train conductor rolling thunder passion,
full harvest moon faith
midnight special holy prayer
thousand hosanna's, yes.
Oh Gospel Train, right on.

Lean On Me

Lean on Me
Soul singer Bill Whither Alabama cottonwood
  strength
calico sister, gone like July garden bloom
big cat racket gangsters
uptown muscle steroid boys midnight fist-a-cuffs
mentally ill soda can ramblers
Canal Street 3 AM dollar hustle.
Lean on Me
Senior citizen holy gray beards
Columbia University tattoo ladies, stove pipe legs
heroin delusion fracture
Joe Skat, Federal Post Office soul two-step.
Lean on Me
Young buck high school dudes
broken family like saltine crackers
Corona 40's bottle binge drunks
86th Street Viande coffee chop
Thursday night ghost rider highway.
Lean on Me
Black high heel style girls
500-dollar uptown trick
like cold blood sexual killing fields.
Baby Boom LSD-25 brain short circuit zombies
1980's cocaine white line promise land addiction
  gulag.
Lean on Me
Yes to overland holy Memphis Bible sanctity
Yes to Vermont loom poetic craft
Yes to railroad heart four-leaf clover emotion
Yes to excellence like high school math wiz.
Lean on Me
Little two-year-old tykes
Central Park stroller scoot
1950's duwop boys
righteous 21st century street corner
four part harmony quiescence
John Lee Hooker buy back Delta cool.

Lean on Me
one night stand tight Levi buttock honey
hip Colt 45
gingham skirt swirl
vengeance like God's old testament thunder.
Lean on Me
Puerto Rico grandmother's stretch budget genius
Second Avenue Key Food coupon magic
Indiana truck stop broad shoulder waitress
Budweiser union work boot construction workers.
Lean on Me
Santa Fe, New Mexico crescent moon ladies
50-year-old sage eyes cinnamon flannel dream
green like September Boston Harbor, Tea Party dawn.
Lean on Me,
that's what I say!

Roll On

Roll On
American hyacinth excellence
opportunity like Memphis short order grill
groove Microsoft computer
flag wave salt tears
1st Armored Calvary freedom time Iraq.
Roll On
Blue ridge mountain mandolin sublime
Baghdad 100 degree heat flack jacket ammo
war on terrorism long haul true grit
heartland combat heroes
New York City, August 5 P.M. silver rain
whole grain bread oven bake.
Roll On
Big John's holy furniture mover outlaw crew
muscle like middle weight Bronx contenders
World Trade Center three years late, break heart
radical Islamic stone cold psychotics on run.
Yes to Kansas City love letters, big old kiss
Yes to Joni Mitchell Saturday night half moon slow
   float
Yes to Claude Debussy WQXR Hudson River serene.
Roll On
Morning Glory staccato bloom
Aaron Copeland American rodeo quiescence
Wyoming tumbleweed self-reliance
Levi's jeans, JC Penney pine green work shirt
Bangladesh Bidyut 85th Street stand excellence
John Ashcroft Attorney General, get tough
homeland justice protect, down right defend
101st Airborne, do a job always.
Roll On
NYPD keep wildcat gorilla city peace
85th Street, Yorkville firehouse ladder 13 can do
No heroin big city hustle freaks
No binge dead end row reefer brain short circuit
No left wing Marxist sheep cadre
No New York University 3 A.M.
ecstasy pop fracture orgies.

Roll On
Yes to pine tree ethics
Yes to Thomas Jefferson Constitution Virginia grace
Yes to Philadelphia 1776 promise land golden
  equality
Iraq desert sand liberation
Yes to Georgia red neck stand by
good old girl calico wife
Texas five alarm chili.
Roll On
Keep Iraq peace, schools open like k-rations
ammonia clean hospitals
U.S. Marines cherry pie combat heroes
No Saadam Hussein genocide
No blood torture chambers
End Satan black snake darkness
War on Terror long haul muscle.
Roll On
Gilgo Beach noon surfers delight
cool Budweiser's
dozen red rose halcyon bloom
American butterscotch optimism
Yes to Terror War, G.I. victory
Roll On, Yes!

Bebop August

Bebop August
Bleecker Street Sunday concrete
pine green plaid shirt
tourist hustle
five dollar Jack Daniels shots
Brigid Murnaghan Back Fence
poetry down and wildcat dirty
sawdust celebration.
Bebop August
Grave yard yellow skin guitar pickers
empty stomach can't find work,
Houston Street soft shoe ramble
thousand welfare check dreams
dignity like Alabama sharecropper
Brooklyn SSI soup kitchen.
Bebop August
Fire eater holy aesthetic
dog run circus side show
scaffold shroud, Washington Square arch
American Flag beatnik Jack Kerouac
on road glory time.
Bebop August
Thompson Street parking garage
20 dollar hustle,
chess shop medieval serenade
white table cloth manga
white cream sauce pasta
New Orleans shrimp curt sauté.
Bebop August
Miles Davis downtown trumpet genius
Monsoon rain like Manila harbor
umbrella fracture
dream on lazy day butterscotch summertime
like ice coffee serendipity
McDougal Street cinnamon road scurry,
Jimi Hendrix purple haze rainbow metaphor.
Bebop August
Tatiana's Moscow monarch butterfly vibration

LaGuardia Place green maple tree grace
holy neighborhood magnolia garden salvation
Mexican five-alarm chili eats
flat bed truck enchiladas
jack cheese tortillas
bring it home frozen margaritas
mythic tequila shots.
Bebop August
Poetic Napa Valley wine easy glide
Allen Ginsberg mythic highway ghost
redemption like holy 1958 finger snap
Gregory Corso touch rainbow sky
black leotard cayenne women
Greenwich Village concrete salvation.
Bebop August, Yes!

Whole Grain 2004

Whole Grain 2004
July Second Avenue wide tooth smiles
downtown holy river run
broad chest poems like Florida Everglades
dreams like orange tabby cat.
Whole Grain 2004
Sandalwood incense tundra
sweet rialto Astor Place tank top caress
let hair down strawberry short cake
afternoon ice chamomile tea passion.
Whole Grain 2004
Drug free, Wyoming road hunger
American cobble stone opportunity
Grand Street midnight rain
like right hand chop sticks,
Egg Fu Yung aesthetics.
Whole Grain 2004
Fresh Union Square farmer's market
bread, blueberry jam baby boom pinewood sisters
thousand straw hat old time beatnik hosannas
Herbie Hancock piano genius.
Whole Grain 2004
U.S. Army, Third Infantry division
Baghdad freedom time quest
Battery Park harbor magic
like 14 year old skateboard sublime
Lady Liberty wartime broad shoulder
protect and down right defend.
Salt Lake City outdoor barbeque, Sunday afternoon.
Whole Grain 2004
Amy Hills guitar pick back beat southern cool
brick by brick magic craft
Bleecker Street pizza slice, garlic, oregano, diet Pepsi
Born Again Christians gospel choir,

freight train transformation
Washington Square Park holy tabernacle
wood bench Marlboro smoke.
Whole Grain 2004
New York cherry wood excellence
Williamsburg canvas stretch, night time
Hudson river velvet dreamtime
Cheshire, mid summer Jones Beach ocean delight
become crimson self
again and again.
Whole Grain 2004, Yes!

Ticket To Ride

Ticket to Ride
John Lennon, Paul McCartney mix a lot
silk groove patchouli oil notions
California dream like magnolia garden bloom.
Ticket to Ride
Moira's upstate wilderness crescent moon ramble
Zen tea hyacinth May dusk
white face carnival clowns Shakespeare eyes.
Ticket to Ride
Youth's sidewinder promise
American in Paris
Van Gogh, vin ordinaire
Moroccan hashish
gendarme hot street pursuit.
Ticket to Ride
Park Avenue yellow taxi glide
white 2004 pansies, Bronx Botanical gardens miracle
  bloom
Tanglewood Music Festival blanket
fried chicken, mythic easy does it Boston Pops Orchestra
Shaker Village singular oak wood faith.
Ticket to Ride
Freewheel Ohio breeze cool down
July clam bake, corn butter
small tykes water wing beach frolic
sun block 45, thousand American promises
like Coney Island cumulus sky.
Ticket to Ride
Fire Island Ferry; cool Budweiser, proud dune grass
heroic Williams Carlos Williams, red wagon luggage tow.
Ticket to Ride
Watermelon vodka spike
dream on like New Jersey Turnpike toll booth clerk
Triboro Bridge muscle construction crew
midtown parking lot Hondo dudes.

Ticket to Ride
Westchester County back road jubilee
nephew Charlie hip hop delight
dusk basketball jump shot excellence
easy glide earth turn.
Ticket to Ride
morning glory highway poetics
blueberry muffin, iced coffee
full tank state line celebration
back to wind, dig it.

Creative Revolution

Creative Revolution
Manhattan artistic prairie fires
highway magnolia excellence
word crack like Texas bull whip
barn fire heart reinvention literary wheel.
Creative Revolution
Wildflower hoots down Lafayette Street
canvas stretch Newark New Jersey
funky blues town painter lofts
Heartland Mississippi river
Al Hirt trumpet cool bop
thousand full moon
Charles Mingus acoustic bass riffs
sleeve roll back beat.
Creative Revolution
Chicago overland apprenticeship
Emily Dickinson April tulip word craft
Saturday night sit at home like pigeon nest
work denim tail off
touch crescent moon night sky
No art scene big time cocaine cats
No computer graphic ego trip painters
No university dull edge paranoid poets
No Yale University ivy vine corpse
graduate school aficionados.
Creative revolution
Red brick foundation formal education
experience like on road tar shack hobos.
pick flannel self up thousand halcyon times.
Creative Revolution
IBM typewriter, spontaneous howl
Puerto Rican conga drum revival
Missoula, Montana big sky cowboy ethics
gingham expression like wide hip pioneer women
Jack Kerouac three square's shot gun aesthetics
shoulder wide flannel muse.
Creative Revolution
Yes to Ernest Hemingway
mud boot literary revolution
Yes to Minnesota northwood's excellence

Yes to Willa Cather heartland Nebraska prairie grace
Yes to 21st century Tennessee two step
Saturday night moonshine celebration
yes to double scoop apple pie
cutting edge San Francisco innovation.
Creative Revolution
Pay price like Bronx middleweight boxer
Sylvia Plath demon lace poetic testimony
James Joyce consciousness language stretch.
Creative Revolution
Yes to New Breeds wide horizon earth planet vision
Yes to Bowery Poets Café grunge, spoken word howls
Yes to young lunch bucket sidewinder
poets steady hands
Indiana straight-line horizon eyes.
Creative Revolution, bring it on!

Crosstown Covenant

Westside freedom train
open dawn sky optimism
ham eggs home fries delight
thousand Columbus Avenue hosannas.
Crosstown Covenant
Jesus Central Park May bloom
Promised land pigeons
holy markers like West Side Highway signs.
Crosstown Covenant
Bob Feldman tenor saxophone el supreme
Times Square groove
big time Disney electric hallucinations
number 1 train Harlem bound
ham hock collard greens
bright eyes grand children marathon read.
Crosstown Covenant
Cherry wood feminists
earth hold fire eyes
year after year Manhattan tundra
ethics like Episcopal minister
Sunday morning cool bop sermon.
Crosstown Covenant
Jim Jennings, American Theater of Actors, drama genius
back garden July Shakespeare
butterscotch Broadway opportunity
hungry new breed actors.
Crosstown Covenant
God's Old Testament 86th Street rainbow synagogue
cinnamon tea poetry gig
outback howls, funky Amsterdam Avenue
Riverside Park Saturday ice coffee dusk
like California blood orange
vanilla ices, small tykes delight.
Crosstown Covenant
Nephew Charles Chelnik's little league third base/mix
  a lot
Clinton District, old time
dirt baseball diamond

Hudson river mythic quiescence
June playoff leather glove drama.
Oh Crosstown Convenant
Lincoln Center New York Philharmonic
Mozart excellence
Alice Tulley hall, Branford Marsallis
magnolia back beat
dreams like Q.E. 2 pier set sail
cobalt blue sky limit
Columbus Circle crimson carousel
Crosstown Covenant, Yes!

Wildcat Independence Day

Wildcat Independence Day
Thomas Jefferson Declaration genius
Monticello grace Creator's apple pie rights
highway big sky eternity.
Wildcat Independence Day
East River firecracker sparkle time
backyard hot dog, burger jubilee
Ben Franklin founding fathers constitutional rights
like cobble stone Philadelphia freedom.
Wildcat Independence Day
Boston Tea party rebellion
like Wyoming free rang mustangs
19-year-old young buck full canvas knapsack
Pacific Coast sunshine salvation, American dream
Detroit City Motown back beat cool.
Wildcat Independence Day
George Washington cherry tree integrity
Texas roadhouse broad grins firm handshakes
pedal steel guitar twang late night
sweet calico kisses.
Wildcat Independence Day
Wal-Mart shopping mall wide open field sales
New Jersey Plaza diner
ham and eggs breakfast special
God's Catskill mountain stream covenant
self reliance, Colorado rocky Mountain crystalline
  vibration
Wildcat Independence Day
bold life liberty, happiness pursuit
Betsy Ross old glory flag sew
Constitution's hyacinth freedom time beacon
Ellis Island steerage hard work sweat dream
City College rosebud quiescence.

Wildcat Independence Day
Mythic Yankee Stadium, Babe Ruth holy ground
ninth inning break tie
Derek Jeter home run excellence.
Wildcat Independence Day
God family big country freedom
patriots t-bone steak vigil
John Kerry, combat Vietnam silver star true grit
watermelon cool July 4th Alabama equality 2004
Lady Liberty's open cotton arms promise
Yes!

Real Deal

Real Deal
November Canadian geese fly south
heat wave oven gingerbread
Hudson River mythic easy glide.
Real Deal
Freedoms wood cracker barrel
Athens, Georgia, Main Street slow down
American destiny, Central Park
yellow maples bold autumn stand
break neck pace, marathon runners excellence
laptop latte steady cash in hand vision
Monday morning rock steady hunker down.
Real Deal
Down U.S. Army Chinook helicopter
Iraq crimson firefight
ultimate bare bone liberty sacrifice
Mid-east freedom road
George W. Bush, Commander in Chief stand tough
like Green Bay packer offense lineman
October Michigan apple orchid pick.
Real Deal
Los Angeles forest fire holocaust
over like celluloid nightmare
demon shroud hell
black smoke sky wrath
rebuild San Diego easy vibration County
Pacific edge eucalyptus
San Bernardino cozy trim lawns
Yes to Jesus glory train salvation
Yes to seedling springtime South California,
    desert magic
Yes to eucalyptus rebirth, eternal sidewinder hope.
Real Deal
Golden dawn honey bear promise
like lover's morning dreamtime kiss
Brooklyn poppy seed bagel, cream cheese
full Johnny Appleseed poem pouch.

Real Deal
Holy 75-degree afternoon
No floorboard bottle cap schizophrenic walk
No Manhattan Bridge suicide leap cowards
No ledge calico cat desolation.
Real Deal
Nebraska liberty large prairie prayer
hobby hose new beginning
cinnamon righteous rebirth
Monday morning
Real Deal

Spiderweb Fog

Spiderweb Fog
November morning black coffee
night time elephant sleep
Election Day liberty fandango
bakers dozen poets.
Spiderweb Fog
East coast line pumpkin pie
Rialto, Jack Daniels serenade
L.L. Bean maroon rag sweater
West Texas, Phillips 66 gasoline pump
freedom time wild west
cowboy honest justice
chicken fried steak aesthetics.
Spiderweb Fog
Chili pepper five-alarm, New Mexico tamales morning
touch Lubbock, Texas
slow float sky
mud work boot traditional values
metaphor's ball point pen fire.
Spiderweb Fog
Heartland grace like World War II
Navy flyboy Norman Duberstein
peanut brittle optimism
South Michigan, farmland gold wheat harvest.
Spiderweb Fog
Night ride Corpus Christi
buy back Coors big dipper
like Moses' old testament holy salvation
No to hundred sophomore promises
No to Saturday night wildcat Vodka drunks
No to high school fry brain marijuana fracture
No to New York University suicide leaps.
Spiderweb Fog
Tulsa, Oklahoma morning dawn clarity
Hank Williams redneck flannel ethics
18 wheel semi broad shoulder salvation
yellow ribbon Utah women, stand by man
Panama City Beach, Florida hot griddle grace.
Spiderweb Fog
U.S. Marines honey jar patriots

bring it on like Mustang corral
protect ad defend cherry pie heartland
roast turkey liberty
Methodist church Sunday School
like straight lace cotton mom
no nonsense, red, white and blue pride.
Spiderweb Fog
Washington Square Park
chess serenade
3rd grade milk, cookies, kick back
hobo tin can Oklahoma melody
bald eagle equality soar
cobra discipline, Fourth Infantry Division
Baghdad cool.
Spiderweb Fog
new calico day, yes

Heartache

Heartache
Candy cane California July kisses
divine patchouli romance
youth's featherbed grace
Santa Cruz full moon 1969
barn fire easy glide magic flesh eros.
Heartache
West Coast touch sky like
holy Catholic Saint
work shirt rosary
Free University hippie redemption.
Heartache
earth hold lentil stew
Pacific Ocean mountain woman cotton hugs
Aquarian holy union
quicksilver bronze flesh
thousand dreams
like cosmic consciousness dawn groove.
Heartache
Oh blond black skirt swirl lady
magic whole grain essence
Zen Satori
ecstasy like cosmic river flow.
Heartache
I walk away purple vibration
soul mate cauldron
ancient brown eyes
Indiana heartland roots.
Heartache
I walk away
like high school sophomore nervous white rabbit.
Heartache
Year after year
Manhattan concrete heartbreak
psycho ward hopscotch
university sweet potato two step
parking lot underground gulag.
Heartache
Diaspora shadow sidewinder path
Byzantine iron rack

CINNAMON REBIRTH

heartbreak golden woman
revolutions miracle wonder.
Oh Heartache
1969 edge of America mythic afternoons
psychedelic window breeze
loves butterscotch jubilee
eucalyptus round breasts
rock and roll lady sublime.
Heartache.
I miss you honey
like catatonic San Quentin prison lifer
Alabama sharecropper poverty train
blonde hair highway lady
34 year heartbreak
Heartache, damn.

Pan Fry Love

Pan fry Love
Cotton pillow wildcat whispers
Texas roadhouse sweet talk
whiskey bar corduroy personal history
one match bake beans camp fire eros.
Pan fry Love
Salt tears like Atlantic Ocean
high tide November night
No cut and run balsa wood romance
No Lithium pill pop isolation
No tabby cat empty milk bowl hunger.
Pan fry Love
Colorado evergreen highway dream
love's banana cake upstate New York grace
bird in hand magnolia faith
clean laundry load promise.
Pan fry Love
Sisters get real like
J&B and Coke big hip bartender
sexy Steamboat Springs sway
Midnight Express Diner
Saturday morning heart on fire waitress
Manhattan tattoo bad girl
Sheridan Square sandalwood incense
quicksilver karmic wheel grace
Jesus' white lily pad redemption
thousand pumpernickel bread loaves
thousand red snapper delights.
Pan fry Love
No to hustle cash affairs
No to Chinese soft shoe opium addict houseboys
No to sharp cleaver groin attack.
Pan fry Love
Respect like pinewood straight back rainbow
Bakersfield, California cotton soft caress
Joni Mitchell guitar pick genius
Friday night cool August meadow kisses
Central Park cumulus clouds
picnic blanket, morning coffee sweet epiphany.
Pan fry Love

CINNAMON REBIRTH

No to oil slick miscues like
Indianapolis hot wire drag race
No to 20-year-old black cat reign of terror
No to typewriter carbon copy plagiarism
Yes to tabletop straight shot New Orleans emotion
Yes to Missouri trout fish morning hugs
Pan fry Love
Sisters let hair down like
Niagara Falls cascade
full antique wood spice rack
cumin, paprika, garlic caress
Atlanta, Georgia open calico heart
season cast iron skillet
New Jersey egg fry promise
crisp Arkansas bacon.
Pan fry Love, yes!

Praise God

Praise God
Rock and roll eternal life
Lafayette Street scoot
holy window sill gray pigeon
green Earth garden planet
spring rainbow gospel.
Praise God
Redemption like Catskill Mountain
cool June trout stream
Holy prophet Jeremiah, rap it down
Harley Davidson testimony
86th Street Daily News tobacco shack
Eastern dawn Massachusetts break heart
easy glide.
Praise God
Chinese seamstresses steady wisdom hands
Williamsburg late night French kiss rapture
faith like number 1 train Sheridan Square bound
Central Park pot smoke
hobo George highway Manhattan fire eyes
Florida Panhandle oyster shuck dream.
Praise God
Jesus' Galilee miracles
Woodstock January snow squalls
hot chocolate
double quilt halcyon afternoons.
Praise God
FDNY light sleep dudes, Atlantic Ocean dream
Montauk salt air
Shinnicock Indian American earth serenade
hardy yellow purple flowerbed pansies
dozen fresh New Jersey eggs.
Praise God
Salvation's East Harlem rice and beans
Easy Rider cool out 1969
magic white swans, Mamaroneck Harbor

Ohio Turnpike Tuesday morning Midwest rhapsody
thousand hosannas
Morning prayer like Mount Sinai Moss.
Praise God
Manhattan Methodist Church toll resurrection
pasta el dente, garlic, Portobello mushrooms
May Walt Whitman Brooklyn Ferry lilacs
purple sky quiescence
American highway full gas tank grace
creation like Vermont loom
butterscotch morning sunlight.
Praise God!

Dead Souls

No to Sodom and Gomorrah
garbage can desolation row
No to California green money vortex
No to Park Avenue marble cows
computer digital gulag
like Satan's double dip hell burn.
Dead Souls
No to shut up and consume kewpie dolls
clinical tape measure paranoia
No dank water narcissism
seamstress quick fix lobotomies
No to psychiatrist sugar land hand in pocket hustle.
Dead Souls
Yes to Prophet Isaiah's righteous testament
Yes to Lebanon green pine valleys
Yes to Gods milk and honey beatnik grace.
Dead Souls
No to Avenue C heroin shoot galleries
uptown tight buttock all girls
No to same sex bizarre purple yarn twist
No to red wine morning holocaust short circuit.
Dead Souls
No to Marxist warrior's penny ante
Yale university cardboard revolutionaries
No to 8-year-old Vietcong, BF Goodrich sandals
play station mind strip search.
Dead Souls
No to blackout 2003 end of world
power grid wannabe sabotage
No to Amsterdam Ave gin drunks
Hitler youth spaghetti top women
No to grunge dudes Brooklyn Bridge suicide
screw parents dead pan leap.
Dead Souls
Embrace Central Park Freddy Hubburd fire jazz

Embrace Norman Riley, magic drum rhythms
rap in downtown Santa Cruz mountains
spoken word saints
Embrace Fern Filner's mythic cross-country odyssey
1977 Toyota camper
Embrace America's freedom highway essence.
Dead Souls
Yes to maple syrup New York Harbor optimism
Yes to Utah wilderness self reliance
August rain soft needle grace
Yes to calico community easy smiles
eye on sky like Bob Dylan's Mr. Tambourine man
Yes to Zen consciousness reckless like runaway freight
always righteous, dig it.

Oak Wood Dignity

Oklahoma crimson pride
Lance Armstrong five Tour de France
long haul true grit medals,
combat American third infantry division Iraq
noontime firefight freedom time heroics.
Oak Wood Dignity
Southern Michigan holy Midwest moms
girl scout merit badge sew
hot brownies, milk
12 year old daughters
young black colt brush shine
Black kids of Southern Illinois University library read
night train homework midterm excellence.
Oak Wood Dignity
Roberts DTUT coffee house cut flowers el supreme
Arturo's hot coffee morning floor mop
Donna Long folk music passion.
Oak Wood Dignity
Jamaican June nanny cool
Campbell's hot soup, half sandwich, childcare
broad grin, cover bases always
Barnes and Noble denim clad store clerk
encyclopedia kaleidoscope brain
Bangladesh lunch on run taxi driver
87th Street Saturday morning
jackhammer quick shot muscle
down right blueberry muffin
cement pour.
Oak Wood Dignity
No to high school sophomore pot party fracture
No to tombstone drugs
Yes to clean and sober like
full Long Island Sound spinnaker sail.
Oak Wood Dignity
Stand tall like eastern Colorado telephone poles
Episcopal church steeple, Woodstock, Vermont
Mississippi river mythic April currents
red checker kitchen table ethics

church pew Sunday holy calico prayer
Ten Commandments like Alabama southern glory train.
Oak Wood Dignity
September honest schoolyard peanut and jelly
Anthony's basketball dream
open highway library card read
like 8th grade top notch cool
union construction worker steam fit pride
Han's Scarsdale garage
35 years auto mechanic magic like
Wright Brothers Dayton Ohio bicycle shop.
Oak Wood Dignity
No to half bake Absolute Vodka sell out
No to back seat gorilla wrestle
No to midnight downtown reefer comatose rambles.
Oak Wood Dignity
Straight and narrow Alabama highway
open August Pennsylvania
dozen red rose heart
Oak Wood Dignity, yes

Coolsville

Coolsville
White Plains Bowl seven ten-roadhouse split
Deborah's eggs over easy, home fries
rolling stones Provincetown salt air essence
kick bottom San Quentin
jailhouse poetry renaissance.
Coolsville
Chattanooga white lace wedding dreams
senior prom June tuxedo get down
Times Square dervish swirl
like miracle top spin
Bob Feldman tenor saxophone
t-bone east coast chops
calico heart liberation
synagogue torah scroll read riot act
Sweet Marin County
back road quiescence
Detroit, Michigan, Midwest United Autoworkers
assembly line pride.
Coolsville
No to Houston Street pool hall
Wrigley's gum hard jive
No to Fort Lauderdale Oxyicotton crush pill
brain fry addiction
No to Fenway Country Club
fat cat elite trash bin snobs,
diamond ring fracture
No to Lexington Avenue mini skirt
nylon party girls dollar bill holdup.
Coolsville
Martina McBride, Nashville
guitar twang country music excellence
stand by me
pinewood Interstate 40 sweet Memphis

CINNAMON REBIRTH

Phillips 66 truck stop country western values
Texas shotguns keep big sky peace
Jesus pork chop Sundays
American bald eagle lock and load pride
Dodge City Kansas prairie schooner excellence
J.C. Penney September
starch clean school clothes
senior citizen clams casino wisdom
VFW Tuesday fish fry
Montana big sky calico promise
Coolsville, Yes!

Silk Glide

Silk Glide
Red raven cherry lipstick
Rivington Street, Saturday sunset kisses
rainbow Manhattan September holy promise
Jesus' peach cobbler
Promised Land hot oven salvation
like westbound Interstate 80 diesel
veggie stew chop bell peppers.
Red onions, carrots, mix a lot.
Silk Glide
No to cocaine Syracuse University sorority sisters
No to madcap insane high tech Dexedrine freaks
No to hit and run Jeep Cherokee
roll over blood corpse clowns.
Silk Glide
Yes to poverty train SSI Prozac angels
food pantry stretch budget
like Newark Star ledge rubber bands
Yes to thousand hot oatmeal hosannas
Bonnie Raitt blues guitar get down ramble
Yes to Sunday afternoon Wrigley Field
Sammy Sosa mythic Chicago Cubs
October play-off magic.
Silk Glide
Hip-hop boys bring down house rapture
spoken word Cork City redheads
Jack Daniels, lower Broadway scat time
Evangelical Bible word of god salvation
Atlanta, Georgia peach tree gospel choir
sweetwater calico redemption.
Silk Glide
Nevada High Sierra evergreen
high altitude serenity
flannel poets rock steady

CINNAMON REBIRTH

Kansas prairie heartland crescendo
Red cross first aid kit relief
Jewish Synagogue miracle stain glass
holy revelation
corn on cob butter love
French kisses like Sicilian garlic cloves
moon dance cinnamon heart alive
Silk Glide, Yes!

Babylon Tuesday Morning

Babylon Tuesday Morning
Hardscrabble New York City unravel
ten Absolute Vodka short circuit shots
junk yard cabbage patch brains
empty scat hipsters
Bedford Styvesant housing tenement
New York University illiterates
Bobst Library shoot out
demon suicide leaps
heroin Avenue C jones
trust fund Katmandu revolutionary
Aries desolation.
Babylon Tuesday Morning
Hearts like thousand dollar call girls
leather Bloomingdales boots,
dirt hill Yorkville psychosis flat tire
Massachusetts, George
Central Park knapsack hobo supreme.
Babylon Tuesday Morning
Mad dog corporate CEO's
like Harlem purple pimps
pill pop East End Avenue psychiatrists
Horace Mann private school chili pepper brats
oral sex high wire two step
nose in air like pink poodle
Park Avenue white tulip wasteland
thousand iron rack S&M cults.
Babylon Tuesday Morning
Yes to Utah wilderness blue sky grace
God's Bryce Canyon morning creation
Yes to mud work boot ethics
Yes to Richmond Hill, Queens
Catholic angels canvas duffel bag
Chesapeake and Ohio railroad saints
Bakersfield Mulligan stew tasty delight
Yes to Santa Cruz, California
Valerie Meier guitar pick kick bottom genius

CINNAMON REBIRTH

drum circle fringe celebration
ham on rye poetry liberation
Yes to morning Marlboro smoke
Yes to laughter like hippie jubilee 1969
Yes to Clemson, South Carolina
blue highway road vibration dawn
Yes to Colorado mountain women,
cowboy boots
Jack Daniels kick back
denim embrace Rocky Mountain hugs.
Babylon Tuesday Morning
No way jack!

Cinnamon Rebirth

Cinnamon Rebirth
late November maple tree
Central Park celebration
hot green tea
blue cotton sheet hand on broad hip
Colorado rainbow serenade.
Cinnamon Rebirth
Nutcracker Suite wood soldiers delight
Jamaica sweetheart June Kingston
cut pie essence
jerk chicken, white rum
down home coconut juice,
corn row hairdo soul sister cool.
Cinnamon rebirth
Sunday morning Tarrytown, New York
Hudson River, small town quiescence
Dutch Presbyterian
400-year stone church salvation
Bella red neck restaurant
flannel old timers
Daily News, hot oatmeal kick back.
Cinnamon Rebirth
Louisville Kentucky, Colleen
silver blonde southern pastel quilt kindness
full moon eclipse,
God's miracle creation
22 story roof top wonder.
Cinnamon Rebirth
Thanksgiving three days
freight train, Concord
New Hampshire
Atlantic Ocean salt horizon
broad Manhattan grins
Girl Scout chocolate mint cookies
cold milk hoe down

ethics like wildcat
Westside reform Rabbi
fire eyes, Kabala wisdom
Prophet Isaiah,
holy Promised Land revelation.
Cinnamon Rebirth
East River crystalline Sunday night
glass mirror sanctity
thousand crimson American night dreams
two comforter honey bear sleep
cumulus cloud city wide gotham joy.
Cinnamon Rebirth, Yes!

PETER CHELNIK - HEY GIRL - COLLECTED POEMS

VIII
MILLENNIUM WEAVE
2000

Highway Time

Highway Time
quick shot Interstate 80
New Jersey George Washington Bridge
electric hot chowder hard drive
metaphor stack like Christmas Barney inventory.
Highway Time
shake and bake Paterson New Jersey
mythic read
Greg Velez's outlaw blue collar cool
cool cat Bob Feldman
tenor sax Kerouac riff.
Highway Time
18-wheel semis Portland, Maine
sweet tooth dashboard Hershey bars
dream Tennessee redhead radiator heat
December silver needle rain.
Highway Time
Macintosh apple satchel
Joe Dimaggio Florida deathbed
heartbreak like raw eggshell.
Late afternoon winter black horse dusk.
Funky Bronx grace bodega ham and swiss
hip hop baggy pants sublime
quilt down jacket
trash can fire vagrant's hand warm
tribe breaths like 100-meter track star.
Highway Time
New Mexico bound red bean burritos
hot salsa margarita delight
crimson Die Hard battery jump-start.
Highway Time
Jesus' cirrus cloud grace
embrace Interstate 25 Denver to
sweet Albuquerque
Motel 6 clean sheet cool out.
Highway Time
hyacinth spirit revolution.
Gym class jumping jacks
first french kiss Georgette
backseat Chevy wagon 1965.

Highway Time
Arkansas apple pie road quest
Christmas Eve half moon salvation
Florida round grapefruits three for
99 cents.
Highway Time
straight line San Diego surf's up
road savvy cabaloosa dreams
tender brain freight train
Susquehanna work horse railroad diesel
internet digital illusion
Manhattan wilderness quiescence
Yes to Alvin Ailey dance genius.
Yes to denim blue collar wide shoulder poetics
Highway Time
high Colorado rainbow plateau
close Gillette exact shave
34 cents postage stamps
California soft shoe horizon dream.
Ford pickup engine hum.
Phillips 76 truck stop
red neck ethics
Highway Time, yes.

Stand Tall

I Stand Tall
like eastern Colorado telephone poles
September horizon clothesline.
Carnegie Hall stage string bass
Patrick Ewing too many championship defeats.
I Stand Tall
like third grader concrete school playground
ex-con futile job search
large ice coffee plastic
buttered poppy seed bagel.
I Stand Tall
like Greenwich, Connecticut back road oak tree
debutante's long gown mom's sweet neck
Tiffany pearls.
James Baldwin's Harlem literacy mythic dream
brown Key Food sack payday groceries.
I Stand Tall
like Miles Davis bebop hey days
World Trade Center Monday morning
elegant sea mist 1997
85th Street corner lamppost
Fitzpatrick's bar, veteran hookers, spike heels,
cheap waist fur jacket.
I Stand Tall
like top shelf poetic manuscripts
no to feminist barb wire snarls
no to mutant dime store anger
no to granite master slave hearts.
I Stand Tall
like God's barn raise sanctity
red, yellow, green traffic light cadence
love's queen size bed devotion
Vietnam era baby boom courage.
I Stand Tall
like 86th Street construction site
third floor genius steamfitter elegant
union craft
George Washington Bridge hell bent
Jersey bound.
I Stand Tall

like hot shot fashion model
city magic manicure hands
Friday night martini straight up
river run.
I Stand Tall
like western sky white puff cumulus clouds
D.H. Lawrence mythic Taos New Mexico gravesite.
Baldwin piano Duke Ellington fire.
I Stand Tall
like parking lot dude
five dollar tip
Mercedes Benz lilac hustle.
Don Paynes' Canadian Navy broad shoulders
mythic roll.
I Stand Tall
like prophetic coffee table angels.
Kellogg Corn Flakes, red checker table
cloth serenade
New Jerusalem white light harmony
Gregory Corso beatific glide
Kansas grain silo's singular voice.
I Stand Tall
like Ezra Pound Pall Mall
cigarette roll Greenhaven Prison watchtower
shift change.
New Rochelle neighborhood steel
water tower
Jimmy's mom's ravioli lunches;
calico notions New Mexico bound.
I Stand Tall
like Lady Liberty's wide angle Nikon lens
Stockbridge, Massachusetts Norman Rockwell
American bone pride.
I Stand Tall.

Have Faith

Have Faith
fringe brothers sisters on Maryland
country lane. Missouri holy
Mississippi River bank
Rikers Island Prison.
Have Faith
in mythic bottle cap road years
mercy's bullwhip crack fire hydrant quatrains.
Have Faith
in Manhattanville College early 1970's
cool blue academic excellence
Carolyn Stoloff Zen stick crack
poetry workshop
Burmashave Bukowski deadpan Los Angeles.
Have Faith
in communion wafer flannel shirt pocket
rosary beads.
Three Jaimison shots madcap Kettle of
Fish Bar howls.
James Joyce buckshot invention.
Virginia Wolf genius weave.
Have Faith
brothers and sisters
in neon Manhattan highway
Blarney Stone short beers hot
corned beef
pocket black bible key ring fantasy
daily journal entry like hot ivory
soap shower.
Have Faith
in God's Jewish wildcat spirit
hot dog vendor lanky independence
cool Central Park Snapple peach ice tea.
Teenage skateboard dialectics
Have Faith
in firm Manhattan handshakes
George Washington cherry tree integrity
Abraham's red-hot barn fire vision.
Teamster union hall repentance.

Have Faith
in parents Ford Thunderbird love
bring home bacon dads and moms.
Vietnam rolling thunder peace,
Bill Clinton whole apple pie green
cash economic boom.
Have Faith
brothers and sisters in Black man's
tar and feather mythic vortex holocaust
cotton pick dark hole slavery. Liberation time.
Have Faith
in mud tire tracks
Katonah red wine salad days
Wayne's fresh made eggplant parmesan
Catholic girls honeysuckle kisses
Moira's elegant dorm room
tea ceremony 1972
preppy Connecticut butterfly seductions.
Have Faith
in magic word on paper
memory like sports page fourth grader
therapist's office rap it down
personal history.
Fire department C-Town Friday morning
food runs.
Have Faith
brothers and sisters meatloaf, mash potatoes,
corn, lit cheroot,
small tank top rainbow caress.
Have Faith
in 12 step dollar in kitty redemption,
clean, sober Bohemian cool.
Have Faith.

Catch As Catch Can

Catch As Catch Can
Duke Ellington Far East suite
silk kimono
Vietnam stir fry
American blood in Central Highlands
Khe San 1968 GI heroics
Saigon nylon stocking affair.
Catch As Catch Can
1998 Sunday radiator heat
sleep in
New Orleans dreams
B flat serenade uptown rap.
Saturday afternoon peppermint French kiss.
Catch As Catch Can
Jesus' bring it home love
full wicker picnic basket
poetic gift like Roy Eldridge
bebop sublime
twenty dollar bill roll
supermarket milk train.
Milk, Jersey jumbo eggs, farmland butter.
Catch As Catch Can
no to World Trade Center
September 11 mass grave
no to al-Qaida psychotic evil.
Catch As Catch Can
City College poetry hoe-down
chicken and rice, coca cola ice shave,
Sweet Marcus, magic Dominican sweetheart Che
mythic Flo Kennedy rainbow starship.
Catch As Catch Can
January half moon
Black day laborer lunch bucket sweat
pay rent fill wide fridge
Cornell University daughter, dig it!
Catch As Catch Can
no Maoist gender snarls
no political correct language goose step
revisionist minestrone soup.

Catch As Catch Can
full gum machine gift
American highway high pin curve
dream time.
Catch As Catch Can
SAT all-night cram.
Library's mythic green garden delight
psycho ward Saturday day pass,
Big Mac, fries, coke-freedom.
Catch As Catch Can
angels delight on 52 year
old city brow
typewriter holds like champion
tug of war team
road kindness Indiana truck stop
Monterrey Peninsula holy vibrations
Santa Cruz Free University psychedelic groove.
Mississippi Delta spring planting time.
Catch As Catch Can
Grass roots creative ballpoint
pen fandango
No publishing house brand name package.
No MFA tin angel discourse.
No Madison Avenue wannabe black couch
leather scams.
Catch As Catch Can
John Coltrane Love Supreme blood passion
wildflower April transcendence
desert water jug integrity
Charlie Mingus bass blue
Memphis afternoon.
Catch As Catch Can

I Call To You America

I Call To You American excellence
stand up string bass
crescent moon millennium December night
restless spirit on truck stop move
Colorado Rocky Mountain flannel shirt dream
Wrightsville Beach front porch veranda
wooden pick up sticks, cool pink lemonade.
I Call To You America
immigrants drive for dollar bill
gold rush opportunity
New York City hope like hot sauce falafel,
Lamb cous cous, Irish stew,
Lady liberty's open embrace.
I Call To You America
U.S. Marines leatherneck freedom quest
Army Rangers can do cool.
I Call To You America
Bill Gate's Seattle mirco chip genius
tough burly Fords off
Dearborn Michigan assembly line
stock market crochet
small business ingenuity.
I Call To You America
cotton sleeve sensible shoe librarians
book publishers eye on poetic
maple syrup sublime.
I Call To You America
Deborah Auer cashmere sweater torch singer
uptown cocktail lounge,
Third Avenue square block movie lines.
I Call To You America
girl's night out draught beer
woo woo shots sassy like
field hockey team.
I Call To You America
mythic Alexander de Tocqueville vision
like birthing cafe innocence
Pinewood cord pile, clean well water
Bryce Canyon Utah frontier grace.

I Call To You America
Main Street Woodworth five and dime
trinket paradise
barbershop politics local corncob gossip
diesel fuel politics
midnight rare cheeseburger Friday night
Chevrolet kisses mini skirt up high.
I Call To You America
garbage haulers ballet grace
construction workers hands on genius
lunch bucket iron piling craft
NYPD, fireman's, EMS World Trade Center
heroism, milky way blood donors.
I Call To You America
Bill of Rights sublime Constitution
founding fathers in God We Trust genius
Vermont woodsmen, Chesapeake Bay fisherman
crab and oyster quest
Yellowstone Park fierce beauty.
I Call To You America
Diz's trumpet ride Gil Coggins
piano delight
jazz serendipity New Orleans
to sweet Chicago
New York City vortex. Ghetto beatitude.
I Call To You American transcendence
Springfield, Missouri handshake honesty
San Francisco bound diesel freight train
small town ethics like cheerleader's
arched back
Mississippi Delta justice flannel dream
Methodist Sunday morning church bell toll.
I Call to You America, yes.

Time To Heal

Time to Heal
Place aside Manhattan chain saw
blood wounds
no oatmeal rat poison
Missouri Ozark muskrat iron trap pain.
No ecstasy tab youth fracture.
Time to Heal.
No tea room fisticuffs
no Bleecker Street Che Guevera
guerrilla war tactics.
no paprika scapegoat cat calls
Number Six-line subway train.
No sawed off shotguns.
Time to Heal.
Put aside sidewinder orange peel cynicism,
digital computer chip rice Crispy aesthetic
cruel barroom bourbon shot bravado.
Time to Heal.
Set aside hundred dollar retribution
gender war's hot tar killing fields.
East Coast night stray dog whelps
roulette red 32 desire.
Set aside chi chi clothes cut
upper class Mercedes Benz Madison Avenue
elitism.
Chicago windy city broad shoulder anger.
Time to Heal.
No Yale University hop scotch
law school notions
no Mississippi straw river raft capsize
no poets room soft machine
sword play.
National Endowment Turkish taffy politics.
Time to Heal.
Allegheny Indians rainbow spirit
green Rock Hill South Carolina azalea garden
touch sky like lover's round hips.

Time to Heal.
Bring home straight lace discipline
morals like third grade yard stick
multiplication tables.
Time to Heal.
Ride freight train Trenton, Philadelphia,
sweet Baltimore.
Cinnamon sweet lady, Queen Anne's Lace
bouquet, full moon Woodstock night stroll
left hand 20 year wedding ring.
Time to Heal.
Call out God's name again and again
hot morning coffee typewriter garlic
clove punch.
Heal brother and sister
no to Jim Bowie knife wound
Mekong Delta napalm
no to Desert Storm nasty chemical warfare.
Time to Heal.
Daily Ivory soap showers,
tooth floss, devotion to stain glass cathedral,
velvet pool hall, synagogue wood pew,
corner butcher shop.
Time to Heal.
Place aside 38 magnum
walk Zen road like cool Texas dawn
highway breakfast May chrysanthemum window
box delight.
Wide tooth smile.
Time to Heal.

Open Road

I am December Hanukkah lights
noon grill cheese sandwiches
iron railroad track copper penny
flannel line seven-year-old
blue jeans.
I am infant Moses
wicker basket riverbank.
John the Baptist visionary faith heal.
Albuquerque cirrus sky desert dream
fresh Ocalla navel oranges.
I am American excellence
straight shot like Bob dole
Kansas Republican Party
Midnight Snickers bar
young feminist toothed smile.
I am cut the pie poet
Saint Patrick's holy communion.
Denim shirt rainbow sage
I-95 Connecticut state line
toss salad russian dressing.
Makeshift Christmas tree
Marine Kandahar air base.
I am old man's downtown
parking lot.
Cadillacs Toyotas hardscrabble brain.
Fire on lake.
I am Kwanzaa Bed Sty delight
Crown Heights cool out
Santa Cruz hilltop Zen patchouli Eros.
I am over easy short order
grill man
Constitutional equality's sweet American promise
Tennessee moonshine glass
pickle jars
Christmas Day Seattle 1989
hot coffee Puget Sound sea breeze.
Red Marlboro carton.
I am child of God
grandpa's empty cigar boxes

potato latkes apple sauce always power
of prayer.
Volkswagen day glo van.
Carlos Santana guitar pick excellence.
I am Ohio highway at dawn
Laura Nyro tapedeck urban soul.
Navy carrier Theodore roosevelt flight
crew savvy.
Goddess spirit tapestry.
Perfection bold 18 wheel essence.
Cherokee tribal land sanctity
I am Duke Ellington's Nutcracker Suite
Christmas Day
prairie solitude like cotton weave
overtime Thursday paycheck
Abraham's holy desert covenant.
I am Washington Square Park
marble arch poets
C-Note Bar Hoe-down calico heart
on sleeve
I am next week's New Year's
full sail soiree
Woodstock Sunday afternoon mythic
drum circle.
Eye on cobalt blue horizon.
American sweet cake optimism
bound for glory grace
Open Road.

God Set Me Free

God Set Me Free
in short bolt gray Manhattan avenues
panel wood barrooms
funky midtown parking lots.
MacDougal Street falafel joints.
Slaughter house Greeley Colorado vortex.
God Set Me Free
in Christmas Paramus shopping mall holocaust
poets room marijuana haze
hot wire Arkansas state line
2 am freak out.
God Set Me Free
in American computer gulag
go go greed stock market
scorched mythic January Kansas prairie
sea shells like diseased cattle
ear lobes
wire trash can stale brioche
silk shirt TV talk show hosts
New Age crystal amulet con game.
God Set Me Free
from December house arrest
Vietnam resistance barbed wire nightmares
Charleston, South Carolina slave auction block
ecstasy tab M.F.A. poets
yes to Amherst Emily Dickinson singularity
yes to Walt Whitman American calico
honey suckle dream
yes to Ernest Hemingway sparse hard drive genius
sweet Walden Pond Thoreau earth vibrations.
God Set Me Free
from crack house aficionados
large suburban bank mortgages
entendo children
thousand spoil brat desires.
God Set Me Free
from Memphis highway rush hour fly by.
Bloomsberg, Pennsylvania Saturday night
Main Street graveyard.

stale Kit Kat bars.
God Set Me Free
from fashion design Methodist church goers
mirror narcissism Gristides grocery lines
poets read like old time
railroad waiting room
incessant stammers
cheap cigars cigarette butts
cold 50 cent coffee.
God Set Me Free
like Illinois night ride
Chicago bound Sunday miracle rain
heartland roast turkey notions
Jesus' Midwest garden providence.
Montana 500 mile freight train roll
Orange blossom honey
Red Zinger tea
Deborah's bedroll kisses.
Ohio River icebound grace.
God Set Me Free
Pacific Coast highway laid back hitchhike
bring on warm magnolia morning smiles
millennium wide brim jubilee
1958 Charlie Parker bebop celebration.
God Set Me Free, Yes!

Fly Away

Fly Away
to California Big Sur ocean magic
funky Lenox Avenue
black hip-hop saint street corner
Brother Marc's Woodstock blue shutter
gingerbread cottage.
Fly Away
to Albuquerque South Valley
moist kisses white light desert heal
round shoulder caress.
U of New Mexico morning coffee prophesy.
Fly Away
to Paris 5th floor flat
American English typewriter hum
hot espresso one sugar.
Cool Sonny Rollins American tenor saxophone.
Fly Away
to Caribbean bound liberation
cotton sail full spinnaker
all day run.
Salt ocean sky providence
tiller right hand firm.
Fly Away
to Terre Haute, Indiana 12 step
soda pop grace
55th Street gourmet Chinese food
with folks.
Bold St. Mark's Place tattoo.
Jane's New Years Eve cool bop kisses.
Fly Away
to late night Herbie Hancock
jazz piano resonance
October velvet New Jersey poet
room courtship.
Fly Away
with prophet Jeramiah's kick back
cherry tomato revelation
providence like Kansas City highway
clover leaf shoe lace incantations

faith like stacked oak wood cupboard.
Fly Away
like western milk train groove,
New Age oracles, Ben Franklin American
renaissance dream, bologna and cheese on toast.
Greenhaven inmates fire visions.
Fly Away
like full laundry cart
corner federal mailbox phone bill deposit
full house poker hand
sweet kings aces.
Wrightsville, North Carolina moist southern kisses
urban frontier voodoo First Avenue.
Yorkville quiet storm.
Youth's Chevy engine resilience freedom.
No digital high tech gulag tar and feather.
No heroin fracture holocaust.
Fly Away
to Quebec City snow boots strong
feminine calves honest clean sheets
fire radiator English French pocket dictionary
B&B cognac shots.
Fly Away
from psychiatrist brain distortion
borderline stance money pocket hustle.
Embrace green poetic delight
cool Nevada desert motel shower
Oklahoma blue sky hosannas,
College Station, Texas rib eye dinner
Cherokee earth wisdom.
Fly Away
to blueberry muffin heart, Cancun shrimp,
full mon dream,
Jane's New Year's Eve knee socks.
Fly Away
like slow simmer mushroom omelet
Laura Boss' April afternoon sweet phone call,
Key Food grocery delivery
full Missouri Exxon gas up liberation
Fly Away, Dig it.

Embrace 1

I embrace God's chicory sanctity
Navy fighters' two o'clock eastern horizon
fourth grade soccer league mud
Chelsea field.
Hot chicken chow mien.
poets clean and sober 12-step serenity.
I embrace sexy high heel women
Emily Dickinson Amherst October
dried flowers.
Glass jar tomatoes wood
farmhouse cupboard.
PTA drive cats eye excellence.
I embrace soulful blues dudes
Memphis to sweet Chicago
Muddy Waters, Sonny boy Williamson
oven gingerbread, black eyed peas,
Delta guitar pick,
Jack Daniels firecracker jubilee, Navaho blanket.
Righteous big bone mama.
I embrace wheelchair Vietnam vets,
honor and valor, football blood scrimmage
Santa Barbara parking lot.
God bless!
I embrace Flo Kennedy cool whip comeback
no chocolate body hospital wires
kick bottom Kansas City ghetto fire
savvy like ham hock, collard greens,
and yes homemade pumpkin pie,
Dashiki mentor, heart queen.
I embrace red neck blue collar
trailer park
crescent moon late light serenity
Carbondale, illinois garden night sky.
Zen meditation.
Ice Maxwell House. Interstate 70 Rocket Ride.
Mississippi River wetlands. Wilderness grace.
I embrace Savoy Lounge, bartender Ellen,
blues lady calico down beat cool.
Tape worm thirst V.O. shot
Johnny Walker straight up

Ninth Avenue frontier glide. Easy smile.
I embrace St. Mark's Church
open mythic reading
bring on ghosts of Jack Kerouac
visionary Allen Ginsberg
hard ride Gregory Corso.
Yes angels hover like truck stop
hitchhiker trash can fire.
Houston Street on road hobos.
I embrace Bob Feldman Central Park
band shell tenor saxophone delight.
Back beat Charlie Parker chops like
125th Street Lenox Avenue fire.
I embrace work shirt passion
Belfast, Maine redemption
Walden Pond self reliance
Mamaroneck winter dry dock sloop,
City Island full steamers basket.
Long Island Sound salt air freedom.
I embrace Myna's cherry pie kindness
Daily Word prayers
Greenwich Village bebop tattersall hip sway
late night West 3rd Street sushi
porcelain saki shots.
New Jerusalem fire
flat bed truck wide load down
Second Avenue.
Bohemian mythic big wheel turn. Yes.

My Ship Comes In

My Ship Comes In
round mouth hooters beatnik
cool bop celebration
American apple pie.
No gift-wrap Lord and Taylors love
no stock market tight lip affection.
My Ship Comes In
Boston cream pie doubles
Jersey side river fresh syrup air
Sturdy Rhodes 19 sloop, Antigua bound.
No November wilderness hit and run death
no Long Island cemetery casket
no 19th precinct strip search
no North Atlantic scurvy.
My Ship Comes In
Ezra Pound metaphor tapestry wail.
Patterson gritty Islamic faith.
Hot dogs on cheap, mustard, Indian relish
velvet California night dreams.
No barb wire corpses
no cold weather sweats
no Q.E.2 wide berth muscle.
My Ship Comes In
no napalm in melon skull
no apple dunk corporate brainwash
yes to free range bound embrace
yes to Montana glory, split pea soup, croutons.
I-40 New Mexico state line.
Cash in denim pocket.
My Ship Comes In
Sweet Pitsfield, Massachusetts cirrus sky
Joan's scotch plaid punk aesthetic
parking lot rubber screech NASCAR crescendo.
My Ship Comes In
City Island fried clams feast
Marjories' fire like round late afternoon
Hackettstown sun.
My Ship Comes In
no to upstate war games
no paint bullets

adolescent tin soldiers.
No to upper class sirloin steak
top shelf snob attitude.
My Ship Comes In
Colorado wildflower Rocky Mountain
afternoon kisses.
Pine cabin cool flesh on flesh.
My Ship Comes In
Mayflower Plymouth Rock first
holy Thanksgiving.
20-year-old poet's young buck
apple pie bravado
Clinton Street Generation X sweethearts
stove pipe legs canter.
Woodstock Tinker Street first snow
Brother Marc's funky blue sutter cottage.
Hot rod Suzuki motorbike.
My Ship Comes In
no more checker table crumbs
no long crow's next night watch
no deadbeat mad dog snarls.
My Ship Comes In
Jesus' rainbow sanctity
J.C. Penney store bought flannel shirt
Lake Hoosatanic dawn bark
canoe paddle
Zen satori excellence
Denver bound poetic freight train
paprika heart liberation always.
My Ship Comes In.

Can It

Can bantam weight red brick
university ignorance
Hollywood Cineplex delusion
fashion model dialects.
Can revolutionary stone masquerade
drive to destroy sacred brain synapses
Reddi Whip nitrous oxide rush.
Can Varick Street Saturday night
sex orgies
film maker just bring cash fantasy
anorexic fascination with dinner time
soup can
internet black hole computer addiction.
Can lust for spandex
pretty people
MTV corporate music aesthetic
40 year march put down,
American green wilderness
spoil brat suicide cop out.
Can quick fix women's magazine
makeup counter cosmology.
Feminist Prozac red wine victim psychosis.
Columbus Avenue ecstasy foot soldier brainwash
heroin nickel bag aesthetic
Avenue A bohemian conformity.
Can iron submarine mind
gray pit bull classroom anarchy
no respect for hard work parents
sixties Vietnam vet Purple Heart valor
black Red Sty gray hair
street corner sages.
Can Second Avenue gorilla yelps
hog-tied hatred
Enron CEO Aspen ski house greed,
Wall Street three card monte hustle
mythic literature, cobble excellence
lunch bucket craft disdain.
Can Sesame Street let it flow commotion
Earth scorch high school ecstasy

mambo narcissism mirror
funhouse.
Jungle mud sexual daisy chains.
Daily Absolute Vodka drunks.
Can American history ignorance
yes to James Madison, New Deal FDR
1930's great dust bowl depression
yes to freedom time America city on hill.
Can Plato's cave barb wire ignorance
hate America crowd
hip hop milque toast poetics
hate parents vortex.
Can revolutionary consumer side show
daddy charge card grease paint jubilee.
Cell phone big time wannabe hustle.
Can punk two bit muscle gangland
cocaine deals
downtown heroin hustle.
Embrace mythic highway angels
Colorado wildflower heart
12-step clean and sober gratitude.
Embrace ethics, morals,
pinewood values like Missouri
soy bean farmer.
Embrace straight line lower forty
October harvest
cherry pie repentance. Amen.

Blessed

Blessed is Noah's Ark holy flood redemption
fragile southbound Canadian geese
New England griddle BLT sandwiches
Colorado rail track horizon virtue
poker steady hand. Straight shooter.
Blessed are derelict poets
eye on New Mexico sky curve
chop and dice metaphors
flannel sleeve ace hot oatmeal smile.
Freedom time America.
Blessed are Vietnam vet wheelchair cadre
Arkansas lightning revelation
Huck Finn mythic Mississippi wood raft
Earl Warren court equality
Madison Avenue corner curb cut.
Winter solstice butterscotch sunlight.
Blessed are grade school kids
penchant for sweet Michael Jordan
Chicago Bulls
Dizzy Gillespee trumpet scales
Tuesday afternoon bebop glide
President George W. Bush West Texas heart.
Eastbound dawn Massachusetts Turnpike
black Harlem corner food co-ops
sassy Eastern Parkway Haitian women.
Blessed are homeless fringe saints
hunger for clean sheets
New Jerusalem spare change
any old time
gingerbread home notions
faith like rainbow lunch bucket providence.
Corduroy Episcopal grace.
Blessed are guitar pickers from cocky
Austin to rock steady east coast
Greenwich Village, green-eyes tears
Cheshire lady silk caress
straight back bedroom chair
cotton skirt spirit trailblazer.
Jack Kerouac textured word on paper

passion, white line Pacific coast
highway satori.
Blessed are mentally ill O.K. Corral angels,
brain synapse, commotion, November
ridge line, Vincent Van Gogh genius.
God's children deep into Manhattan night
broad chest hospital gown
God's carousel delight compassion.
Blessed are Marion Federal Prison
hoodoo boys
discipline like Benedictine monks
jailhouse lawyers
mythic novel on hunt and pick typewriter
taut clothes line.
Saturday night blood impulse redemption.
Blessed are Yorkville moms
Second Avenue coffeehouse
blue river run strollers
warm milk bottle wizards
nursery rhyme poetics.
Clean cut honeycomb choir girls
straight line 10th Avenue wind chimes.
Blessed are can-do US Marines
cherry pie Delta Force
F-16's over Afghanistan
12 step prayer St. Mark's Place
T-bone serenity.
Fallow Iowa pasture
thousand pine tree resurrections
toothpaste over white teeth.
Blessed are Joseph Brodsky elegant poetic texts
bound like easy Martha Graham
dance glide
Radio City Rockettes leggy cool
Sweet South Carolina fried chicken perfection.
Gospel black eye peas.
Blessed, bring it home!

East Coast Underground

I Am East Coast Underground
round shoulder flannel shirt warrior colors
hot wire down I-95 Maryland
crab cakes hot sauce God's easy
harness covenant
beatific back beat 52 year old
hand slow motion
South Carolina easy glide.
I Am East Coast Underground
pinewood consciousness
Richmond bound denim lap
T.S. Eliot poems.
Motel 6 door sawed off shotgun
Fordham University alternative radio
Claudia Marshall WFUV velvet morning delight.
No ecstasy trip city freaks
no cocaine fashion model
no steroid weight lift gorillas
I Am East Coast Underground
Manhattan straight fix avenue
beatitude Bleecker Street Cheshire muse
Brigid Murnaghan gin joint
Washington Square Park hoe-down.
No Mick Jagger parody
no lite FM cauliflower car
no black leather gangster hip hop poetics.
I Am East Coast Underground
beat down AIDS plague
grass rooms C-Note Bar guitar pick
open mike.
Washington Square Park fire leaves.
Delta blues Tribeca Saturday morning
coffee raps 1979.
Hot lentil soup December wool mittens.
East Village serendipity.
I Am East Coast Underground
no corporate death grasp
no Washington DC politico's fandango
No left wing revolutionary cadre heroin

addict suicide.
I Am East Coast Underground
Nags Head salty air sublime
Wright Brothers' Kitty Hawk genius.
Wrightville Beach southern kisses.
Jewish chicken soup rebirth.
I Am East Coast Underground
Scotch plaid punk rockers serenade
Rock Hill, South Carolina easy April
spring vibrations kaleidoscope wonder.
Poetic flame keeper
Greek diner shish kabob.
I Am East Coast Underground
cirrus sky flight angel
no black hole internet
no Vogue magazine fashion brain wash
Barnes and Nobles corporate censorship.
Brown University illiterates.
I Am East Coast Underground
Virginia Beach cognitive thought
red brick Abraham Lincoln courage
south Georgia barn raise
New Jerusalem dream
tribe's heroic road quest.

Nation Building

Nation Building
Philadelphia mortar colonial brick
broad shoulders Monday night football
barn raise Iowa pasture
Lafayette Street wildcat poets.
Nation building pinewood Kentucky log cabin
God's Karo syrup
sweet Houston Street pool hall finesse.
Mythic John Glenn space
lemon meringue orbit
Oneida Indian hi-rise steelworker grace
back beat Charlie Mingus excellence.
National Building
Pony Express depot shower
hot grub prairie deep sleep.
Bronx hometown shanties
patchwork aluminum siding
kerosene lamp prophetic glow
like holy Catholic angels.
Nation Building
Baggott Inn acoustic jam
Sunday steel string afternoons
American cobble genius
President Bill shucks clams
Monica's high stakes puppy love.
Nation Building
Peace Corps volunteers tangerine hearts
2nd grader library card sanctity
St. John's University basketball
hip savvy.
Nation Building
heroes fall like stale potato chips
rooftop dive bomb pigeons
heroes gone Martin Luther King
sweet Bobby Kennedy.
No mix master dream
no internet digital harness
no hip pocket rattle snake

jeep four by four yuppie gorillas.
Nation Building
Tuesday night long hair revolutionary's surface
Gibson guitar broad hip.
California righteous reefer.
Baby boom laid back blues riff.
Yes to life, liberty, pursuit of
railroad happiness
American sweet water dream, thousand hosannas.
Nation Building
Jones Beach autumn dusk jam
wet navel orange caress
November knit sweater
Jack Kerouac literary bebop.
We the People amen.
Grass roots Turkish Taffy highway revelation.
Oklahoma Interstate 40.
Embrace Huck Finn outlaw soul
Apple pie Becky Thompson
Memphis trumpet boys
wino beat saxophone poets
Nation Building
knock out corporate three-card monte game
Babylon's tar pit university holocaust
embrace W.E.B. Dubois kick bottom
salvation quest
James Baldwin Harlem literary excellence.
Delaware Water Gap garden green ecstasy.
Nation Building always.

Too Early In Morning

Too Early In Morning
for Sunday Second Avenue bebop serenade
diamond head church choir
senior citizen's hallow trek
Gristedes super market 5 am.
Too Early In Morning
for cool breeze featherbed dawn
hemp rope leash collie
corner Greek diner Sunday
Chi chi brunch menu.
Too Early In Morning
for Horrace Silver Quintet jazz weave
phone call to Laura Boss
New Jersey Hudson River sanctity.
Pagan earth hold magic ritual
paper clip logic.
Too Early In Morning
Mohammed's tobacco kiosk.
Sunday milk craft watch.
Morning ocean salt kisses
Bette's Portsmouth, New Hampshire pinewood
friend letter write
puff cloud thigh caress 5 am.
Too Early In Morning
for Sunday I-40 Oklahoma highway dream
Gil Scott Heron D.C. poetic fire
truck stop virtuoso red neck integrity
Fort Lee gas jockey like bebop sage.
Manhattan Sunday downtown madcap
bus rev up.
Too Early In Morning
for funky Tony's beatific whiskey rap
Joe Williams croon 1958.
Fitzpatrick Bar
hitching post holy alcoholic vortex,
clinical brain chemistry paranoia.
Double dose pink lithium tabs.

Too Early In Morning
for thick ten pound Sunday
New York Times
fresh red Marlboro pack
cut rate poetry gossip
velvet Greenwich Village barroom
Bleecker Street cowboy resonance.
Too Early In Morning
for NFL pro football warrior
blue tango
block long Chelsea Pier overland trek
buttered daybreak sesame bagel
hot Yorkville coffee 5 am.
Too Early In Morning
for Volvo liberation from cousin
Stevie Gold's parking garage
November Central Park pumpkin harvest
trail quest like Lewis and Clark expedition.
Too Early In Morning
for 1969 Vietnam era fracture
blood ritual nightmare vanish,
Texas panhandle America howdy.
86th Street homeless Bobby
odd job hustle.
Too Early In Morning
for Miles Davis excellence vinyl record
Times Square juke joint quintessential cool
last call.
Too Early In Morning
for promised land Colorado tumbleweed dream
salvation's angelic stovetop hot
Cream of Wheat
firm hand on karmic wheel.
Yes, 5 am. Too early.

Pinewood Sanctity

I am dry vermouth
Staten Island open air landfill
gray January afternoon. Marlboro Cigarette smoke.
I am Tholonius Monk electric
piano delight
Macaroni and cheddar oven bake.
I am computer free cognitive
Rand McNally road map serendipity
college of hard knocks
East End Avenue 26 year psychiatric gulag
I am union high rise welder Tom's
rock steady craft
open gate iron graffiti parking lot
Manhattan fandango.
I am child of calico God
canvas gunny sack magic tricks
surburban swimming pool terra cotta tile swan dive.
I am desolation angel's cobalt passion
firm hardware store handshake
diner glass door seven layer cake
Myrna New Testament bible faith.
I am Count Basie big band
jazz swing excellence
Gil Coggins piano sublime
senior citizens plaid dignity
like upstate Rhinebeck oak tree.
Nevada desert flatland sonic boom.
I am Lexington Avenue taxicab
downtown midnight scoot
meat loaf, mashed potatoes, illustrious corn,
always seconds.
Ford pickup gun rack, hunt rifles,
barroom plywood wall deer antlers.
Bathroom rococo cabinet, dental floss.
I am garden providence faith
tape measure Shea Stadium home run

I am flannel shirt patriot
John F. Kennedy American vision
hot coffee no sugar
Mary Lou Williams piano damn
straight genius.
I am poet on wood stage
literary reins taut like
Montana rancher
heartbreak like saltine crackers
frozen Milky Way candy bar
Saturday night New Jersey Red Oak
Diner cheeseburger.
I am skateboard cacophony
mental illness blood cake warrior
Central Park winter tundra. Violet surprise.
Black bible revelation.
I am sweet pinewood sanctity.

Oh Big River

Oh Big River
cathedral excellence hot Sunday biscuits
white picket fence
black school notebook
New Rochelle sublime baseball
pick up game.
Oh Big River
Keith Jarrett bring it home genius
baby boom generation blood holocaust
magazine perfume samples.
Mark McGuire home run supreme.
Oh Big River
soft November current riverboat delight
white poodle faith
Hannibal, St. Louis, Sweet Cairo
roll on promised land wonder
Omaha Beach kick bottom heroes
Khe San Vietnam rock and roll valor.
Oh Big River
Mark Twain Missouri big river
literary genius.
Bring on three card monte poetics
soft shell crabs, potato and salad
nine bucks flat out.
Oh Big River
heartland texture Ford pickup
sturdy gun rack,
psycho ward soft boiled eggs.
Oh Big River
American Moses Thomas Jefferson
Declaration of Independence genius.
New York City hot dog and mustard
11th Avenue overdrive longshoreman
muscle banter
classy lover's crows feet

Queen Elizabeth cruise ship
Laura Boss' Hudson River horizon eyes.
Oh Big River
iron ore barge bark canoe
Memphis black street corner prophets
W.C. Handy trumpet blues get down.
Elvis pre U.S. Army brilliance. 1956.
Oh Big River
destiny like Tennessee short order cook
Carbondale, Illinois red white and blue
holy American flags
gift shop magic trinkets.
Brown delta thighs. Soft breast curve.
Oh Big River
Mississippi, Ohio, Missouri,
bring it on home like pioneer vortex.
Huck Finn outlaw heart.
Black Jim's New Orleans freedom quest.
Oh Big River
grand calf birth republic's liberty
a million heartland dreams.

Gabriel Blow Your Horn

Gabriel Blow Your Horn
in Constitutional America, hometown
barber shop, VFW plywood halls,
local Woolworth five and dime.
Gabriel Blow Your Horn
in western Pennsylvania green valleys
tobacco shops worn girlie magazines
automobile repair shops
square deal tune up oil change.
Gabriel Blow Your Horn
for Allen Ginsberg desolation hipsters
14th Street after hours gin joint
elegant Park Avenue cat house
corporate board rooms like Rubic cube.
Sunlight psycho ward January gymnasium.
Gabriel Blow Your Horn
for broken souls garbage dumpster quest.
4th grade soccer champions
World Cup trophy glory dream teamwork
like kick bottom Army 101st Airborne.
Gabriel Blow Your Horn
for car-pool moms twenty hardscrabble
miles each corn flake day
kid's ballet lessons karate sweat workouts
Nighttime spiral notebook homework.
Gabriel Blow Your Horn
in God's infinite glory
Tennessee pine top providence.
Bob Feldman magic saxophone
French avant garde cinema
Bleecker Street buy back cool.
Gabriel Blow Your Horn
for hyacinth Zen madmen
New Jersey crack addicts
down east Maine blueberry patch rehabilitation

Jack Kerouac typewriter imagination hum.
Dizzy Gillespie bebop trumpet grace.
Gabriel Blow Your Horn
No September prairie roadhouse dice load.
No quick talk used car lot
carney dudes.
No dinnertime telemarket hustle.
Gabriel Blow Your Horn
in Rocky Mountain April wonder
mountain stream cold water like country
porcelain bathtub.
Cherry high altitude crystalline air.
Baby boom women's apple pie grace.
Gabriel Blow Your Horn
for America's promised land heart
freedom like bald eagle big sky
northern California
hot home cook meal
gingham Louisiana delta skirt caress
Manhattan holy covenant night wind chimes.
Gabriel Blow Your Horn.

Embrace 2

I embrace Laura Boss's beatnik black
skirt hips
round goalkeeper shoulders
Hudson River edge passion
pantry shelf can of corn
crisp January afternoons.
I embrace poetic excellence
Billy O's downtown golden oldies night ride
beatific Fitzpatrick Bar raps like
Yorkville outback tapestry weave.
I embrace post office runs for American
flag halcyon stamps
20 cent post cards
always soulful smile California dream
postal clerk.
I embrace Betsy Harrington's elegant
poem craft like Oklahoma gingham
clear heartland cirrus sky,
I embrace revolutionary karmic wheel turn
vintage Triumph sports car
52nd birthday nine days resonant
morning horizon.
I embrace God's gun tote justice
ten commandment Georgia riot act
bread truck essence.
Lower East Side Saturday afternoon
cobble joy.
I embrace calico metaphor
empty old time milk bottles
June lace curtains Santa Cruz dream
thick chocolate milkshake home fries
Illinois prairie freight train thrust.
I embrace East Coast Jazz Poetry
Explosion cool
Bob Feldman's tenor sax easy glide

all day suckers
Nuyorican Poet's Café hardscrabble mambo
twilight crystalline vibrations.
Julio's two-fisted wit.
I embrace mythic Martin Luther King
Civil Rights liberation quest
non violent Mississippi resistance
arch back sharecropper liberation
poetry road freedom.
I embrace mom with metal stroller
kid's break down brick wall love
milk bottle
sanctity carrot sticks scotch plaid
small blanket.
I embrace American jazz consciousness
Ben Sidron vocal bebop like
Kyoto silk kimono
Horace Silver revolutionary kick bottom 1970
New Paltz country road excellence
cool tap Budweiser
cocktail waitress's sturdy ankle
juke box Joni Mitchell brilliance
snowbound Vermont winter field.

Free

I am
no Fifth Avenue apartment silk sheets
chestnut hair elegant dame in arms
Metropolitan Museum thousand dollar ticket
black tie open snap to
monkey suit doorman
I am
no Brooks Brothers button down
London Fog tan trench coat
cocktails at Westbury Hotel.
I am
no New York City class act
Christmas Day Don Pedro cigar eloquence
Lutecé table for two.
I am
no upper class cashmere sweater
blue moon Sundays honcho's, rare like
Sparks Steakhouse sirloin
Madison Square Garden courtside tickets
sweet Knicks rolling thunder.
I am
no Ambacrombie and Fitch telescope
wicker basket champagne set
Four Seasons Restaurant New Years'
three martini literary talk.
I am
no top shelf Remy Martin
Oak Room hardwood Plaza Hotel clan.
I am
no old man's five star world
Grand Central Oyster Bar
Algonquin Hotel Dorothy Parker
round table tae.
I place aside raspberry soufflé
10 dollar Italian cheesecake

shiny green forest Rolls Royce
French Champagne.
Bring on brother Colorado highway brilliance
hobo fires down by mythic Hudson
bring on brother homeless fringe oracles
Brooklyn Sister Teresa waitresses
beehive hair cocaine beauticians
bring on brother late 20th century howl
poetic Marlboro cigarette
Avenue A cheap wine night ramble
bring on brother parking lot
Dominican sidemen
golden racket boys.
Fitzpatrick Bar holy Budweiser
and shooter oracles
bring on brother Saturday night downtown
Number Six-train rolling thunder rumble.
Lexington and 29th Street righteous
street hookers.
I am free like Battery Park sea breeze
feather in thin hair
hand on Cheshire lady's small waist.
Pacific coast highway hitchhike groove
Colorado wildflower grace
Woodstock October fire tree magic.
I am free, yes.

Millennium Weave

I am millennium weave
Georgia gospel choir
God's miracle quicksilver grace
whole wheat pancakes stack
old man's Dick Tracy hat
clip on bow tie
Jesus' Galilee miracle.
Gospel highway melody.
I am millennium weave
Beach Boys good vibrations
Huntington Beach mythic surf
Crosby Street narrow back alley providence.
Albert's Washington Square Park comedy outrage.
I am millennium weave
Joseph's multi color dream coat
New Hampshire cherry wood loom
rainbow tapestry.
December Tuesday morning alive like
Emily Dickinson Amherst forsythia garden
small snake.
Walt Whitman Brooklyn Ferry salvation
I am millennium weave
egg rolls, duck sauce, cool Pepsi
24 liter bottle.
Robert Frost poetic passion
mended wood fence
Middlebury, Vermont snow squall.
I am millennium weave
Georgia O'Keefe bold flowers
New Mexico desert magic pastel Eros.
86th Street cowpoke Lexington serenity
hopscotch Second Avenue
I am millennium weave
Guggenheim paint on canvas grace
American artistic vision like Kansas sunflowers

full bloom serenade.
Norman Rockwell Thanksgiving grace.
I am millennium weave
garden hyacinth excellence
corduroy tykes
chocolate ice cream smiles
grade school crowd nylon knapsacks
key chain breakfast sesame bagel
and cream cheese.
I am millennium weave
long cobble road years
God's holy heart covenant.
Satan's battle scars like 1945
Okinawa shrapnel.
Joni Mitchell genius vision
clamshell word clip T.S. Elliot
crystalline images lily pad
fire in brain like old time
railroad coal furnace.
I am millennium weave
resonant string bass hope
compassion like Salvation Army shelter
parking lot beatitude
ecstasy's Navaho spirit wonder.
City on round hill.

Rooster Crows

Rooster Crows
highway song head shave California
skate board ocean boardwalk dream
Hanukkah Morse code like potato latkes
purple sidewinder candles.
Rooster Crows
ball point pen ironing board
legal pad jump start like Mt. McKinley
trail ascent.
5th grade Christmas vacation school return.
Rooster Crows
dawn breaks
no overland demon, boogie man darkness
no anorexic Chanel style girls
no office Yule tide party
slow float.
No computer combine straightjacket.
Rooster Crows
joy like blueberry muffins hip pocket cash
grandma's sugar coat wolf baby boom
ecstasy weave.
Rooster Crows
begin like Andrew Wyeth blank canvas.
Saint Peter's Jesus' chicken scratch denial
December horizon wax candles
home made four-alarm chili.
Rooster Crows
push aside yellow starch sheet
square Kleenex box, cornflakes and
milk always.
Demons hand man noose.
Rooster Crows
kick despair like flat tire delay
bring home fluffy calico cat
rev up new millennium weave.
Haul across west Texas plains
become crimson self
again and again.

Straight Shooter

I am straight shooter
New Mexico tough desert wildflowers
hands on blueberry patch poetics
right 13-year-old wrist I.D. bracelet
Las Vegas ace of hearts blackjack
hole face to face
Allen Ginsberg revelation.
I am straight shooter
barroom Johnny Walker shuck and jive
Indian pine grove quiescence
Moses' promise land holy salvation quest.
Baked ziti, garlic bread, Chianti, checkered
red tablecloth.
I am straight shooter
erotic love passion baby oil
puff cloud.
Flannel layer railroad man integrity.
Manhattan night kick bottom bravado
Congressman John Conyors Michigan
ghetto fire.
I am straight shooter
Zimbabwe elephant memory
Charlie Parker bebop quiescence cool.
Christmas Jesus' manger holy birth
Hosanna Hosanna
velvet Laura's short order late
night raps.
Yorkville moist riverfront kisses.
I am straight shooter
call red spade damn trick
red spade.
No ivy university ecstasy tab linguistics
no Yale University grunge sidewinders.
No ice coffee shots, words like mud
New Rochelle anthill
no Metro North Grand Central bound
rush hour gulag.

I am straight shooter
humble like Zen beggar eye like
painter Marc Chagall
God's Montogmery Alabama back beat redemption
Charlie Mingus 52nd Street juke joint bass.
I am straight shooter
No Louisville Kentucky bourbon excuses
no power plays like cocaine
Yorkville bartenders.
Yes to Sardi's velvet nightcap
yes to Greenwich Village 4am ham and eggs.
I am straight shooter
cut the apple pie
Bronx schoolyard bone dice
Mark Twain Mississippi River quiescence
no double entendre
no knife in flannel back
no French semiotics slow boat metaphor
political correct chairman Mao party line.
I am straight shooter
slow simmer leg of lamb
Diet Coke six pack
Denver August nights.
Big Sur beach head wax candle
highway passion like red Colorado
horizon surge
Sunday breakfast special.
A thousand rosary beads.
I am straight shooter, yeah!

Write A Poem

Write A Poem
on American fertile topsoil
dime store spiral notebook
greasy brown paper lunch bag.
Write A Poem
on Portsmouth, New Hampshire harbor mooring
Woodstock Jerry Garcia tie dye t-shirt
December caterpillar spine.
Write A Poem
on lovers milk breast
Con Edison electric bill
Miami barbecue rib joint menu.
Write a Poem
on Guernsey cow wide flanks
Minnesota publisher rejection notice
IBM low-tech typewriter
Saturday afternoon upstate New York
snow squall.
Write A Poem
on Avenue B downtown graffiti wall
Columbus, Ohio Days Inn Motel room
bed cover
inner thigh elegant like pearl necklace
museum opening.
Write A Poem
on Jones Beach Coppertone white sand
Montauk lobster shack
sexy truck stop waitress's firm forearm.
Write A Poem
on sweet Tomasso's starch white shirt
western Kansas fallow wheat field
San Francisco Mission District greasy
spoon napkin
Thorazine medication tray.
Write A Poem

on singer songwriter Joni Mitchell's long
calico road years
Montclair State student cafeteria ride board
ballet dancer's ebony spine arch.
Write A Poem
on Federal courthouse steps
cereal corn flakes box
wide english umbrella
Timberland shoes sales receipt
Washington Square Park green wood bench
subway Metro Card
John Coltrane sheet music.
Write A Poem
on Tennessee whiskey still
House of Representative's daily docket
Visa card shopping binge bill
junk man's Rube Goldberg soda
can rig.
Write A Poem
on cirrus sky spirit integrity's straight
line road passion
Yale University bound senior thesis
wings of a dove.
Write a poem, yes!

Take My Heart Poems

Take My Heart Poems
like Greenhaven Prison poet laureate
hunger like Salvation Army soup kitchen
biscuit smells thick gravy satori.
Utah's silver mercy vibration winter
oak wood lean-to.
Take My Heart Poems
language like Marlboro lighter spark
wide eye gingham country ladies
ace of diamonds in long finger hand
leather bag cash
Dentine poetry text.
Take My Heart Poems
like city limits funky gin mill
Bronx go-go joint, Woodstock dream
Rosa Parks freedom ride courage
November Thanksgiving providence.
Take My Heart Poems
A Train subway late night ramble
El Paso, Texas east January dawn
school yard fence in
basketball hoop delight,
red lips hot chocolate down
parka sleeve.
Take My Heart Poems
like Irish Tom's crystalline wit
Central Park next month sleigh ride
bowling pin metaphor
player piano keys magic hum.
Take My Heart Poems
read *Wildflower Serenade*
holiday mad spree quiescence
beef barley soup on slow simmer
Irish Woodside Caily dance celebration
Angelo's Cornelia Street mythic poetry read.

Take My Heart Poems
Harlem beatific vision brown bag
hot chestnuts.
New York City gotham beatific revelation
nephew Charlie soccer player supreme
Hudson Pier riverfront serenity.
Take My Heart Poems
simile's broad horizon stretch
harvest moon eclipse Hale Bopp comet
whole grain pancakes short stack.
Take May Heart Poems
mythic kitchen table milk and cookies embrace
Brigid Murnaghan Back Fence poetry
barn raise.
Home boy wildcat fringe oracles
mythic words high tide slam poets.
Take My Heart Poems
revive hula-hoop antics
Pentecostal holy frenzy sharecropper burn
Round house passion.
Fire like Gregory Corso West 3rd Street howl
3am Hudson Street aesthetic raps
William Butler Yeats paper back brain
synapse groove.
Take My Heart Poems
leather bull whip liberation
Arkansas winter soul weave sanctuary
word on paper kaleidoscope transformation.
Read me

Revolutionary Kindness

No to President Bill Clinton easy
glide silk stocking hide out
stock market Wall Street double
deal hallucination
no to first grade computer semi
conductor gulag
no to fifty dollar bill mercenary
trumpet dude, mad Prozac poets
Lexington Avenue literary cut rate corpses.
No to feminist consciousness raising
velveteen cocaine victims 1998.
No to Palm Beach County hanging chads
no to marijuana Buddhist sandstone Maya,
New York Yankee World Series steroid
three Budweiser goosestep.
No to Barnes and Noble censorship
like 38 magnum silencers.
No to literary nepotism like
late August Eureka Springs flash floods.
No to Philly blunt high school
Hip-hop poets, Tommy Hilfinger charge
card consumer rebels.
No to paranoid cherry pie slice
no to out of orbit incest fantasy fracture
no to sexual harassment steel blue criminal court
law suit.
Hand in pocket East End Avenue psychiatrist.
No to $300 Italian soft leather loafers
Waldorf Astoria half shell power lunch.
I say yes to John Kennedy Hyannis, Massachusetts
resurrection
Colorado open freedom highway
American oatmeal excellence.
Fort Lee Mobile gas up.
I say yes to high heel corporate women

Tupelo honey cool grace
God's straight line First Avenue
holy markers.
Front burner beef stew simmer
whole grain oven fresh bread
love's sweet New Mexico roadhouse embrace.
I say yes to stand by me
flannel friends
lunch bucket aesthetics
holy homeless oracles
mom's pinewood no nonsense spirit.
I say yes to wide angle
Indiana road smiles
fresh Ivory soap bar
Vermont maple fire trees
prophetic horizon like
prophet Isiah Old Testament cut pie witness.
I say yes to fallow Pennsylvania field,
denim shirt roll lace
mud Missouri workbooks
Wyoming cowboy ramble
soft boil egg glory train
Susan's upstate wildflower grace.
I say yes to sweet bluebird notions
round cheek salt tears
revolutionary kindness. Yes.

Breezin'

I am breezin' through
ginger bread house poetic ecstasy
Black Panther ham hock soul jubilee,
rabbit stew July Aix en Provence 1973.
National Rifle Association patriots
sassy 1960's ladies Rehoboth, Delaware
boardwalk April promise.
I am breezin' through
warrior feminist prairie fire gender
equality quest
Avenue A tire skid marks heart
I am breezin' like
I-40 Tennessee Smokey Mountain
corncob hillbilly beatitude.
Thanksgiving turkey candy yams
wide open cranberry sauce celery stuffing
home boy chops
Mayflower promise land salvation.
I am breezin' like George Benson
guitar sublime 1982.
Columbus, Ohio rock steady Republican quiescence
Friday night Bronx mad dog
twenty twenty.
I am breezin' like Baptist bible incantations
bake sale excellence
poetic down beat resonance
drug free holy bohemians
Thompson Street Wednesday afternoon
French kisses.
42nd Street shoe shine boy savvy
Manhattanville College library open stack
north star wonder.
Bob Dylan burn down house poetics 1965
late night cheeseburger deluxe.
I am breezin' beyond Satan's millennium

MILLENNIUM WEAVE

Hollywood cinema demon
three dollar bill
West Side heart bleed hypocrisy
charge card upper class polyester ball
and chain.
I am breezin' through Kansas
winter wheat mythic heartland
George W. Bush straight shoot courage.
Lincoln, Nebraska truck stop hot coffee
Table Talk cherry pie
homeward bound like calico cat.
New Orleans jambalaya good eats.
Tennessee Williams mythic dramatic text.
I am breezin' through frozen
lace boot New York Hospital
jailhouse solitude
Torah scroll sanctity God's chaparral grace.
I am breezin'
into orange prairie dusk highway glide
work a day heart language cadence
Saturday afternoon quilt comforter whispers
magic millennium weave limbs.
November half moon night.
I am breezin', dig it!

Stride Piano

I am Fats Waller barrel house
Stride Piano
Cotton Club finery 1936
God's infinite sugar donut deliverance.
I am lentil stew, turkey franks chow down
New York State Thruway
Suffern, New Paltz, Kingston.
Halloween candy leftovers Muddy Waters
blues jam.
I am highway night ride soul
denim long way home.
Marlboro dream.
Ella Fitzgerald scat delight cheap California
red wine
3 am night telephone rambles.
I am Niacin dose Valarium capsules
mental health high Sierras cure
instant Maxwell House cool ice coffee
Hank's Yorkville Fitzpatrick Bar raps.
Poetic azaela metaphors
word economy like Tide Detergent box.
Round shoulder velvet caress.
Che Guevera olive fatigue t-shirt
round breasts.
I am Sunday rain bone cleanse.
Susan's magic spirit Livingston Manor
letters 1970.
November morning Mr. Laydensack's senior
English class
J.D. Salinger fire, James Joyce consciousness
river flow.
4 pm kitchen daydream. Milk, cookies,
New York Times sports page.
I am push come to shove
steel wool discipline

Army Rangers Afghanistan heroics.
Special Ops valor.
Goodyear Tires, hot split pea soup.
San Francisco North Beach strip joint
watered down bourbon, spangles,
pasties wide hips, sugarland express.
I am Steinway piano mom's formal
living room
cool jazz dreams cocky fingers
wind chime ear melody texture.
Paul McCartney groove 1964.
Tribe's Taos New Mexico rainbow quest
clarity like Nikon camera lens.
I am Promethean fire
jailhouse ball and chain white
sock ankle
ball cap poetics.
I am black cloak angel
Bradley Beach wood boardwalk 1967
straight shot like 59th Street Bridge
promise land Manhattan bound
Lafayette Street morning bacon and eggs.
Chapel Hill, North Carolina dream like
hot blueberry muffins
Yellowstone Old Faithful geyser magic
American deep well excellence.
I am Stride Piano on fire.

American Genius

American Genius
Elizabeth, New Jersey tool and die shop
lightning IBM mail room
beauty parlor Saturday afternoon commotion
Kankakee smooth silk freight train.
NYFD, police, Army Reserve, sweet EMS mythic
World Trade Center heroics.
American Genius
bebop jazz black Philly lunch
bucket soul
garbage man's elegant Viennese waltz.
Tough Delta Force kick bottom valor.
American Genius
teenage computer hackers
cognitive layer cool cobalt blue brain
Chelsea soccer field straight out heroics
shin guard mud oversize fray jersey.
American Genius
sassy singular leather sisters
Oak Room vodka martini straight up
clamshell, dream.
Hot milk bottle December infant
bundle up.
First Lady Laura Bush reading passion.
American Genius
Illinois heartland green garden
Little League Louisville slugger
home run crack
Richmond, Indiana ruck stop cheeseburgers.
Hoosier Interstate 70 heartland glide.
Waitress saint soothe road fever
coffee refill again and again.
American Genius
nephew Charlie's corduroy touchdown catch
November grid iron delight

old man's World War Two 45th Infantry
five battle stars.
GI's Vietnam rolling thunder valor.
Manhattan glory night Hindu taxi thrust
like barroom pinball machine.
American Genius
senior citizens greatest generation
Santa Fe, New Mexico Elk's Club
always card game schnapps shot
on sly.
American Genius
Korean sweet 86th Street stationery store
Ballpoint pens, jiffy mailers
funky fur bears.
Saint Ignasus Church Sunday communion.
American Genius
flannel Chevrolet outlaws
Jane's sculptor rack and pinion grace
Quaker quilt circle December wisdom.
President George W. Bush big sky
west Texas plain talk.
American Genius
in God we trust
Capital Hill silver trout excellence.
House of Representatives Speaker Danny Hastert
wrestling coach hard drive.
Tom Daschle South Dakota common
man ethics.
Oh American Genius
Pittsburgh steel mill
Hutchinson, Kansas holy wheat field
Harlem street corner gold tenor sax
always sublime chops.
American Genius.
Yes.

Cut The Pie

Cut The Pie
like Alabama sharecropper Mile Davis
bebop trumpet
wet sugar daddy lip suck
Corpus Christie midnight beach big
dipper dream.
Cut The Pie
like librarian sage, Mr. Clysennes sophomore
George Washington U.
tweed English teacher kick bottom passion.
Cut The Pie
Heartland America kid's lemonade stand.
city limits poetry crescendo Newark
literary frontier.
Combat boots multiple silver earrings.
take on technological three card monte dudes
sexy party girl's claim check heart
yuppie day trip cocaine power play.
Take on Hollywood brainwash
five dollar chi chi coffees
picket fence top shelf obsession.
Cut The Pie
like i-80 Ohio green August hillside
sweet Cleveland, Toledo, blues
time Chicago.
November Philadelphia hoagie
pretzel hot mustard
wacky street corner Mummers.
Cut The Pie
like Duke Ellington Band
A train sublime.
William Faulkner Mississippi September afternoon
veranda ice tea.
Bring on brain synapse photograph memory
calico cat curiosity heart on

sleeve aesthetics.
Bring on Wall Street mambo
Triboro Bridge breezing work shirt
fresh Wrigley's gum
James Joyce stream of consciousness genius.
Cut The Pie
like young Charles Bukowski hipsters
mythic Manhattan prairie quest
Jerry Garcia west coast cathedral excellence
California full moon July sanctity
corduroy pocket green cash
Miami sugar can low riders.
Cut The Pie
like dousing rod well water
prophetic quest
Las Vegas slot machine paradise
three lucky cherries.
Isiah's fierce homeboy vision
East Harlem rice and beans
D train Brooklyn bound.
Cut big old apple pie
like Michigan wolverine fire
New York Fire Department break down door
muscle.
Cut The Pie
like St. Valentine's Day's velvet hugs
Kansas City T-bone cool flesh
on flesh.
Cut The Pie, yes.

America Call My Name

America Call My Name
like cobble bebop Avenue A blood
red dawn.
D.C. Pennsylvania Avenue cheap burgers
overland Amtrak freight train.
Can do excellence.
American Call My Name
like Hudson River sublime essence
Kittery, Maine tar shack blue
collar liberation.
Hardscrabble opportunity like dozen fresh eggs.
Mass Pike easy dawn overdrive
Constitutional liberty's sweet pinewood essence.
America Call My Name
like madcap whiskey rappers
holy New York Hospital psychotics
paper slipper oracles.
Atlantic City gambling quick fix boys
whole wheat bread fresh strawberry preserves.
Hot January radiator.
Mike's SSI check on time like
Boston U.S. Air Shuttle.
Small town Main Street
Norman Rockwell genius.
America Call My Name
like Chicago gratitude, God's flannel
shirt grace.
Brooklyn chocolate egg creams
Sheepshead Bay fishing boat delight.
Samantha's China cut hair do
serenity like midnight Pacific Ocean dream.
California hitchhike 1969.
American Call My Name
I, a native son search for
carrion, warm Cheshire smile, Harry Truman

buck-stops-here courage.
No Vietnam era Jersey Turnpike psychosis
no politically correct tar and feather
no cold lentil soup
ball and chain.
America Call My Name
in urine tenement hallways
cat house plywood back rooms
Madison Avenue coffee kiosk
uptown prize fight liniment gym.
Mohammed Ali black man's poetics.
Vermont quilt cadence whispers
Ozark hillbilly twang.
One nation under God.
America Call My Name
no World Trade center mass murders
no Al Qaeda opium addicts
evil fracture terror.
No blue steel ambition freaks
Times Square bare Jack Daniels haze.
America Call My Name
Charlie Parker mastery like hot
wood stove.
Pakistani taxi driver green light fantasy
vagrant's rough sleep.
America Call My Name
in Plymouth Rock October.
Fire leaves tin can redemption.
University of Michigan Ann Arbor
Saturday football.
Bring it home like Sioux tribal ritual.
Soft shoe vaudeville innocence wide eye
first grader. Lunch box peanut butter
and jelly.
God's Washington Heights tabletop glory.
Sweet wide earring hoop
Latino ladies.

America Call My Name
like Tucumcari strip down desert road
32 road year outlaw heart
Manhattan East River heart
Colt 45 party on.
Marlboro morning outback smoke.
black street corner blues cats
ice bound Portland. Maine spinsters.
Cowboy poets Missoula to Laredo, Texas.
America Call My Name
like Ponderosa free-range optimism
freedom like Norfolk Navy liberty fandango.
Lester Young saxophone cool.
Call to me America
like youth's wildcat ideal notions
part-time job, Ford Mustang hot rod quiescence.
God, family, sweet country Iowa
corn field
Walden pond cathedral wilderness.
America call to me
I am yours.

Do Something Do Anything

Do Something Do Anything
read D.H. Lawrence into early morning
flannel dawn.
Learn French from elegant chic madam
cut Bartlett pear
place postage stamp on white envelop.e
Do Something Do Anything
rap with Savoy Lounge jazz cats
commit lilac revolution act on Astor place
subway station platform
make grill cheese sandwiches
for best friend's sister
watch Mississippi river like mad oracle
talk hog prices with Missouri farmers.
Do Something Do Anything
catch gypsy cab Harlem bound
dream through Metropolitan Museum like
gold angel
unclog bone porcelain sink.
Do Something Do Anything
learn new computer program outrage
cut waist high suburban Woodstock grass
discuss local hardware store ratchet and
screw driver aesthetics
drink three coffees buzz on
electric typewriter.
Do Something Do Anything
visualize one act dramatic play
8 am Second Avenue clarity.
Put twenty on Aqueduct Philly
suck on Budweiser bottle.
Do Something Do Anything
play magic saxophone Washington Square
Park vortex
kiss green eyed mountain woman
beyond velvet eternity road crescendo

howl poem at Brigid Murnahan's beatnik
home girl read
pan fry green okra.
Do Something Do Anything
hang Van Gogh print in four
corner bedroom
pick mentor's Illinois prairie brain
gas up at truck stop cathedral.
Do Something Do Anything
become self in thousand Buddhist wheel turn
express devotion to God funky beatnik prayer
shoemaker's hardscrabble craft.
Do Something Do Anything

God Sanctify Soul

God Sanctify Soul
hop cross-town bus Central Park
sky curve
hot wire Route 46 New Jersey.
God Sanctify Soul
Barnes and Noble grocery store books
crisp new twenty-dollar bills
Jack Kerouac Greenwich Village
spontaneous creation
apple crumb pie glass shelf
last solitary hearty slice
Hal Sirowitz deadpan read.
God Sanctify Soul
elegant banditos ear pierce outlaws
literary home girl soul mate.
86th Street holy homeless prophets.
Yugoslav Mikey's overnight raps.
God Sanctify Soul
green down vest flannel highway coat
full Mobile gas up.
Hemingway quick feet bullfight
K-Mart cashier
AFL-CIO black electrician beyond cool.
God Sanctify Soul
large white thread spool
pin cushion fluff
November Oklahoma red clay hills
wilderness dream.
Salvation Army soup kitchen compassion
elevator smile Bloomingdale's shopping bag.
Fulton Fish Market early morning
blue fish
long john's December wear.
God Sanctify Soul
Fort Lee Rad Oak Diner serendipity

Mississippi Civil Rights kick bottom courage
baby boom Vietnam resistance
Santa Cruz backcountry groove 1969.
God Sanctify Soul
spirit pumpkin pie repentance
front port cool
George Washington Bridge toll cashier
singular rainbow fantasy.
God Sanctify Soul
60 year old handsome racehorse women
like North Dakota plains stallions
New Mexico desert windmill field.
God Sanctify Soul
road long like Norfolk navy mooring.
Cornell Medical School surgeon's degree
Jesus' flat out faith heal.
God Sanctify Soul
Zen Buddhist zazen satori
wild blossom honey Hindu nirvana
5 am July Manhattan purple dawn
unlock thousand doors quicksilver begin.
God Sanctify Soul, dig it!

Wilderness Seekers

We are wilderness seekers
northern Arizona holy children
Jewish Sunday School starches shirt
daydream faith
midnight mustang corral.
We are wilderness seekers
rainbow essence like Tupelo honey
New Orleans April rain
square oven, hot cross buns.
Ben Franklin kite key electricity.
We are wilderness seekers
Mississippi River ethics
no wind up alarm clock
no Wall Street phone bank
ball and chain
No subway Number 6 Train breakdown.
We are wilderness seekers
essence like Pennsylvania July green valley
chamomile tea. Haight Asbury patchouli
incense burn. White light Islamic passion.
Warm gray army blanket. Pork chop dinner.
We are wilderness seekers
Zen mediation serenity
quest for eggs over easy truth
Hollywood Boulevard Motel 3 hour
sex it up stint.
Yes to sacred Hopi tribal rituals
reverence like Catholic choirboy
baby boom women's 1970 Cheshire heal
Louisville slugger faith
Martin Luther King's equality fire vision.
We are wilderness seekers.
Yes to America's more perfect union
yes to Ear Inn mussel steam Bordeaux red wine.
Baudelaire poetics.

We are wilderness seekers
sweetheart's pinewood hands, Colorado cumulus
cloud body, hazel eyes, ready hobo
railroad yard fire.
We are wilderness seekers
High Sierras snow melt dream
Steamboat syrup April afternoons.
125th Street saxophone small Latino kid
reading wiz.
We are wilderness seekers
warrior flannel soul mate quest
easy bell bottom laugh
Sylvia Plath poetics mythic
T.S. Elliot text, down beat Paris
Henry Miller.
We are wilderness seekers
marble Lincoln Memorial steps angel.
Gettysburg Address blood revelation
hip pocket cashews Bobby Kennedy
prophetic resonance midnight special
freedom train.
Georgia bound gospel barn raising faith.
Always American highway hot
oatmeal covenant.
We are wilderness seekers, yes.

Long Way Home

I am long way home
through God's January pine grove desolation
lit white Sabbath candles
Newark bebop jazz radio.
I am long way home
through acerbic computer hackers' grand delusion
plastic surgery hondo gals
500 dollars blue jean call girls.
I am long way home
through Michigan militia lock and load
outback left brain fracture cadre.
Mercer Street Manhattan deep kisses.
I am long way home
beneath L.L. Bean maroon quilt
full cancerian moon 83rd Street
Cherokee Trail
Montpelier Fred Lee's vodka glow
Hershey bar Route 3 sugar rush.
I am long way home
Prophet Isiah's apocalyptic vision
interstate highway flesh. Rose thorns.
Woo Woo shot, Shooters.
Miles Davis genius beyond ghetto
tenement despair
Jim Crow hang noose.
I am long way home
through Maryland highway markers
Saturday night Oklahoma City
Days Inn slumber
Sonny Bono hardscrabble heal 1970.
Palm Springs long hair hippie quiescence.
I am long wy home
through New Jersey Holland Tunnel Texaco
gas up
Jehovah's witness concrete 51st Street

subway platform testify.
I am long way home
like Jane's unclasped brassiere, New Year's Eve
1991.
Back seat young buck virgins.
San Diego California red hot burritos
linoleum floor bedroll camp out.
I am long way home
through William Blake prophetic vision
Mescalito golden July afternoons.
Virginia Beach gentle surf
Jack Kerouac literary beatnik hipster grace.
I am long way home
through Sunday paper stack
cheese omelet delight.
Vietnam Veterans bound for glory
true grit
Philadelphia liberty bell freedom.
I am long way home
through Indiana pine grove quiescence
Bellevue straight jacket lock up
sleeping pill hard core short bolt
magnolia heart demon fracture.
I am long way home.

Parking Lot Satori

I am parking lot satori
old man's GI Bill business savvy genius
God's flannel shirt redemption
Solomon's desert wisdom.
November Manhattan cirrus sky.
I am parking lot satori
hot breakfast wheateena
North Carolina moist kisses like angel
food cake.
I am parking lot satori
Lincolns, caddys, nifty toyotas, computer punch
tickets, Dean Moriarity foot on gas
pedal rage.
I am parking lot satori
Gypsy prayer concrete car stack salvation
like miracle labyrinth. Checkers game.
I am parking lot satori
jailhouse black Latino holy saints
midtown tire screech fire.
White upstate gun tote flannel
old timers.
Always lit stogy.
I am parking lot satori
Jeep CD player Anita Baker dignity
like coffee, bagel and butter
time card punch.
I am parking lot satori
Hegel dialectics general manager Archie
Bunker Clem.
Greg's Fifth Avenue Marlboro Newark
Fourth Ward cool.
I am parking lot satori
twenty dollars tax five-dollar president
Lincoln tip.
Metal locker metal Saturday Night Special

Four Roses whiskey bottle
funky Campbell's Soup hot plate
Manhattan freedom time
old man's back break business creation.
Gas fume holy revelation
concrete ramp black Knapp shoes
6 pm lockup quiet time delight.
Do a job. Cash and carry outlaws.
Holy parking lot satori. Yes.

Home Grown New York City Poet

I am home grown New York City poet
Colt 45 straight shooter
flannel metaphors like K-Mart chain saw
Bleecker Street narrow sky
elbow work shirt roll.
I am home grown New York City poet
born 1950 East 77th Street
January cold spell like witch's bottom
wooden spoon in mouth
trim lawn suburb childhood
Davis School hoe hearth
16-year-old Saturday night GTO beer runs
backseat erotic seduction.
I am home grown New York City poet
Manhattanville College trial by fire shoulder to
shoulder
Carolyn Stoloff mentor 1972 poetry workshop
bold prairie fire images like mad
oracle
cheap California wine holy vortex.
Highway time sanctity.
I am home grown New York City poet
Yorkville overripe green eye saint
Central Park ball cap bravado
parking garage muscle penance
blue collar cut the pie workplace.
I am home grown New York City poet
spirit like black folks mythic
born again passion.
Number Six Train hard drive promise
land heart.
Manic depression 2 year hard time upstate
lock up.
Thorozine tray occupational therapy poetics.
Ezra Pound Pall Mall howls.

Latino Young Lord Lower East Side
revolutionary street fire.
I am home grown New York City poet
seven plays Jim Jennings W. 54th Street
off-off Broadway funky theater
13 years electric poetry circuit.
Up against wall railroad craft
God's beatific calico grace
word angels
downtown hyacinth revelation
no to weak tea poetry politics
no to bad text like fools gold.
I am home grown New York City poet
3 am typewriter rides.
Demons like mad East Harlem chickens
literary courage like Sylvia Plath
shadow demons
New Mexico Hopi Desert faith
Walt Whitman American optimism.
I am home grown New York City poet
32 year literary road quest
bricklayers craft metaphor rubber band similes.
Language economy like carry on luggage.
Word on bond paper
mythic ramble like McDougal Street
Gregory Corso magic concrete voice
American halcyon prairie vision.
I am home grown New York City poet, amen.

Laura Boss's Heart

Laura's heart
5 am Cross Bronx Expressway easy glide
fresh Godiva chocolates
shopping mall free fall
New Jersey highway quiescence.
Laura's heart
high school teacher's belief
in cathedral sublime poet workshop
wizard like salt cashews.
Laura's heart
mad swirl beatnik black long skirt
eyes like universe starts
Annie Sez bargain. Tiffany pearls passion.
Hot rod blue Saab pinewood goodness.
Laura's heart
November poetry excellence, dog Coco
nylon leash down Boulevard East
eye on sleek metaphor
Pathmark roast beef on cheap.
Laura's heart
steel girder poetry workshops narrative craft.
gingham personal histories Woodbridge,
New Jersey childhood.
No to university door lock
no to trim law marriage.
Laura's heart
no to sidewinder scam up
mythic mountain
no iron ball and chain tether
yes to Fairleigh Dickinson poetic passion
pinewood genius.
Heart of heart you snatch me
from cold water ditch butcher
cleaver demons
Dayton Ohio Pizza Hut.

Yorkville blood wounds. Thousand Hudson
River affirmations.
Laura's heart
bring it home Lips Magazine long
haul beatitude mad genius poets penchant.
Ballet slipper language wide berth.
Faith like three Hershey bar binge
late night Colombian coffee jag.
Left bank Parisian February ramble.
Laura's heart
they do not break cotton sheet spirit
rip green eyes out of 1950's
dowop child
no granite soul
no poetic born again holy
roller pretense.
Angelic grace two pinewood sons
Two honey bee granddaughters
wildcat carpool.
Bold literary flame like Florentine fresco.
Laura you carrier pigeon hind leg poem,
rolling pin thunder.
Fandango highway sister always hyacinth heart
straight east coast shot.
Love's April honey redemption.
Laura's heart.

Fever Time

Oh Fever Time
dry Bayonne, New Jersey heaves
mad swirl delirium rancid chicken cutlets
cut and dice shouts down
Second Avenue.
Oh Fever Time
New York City dry wall lock in
no Albuquerque desert flat land dream
no round shoulder silk blouse caress.
No Harvard University poet laureate
pay check gig.
Fever Time
July memory like concrete pigeon collective
sour milk beyond expiration date.
Oh Fever time
hard drive God's licorice salvation
parking lot fandango psychiatrist's
Connecticut dry flower shell game.
Fever time
Long Island Mary mental illness
lock jaw paisley heroics
Triboro Bridge three fifty toll
freedom distance like Jesus' second coming.
Fever time
Advil pop hot honey tea
damp flannel bedclothes American round
house dream on hold
Freddie Hubburd radio soothe
Bette cuts southern Maine pinewood
New York Post shouts street
corner obscenity
slick yellow journalism propaganda.
No Babylon Channel 4 brainwash
no generation X maple syrup ecstasy addiction.
Oh Fever Time

old man Shanghai's spirit like
New York Hospital head nurse
key rings on wide hips
Prolyxin shot straight jacket
cut squash, holy sweet potatoes, zucchini like
tough local judge.
Winter moves in double bill movie
black knit navy watch cap
Number 4 Train on 14th Street
subway planform derail.
Oh Fever Time
yes to blue highways cinnamon quest
yes to Greenwich Village April jubilee
East River strawberry preserves harbor
tug boat.
yes to Sweet North Carolina kisses.
Oh Fever time
take me home
East Side marshmallow quiescence
Soft-shoe dream.

Sometimes

Sometimes
I'm stone crazy jailhouse blues
empty refrigerator.
Hallucination, wide barrel torso
pine tree storm demon damage.
Sometimes
I reel in Dante's 9-layer hell
thin finger tobacco stain
no prairie fire sanctity empty
tin cup.
Sometimes
demon blues close down August garden
tomatoes swipe by neighborhood thugs
short Green women in dandelions pick.
No metal storage bin fertilizer.
Sometimes
no sweet New York City rain
western New Jersey horizon
pigeons avoid square terrace
no tight buttock women notice
blood wound
biceps cobra snake memory like
wood splinters.
Sometimes
I cry from night terror
Marlboro hardscrabble depression empty
queen size bed life raft
barbecue fence backyard stranger.
Sometimes
pain like opaque demitasse cup
Star Wars galaxy
Manhattan crucifixion too many years
sweet resurrection shut down
no God's Sunday morning
Billie Holiday grace

canvas Bellevue straight jacket
tight on defense nose tackle chest.
Sometimes
cattle wander barb wire fence
Halloween children trick or treat
home return terror small face
tears hobgoblin egg toss.
Sometimes
Poetic rack beyond lunch bucket knowledge.
God why do you crucify me
Oh schooner mast Melville's Billy Budd.
Cut vocal chords like butcher
cleaver executioner.
Sometimes
pain like hot tar Memphis blues
midtown traffic snarl, I-70 Indiana
flat tire.
Sometimes
I am rooted in Carrara marble,
crazy glue, Hawaii hot volcano lava.
Sometimes
I wait for sweet mythic release.

We Are Born

We Are Born
like back beat jail juke joint
Monday night quiescence, pinewood swirl.
Harley Davidson madcap outlaws.
Black home girls satin sheets
Malcolm X Harlem November radiator heat
up high.
Are Are Born
like James Brown soul strut Sugar Hill Harlem.
Lemon sole fry spaghetti mom's
mythic recipe.
Cannonball Adderly Alto saxophone sublime.
We Are Born
like 4 am Hartford, Connecticut machine
gray hum
sweet New Hampshire bound like
hardy Quaker quilt
prairie renewal typewriter faith
God's crimson salvation.
No to flower bed death wish
no to psychedelic thin shadow
brain fracture.
We are born again
like Cassandra Wilson highway silk vision
Friday afternoon fish and chips deluxe
down vest barrel chest Canada wind
Kankakee railroad lantern illuminations.
We Are Born
like water cooler confessional
colonial Williamsburg, Virginia candles hand dip
serene inner sandbox fat cheek child.
Dizzy Gillespie trumpet ghetto fire.
We Are Born
like first Manhattan winter snow
Central Park cross country ski

cognitive rumble.
Flannel shirt wildcat dream
New Mexico Hopi drum circle
holy land America.
We Are Born
like bold Piscataqua River
Puritan covenant New England glory.
Poet Walt Whitman walk mythic
land democracy
poetry satchel like apple seeds.
We Are Born
like canvas gunnysack
Moses Mississippi wicker raft
Scotch plaid cap taxi cab
back seat
Charles Mingus bebop string bass.
Jack Kerouac Lowell, Massachusetts
Dunkin' Donuts morning grace.
Back pocket Tokay wine.
We Are Born
in 42nd Street beat black cool
Sunoco tank one dollar twenty
New Jersey crescent millennium moon prophecy
always a night ride home.

Rev Up

I Rev Up
Vermont Green Mountain August blueberry patch
hard drive lady liberty American excellence.
I Rev Up
86th Street sweet bartender Pilar
Saturday night full moon essence
southbound New Jersey Turnpike
New Brunswick, Hightstown, sweet Philly.
Bring on easy redneck smile
Georgia women soft thigh cotton curve
rainbow no nonsense hands.
I Rev Up
to truck stop hot coffee
Stuckey's Curio Shop, New Mexico desert,
Turkish taffy, miniature license plates,
Paul's Beth Israel Aids hospice grace.
I Rev Up
to Arizona Navaho fire
sacred land consciousness tribal justice
large midnight barn fire.
Bring on Amarillo big sky
I-40 Texas tumbleweed affirmation
country grill T-bones
God's milk bucket sanctity.
Bring on 8-year-old kid's
Thomas Jefferson awe,
Colorado Rockies box scores,
fascination Seneca holy land beatitude
ball cap on round head
cumulus cloud
January beauty.
I Rev Up
like Romeo heart resonance
Manhattan hallway moist kisses
tabby cat milk dish.
Wrightsville Beach oyster fry

Key West bound Southern Comfort
back beat.
I Rev Up
to Northern Michigan wolverines
beaver dams long wilderness outback
synagogue holy Sabbath delight
Methodist Sunday bake sale chewy walnut
brownies.
Bring on God's magic gingham weave
angels of mercy surface like
Mission Beach, San Diego
faith eucalyptus fragrance Coppertone lotion
lower back sweetheart groove.
I Rev Up
to September school haircut
spiral notebooks thin leg 3rd grader.
knapsack overstuff.
Take it home America road essence
steel railroad line Chesapeake and Ohio
Railroad line plain talk.
Hobo jungle mulligan stew celebration
New Orleans street corner mad poets
common man's constitutional virtue
fire burritos West 3rd Street Tex-Mex.
I Rev Up
President William Jefferson Clinton
Little Rock, Arkansas baby back rib delight.
Mississippi Delta fertile black soil
straight line tar shack horizon
honor student's hard drive
top gun knowledge.
I Rev Up
like Chevy pick-up
Colorado state line liberation
denim lap Seven Eleven slurpy
52 year old hand always on
the American wheel. Yes.

Flannel Warrior

I am flannel warrior
watershed Adironack passion lit
contraband match.
Marlboro morning smoke mental hospital
day room
eye o nurse Becky's strong
Pennsylvania legs
front porch pick up sticks
elementary school bound 3rd grader.
I am flannel warrior
Cole Porter silk stocking quiescence quest
rap around cool daddy sunglasses
quiche Lorraine red Beaujolais.
I am flannel warrior
poetic Denver hopscotch darning needle eye
like Green Bay Packers offensive line thrust
November calico Kansas fields
Gracie Station commemorative postage stamps.
Gay boys' Italian loafer creative verve.
I am flannel warrior
Horace Silver Jazz Messengers
cool bop mint tea deluxe
flannel front pocket rosary beads
Friday night payday Number 4
Subway train three beers bound for
fried chicken Bronx home.
I am flannel warrior
Manhattan tobacco stain saint
broccoli on sale 99 cents line
Silinas migrant field labor.
Roselle Park, New Jersey cool maple syrup
poetry read.
Mountain Dew quench thirst
straight back chair mythic scotch
plaid blanket
Harlem road fever like City College

hip hop madman
cool Colt 45 Malt liquor poetics.
I am flannel warrior
October fire tree kisses
pale yellow rent check on time.
Visa car shylock payoff.
Depokote blood drawn like
Great Lakes Michigan oil rig
green felt poker game full house
jacks and aces.
I am flannel warrior
Gregory Corso beatific angels
Jesus' resurrection Manhattan Bic razor shave
late night Second Avenue taxi cruise
bedrock Taurus full moon Vietnam
era flashback
down vest nose tackle shoulder
2 am Ambien sleeping pill pop
Robert Frost poetic Vermont
snowfield word economy.
I am flannel warrior
Plaza Diner salmon grill with
velveteen Laura sweetie.
Three coffee poetry circuit gossip.
I am flannel warrior
bold like Texas wildcat Velvet Hammer Band
Austin kick back perfection
Jack Kerouac flannel blue collar riff
open New Mexico I-40
hot wire T-bone hunger
always river run passion. Yes!

October Cool

I am October cool
round shoulder autumn knit sweater
lace timberlands hot red zinger tea
American dream.
Pauli Arroyo's 20 year old jeep
First Avenue maple syrup groove
cat's cradle brain weave
Marc Chagal stain glass grace
hot fudge Sunday excellence.
I am October cool
Baltimore Orioles hot crab cake
Tennessee biscuits and gravy
gymnast's high school discipline.
I am October cool
Grover Washington Philly soul cadence
Newark crescent moon poetry read
Hip-hop outlaws New Jersey
contraband run
clean cut prep girls chestnut hearts.
Jesus' hot muffin salvation.
I am October cool
street corner grace devotion.
Easy rice and beans
East Harlem funky discount clothes rack.
Yes to Nuyorican Poets Café
spoken word ramble
silver passion poetry heroes wildcat youth's
ideal quest.
I am October cool
Pete Hamill Marlboro pack
Daily News editorial room
Central Park open sky wonder
garden glow.
Yes to leather outlaw passion
Deborah's dramatic Rolling Stones aesthetic 1972.

I am October cool
brown bag Budweiser eight hour
work harness
Holland Tunnel easy glide
turnpike serenity three Jack Daniels glow
ham hock freedom.
I am bolts and nails
slow Pittsburgh poetic burn.
French fries, cheese melt, cool Coca-Cola
Friday gymnasium dance Ford Mustang
backseat neck and pet 1966.
I am October cool
Andrew Wyeth Whitney Museum
FDR downtown C-Note Bar
Tuesday guitar pick open mike
medicinal herbs, passion flower, valarium,
pink Depracote tablets.
Joni Mitchell tap American providence
highway resurrection
thick mushroom soup cherry wood
poem craft.
I am October cool
western Massachusetts Joan soul
like Medieval tapestry
high wildflower ground quest
flannel hugs like lemon meringue pie
cool milk.
I am Ohio truck stop
red neck hot southern biscuits.
Prospect Park box kite
mythic St. John the Divine sermon
God's straight shot grace.
Yes I am October cool
I-95 Connecticut Greenwich, Stanford,
New Haven, Sweet Moses' salvation
Christian born again Greyhound funky
bus station

crimson dawn eggs over easy
rye toast
straw hat tourists Hyannis dream
Mexican delivery boys proud mambo.
I am October cool
blue jean sophomore fraternity football
nose tackle.
Yorkville short order cook
Heaven's eternal life's promise.
12 gate gold city, American excellence.
Summer passion harvest, Montauk cobble daydream
the long way home. Yes!

IX
RIDGELINE ETHICS
2001

PETER CHELNIK - HEY GIRL - COLLECTED POEMS

Halloween Trick Treat

Halloween Trick Treat
Ghost miracle hobgoblins
sassy French maids
bourbon howls along Second Avenue,
terror blood artery.

Halloween Trick Treat
Chicken wing dinner cool Coors beer
Archer's Bar karaoke down right revel
October election crunch,
glory train American pagan velvet
wide hips. Donna's gothic wide eye magic essence.

Halloween Trick Treat
snickers bars, cool daddy Hersheys
pumpkins carve computer
mid-town Manhattan Saturday night
reefer glow.

Halloween Trick Treat
denim ghost riders
bohemian low riders like
butterscotch all day suckers,
Big Red gum,
small tots bunny rabbits delight,
yellow black bumble bees
grade school spiderman, orange Jack-o-lantern plastic buckets.

Halloween Trick Treat
Salem witches burn down house
cast spells like Broadway short order
cook.
Greta Garbo, Marlene Dietrich
bring on Marlon Brando, purple wigs,
sexy fishnet stockings, racehorse golden legs.
Upstate New york magic potions
sandlewood incense serenity.

Halloween Trick Treat
Apple pick Macintosh
Gala yes delicious apples
crunch out like cool daddy river
beaver.

Halloween Trick Treat
Greenwich Village
big dog parade, drag queens
grey cloud mummies, prairie women
broad tooth smiles. Barrelhouse floats.

Halloween Trick Treat
New Hampshire Wicca Pagans white light
fire glow, wood nymphs
costume delight transformation
like fresh back whole grain bread.
Yeast rise, kaleidoscope hearts on fire.
Halloween Trick Treat, yes.

Willow Weep Eros

Willow Weep Eros
Thousand Hudson River corduroy good-byes
Siamese cat gaze like Greenhaven
Prison convict
seamstress hugs sandbag cut and run
semi-conductor romance, Lexington Avenue
street corner blood snarls.

Willow Weep Eros
Side swipe hand on narrow denim waist,
blood cascade medieval tapestry,
schooner mast Lake Superior broken promises
Sheepshead Bay blind date manic
depressive deep six catatonia.
Crap shoot Saturday night ice coffee jags,
lolly pop psychosis. Delusion like runaway
oak wood stage coach.

Willow Weep Eros
Party girl Yorkville roulette wheel turn,
gold dig straight up martini, hard steel girder eyes
cocaine top down silver grey BMW's.
Frank Sinatra salt tears like Hoboken, New Jersey
last call Johnny Walker short bolt.
Alone like gangly acne Ohio State freshman
ghost rider terror.

Willow Weep Eros
Yes to Pacific Coast Highway orange sunset
quiescence.
Yes to Gladys Knight soul sister kick back
patchouli hugs, revolutionary renegade north star delight,
whole grain Vermont passion.
Yes to pork chop full belly, immense love
youth's cumulus cloud Kansas Interstate 70
singer Joni Mitchell heart, man and woman blueberry patch
mythic rhythms.

Willow Weep Eros
Yes to Glory Time overtime Union Station
Washington, D.c. moist poundcake kisses.
yes to October bronze flesh on flesh
like D.H. Lawrence afternoon
cupcake dream.
Taos, New Mexico old desert wonder, 1978.
Yes to hot chamomile tea creative
typewriter roll, overnight prairie fire verbal poetry riffs.

Willow Weep Eros
Hand in hand bluejay autumn
salutation, soul mates like spicy quesadillas
brown hair ridgeline sweethearts. Chick beauty
honeycomb Madison, Wisconsin grace
God's holy gingham union always!

Spirit Humble Pie

Spirit Humble Pie
Friday afternoon patchouli
incense burn,
Albuquerque New Mexico piñon wood
fireplace earth hold quiescence,
Cirrus cloud February
desert muse like
God's roundhouse oneness.

Spirit Humble Pie
Quiet bar room Budweisers,
jukebox silence.
Thousand tumbleweed late 1970's
hosannahs.
Crimson optimism,
calico notions like
Hopi Indian holy drum circle.

Spirit Humble Pie
No to psychedelic sophomores
ball jack aesthetics
No to mushroom brain chill
No to lanyard fracture
boy scout runaway coyotes.
Yes to Santa Fe bring home
burritos,
Yes to Georgia O'Keefe paint genius
Yes to America's southwest
renegade Latino salvation.

Spirit Humble Pie
Cowboy boots Tony Lama specials,
five alarm chili, full Leo moon
bring home southwest pine tree magic.
Moist afternoon kisses,
twenty seven year old
pancake dreams.

Spirit Humble Pie
Interstate 25 Taos bound
winter like Catholic Mass,
vinyl 33 records, Jackson Browne salt tears
veggie soup whole grain
bread renaissance.
Flannel poet heartland integrity.

Spirit Humble Pie
America's pioneer rainbow
covenant, bald eagle
halcyon flight,
leather chaps, silver spurs
like John F. Kennedy silver dollars.
Shot gun keep ranchers fallow
field peace,
Pow Wow peace pipe does it grace,
Spirit Humble Pie, Yes.

Chevrolet Dreams

Chevrolet Dreams
Backseat calico french kiss
high school passion,
wildcat literary paperback desire,
eye like Nikon camera
f-stop focus, Kodak film redondo
Union Pacific rail line personal history.

Chevrolet Dreams
Youth's kick can touch sky like
Central Park Mad Hatter,
Joy Leftow Columbia University
high school bad girl drop out
pick self off Washington Heights
cruel concrete again and again.
Cap gun cowboy and Indian
rumbles.
Hand on Levi thigh like stove pipe
7th Avenue fashion model.
Heel spike Manhattan passion.

Chevrolet Dreams
Read read read
No to snob ivy league Brooks Brothers
eat clubs.
No to Triumph sports car
frat boys ring a levio
dead beat poetics.
No to daddy Exxon credit card gas up
like Washington, D.C. Georgetown
chi chi eats.

Chevrolet Dreams
Pacific Coast Highway rainbow quest 1969
Khaki Jack Kerouac Dharma burn knapsack,
Full Moon electric wine,
lentil stew peace vibrations.
Home girl cosmic eros.

Chevrolet Dreams
Daily journal entry like
65th Street grocery shop spree
massage parlor hot flesh desire 1975,
East coast parking lot exile
Village Vanguard
Joe Farrell Alto Saxophone supreme.

Chevrolet Dreams
Yes to Memorial Day 68th Street subway station
San Diego blond hook up
like cherry cheesecake,
Yes to young buck's clean and sober
New School Robert Phelps mentor cool
literary quest like
Pentecostal minister,
Yes to IBM electric typewriter
holy February morning hunt and peck.

Chevrolet Dreams
Fame like aluminum tin foil,
tight lace worn Missouri work boots,
Hungry Man turkey t.v. dinner.
Bring on poetics resonance like
Brattleboro Vermont downtown
morning blizzard.
Bring on Singer Sew machine excellence
like 85th Street Nimpha genius.
Bring on subway number 6 line conductor 8 hour
underground hard grind.

Chevrolet Dreams
Cotton sheet weekend paisley romance Jane's
WQXR Vivaldi maple syrup beauty,
spark plug tune up love.
Pennsylvania beaver tooth
smiles, soul mate like
south Florida 85 degree blue
sky afternoon.
Valentine's Day Godiva chocolate delight.
Chevrolet Dreams, always!

Blue Ridge Crossroads

Blue Ridge Crossroads
rosary bead flannel shirt pocket
revolution.
Southbound spirit quest like
May spring break heart, eggs over easy
grits, butter,
concrete city demons 1997.
Maximum security jail time soul,
thousand hosannahs.
Hope eternal red rose,
noon time mythic novelist James Baldwin read.

Blue Ridge Crossroads
Manhattan Lisa S. three dog jubilee,
Hip hop nephew Charlie's
Brandeis University kick back
Gotham Friday night June serenity.
Hamptons explode like crack pipe,
Dutch Masters reefer roll.
Merlot wine addiction 2005.

Blue Ridge Crossroads
Fifth grader straight back multiplication
table, discipline.
Pledge of allegiance glory train.
Bluegrass oak wood fiddle twang,
banjo pick feet shuffle delight
Roanoke, Virginia Jesus holy Sunday
Baptist church sermon. Flat wave American grace.

Blue Ridge Crossroads
Hillbilly gospel moonshine country
back roads, Virginia Tech rock steady
conservative university educate
pursuit,
Good old sorority girls apple pie bake, pink nail chatter.

Blue Ridge Crossroads
Manhattan June weekend computer cool down
Madison Avenue quiet like milk fed
midnight infant,
yellow taxi cross town east side scoot,
three martini business suit week long unwind
like highway BMW.
Noah's Saturday little league baseball
compete, second base excellence,
ice cream sunday, whipped
cream chocolate syrup, family
maplewood weave.

Blue Ridge Crossroads
Rebel Ford pick up, deer hunt
season like 200 year buckskin pioneers,
Andrew Jackson old Hickory woodsman quiescence,
ham smoke dignity.
Yellow ribbon moms, honey blond wives,
U.S. Third Infantry Division Iraq valor,
Patriots red neck green hallow faith.

Blue Ridge Crossroads
Christenburg, Virginia one week
easy beat, Heal like break wind blue jay
New York City blood wounds.
Return home Interstate 81
garden spirit God's rainbow love,
Blue Ridge Crossroads, beautiful!

Holy Sabbath Lights

Holy Sabbath Lights
October ragtime cool bop worship
cats claws, taxi scoot
crosstown fire leaves.

Holy Sabbath Lights
Israeli promised land Red Sea virtue
cap guns like Arizona desert
Southwest frontier spirit.

Holy Sabbat Lights
Election fandango President George Bush
bring it home muscle,
White House homeland rock steady
essence.

Holy Sabbath Lights
No to grim reaper poetry aesthetics.
No to kool aide Columbia University
crack whip professors.
No to rib condom ecstasy no name sex.

Holy Sabbath Lights
Bring on Tom Waits tenderloin district
ramble
bring on young buck clean and sober
Wyoming ranch-hand ethics
bring on Cincinnati, Ohio homemade cherry pie
American virtue.

Holy Sabbath Lights
Torah scroll Temple Emanuel
calico knowledge,
God's pine tree oneness like miracle Taurus moon
eclipse
cameo hearts on fire,
bedroom easy kisses, cotton sheet serenade.

Holy Sabbath Lights
Day of rest matzo ball soup
logic like potato knish synagogue prayers,
thousand atonements,
Albert Einstein relativity time genius.

Holy Sabbath Lights
Candles river-run redemption like horizon dream,
green valley grace over and over, yes!

Heaven's Gate

I am heaven's gate
New Mexico desert magic jewel dusk
Albuquerque night sky like
Tiffany pearls.

I am Santa Cruz, California
cool out cosmic ecstasy Top cigarette roll
playground kisses
big dipper dream time like
Madison Avenue Rolex watch.

I am homeless saint Central Park
July camp out, hot morning coffee
Gotham on the rod hobo satchel quest.
Phil Hughes Bar hard core beer boys
mythic juke box serenade.

I am love's holy angel, tree top
blue jays,
South Carolina lemonade soft Dixie laughter,
Martin guitar twang, Memphis to Little Rock
Interstate 70 halcyon highway dream.

I am sugarland Chicago Rush Street
blues time, Muddy Waters down and dirty
American genius, Lake Shore Drive
hob knob quiescence,
Old Town singer John Prine cut cherry pie
1972.

I am Jeff's South Fallsburg, New York
handyman special, three great kids,

home girl rock steady Magnolia wife.
I am opportunity like New York Times
Sunday want ads, Ithaca College coed
first job Manhattan open universe
crimson Yorkville desire.
No to Satan's subterranean black
hole tunnel addiction.
No to hypocrite narcissistic tar
and feather SUV yuppies.
No to trendy School of Visual Arts
painters, morning heroin jones.
Yes to brother Marc's Woodstock
funky house renovation glory project.
Yes to Dad's swimming pool physical
therapy 85 years old keep trucking
hard drive.
Yes to mom's sculpture summer bring
it home hammer and chisel, God bless.

I am five year old Eliot's chocolate
candy bar sublime summer camp rebellion,
Coney Island quiescence,
Nathan's hot dog hoe-down,
Brooklyn Cyclone's home run crack
Chelsea bicycle messenger day-glo cadence
9th Street cross-town bus cha cha.
I am a thousand summer dreams. Yes!

Taurus Sun Glory

Taurus Sun glory
May spring blood rites,
paralysis like electric prong
Montana cattle.

Taurus Sun Glory
Desolation Row Brown University
daisy chain sex
ecstasy tab brick wall
incandescent leaps
document forge xerox signatures.
Identity theft surfboard wipe-out.

Taurus Sun Glory
Bring on New Hampshire calico cat female hearts,
Bring on south Michigan double rainbow jubilee
Bring on Poets Atlantic Ocean
sea breeze excellence.

Taurus Sun Glory
Computer hi-jinx Starbucks cafe
nose in air attitude pose
semi-conductor mental illness,
Ambien sleep pill pop like
old fashion red hots, Halls menthalyptus candy.

Taurus Sun Glory
Neversink River log jam emotion,
immigrants square peg round
hole rialto hide out,
Sunday brunch Panorama Cafe
waitress Meagan good old girl Rhode Island
customer tip hustle.

Yes to New York Thruway miracle
night rides, Newburgh, New Paltz, Kingston jubilee.
Yes to Palomino word play, leather saddle cow-poke
language.
Yes to American excellence like Lewis and Clark
westbound courage.
Yes to corporate honchos fifty hour
suit tie hard grind,
house mortgage, trim lawn.
Yes to Silverado dream, kids like Dora the explorer
wind at back innocence.

Taurus Sun Glory
No to Jaimison whiskey
wedding music band cellophane robots.
No to weekly new sex partner bullwhip anorexic
mud-pit aesthetic.
No to Mulberry Street 3 A.M. May night chill
  psychosis,
reefer yarn tear fracture.
Yes to tears of joy Alabama Bible belt
friendships, 5th grade Demitri mythic
fencing lessons.
Yes to broad shoulder optimism like
full hereford cow milk tie.
Yes to kick-back Timberlands,
joy like Big Apple Circus high wire act,
Taurus Sun Glory!

Cherry Pie Creative Revolution

I am cherry pie creative revolution,
parachute Rocky Mountain free fall,
green Pennsylvania April scotch plaid blanket,
fried chicken picnic,
birthday Wichita, Kansas sky
blue balloons.

I am flannel poet Austin City Limits bound
like pit bull terrier,
thousand karate chops at thin neck,
Levi jeans fray, Eurikas Springs, Arkansas
Don Payne may he rest in pease
American hardscrabble muscle.

I am IBM typewriter ride,
Jack Kerouac gin mill late afternoon
beatific howls,
Jewish sabbath candle light, white wax tears
Prairie Fire DTUT cafe one year
mythic poetry excellence.

I am eye on Yorkville tight buttock
party girls, vacant bed like
Huck Finn Mississippi River raft,
tree bark canoe Lake Hoosatonic dawn
easy glide, sunrise crescendo
Joan's Santa Fe, New Mexico acrylic
on glass artwork excellence.

I am United Sates Marine uncommon Iraq
valor, Apache helicopter Mosul 2 A.M.
victory strike,
Valentine's Day Napa Valley champagne
side-pocket engagement ring,
Paramus, New Jersey Fortunoff
diamond cash and carry.

I am May Walt Whitman Brooklyn Ferry lilacs,
Coney Island Cyclone,
Yugoslav Mikey's Montenegro vacation quest.
New York Mets Carlos Del Gato first base
Latino best May team record in majors.

I am Friday night teen-age posse pizza
hang-out, cool cokes, frisky romance
like Persian cats.
86th Street back row neck and pet.
January 23rd 56th birthday Tal Bagel cold cut delight,
Barnes and Nobles gift certificate serendipity,
Middle School teacher Sara
Baylor University Waco, Texas prairie values
honest like cowgirl straight back ethics.

I am Manhattan down-home t-bone steak
optimism, angelic illumination like
Michelangelo fresco. Metropolitan Museum
Tuesday afternoon easy beat,
pine wood renegade poetics.
Danny and Eddie's Bar pool table Budweiser hustle.

I am mom and dad's senior citizen
oakwood California ranch house
rock steady rialto.
Cool Catskill Mountain May butterscotch night,
cordwood pot belly stove quiescence, yes.

Ridgeline Ethics

Ridgeline Ethics
Caribou, Maine May spring
sassafras delight,
easy breeze like dirt road frame
cottage lack curtains,
firm Jamestown, Rhode Island
harbor grace.

Ridgeline Ethics
Penombscott Bay dusk magic schooner
glide.
U.S. Constitution rock steady
American excellence.
Bible pecan pie values
like Charlotte, North Carolina Baptist minister
God's white light revelation, ten commandment
straight and narrow highway
thousand Gillette shaves,
shoe-shine morning glory,
late Johnny Cochran
pull no punches honest courtroom cadence.

Ridgeline Ethics
Yorkville clean and sober
NYPD keep 19th Precinct peace,
pork chop, mashed potato morals.
No to shyster ambulance chase lawyers.
No to keep up with Jones' Mercedes Benz
corporate swindle.
No to left-wing pistol whip delusion.
No to New School John McCain commencement
freak-out protect tantrum.

Ridgeline Ethics
Boy Scout truth and justice
one match camp fire,
can man twenty dollar bill
all night scramble, 1st Avenue ramble.
Small businessman stand behind product
like Local 32B union delegate
April late night rank and file contract
negotiations.

Ridgeline Ethics
Bring on Harry Truman buck stops here
tough Missouri common sense.
Bring on Ronald Reagan sweet America plain talk.
Bring on John F. Kennedy PT 109 World War 2 heroics.

Ridgeline Ethics
Christian's La Guardia Community College
immigrant English class east coast
rainbow opportunity.
Shirt sleeve 14th Street Little League Saturday
afternoon dads,
hamburgers and hot dog Sunday
miracle barbecue.
Saint Joseph's Church communion
like East River rainbow quiescence.

Ridgeline Ethics
Mother's Day Gold Club shoot the moon
bring it home buffet.
Front porch Newburyport, Massachusetts
senior year high school world is oyster.
Right and wrong moral ladder to sky,
curlicue midnight curfew
University of Michigan freshmen like silver bread truck,
morning fresh bake.
Ridgeline Ethics, yes.

Satisfied Mind

Satisfied Mind
Manhattan west side Riverside Drive
May miracle sunset,
purple incandescence,
horizon holy like Jesus
sugarland resurrection.

Satisfied Mind
85th Street park bench classic rock radio
flannel shirt fandango.
Sonya's home brew peppermint
iced tea Moms infant stroller
milk bottle groove,
Led Zeppelin guitar wail
Santa Cruz, California 1969.

Satisfied Mind
No to psychotic Brooklyn Bridge
suicide leap.
No to Ambien sleep pill three martini frazzle.
No to dead-pan mud ditch blues.
No to mad dog gyroscope non-stop manic swirl.

Satisfied Mind
Gingham skirt city girls
hip sway, afternoon rainbow caress,
Sara L's New Hampshire
down home country vibration.
Concrete brown sparrows like
God's holy neighborhood Jerusalem markers.

Satisfied Mind
Embrace gung-ho mythic Corey's New York Mets.
Embrace home fried egg on roll devotion.
Embrace Buddhist meditation like May spring rain
incandescence,
George's fruit stand green bell peppers 99 cents a pound,
white cloud sky serendipity,
68-degree east coast holy easy vibrations.

Satisfied Mind
Tuesday day-glo Jennifer's Canarsie, Brooklyn
Beatnik nomad cool.
Clean sheets squash pasta dinner
oasis shower,
Crown Heights Bible read like born-again Christians
straight back pinewood faith.

Satisfied Mind
Shake and bake Haitian Yvon hip
mountain-top groove,
1 A.M. liberty Yorkville Towers lobby
rap it down.

Satisfied Mind
Yes to dawn Central Park boat house
robin chirp quiescence.
Yes to brother Marc's Woodstock 7 A.M.
deer freedom train.
Yes to husband wife Saturday morning
magic bedroom pillow talk.

Satisfied Mind
Mom and Dad easy does it senior citizens
soft-shoe serenade, Jewish Torah redemption.
High school freshman algebra achievement
Lords oneness. New York Harbor denim sea breeze
old time Moran tug boat.
Serenity, corduroy joy.
Satisfied mind, dig it.

Optimism

I am Union Pacific freight train
hell-bent west bound,
Budweiser pitchers 12 dollars
Wednesday evening silk smooth,
Mississippi River Huck Finn, black Jim
American outlaw courage.

I am New Orleans sugarland express
rebuilt like 9th Ward miracle,
youths upstate New York fire glow
Vic's skateboard genius Orange County
California easy beat essence.

I am Jonelle's sweet home
Philadelphia dream quest.
Bring bacon home corporate
moms dads, special education kids
tutor excellence like Central Park
robin red breast, holy Presbyterian Church choir,

I am America's cash in pocket
Queen Anne lace opportunity,
immigrants 12 hours haul bottom
work load
young Mohammed hip-hop Hot 97 FM youth grace.
Local 272 parking lot straight back
car jockey.

I am House of Representatives
people's house rock and roll
preserve Republic like
Iowa corn silo,
John Deere lizard green tractors.
10th Mountain Division
Fort Drum, Afghanistan combat devotion,
Bill Gates computer honeycomb genius.

I am Rock Hill, South Carolina
butterscotch May sublime,
Anne and Alex same sex cirrus sky glow
cool mamas,
Latino Coronas and lime quitting time
chill-out, mellow like Los Lobos Mexican
music sublime.

I am 21st century Myrna's Miami
cover bases friendship, overland
phone calls, Ford Explorer halcyon glory.
2007 Puritan individualism,
Massachusetts Bay Colony wilderness dream.
Don't trend on me, Chevy pick-up gun rack
independence.
Home bake bread, fresh strawberry jam
Tennessee hickory ham smoke.
Optimism like 79th Street Catholic priest
smile on face, eye on God's miracle dawn.

Hope Eternal

Hope Eternal
Nebraska prairie ethics,
cherry pie June faith
like minor league
Albuquerque Dukes high altitude
home run crack.
God's July fourth America
barbecue kick-back.

Hope Eternal
Great Niece Jordon funky
rainbow heart, safe brown eyes,
Bedford, New York wide open
playground world.

Hope Eternal
Yes to banjo faith, West Virginia
Blue Ride mountain quiescence,
Yes to 86th Street fruit stand blueberry
jubilee
Yes to Roberts DTUT businessman's
cool daddy cash and carry excellence.

Hope Eternal
Pine Sol floor mop each
holy Thursday,
arts and craft ice cream popsicle
stick canoes, Mark Larsen Jackie Gleason
Illinois clean and sober ethics.

Hope Eternal
Brandeis University nephew
Charlie freshman honeycomb
dream, Budweiser can glory.
American history Civil War
Abraham Lincoln rock steady glory.
Parmalat milk bran flake late night
home boy delight.
Yes to great nephew Tyler ever ready
pancake smile.
Yes to corn on cob golden sunlight
optimism.
Yes to highway prayer 2 A.M.
Denver bound talk radio Bible belt essence.

Hope Eternal
Kisses like wedding day honor and cherish
forever,
Ohio wind on flannel back
touch sky like poet warrior,
a thousand wildflower notions.
Yugoslav Mikey Mineola
class act ramble, Saturday night meat packing district
rock and roll hodad.
Laura Boss' Hudson River miracle aesthetic.

Hope Eternal
Denim sanctity, summer solstice
butterscotch dawn,
Second Avenue M15 downtown
bus supreme,
home-made lasagna
California red wine breezin,
horizon eye, future like Courtney Collins
Colgate University excellence. Yes!

Holy Redemption

DTUT Cafe 5 P.M. September afternoon
happy hour. Merlot wine ike
maple syrup pour,
laptop hide and seek high tech
bugaloo.

Holy Redemption
Brig home Second Avenue rainbow
howls, green eye ladies.
Bring home gingham Texas pride.
Bring home creativity's Missouri highway
autumn touch sky jamboree.

Holy Redemption
Temple Shari Tafela slow boat Friday
night sabbath service
Torah scroll magic like Allen Ginsberg poem.
Quicksilver Albuquerque waitress,
eggs over easy, crisp Wyoming bacon
black coffee redondo.

Holy Redemption
No to New York Public Library
spider web queries.
No to Hollywood celluloid shave
head gang honchos.
No to private school grade kids day-glo
paranoia.

Holy Redemption
God's cash and carry honey bee pick self
up from Kentucky strip mine ditch,
twelve step dollar in kitty
clean and sober 13 years straight
line heroics.

Holy Redemption
Brother Marc's
American dream Woodstock mythic house
renovation,
cobble stone logic,
San Francisco Haight Street
key chain faith, cinnamon stick ecstasy.

Holy Redemption
Hudson Valley Gala apple
crisp bite joy,
Mary M's tango back-beat
Manhattan eloquence.
Rise like Continental Airlines
Paris-bound 747.
Rise like Montana bald eagle
sanctity,
whole grain Burlington, Vermont bread bake in.
Rise like Friday afternoon
bedroom kisses, clean cotton
sheets, loves pine tree delight.

Holy Redemption
18 wheel semi New Jersey Turnpike
Brooklyn-bound,
Ricks environmental masters
degree
Atlantic Ocean bait on line desire.
Blues, porgies, striped bass down east catch.
Rumanian scaffold muscle boys
erector set genius, June's Jamaican nanny cool out.
Harvest like Las Vega slot machine
silver dollar cash in.
A thousand pillow case prayers.
Holy Redemption, yes!

Shining Star

I am God's silverado shining star,
black iced coffee, Marlboro
cigarette soke
Arizona highway
shotgun laugh lines.

I am Atlantic sea breeze,
Toledo Charlies' dream quest
like London hardscrabble Shakespeare
actor,
burning bush Abraham's holy Isaac
sacrifice edge close.
Empty canvas handshake,
Beethoven music note palette joy.

I am Courtney Collins twenty
three year old Bronx ghetto
school teach heroics
Brad's outlaw west side New York Mets
holy holy passion.
Daily News true grit sports page
Porterhouse steak get down
Lubbock, Texas Sunday afternoon
barbecue.

I am warm caresses like back seat
Brooks Brothers shirt teenager,
moist Westchester kisses, 1965 Mustang convertible.
Lancaster County fresh bread
butter melt. Eggs over easy delight.

I am Walt Whitman Brooklyn Ferry
American poetry quest.
Bourbon shouts Mulberry Street pizza slice,
Bridget Murnaghan journey woman
Beat Bleecker Street howls.
Dads 87 year old rock steady
Greatest Generation can-do wisdom.

I am Rosh Hasshanna Jewish
New Years roast chicken,
potato kugel, keplach soup holy
fandango,
Homeless can man Baptist church
Park Avenue chow down.
Dreams like high school freshman
easy rider punk rocker.

I am Pacific Coast Highway morning haze,
Carmel, California illegal sleep on beach
easy glide notions 1969.
Knit scarf Yorkville style girls.

I am black leather shaved head gangster, eight ball
pocket cocaine,
lite FM Rod Stewart back-beat jam,
magnolia serenity,
Central Park September wind chimes,
like calico notions.

I am NYPD keep gotham peace 5th precinct
squad car late night patrol
Dean Moriarity parking lot heavy foot on pedal
hodad dude
God's infinite covenant, always.

Chick Pea Notions

Chick Pea Notions
FDNY ladder 13 fire rig
Second Avenue cool flame stake out
Mexican delivery boys Gracies Corner
Diner cool daddy class,
fried egg American dream like trout
fish river deluxe.

Chick Pea Notions
romaine lettuce, carrot shred,
cucumber Russian dressing
health chow down,
late night Wednesday cameo hearts on
fire, Union Square youth riff,
skateboard teen-age break rock
celestial star dream.

Chick Pea Notions
Baby back rib Arkansas poetics,
Andrew Wyeth Christina's World
heartland dream,
United Nations September taxi snarl
like knitting circle purple yarn.
Nell's acting dream, NYU excellence
Hershey bar proscenium cool mama.

Chick Pea Notions
God's side saddle covenant,
Mount Sinai Moses Ten Commandments
holy tabernacle hoe-down.
Nightingale Poetry read, David
and Su rock steady compassions
hearts like cheshire cats.

Chick Pea Notions
Autumn equinox ham hock delight,
fire leaves Woodstock
glory train delight.
Freedoms infinite virtue,
Capital ill Republic's easy beat,
E Street hot dog stands, Washington, D.C.
Metro urban scoot.

Chick Pea Notions
Bring home straight and narrow sober
teenagers.
Bring home Boy Scout eagle scout wilderness
trail hike self reliance.
Bring home Town Hall good peanut and
jelly local government.

Chick Pea Notions
Jennifer's photographer Hunter College aesthetics,
touch Oklahoma sky
highway morning delight, hot coffee
horizon destination.
Chick Pea Notions, yes!

Patchwork Quilt Emotions

Patchwork Quilt Emotions
Red rose halcyon love,
highway hugs like beef jerky sticks,
Wrigley's chew gum.
South Carolina wet back seat
kisses.

Patchwork Quilt Emotions
Forever after tea cup
Emily Dickinson conversations,
butterscotch whispers,
Tennessee country smoked ham
mayonnaise sandwiches.
17 year old Shane's rainbow
soccer quest, Rio de Janeiro
August lovely lady hook up.

Patchwork Quilt Emotions
Daybreak faith, east Harlem
4 A.M. night bicycle
ride mama, camouflage jeans,
eye on Greenwich Village
easy beat.

Patchwork Quilt Emotions
Mary M's tango dream quest,
Columbus, Ohio weekend
scoot,
bubblegum passion.
No gender war blood letting.
No upper east side Saks Fifth Avenue
snarls.
No Mount Holyoke watercress
sandwich nose in air snobs.

Patchwork Quilt Emotions
Calico heart open like
Isleboro, Maine gate swing
ferry delight cool Penombscot Bay
easy breeze.

Patchwork Quilt Emotions
Wonderland bodies baby oil
get-down massage.
Love letters across state lines, dig it!

Peace of Mind

Peace of Mind
Blueberry pie, New Jersey
cool farmland milk
Buddhist zen meditation
like 2 A.M. deep blue comforter kisses.

Peace of Mind
Cheshire cat smile
Kansas City Charlie Parker be-bop
excellence.
No to roundhouse soft shoe Manhattan
critics.
No to ecstasy pill pop Amherst College
freshman.
No to New Age same old road gangsters.

Peace of Mind
Hoots dow update dawn
Woodstock country lane.
Long skirt denim Oregon women
yellow ribbon chestnut hair
stay at home moms cheerio breakfast
tuna lunch pack, 3rd graders reading trout fish joy,
love old man up like
meatloaf dinner, lemonade, hot biscuits.

Peace of Mind
Angels calico magic,
radio lite FM easy glide like brother Marc's
White Plains Ebersole Ice Rink hockey team heroics.
Noel's Haitian cool hip uptown
spiritual quest.
Jewish Yom Kipper Day of Atonement
family magnolia pow-wow, 24 hour fast
like Hopi indian peyote vision.

Peace of Mind
57 year old prairie fire hard drive,
Hudson Valley Gala apples, cranberry
juice like Jesus holy blood,
Mississippi River Huck Finn river
raft quiescence,
Black Jim's liberation quest like
ham and egg freedom time breakfast.

Peace of Mind
No junk yard whiskey bottle
cognitive fracture.
No to egomaniac purple tights Oberlin College
shuffle.
No psycho ward blood red fist de cuffs.

Peace of Mind
Yes to New Mexico Desert Tucumcari highway
west-bound delight.
Yes to daily journal entry like Los Angeles soup
kitchen full belly.
Yes to baby-boom brother and sisters
back to pine tree roots
thousand penny loafer dreams.
Yes to Clams Casino white wine come back baby
  excellence.

Peace of Mind
Nikon camera photo memory essence,
Big Ricks soul mate quest like wishing well
penny toss,
Grestides check-out girl easy 86th Street
smile.

Peace of Mind
Catskill Mountain breeze,
Orions belt, Big dipper Cosmic creativity
Laura Ludwig poetic prairie fire.
Jones Beach October kite fly,
little tykes bedtime story,
Curious George, Willie Wonka and the Chocholate Factory, sleep tight, you hear!

Peace of Mind
Orly's newborn Itai orange carriage
Rainbow scoot,
Second Avenue promised land miracle delight.
Love's October Irish sweater trail hike,
golden sunlight.
Peace of Mind, yes!

Flat Out Smooth

Flat Out Smooth
Halloween kick back
soft jazz Al Jarreau
immense vocal chops,
Eastern Standard time change like Union Pacific
rail car hook-up, Charlotte, North Carolina bound.

Flat Out Smooth
Johnny Z shell steak Pelham ramble
thousand pumpkin carve notions,
4 A.M. leaf fall like
dirty hamper clothes. Toddler's eyelid sleep.

Flat Out Smooth
I-95 Connecticut highway jubilee, God's
cinnamon heal like epson salt hot bath.
Calico transcendence mid-term election
day 2006 moves in life
Hyannis, Massachusetts breakwater floods
60 miles per hour wind,
Elmsford, New York power lines down,
autumn dark cave Long Island
darkness. Candle light kitchen table cold roast
  chicken.

Flat Out Smooth
Monday oh Monday
corporate moms, blue business suit
savvy, overcoat dads bee-line commute
like pork chop defrost.
Number six subway line heat up,
cross town 42nd Street bus
on Mayor Bloomberg's metro card
money.

Flat Out Smooth
Jamaica June sends
Canarsie kids to red brick school house,
lotto quest, own house
like American Dream redondo.
Viande Diner Alex and Vin scoot home,
grave yard shift Sunday
night Second Avenue traffic hum,
deep butterscotch morning sleep.

Flat Out Smooth
New York Giants victory Meadowlands
Big Blue excellence, stonewall burly defensive line.
Edge shave, Gillette razor magic,
Cheshire Manhattan mascara women
almond Chinese eyes.

Flat Out Smooth
Begin again like Harriman State Park
trail hike,
HIV patients bus run,
New York Presbyterian Hospital
blood work, X-rays.
Fresh start like Tal Bagels oven fresh.
New week like brown bag tuna sandwich.
Flat Out Smooth, always!

Travel South

Travel South
Poet strawberry poems
Florida panhandle bound
workshirt cotton, 5 year old worn
topsiders,
breeze on back like
twenty something tight jeans gunge outlaw.

Travel South
No Manhattan steel tooth
November cold.
No long john hot cocoa
bootleg dreams delusion.
No fat cat Thanksgiving
East Hampton turkey dinner.

Travel South
Freedoms Gulf of Mexico
key lime pie delight,
God's orange ball magic sunrise,
highway quiescence Texaco fill-up,
pearl clothes like artichoke lunch
front porch veranda Palm Beach
bleach white guest house 1982.

Travel South
Dixie's kick back,
easy does it like dawn 18 wheel semi
Chattanooga bound, hot coffee thermos
CB radio breaker breaker.

Travel South
No tin solder Rockefeller Center
Christmas chaos.
No monkey suit tuxedo aficionados.
No East Village cash flow heroin
snort.

Travel South
New Orleans Bourbon Street American cartwheels
post Hurricane Katrina jubilee
Tulane University honey bee
butterscotch coeds,
Lake Pontchartrain skim stone rainbow love.

Travel South
Fort Lauderdale get lucky
warm moist chocolate chip kisses,
bourbon cameo delight, 1982.
Rock and roll liberty train like
Macon, Georgia Allman Brother
jump start genius. Cathedral Dickie Betts guitar pick.

Travel South
Bring on redneck straight shot like
shotgun target shoot.
Catfish fry Pabst Blue Ribbon ho-down,
NASCAR start your engines gentlemen true grit.
Spring's long distance monarch butterfly magnolia
promise.

Caramel Compassion

East Harlem soup kitchen
hot past salvation lunch,
can man dollar bill,
homeless like Central Park
December squirrels.
Poverty's cruel metal vice.

Caramel Compassion
Highway wildcat delirium,
pink waitress easy Oklahoma smile,
Holy hosts Jesus whole grain mercy
New York Hospital
psychedelic rehab, redemption.
Playboy Magazine mattress hide.

Caramel Compassion
Jamestown, Rhode Island mistletoe
Meagan's white and maroon
Christmas tree holy spirit faith,
Hanukkah light potato latkes,
white light God's holy miracles.
Theodore's Belleview men's shelter
three squares messenger job
dreams Princeton University
low-rider academia.

Caramel Compassion
Clean and sober twenty something
Yale University forsythia
medical students,
American pan fry excellence,
Jacksonville, Florida talk radio
calico pride,
New York City
classic rock Led Zeppelin
D.J. Carol Miller night ramble.
12-step dollar in kitty hot decaf.

City Harvest tin can food pantry.
no to hungry chocolate pre-school
tykes.
No to senior citizen shut-ins like zoo tiger.
No to cocaine string-out
fashion models.
No to mental illness free wheel
off medication, mail time lock up.

Caramel Compassion
Bring on Salvation Army New Years
2007 rehabilitation.
Bring on Houston, Texas
Sugarland Methodist Church
yard sale charity, greenbacks.
Emergency room Mexican health care.
Bring on Missouri show me state faith.
Bring on Milwaukee, Wisconsin
Miller High Life integrity.

Caramel Compassion
Pick fringe torso off ground
again and again like George Foreman
heavy weight prize fight,
heart on fire like Salem, Oregon sunrise,
Rock Hill, South Carolina fish fry.

Caramel Compassion
86th Street midnight prayers,
Chinese seamstress twelve hour
cubby hole steady hands,
Baruch College senior
immigrant genius,
Turkish corner fruit man
white stallion American dream.

Caramel Compassion
Mulberry Street December corner wind gust,
97 year old John Briggs dies like Yorkville
angel, cheshire heart always
white lily hope, easy Jesus grace.
Blues gone like winter Canada geese,
thousand Massachusetts rosaries,
warm radiator heat apartment,
quilt bed prairie dreams.
Ghetto hope!
Caramel Compassion, dig it.

Woodstock Field

I am Woodstock field
York peppermint patty,
cameo hear fire like
paper Waldorf Astoria matchbook.

I am Bowery night train
vagrant, Fifth Avenue tuxedo out on town
like gypsy mad hatter.
Carnival Marlboro smoke,
afternoon rainbow siesta, Christian radio,
Nell's elegant Hartford, Connecticut
debutante square shoulders.

I am Eastern Colorado 18 wheel trucker
blizzard highway turn-around,
beef jerky night dreams,
Manhattan roots like
Declaration of Independence 1776.
American Constitution free speech
rialto.

I am 101 Airborne Iraq heroism,
Christmas turkey, Louisville, Kentucky
broad grins. Jack Daniels straight up.
Hot homemade butter biscuits.
Kenosha, Wisconsin small town football full back,
six pack Budweiser run.
Algonquin Hotel high tea,
workboot prophesy, mudcake like
homemade cherry pie slice.

I am 86th Street and Second Avenue
3 A.M. bar room brawl, guerrilla blood fist de cuffs
Botanical Gardens Christmas railroad train magic.
Macy's Herald Square sales crunch,
Winter Solstice like ghost rider
7:22 P.M. blanket cover miracle glow.

RIDGELINE ETHICS

I am U.S. House of Representatives
Nancy Pelosi Speaker firm hand.
San Francisco Nob Hill morning justice.
Pillow whispers like winter
LaGuardia Place sparrows,
poet Gregory Corso tequila buy back.

I am flannel poet, journeyman
aesthetics like Montana pine tree,
lunch bucket New Years Eve dreams.
Ryan's white Russian rock and roll stand tall.
God's rainbow Mississippi River faith,
barn silo ethics, youths baby back ribs optimism
calico cat gentle grace, yes!

Hog Heaven

Hog Heaven
Zen Buddhist sublime incense meditation
honey bee empty mind like
Utah Bryce Canyon,
Fish and chips
Fiona's Irish Bar lunchtime jubilee.
Myrna's Miami Christmas pork roast.

Hog Heaven
Hot chestnuts, Fifth Avenue
Christmas lights, wide-eye tykes
ski parkas, mitten fasten,
end of year 2006.
Hope like Hannuka candle magic quiescence.

Hog Heaven
Peace on Earth,
Wollman Rink skate grace
hot dog vendor, mustard sauerkraut
hot chocolate faith
Hindu mythic prayers,
Tobacco Shack young buck Mohammed
Jackson Heights, Queens posse,
afternoon romance like
Kama Sutra buy-back plum wine.

Hog Heaven
C-Span politics on New Years Hold,
NBC Nightly News Brian Williams
day-glo America, baby boom
shake and bake wheel turn.
LaGuardia High School Seniors' university quest
Texas Hold 'Em hard drive.
SAT lead pencil crack books.

Hog Heaven
Night crook halcyon Manhattan slumber,
DTUT neighborhood iced
coffee cowboy ramble,
big sky Wyoming ranch hands
baby back ribs dinner chow down,
God's bread and butter
tumbleweed salvation.

Hog Heaven
Doorman Jeff's karate skill,
late night rap on jubilee joy
morning coffee like methedrine shots.
Denver snow blizzards like cotton ball
non-stop deluge,
airport sleep in, gin rummy insomnia.

Hog Heaven
New Years solitude, typewriter
rides like Aretha Franklin vocal chops,
sweet Los Angeles soul sister 1968.
American troops combat cool
War on Terror long road victory.
Crimson Latinos easy glide delivery bicycles,
African dudes Gristedes ebony saints,
easy beat poets, wind on back curve,
always eye on American horizon. Amen.

New Beginning

New Beginning
2007 New Years Day firecracker
poetry marathon.
Bruce and Joanne Weber
wordsmith organize genius,
Bowery easy jam.
Needle point drizzle, hope
like hot red zinger tea.

New Beginning
Democrats take Congress
like Omaha Beach G.I.'s,
candy cane Christmas trees mulch,
President Ford laid to rest
Grand Rapids, Michigan
midwest flatland holy ground.
Heal American saint 1974.

New Beginning
Bacon and beans go-go stock market prosper,
SSD Checks savings bank bound,
mythic corned beef sandwiches,
thousand Jewish holy land prayers.

New Beginning
January day-glo heat wave,
70 degree global warm hot milk bottle
quiescence.
DTUT Cafe Nell and Blake's coffee serve
top-notch class,
Sister Roberta's 58th confetti birthday
white mustang
football dudes, concert choir soprano excellence 1966.

New Beginning
Mohammed Ali prize fight tumbleweed discipline,
hearts on Salt Lake City, winter breeze
Manhattan computer midtown
digital engine hum, hard drive deluxe.

New Beginning
Hope like Fresno, California hot oven apple pie,
Chevron Chevy gas-up, Indianapolis
clover-leaf perfection,
Canadian geese Palm Beach January nest.

New Beginning
Oh poets words flow on page
like porterhouse steak genius.
Six shooter outlaw craft
revolutions tan buckskin coat
Pacific Coast Highway magic aquarius moon night
cosmic dream.

New Beginning
American highway oakwood optimism,
clean and sober dollar in kitty,
Methodist Church wood pew prayers
like calico cat, baby boom
prairie women grace,
Grandmothers pearl gate
fence mend wisdom, yes.
New Orleans two-by-four house build.
New Beginning, yes.

February Rain Freeze

February Rain Freeze
Talk radio Thursday afternoon
chocolate donut rialto,
Amy and Leigh's honeycomb theater open
Bond Street downtown excellence.
House-sit dog Los Angeles return
like lightning speed race car.

February Rain Freeze
Presidents' Day hot oatmeal
serendipity, White House Washington, D.C. courage
Gods bring it home
cumulus cloud Catholic angles transcendence.
Cameo hearts on fire like
Montana Saturday night square dance grace.
Big Sky pick-up truck excellence.

February Rain Freeze
My "Prairie Fire Poetry" read
Yorkville cool daddy quiescence,
word howl Second Avenue heartland
rainbow sublime.
Home-grown New York City create.

February Rain Freeze
Radiator heat warm bones
like Albuquerque hot five alarm chili,
brother Marc's 53rd Hudson Street
birthday hoe-down,
Brazil ladies elegant samba,
hearty Manhattan bravado.
Red wine flow like Jesus magic
Jerusalem Last Supper.

February Rain Freeze
Jet Blue JFK airport snafu,
tangle like knitting yarn
third grader knot failure.
Yes to winter's strong arm muscle
Riker's Island jail house faith.
Yes to East River purple dawn,
hope like Britney Spears rehab bound
clean up act.
Addiction black hole demon, cupboard shelf Vivaldi
quarter-note hope.

February Rain Freeze
Missouri ice storm, week long
power out like flea flicker July firefly.
Interstate 40 18 wheel semi close down.

February Rain Freeze
Embrace hassle free Dartmouth College
sophomores.
Embrace Walt Whitman Brooklyn Ferry immense
American optimism.
Embrace Bleecker Street Budweiser
glory train ghost riders.

February Rain Freeze
Poets like sufi dervish,
Catholic saint, Baptist holy roller minister.
Long johns, Timberland work boots,
Dutchess County monastic retreat
snow ridge line souls
dream soft shell crab spring,
Lent's candy cane sacrifice,
Canal Street year of pig
singular Buddhist satori
February Rain Freeze, yes!

Friday Sunshine

Friday Sunshine
February dry bone rococo fruit stand morning,
one dollar papaya,
two dollar Chilean cantaloupes,
miracle red ski parka dream time.

Friday Sunshine
Overnight doorman Jeff
cool Yugoslav kick back vibration,
corporate suit and tie boys cut
cherry pie pay check,
toddlers arise like muffin bake,
stroller moms breast feed rock steady heroism.

Friday Sunshine
Second Avenue be-bop coffee cart
croissants, hot black coffee,
Marlboro smoke like Ohio cirrus clouds.
Tobacco harmony,
hot oatmeal, Greek diner break day
like morning canine walk.

Friday Sunshine
Laura Boss's New Jersey computer repair,
poets bear cut like Jackson Heights
April front lawn trim.
Penthouse Magazine easy glide,
no sweetheart flesh and flesh
chop suey rialto.
86th Street jackhammer shake and bake
noise shatter.
Hobo George can-man seven year Manhattan ramble.

Friday Sunshine
Thousand Hebrew prayers,
sabbath dusk synagogue Torah sanctity
candle light roast chicken
God's desert prophecy.

Friday Sunshine
Texas Blake's cheapo haircut,
DTUT coffee house computer zombies,
souls shatter like Grey Goose Vodka breakfast,
youth brick wall delusion.
Rehabs full like jelly bean baskets
Jet set go go cocaine heads
flip city ramrod desolation.

Friday Sunshine
Yes to Bronx Science High School senior year
 discipline
honey bee calculus excellence.
Yes to Antoine Chekhov *Cherry Orchard*
dramatic read.
Yes to *Moby Dick* Herman Melville whale.
Nantucket sleigh ride.

Friday Sunshine
Roanoke, Virginia fry pan humility,
American optimism
like spring training Yankee short-stop
Derek Jeter. 2007 new beginning.
Pinewood integrity, calico cat,
keep flannel faith.
Friday Sunshine, yes!

Daybreak Express

Daybreak Express
Ham and eggs St. Marks Place scoot
mellow jazz like Saturday morning eros,
Jesus' infinite Brooklyn miracles.

Daybreak Express
Alta, Utah February family
ski rialto, snow-board quicksilver
youth cool,
hot chocolate breakfast
American Olympic dream.

Daybreak Express
No to Friday night sidewinder
cocaine aficionados.
No to call-girl turn trick
on new George Washington
dollar coin.
No to Yale University new-age whole
grain know-nothing reefer heads.
Bring on American history fifth
grade passion.
Bring on senior citizens open highway
rock solid wisdom, greatest generation!
Bring on Swiss watch repair genius.

Daybreak Express
Myrna's Miami Wednesday evening Bible
study excellence
black crows telephone line
chit chat,
God family country like
hot Memphis pecan pie,
82nd Airborne Iraq do a job cool,
Waldorf Astoria 500 dollar a night
digs, homeless Harry's
crossword puzzle street-wise obsession.

Daybreak Express
Union Pacific freight train
Chicago to sweet Phoenix,
Centrum Silver vitamins,
faith like Vietnam veterans
Da Nang fire fight,
top flight freedom time victory,
homecoming like carrier pigeon return 1970.

Daybreak Express
Embrace Andreas' deli short order
cook quiescence,
Taos, New Mexico high desert dawn,
Methodist Church straight back
honeysuckle Sunday sermon.
Starch collar Christian family unity.

Daybreak Express
Fresh Direct clean cut make a buck delivery boys,
Union Local 917 truck driver, muscle.
Thomas' English muffin butter and jelly aesthetics.
Winter 36 degrees weekend like honeybear hibernate.
Workbook flannel metaphors.
Daybreak Express, always!

Wilderness Redemption

I am God's wilderness redemption
one match Boy Scout camp fire,
expert bowie knife
survival jamboree,
Springfield, lllinois Am-Track signal cross.

I am Saturday night WINS-AM all
news radio,
Ames, Iowa hoe-down,
corn husk courage like next year president
caucus politics.

I am needle and thread pin cushion excellence,
Wal-Mart budge Saturday shop.
John Z's Long Island Sound miracle
spring blue fish quest
Hudson River New Jersey magic
Palisades like England Dover cliffs,
D-Day G.I. Normandy Beach
freedom time heroics 1944.
Gold Star Moms ultimate sacrifice
cheshire sons, pig tail daughters.

I am Laramie, Wyoming rodeo,
beer on sky like cloverleaf
bandit 1965.
Alternative fuel solar panels,
easy does it wind mills, ethanol corn process fuel.
Kansas Interstate 70 sunflower
July excite, full Exxon Mobil
tank, puff cumulus cloud
Colorado state line.

I am Malibu beach bikini
ying-yang, beach house
million dollar glory train haciendas.
Morning Pacific Ocean cosmic fog.
Yorkville Saint Patrick's Day
corned beef and cabbage,
Alcoholics Anonymous meet like
zen incense temple, sobriety.

I am Cornelia Street Roxanne Hoffman
wheel spoke publishing genius,
prairie fire zoom lens aesthetics.
10,000 glacial Minnesota lakes quiescence.

I am Tidal Basin Jefferson Memorial
early April spring, cherry blossom delight,
Park Slope four year old tyke
pre-school nap time.
March Madness basketball hoop skill
Big East Georgetown University
knock off Pittsburgh final tournament
victory.

I am Pensacola, Florida panhandle
key lime pie, Navy top gun fly boys.
Florida State baby back ribs,
Joanna's Holy Cross College freshman
pre-med hard grind dream.

I am Girl Scout cookie delight,
American Idol Fox 5 kaleidoscope youth,
orange sunrise Mexico Gulf
Smooth Maryland turnpike south-bound, yes!

Riverrun Wednesday

Riverrun Wednesday
Brewers Yeast energy rush,
spring equinox like raw egg
balance,
butterscotch sunlight
Saint Paddy's Day corned beef leftovers.

Riverrun Wednesday
Fruit stand man Ali Bangladesh.
Magic Mississippi River, southern Illinois
March easy glide 86th Street corner grace,
God's fresh laundry wash redemption,
Jamaican June's Brooklyn cool sister
vibration, white rum sanctity.

Riverrun Wednesday
Chicken cacciatore weekend hoe-down,
New York Mets spring training
afternoon magic slumber like
grizzly bear hibernate,
Sara Liebling Disney publish can-do.
Rock and roll cut pie 3 A.M.
guitar twang,
iced coffee early morning jag.
Ryan's heavy metal serendipity.

Riverrun Wednesday
Stock market Wall Street tango,
U.S. House of Representative pick
ax subpoena, spring thaw like
Kansas plant time corn seed,
hot biscuits honest handshakes.
High school seniors college straight back
reply notice.

Riverrun Wednesday
My "Prairie Fire Poetry" read like
state of Maine lumberjack, chain saw
aesthetics.
Saint Thomas Park Avenue choir
baritone excellence,
Central Park rain delight
wood park bench lovers eye
hyacinth serenade.
Midnight Manhattan eros.

Riverrun Wednesday
Johanne Sebastian Bach birthday,
music honeybee genius like
Vermont weaver's wood loom,
Chelsea afternoon moist kisses,
Jesus sheep herd compassion.
Montauk lobster dinner holy crusade.

Riverrun Wednesday
Aries sun bring it home
fire like New Mexico
hispanic angels, ruby red rosary beads.
Noah's Little League practice
American dream start up.

Riverrun Wednesday
Spring arrives like Denver, Colorado freight train,
dawn chill-out.
Hunts Point Market 18 wheel produce
haul.
MacDonalds pancake maple syrup hot java breakfast.
Riverrun Wednesday, bring it on!

X
SLOW RAMBLE
2002

PETER CHELNIK - HEY GIRL - COLLECTED POEMS

Jack Kerouac Highway Genius

Jack Kerouac Highway Genius
Daybreak two coffee redondo
bootstrap rise and shine
like Lowell, Massachusetts blue jay,
July hell bent like Kansas Interstate 70.

Jack Kerouac Highway Genius
No Gary, Indiana peppermint smokestacks
No Pennsylvania coal mine
on union labor
Bring on Mississippi River
Hunk Fin outlaw linen flatlands.
Bring on cameo heart Walt Whitman
American embrace.

Jack Kerouac Highway Genius
Allen Ginsberg downbeat poetry revolution
Gregory Corso back seat Rand McNally map
Jack Micheliene Thompkins Square Park
daddy-o riff.
David Amram keyboard grace,
Bridget Murnaghan poetry passion.

Jack Kerouac Highway Genius
Magic typewriter rides, spontaneous create
beatific seraphim fire
Charlie Parker be-bop alto saxophone sublime.

Jack Kerouac Highway Genius
Sweet Memphis blues angels
East Village Avenue C
cool brown bag Rhinegold beer.
Subterranean North Beach
San Francisco juke joints
afternoon fourth floor walk up eros.

Jack Kerouac Highway Genius
No iron brainwash media wave circus.
No ivy tower starch shirt square cats.
No suburban money slumber
brain warp.
Yes to Detroit black street corner prophets.
Yes to black leotard crystalline
Bleecker Street women
rainbow hearts always.

Jack Kerouac Highway Genius
Prairie liberation like Illinois
big dipper sky,
salmon pan fry, hobo mulligan stew.
Kettle of Fish
MacDougal Street Jack Daniels
and soda April howls.

Jack Kerouac HIghway Genius
On the Road Literary Exposition 1957,
Dharma Bums Kelley green shamrock Denver
short beers,
Big Sur buckshot desolation angels.

Jack Kerouac Highway Genius
Yes to Goodyear tire rubber sublime
Neil Cassidy hot wire vision
big sky desert American excellence.
Green Iowa corn, Bourbon Street
key lime pie poetic opportunity.
Cheshire providence, diamond metaphor.

Jack Kerouac Highway Genius
Kansas City Lester Young saxophone can-do
Arkansas white lightning quiescence,
Harlem ham hock go cat rhythms.
Jack Kerouac Highway Genius, dig it!

Oakwood Democracy

Oakwood Democracy
We the People
New Rochelle, New York basecard flip.
Vote booth secret ballot
cherry cheese cake honor.
U.S. Marines can-do.
Paisley red brick school yard kisses.
Vinnie Marino WQXR Brahms
2 A.M. Gotham chill out.

Oakwood Democracy
Life Liberty pursuit of
renegade happiness
Saturday morning September apple pick,
SUV upstate Rhinebeck honey bee bound.
4th grade patriots love of country
like Lexington and Concord
revolutionary fire fight.

Oakwood Democracy
Roxanne Hoffman magic Poets Wear Prada
public genius,
honeydew sew machine aesthetics,
Hoboken prairie fire cool bop.
Hudson River Lady Liberty American excellence.
Pacific Coast Highway Santa Barbara hip laid back
  serendipity.
Wildcat independent bookstore.

Oakwood Democracy
18 wheel semi Interstate 25 straight back ethics.
Albuquerque to sweet Denver.
Desert heal like
immense golden glow message.
White House rock steady
war on terror,
Republican, Democrat AFL CIO Union heroes

hardscrabble president election 2008.
Oakwood Democracy
CNN, Fox Cable News rialto
freedom of press
like George Washington
Virginia humility.
T-bone steak charcoal grill liberty.
Ithaca good old girl knitting circle.

Oakwood Democracy
Charlie's Brandeis sophomore
freight train hard sweat hit books
like George Foreman heavy prize fight,
Dora's Merrill Lynch immigrant Brazil classy
American dream
Manhattan big apple Greenwich Village
bohemian howls.
Teenage Huntington Beach surf's up notions.
Flower jams, bikini wildflower wet suit rialto jubilee.

Oakwood Democracy
Supreme Court preserve
rock steady Constitution,
Judy's woodstock elegant roll your
own tobacco grace.
Jesus' open road gospel faith,
Minnesota cool down like mom's banana
cake delight. Buffalo Poets steamroller fire.
Blue Ridge Mountain Roanoke bluegrass banjo, fiddle
hickory ham smoke country jam.
American freedom time glory train,
Oakwood Democracy, yes!

Scarsdale High Excellence 1967

Scarsdale High Excellence 1967
Trim rococo suburban lawns,
Tudor Greenacre houses,
Fox Meadow Murray Hill Road big cat spreads
Heathecoate five corners snicker
bars haciendas,
Quaker Ridge new breed wildcat shacks,
Edgewood gingerbread cottages,
Village Pierce and Shiller Stationery.

Scarsdale High Excellence 1967
Advanced Placement physics,
sweet dream A.P. History
Merit Scholars three hour nightly
homework grind,
Ivy League, Seven sisters
Freight train best and brightest bound.

Scarsdale High Excellence 1967
Muscle football break-even mud record
cross country open ridgeline heroics,
girls field hockey bring it home, yes.
Maroon and white cheerleaders can-do cool.

Scarsdale High Excellence 1967
Open house beer keg Budweiser rialto,
Ford Mustang cotton candy halcyon kisses
concert choir soprano cameo voice chops on fire, yes.

Scarsdale High Excellence 1967
Yes to Candlelight, Tennyson's gin joints.
Yes to Bass Wejuns, Peter Pan collars,
button-down shirts, Levi easy glide.
Yes to maroon ink on paper journalism supreme.
yes to pink corsage, tuxedo optimism
senior prom end game.

Scarsdale High Excellence 1967
Bring on bottom half down low academic
kaleidoscope achievement, late bloom
like Duck Pond tulips.
Bring on engineer boot hipsters
rock and roll English mods, rockers leather
boys.
Bring on Jay Shulman's Offbeat Band true
grit passion.

Scarsdale High Excellence 1967
Twenty plus honeybee classmates pass on
like Canada geese southbound,
death like bad literary pun.
Too much Vietnam blood carnage.
Too much cut marijuana,
tape worm madness.
Too much LSD 25, cheap bourbon shots
San Francisco down and out fandango.
Too much 1980 cocaine dream fracture.

Scarsdale High Excellence 1967
Twenty plus cheshire hearts not on
green garden planet.
Black Hole disease like New Jersey Turnpike
chemical works.
Heaven bound like Jesuit priest,
Cleveland, Ohio rabbi
humble black Alabama sharecropper.
Karmic wheel reincarnation,
Holy redemption spirit break
like cherry jawbreakers.

Scarsdale High Excellence 1967
Yes to America's infinite promise.
Yes to magnolia education.
Sweet yes to apple pie greatest generation
moms and dads.
Yes to baby boom whole grain warriors.
Bring on Long Island Sound ashes spread.
Bring on Valhalla cemetery rest in peace.
Bring on Brite Avenue magic Saturday dawn
Leatherstocking Lane April serendipity
God's rainbow grace
Scarsdale High Excellence 1967, always!

Harvest Home

Harvest home
4-H club Nebraska cow milk'
farm excellence,
pumpkin patch orange ball rialto,
hot chocolate warm small tykes bundle
like red Vermont flannel shirts.
Woodstock oakwood cabin warmth
magic wood burn stove quiescence.

Harvest Home
October Christian Family Radio chill out,
faith like cotton candy delight.
Late night Bible read.
Beef stew-carrots, celery, onion
slimmer,
baby boom wet French kisses
night time Fifth Avenue silk stocking solitude.

Harvest Home
Vision poets bricklayer craft,
ink on paper lone Texas coyote aesthetics,
America's freedom time talk radio
A.M. grace,
RV trailer park common man
campfire tall tales,
Jefferson City, Missouri Mobil fill up
iced coffee eastern bound like
World War Two Red Ball express.

Harvest Home
Kansas scarecrow north wind logic,
Illinois prairie flatland Lutheran church
hymn sing,
local judge keep law like hoot owl
2 A.M. coos.
Ladder 13 85th Street
FDNY cool daddy heroism,
Putnam County beer runs,
ball cherry pie jack,
Jewish sukkoth autumn joy.

Harvest Home
Scarsdale High School undefeated football season
glory time 1968,
sweat muscle Vietnam true grit.
Cheerleaders firm legs maroon and white
pom-pom eros.
Miami two day monsoon liberation
sweet Myrna's real estate halcyon quest,
Cuban coffee, Ford Explorer
supermarket scoot.

Harvest Home
Security guard Thomas Gayana laid
back cheese danish wisdom.
Fire leaves like Grandma Moses paint palette,
Jesus blessed rock steady savior,
Zen Buddhist incense buy back
mediation.
Wrigley Field Chicago Cubs
playoff can-do midwest excellence,
Marlboro cigarette smoke
chill out,
Girl Scouts merit badge sash hardscrabble
　achievement
mom and dad bring home bacon
forever Mississippi River love, yes!

Corduroy Faith

Corduroy Faith
Jesus' New York Harbor miracle
pound cake notions.
Tennessee good old boy rock steady ethics,
October 1st Ohio horizon dream time,
Navy bosuns whistle,
F-16 two o'clock high, fly boy top gun cool.

Corduroy Faith
Lords Day peace of mind
like downhill Adirondack bicycle glide,
Hunter Mountain rock climb,
hot coffee early morning surrender.
Stamford, Connecticut Dr. Hayley tooth
drill genius, Shippan Point half-way house 1971.

Corduroy Faith
American excellence
deer hunt season camouflage hopscotch target shoot.
Kansas sunflower halcyon grace,
Michigan State football noon time
shoulder pad muscle crunch,
Metropolitan Opera House busty
soprano, voice chops,
Channel's classical tuba stick to guns
supreme Big Apple can-do.

Corduroy Faith
All Souls Unitarian Church soup kitchen
Transcendence Henry David Thoreau
fire leaves passion, Walden Pond social justice.
Transcendence like Cheerios and milk,
grill cheese Italian bread grape kool-aid.

Corduroy Faith
June's Brooklyn jerk chicken
salvation like cotton bed time prayers.
God's New Jerusalem grace,
tea cup logic.
Flannel poets word resurrection,
Jim Jennings American Theater of Actors
heart open proscenium stage excellence.

Corduroy Faith
Saint Monica's Church rosary bead candle
light prayers,
New York Yankees A-Rod 2007 excellence,
Supreme Court preserve Constitution
fall maple leaf, Burlington, Vermont grace.
Thousand glory train howls,
six lane highway midnight
Interstate 80 Indiana cool glide,
born-again Christian Sunday morning pine chapel faith
steady hand on Chevy pick up-wheel, always!

Honey Bee Commotion

Honey Bee Commotion
Grand Central Station madcap break dance.
Queen bee like Marie Antoinette
eat cake rialto,
sweet honeycomb delight,
Knoxville July buzz swirl.
East Stroudsberg, Pennsylvania new morning
honey harvest quest.

Honey Bee Commotion
Gyroscope spin like Salt Lake City, Utah
concrete playground,
gangster's brown eye noon time stings,
Burlington, Vermont sweet nectar bee harvest
peanut butter whole grain Tupelo honey
Beethoven symphony magic hum.

Honey Bee Commotion
Magnolia field, Navy F-16 flight
pistil stamen fertilize
like 4-H Club Guernsey cow.
Nose dive bee like Japanese Kamikaze,
Space Shuttle Discovery American heroes
earth return.

Honey Bee Commotion
Beekeepers errant English knight
mask gloves, knee-high boots
like Missouri trout fisherman.
Swarm on exquisite bees like football fans
enter Giants Stadium
Sunday blood jousts.
Yes to honey San Francisco bound glory train redondo.
Yes to Alvin Ailey Ballet easy glide.
Yes to God's Fresno, California
purple creation frenzy.

Honey Bee Commotion
Massachusetts green nature balance
like Emily Dickinson spring equinox egg miracle.
God's forsythia flower grace,
trellis rose hybrid bloom,
bee hive hold Hopi desert tabernacle
sweet Putnam County garden serendipity, yes!

Night Song Heart

Night Song Heart
Sundae morning standard clock time change
  revolution
Jesus miracle salvation like
water to wine Bible transform,
U.S. Army 10th Mountain Division Afghan
heroics.
Sweet radiator heat November
afternoon halcyon slumber,
dreams like fleece lambs over
wood Vermont white fence.

Night Song Heart
86th Street Pizza amigos
carrot juice pit stop,
corner fruit boys get lucky high fives.
Mythic Greenwich Village Halloween parade.
T-bone steak, brick school yard kisses like
pumpkin pie bleach white whipped cream.
Charge card Madison Avenue resurrection.

Night Song Heart
October Van Gogh paint palette fire leaves change,
upstate cathedral brilliance,
down comforter Marlboro smoke.
Lincoln, Nebraska computer hum,
American genius Hudson River iron muscle barge
blue sky adventure.

Night Song Heart
No to European heroin heroes.
No to doom and gloom Prozac prop poets.
No to hate parents, Yale University phd's.
No to radical Islam blood vortex.
Bring on Maria and Peter's rock steady
blue collar chicken shack.
Bring on 69th Street James' and Greg's
hardscrabble parking garage cool.
Bring on Boy Scout merit badge wilderness
crescendo.

Night Song Heart
Eliots dog walk Museum High School hip
vibration.
Brina and Puerto Rican John love doves
like honeysuckle eternal spring,
M-15 downtown bus groove,
twelve step AA freight train sobriety.
Fox News hot blueberry muffin heartland
Missouri oak tree ethics.

Night Song Heart
Righteous cameo heats,
Laura Ludwig's Cairo, New York
wood burn fireplace aesthetics.
No to San Diego fire holocaust.
No to Governor Spitzer illegal immigrant
drivers license delusion.
No to public school 50% drop out rate
head on crash.
Yes to U.S. Navy Seals muscle valor.
Yes to family time dinner
political debates like Lincoln Douglas mix a
lot.
Yes to sixth grader math whiz like
Coney Island Cyclone roller coaster jubilee.

Night Song Heart
God's small Catholic women Sunday
Saint Elizabeth's Church revelation,
Mom and Dad classy Greatest Generation
straight back discipline.
Gold school like 1930's depression
Hooverville hobo camps.
American history rock solid Constitution
protect and defend
like Monticello Thomas Jefferson homestead,
thousand 2 A.M. 18 wheel semi truck stop
highway grooves, southbound, dig it!

Sleeve Roll Aesthetics

Sleeve Roll Aesthetics
Raw bone south Bronx metaphors,
Nautilus machine pump iron
U.S.A. Olympic javelin toss,
straight shot poetic rhythm like
East River Coast Guard rescue boat.
Arkansas morning late autumn hot coffee
buttered roll.
Green workshirt poetic language economy.

Sleeve Roll Aesthetics
Norman Mailer muscle fiction like
Brooklyn mob waterfront rialto,
noon time Marlboro cigarette smoke.
No to Nanny state weak spine infant drool.
No to culture chickification.
No to Greenwich cosmopolitan
cocktail drunks.
Yes to 10 pound chunk big hip ladies,
cheshire Wyoming hearts.
Yes to Omaha, Nebraska heartland
stand by man ladies.
Yes to October little league hard pitch
aluminum bat heroics.

Sleeve Roll Aesthetics
Guyana Thomas' blue collar
thermos coffee jug, overnight hardscrabble cool.
Porterhouse steak grill sizzle like
Birmingham, Alabama November outdoor
barbecue,
Florida Everglades big daddy crocodile
push comes to shove purple survival quest.
Desert highway, Nevada rolling thunder
Ford pick up truck stop shower, shave, flapjacks.

Sleeve Roll Aesthetics
Serbian Chris big heart First Avenue
86th Street rainbow spirit,
hard hat construction crew like
U.S. Marines ut American apple pie.
God's fear like Bay Area oil spill,
fire and brimstone Monday morning
short circuit environmental holocaust.

Sleeve Roll Aesthetics
Jack Kerouac Denver tokay wine big horizon quiescence
Springfield, Illinois pistol pack
blue uniform Pinkerton Bulls.
Hard love women like 3 A.M. typewriter
rides, Nashville country western
pull no punches guitar twang.
God's hot asphalt, Tucson, Arizona jubilee.
Speak mind like old school
black NAACP field organizer Freedom Riders'
North Carolina courage.
Steel mill union jobs excellence,
poems like Oklahoma hot wire tornado.
Sleeve Roll Aesthetics, always!

Gravy Train

Gravy Train
Green cash roll thunder road,
Jack Daniels and soda Friday night
Memphis Beale Street get lucky
sugar babes,
over roast beef, sweet potatoes
Christmas Day family high on hog like
sugar plum fairie Boston saints.

Gravy Train
American Express credit card shoot moon holy rialto,
Flat Iron district barbecue ribs,
Saks Fifth Avenue noel windows,
wide eyed tots bundle
like panda bear deluxe.
Wood cupboard dreams,
New Haven, Connecticut yankee
Italian lasagna,
Catholic Mass like cheshire cat
Jesus miracle wonder.

Gravy Train
No to ice storm Oklahoma electric
power outage.
No to Britney Spears' sister 16 year old
pregnant whack out.
No to Isaiah thomas New York Knicks
bottom eastern division lose streak.
Embrace sweet third grader math skill.
Embrace talk radio 18 wheel semi
red neck common sense.
Embrace Bill of Rights Valley Forge
Revolutionary War ultimate sacrifice.

Gravy Train
Cool mama Colorado homestead,
Marc and Dora's mythic New Mexico
Land of Enchantment desert heal,
Lancaster County Amish ethics like
fallow Pennsylvania farmland field,
Ryan's psychedelic white
Christmas tree,
Second Avenue Swig Bar Dundee, Scotland Scott
young buck Jamison shots,
24 year old blond sweethearts,
Saturday night Manhattan ramble.

Gravy Train
Holiday Microsoft corporate greenback bonus,
mink coat mamas like baby boom
sophisticated lady rialto,
Laura Boss' poetry quest Mendham, New Jersey
pine wood workshops,
41 cent American flag stamps,
Post Office Gracie Station mad commotion,
Iowa caucus honeysuckle democracy
straight edge president campaign.

Gravy Train
God's faith like Channuka candle
light rabbi.
No to Omaha, Nebraska shop mall blood carnage.
No to teenage Vicadin pill pop mess mind
like 1969 Play station desolation.
No to jet-set youth cult fame quest
Los Angeles tabloid fracture.
Bring on Mom and Dad's granite rock steady
Manhattan character.
Bring on Portland, Maine front door Christmas
wreath dignity.

Gravy Train
Shoestring butterscotch winter solstice.
Sedona, Arizona holy afternoon tumbleweed joy.
South Carolina Baptist wood pew holy hymns,
Hosannahs like string bean casserole,
gift wrap aesthetics,
Tiffany turquoise box engagement ring sparkle
Marin County high speed BMW mountain road scoot.
Gravy Train, dig it.

New Years Rialto

New Years Rialto
Jig saw purple haze logic,
porcupine persuasion like back seat
Ford Explorer kisses,
hardscrabble new beginnings, half shell
faith like Crosby Street cheap wine swig.
New Hampshire primary vote booth presidential
Democrat Republican democracy.

New Years Rialto
God's Saint Patrick Cathedral
sweet charity candle light,
Rocky Mountain leather saddle hope,
rosary beat champagne cool daddy resurrection
Mary's straight back tango jubilee,
full moon wicca peace train.
Bellevue psyche ward freedom time release.

New Years Rialto
No to 7 A.M. early bird cocaine bartenders.
No to non-stop locomotion
Manhattan Bloomingdale's divas.
No to three divorce baby boom
keep party going suburban Briarcliff Manor
desolation.
No to e-mail ball and chain poseurs.
Yes to Boro Park orthodox Jewish holy men and
women torah sanctity.
Yes to Provo, Utah Mormon western ethics.
Yes to Dominican Cheli
kids' grade school excellence.

New Years Rialto
Marathon New Years Day poetry magic,
fringe sages, touch celestial sky
like Catholic saints.
America's holy winter North Dakota warriors,
O'Hare Airport checkerboard
flight patterns,
New England Patriots undefeated
season muscle quest,
Huntsville, Alabama turkey baste,
sweet potatoes,
2008 cheshire cat shoulder caress Barrow Street
salvation.

New Years Rialto
86th Street Apartment bleach floor mop,
Gristedes grocery run like
honey bear December hibernate.
Beatnik howls Back Fence Bar
sawdust floors,
Seattle patchouli white light grunge emotion,
Hopi Indian arrowhead pow-wow
Humboldt County, California fireplace kisses,
cordwood rainbow finesse.
Eugenia's Woodstock velvet psychic vibrations
New Orleans' French Quarter southern comfort
bar room shots,
New Years Rialto, yes!

Boy Scout Compass

I am Boy Scout Compass westward bound
wishing well notions
like Shakespeare's Romeo and Juliet.
Reading glasses front flannel pocket
poetry room miracle vibration.
Fairbanks, Alaska morning winter ember fire glow.
General David Petreas' sweet Iraq U.S. Army excellence.

I am salmon bake Pikes Market Seattle
Pacific catch,
Goose Gossage Yankee relief pitcher
Hall of Fame election,
Rhinebeck Lisa permit drive test,
Chinese cuisine full belly satisfy
La Jolla, California oil massage chill out.

I am downtown Fulton Street
Kosher sandwich shop, South Street Seaport
mythic sail sloops,
God's Colorado snow blizzard pine tree
beauty,
New Year's Eve desolation row solitaire round
  house blues,
down and out like frat boy Budweiser drunk.
Madison, Wisconsin State Street,
Sunday morning hosannahs.

I am salvation's blue arctic parka,
Ohio tornado tragic like lost west coast San Barbara
love letter.
Number 4 subway line downtown bound,
no hold barred, rush hour rialto
Grand Central Station 42nd Street
Suburban high roll corporate
cats Wall Street shake and bake,
Montana wilderness Baptist redemption,
Big Sky Country Interstate snow storm glory.

I am Centrum multi vitamin
morning dose like peyote Navaho Indian,
Miami Kendall section Myrna's latino
spice food deluxe, mom Carmen's senior citizen
whole cloth spirit,
morning Bible read like Jesus
born-again sanctity.
Brunswick, Georgia truck stop American virtue,
meatloaf, mashed potatoes
holy self-discipline.

I am pool hall side bet,
86th Street Burger King dollar special,
Scott's Swig Bar broad Dundee Scotland banter.
January east Harlem corner bodega, Wise potato chips
Yorkville soup kitchen homeless survival.
Joanna's Holy Cross pre-med sophomore year
buckle down excellence.
Rent bill mid-month Manhattan payoff.
Louisiana State University national football muscle
 victory.

I am cross country New Orleans easy beat
Wild Turkey bourbon,
church pew faith like New Hampshire primary
democracy supreme.
Greenwich Village movie lines like
cobra snake,
back seat Auburn, Alabama caress,
U.S. Navy Persian Gulf stand fast.
Photo memory, sharp as tack, always.

Wind at Back Groove

Wind at Back Groove
Bob Feldman cool daddy tenor sax,
twenty dollar bill hi-jinx
2 A.M. jazz rainbow celebration,
Jewish synagogue Torah glory,
matzo brie winters short days like capri pants,
thousand hymn book prayers.
Sabbath west side candle light virtue.

Wind at Back Groove
Log cabin cotton sheets,
wood burn stove
blizzard warmth Boulder, Colorado kick back
58th birthday like eggs over easy
turkey sausage, rye toast,
freight train logic Phoenix bound.
Liberty's straight back conservative heartland stand tall.

Wind at Back Groove
Wisconsin hereford cow morning milk,
Western Union money order,
needle and thread metaphors like
Roxanne Hoffman Hoboken easy beat
publisher honeysuckle genius.
Catholic communion wafers,
Jenny and Rudy senior citizen
rock steady 85th Street wisdom.

Wind at Back Groove
Mexican Georgie tequila east Harlem ramble.
Duane Reade pharmacy
medication big time scrip refill,
unused Trojan like cupboard
flour, red zinger tea.
2008 teapot Harvard Yard ivy league excellence.

Wind at Back Groove
Dollar in kitty twelve step
sober hipsters,
mid-January flannel
integrity work boot steady stride.
Regular coffee two sugars, Mikey's Toyota Mineola
   late night
homeward return.
Ryan's cheeseburger holy
Manhattan heavy metal quest
Hudson River miracle sunset.

Wind at Back Groove
No to trust fund kaleidoscope radicals.
No to 300 pound Boston Red Sox fanatics.
No to middle aged child predator.
Bring on self-reliance like Lexington and Concord
revolution victory.
Bring on Veteran's Hospital top notch health care.
Bring on capitalism freedom time
pull self up by bootstraps.
Hardscrabble poverty motivation.

Wind at Back Groove
Houston big rig oil refineries,
clean coal gas station Interstate 70 fuel up,
peanut butter and jelly lunch time.
Kansas City bound like AmTrak bullet train.
Supreme Court Constitution clarity,
CBS News Portland, Oregon
whole grain essence.

Wind at Back Groove
Sandalwood incense late dusk kisses,
California wine notions
snow ball fight like Battle of Bulge America's victory.
Peace train Mississippi River ice flow,
barge Gulf of Mexico bound.
Toddlers french toast dream time
love's cheshire heart open highway quiescence,
Wind at Back Groove, dig it!

Marmalade Tuesday

Marmalade Tuesday
Ground Hog Day Staten Island Chuck
no shadow, spring like warm Georgia breeze.
Park Slope carousel poetry read,
Patricia Carragon Brooklyn magic
like cameo fire heart.

Marmalade Tuesday
New York Giants super bowl Budweiser
cool daddy victory, Plexico Burris
sugar touchdown catch.
Second Avenue wildcat frenzy,
Big Apple gotham commotion.
Winter's damp long leash like state of Maine
brown muskrat.

Marmalade Tuesday
No to off-beat rock and roll
stomach virus, Tylanol pill pop.
No to heavy metal blow ear drums
out like runway 747.
No to maniac neighbor's sex bounce
2 A.M. Manhattan redondo.

Marmalade Tuesday
Yes to Super Tuesday primary
president elect.
Yes to 6:30 A.M.
Mormon Church vote scoot.
Yes to 2008 White House democracy
we the people Democrat, Republican wrangle.

SLOW RAMBLE

Marmalade Tuesday
New Orleans Mardi Gras Coors light
blow out,
Ash Wednesday solitude
like rainbow heaven,
spring promise like frisky
tabby cat,
February dry dock afternoon,
easy does it wind Mamaroneck Harbor
New England clam chowder delight.

Marmalade Tuesday
Sprain Brook Parkway northbound, bare maple trees
like debutante's shoulders,
Great Nephew Brandon's Jewish circumcism
prophet Abraham holy covenant,
lox bagels chow down works.
February aquarius sun spirit glide
always on cash roll,
Barrow Street beatnik beatific howls,
Marmalade Tuesday, yes.

Slow Ramble

Slow Ramble
Northern California immense
redwood tree magic
Humboldt County hippie woman celebration
wood burn stove caress,
Pacific Ocean high tide blossom
like Jesus miracle Galilee water walk.

Slow Ramble
St. Louis alleyway kisses,
record New York City February warmth
like Ohio maple syrup air,
Ash Wednesday black forehead dust to dust
holy God's spirit,
Zen roundhouse meditation
New Age computer genius
like romaine salad, mung beans.

Slow Ramble
Sedona, Arizona adobe homes,
desert heal like epsom salt bath,
touch Grand Canyon sky
America deep crevice wonder,
denim Levi's, Main Street Eureka Spring, Arkansas
  delight.

Slow Ramble
No to Tennessee primary election day tornado.
No to Hollywood coke head baby boom delusion.
No to Santa Monica Beach oil muscle boys.
Bring on American invention.
Bring on Apple I-pod high tech genius.
Bring on high school sophomore
saxophone passion.

Bring on needlepoint steady hand excellence.
Slow Ramble
Meridian, Mississippi apple pie family
dinner
Second Avenue Con Edison water pipe fix
construction hondos,
41 cent stamp red white blue flag redondo.
St. Valentine day dozen red rose get lucky
down on halfback knees marriage propose.

Slow Ramble
Low key notions like M 15 downtown bus,
Hillsdale, Michigan rock rib conservative
college educate,
Amy and Leigh's NYU actresses big time
honeysuckle craft,
serenity like Texas tumbleweed highway
dawn easy does it.
Fourth grader homeward bound milk and
cookie cool out,
Slow Ramble always!

Needlepoint Joy

Needlepoint Joy
Indiana Girl Scouts
pillow cover revelation,
wool shetland sheep glory train
yarn aesthetics,
American folk art craft like
Campbells soup and sandwich snow squall
home lunchtime warmth.

Needlepoint Joy
5th grade school teacher
cotton arm cheshire reading delight,
Gospel train harmony like Detroit City
blueberry muffin bake,
General Motors assembly line
lunch bucket excellence.

Needlepoint Joy
Myrna's butterscotch warm Miami
rice and beans afternoons,
South Street Seaport German long leg
tourists, fur hats, muffler necks.
Republican Party stand fast
War on Terror U.S. Army can-do,
82 degree Baghdad afternoon foot patrol,
secure rainbow bazaars like canvas belt notch.

Needlepoint Joy
Sunshine spring daffodils,
March easy go clock time change,
Santa Monica Beach lovers hand hold
like Buddhists saints.

Needlepoint Joy
Second Avenue subway avenue street
asphalt break up, mom and pop
pizza shop business down like
Dow Jones Industrial Average,
truant 8th grader cheap wine
hide out.

Needlepoint Joy
Nebraska calico grandmother hands
steady like hospital heart surgeon,
pattern books kitchen table
busy bee hobby,
arts multi-color serenity,
toddlers late winter down parka
bundle up.
Family grace
Needlepoint Joy, always!

New Morning

New Morning
Liberty's sweet cake optimism
Cheerios and milk breakfast,
Friday afternoon honeycomb siesta,
calls to Woodstock Eugenia,
psychic goddess,
ridgeline purple clairvoyant.

New Morning
Butterscotch Bible read,
Christian radio roundhouse 8 A.M. tenderloin
faith like Jesus' sugar grace.
Late winter Gemini moon easy beat,
denim radiator heat begin.
Mike's Viande Coffee Shop Yorkville
late night tea cup chatter.
Dallas, Texas wine bar bartender
tough blond downtown dominatrix.

New Morning
Holy South Carolina paper mill prayers
lunch time Hindu chutney, poori bread,
tandoori bring it home chicken.
Gods' oneness.
New Mexico desert jubilee,
Saint Patrick Day Blarney Stone
corned beef and cabbage
Second Avenue halcyon shouts.

New Morning
March fifteenth Ides of March
blood-let like John Kennedy
Dallas assassination 1963.
Big cat betray,
Satan's skull and bone heavy metal
Saint Marks Place roundhouse rebels.

New Morning
New moon March begin tapestry weave,
Rhode Island dry dock
wood hull patience.
Jewish Torah roll holy Friday night inspire,
Gospels' Tennessee Sunday 9 A.M.
calico hope,
New Morning, yes!

Saturday Night Clean and Sober

I am wilderness Marlboro smoke,
Kentucky two-step redemption,
Supreme Court rolling thunder
big cat yarn spool
like spring Washington, D.C. dawn.

I am CBS-FM ring a levio oldies,
hot dogs and mustard south Michigan Dairy Queen
delight,
Palm Sunday ham glaze Pentecostal minister
fire sermon like God's bush burn.

I am Saturday Night Clean and Sober
denim heart steady like
Plymouth Rock pilgrim first Thanksgiving,
doorman Jeff New York Post governor scandal
sex velvet room hi-jinx read,
Atlanta, Georgia split rain tornado,
Manhattan 20 story crane collapse.

I am 2008 late winter March Chicky's Chicken Shack
quarter dark meat, mashed
potatoes,
faith like 13 year old Bar Mitzvah teenager,
bark canoe Missouri lake paddle,
Fort Smith, Arkansas truck stop
miracle sleep in.

I am Laramie, Wyoming gingham celebrate like
prairie tumbleweed, Bob Feldman
tenor saxophone hucklebuck genius,
American Theater of Actors big cat
poetry read,
twenty dollar time piece,
Duane Reade Tuesday morning blue collar special.
Laura Boss' sweet cake eleven year Hudson
River friendship.

SLOW RAMBLE

I am Beach Boys *Pet Sounds*
Hawthorne, California surf's up fandango.
Wal-Mart 4 dollar generic prescription
drug American square deal.
Carley's dad's Ford hybrid Detroit
technology genius,
Albuquerque highway outback
cumulus cloud redondo, always!

Cash and Carry Aesthetics

Cash and Carry Aesthetics
Poetic timberline magic
two dozen St. Valentine Day red roses,
winter's long night ride
Pennsylvania Interstate 80 finish.

Cash and Carry Aesthetics
Bold March winter Columbus, Ohio
20 inch snow blizzard,
patchwork quilt rhythm
like Bleecker Street jazz 1963.

Cash and Carry Aesthetics
No to bootleg east village soothsayers.
No to psycho medication five beer
paranoia.
No to Bear Stearns three card monte
mortgage hustle.
No Visa card Bowery poseurs.
Yes to blue color honeysuckle construction worker
hard hat skill.
Yes to stand tall Colorado pine
valley dignity.
Yes to Marianne's U.S. Mail
cool lady afternoon smiles.

Cash and Carry Aesthetics
Fly fishing similes like upstate
New York bass catch.
Brother Marc's Hunter Mountain homestead
renovate craft.
Poetry word economy like black weekend wheel
  suitcase.

Cash and Carry Aesthetics
Elaine Minionis' ferris wheel
documentary shoot out.
Venezuela can o' sardines genius.
Sweet justice's muscle forearm.
DNA 20 year Attica prison jailhouse

innocent freedom.
Cash and Carry Aesthetics
No to matchbook small time poems.
No to internet journals like
April gypsy moths.
No to workshop teachers wilderness
fracture.
Bring on prairie fire burn down house
can of corn poetry.
Bring on Thoreau self-reliant cobblestone
words.
Bring on Salt Lake City, Utah Mormon
cut apple pie cadence.

Cash and Carry Aesthetics
Ezra Pound consciousness stream.
Hudson Valley Sunday afternoon snow melt.
Canvas stretch like New School
excellence.
Touch west side purple sky.
North Beach beatnik howls.
Shake up white Wonder Bread conformity,
awake Hindu heart chakra like
Ravi Shankar miracle sitar.

Cash and Carry Aesthetics
Wind at Manhattan back curve,
youth fandago, Bradley Beach
wood boardwalk five and dime
cornerstone confessions,
April poetry month inspire.
Cash and Carry Aesthetics, dig it!

Glory Promise Land

Glory Promise Land
Telluride, Colorado pine
trees,
Moses Red Sea Egypt escape
Chosen People liberation scoot,
matzo bake desert ramble
like Billy the Kid outlaw Oklahoma
high tail.

Glory Promise Land
Virginia bluegrass fiddle reel
Friday night sabbath candle light
Mom's roast chicken potato bake
fancy peas, apple sauce.
Synagogue White Plains bound
Rabbi Davis' Indiana bring it home
sermons. Dayton, Ohio spring planting green pastures.
Hudson Valley Yaweh hold fast miracle.

Glory Promise Land
Abraham Sarah hold God covenant
like rainbow calf sacrifice,
sweet Manischevitz wine
wide passion,
marshmallow kisses Lanesboro, Massachusetts
funky motel room.
Star of David holy meditation
God's April oneness Passover bound
seder books.

Glory Promise Land
58 year old Vermont thunder calico
wisdom,
tortoise shell read glasses,
Five Moses Books bring it home
Manhattan ethics,
Ten commandment honeycomb
Alabama stone engrave
Mount Sinai brimstone like
cherry pie ridgeline meditation.
Fire angels Kabala prophets.

SLOW RAMBLE

Glory Promise Land
Kentucky Saturday night jib,
moon shine swig like God's
rent bill three month late hand tremble.
Saturday morning Torah read,
Challah break come of age
like panda bear.

Glory promise Land
Cheerio box Wednesday breakfast,
Andrew's 79th Street Hebrew lessons,
fur cat springtime notions,
Canaan milk and honey bound,
Dream time cinnamon reality always!

Heart Glow

Heart Glow
Round shoulder North Carolina women
sweet Wrightsville beach April
kisses,
half moon Aquarius 5 A.M. honeysuckle
magic, highway delight like
potato pancakes apple sauce.

Heart Glow
Albuquerque El Dorado High School
desert excellence,
school yard 17 year hand hold,
ice cream Dairy Queen quiescence,
thousand highway miles like
Alaska bull moose antler beauty.

Heart Glow
Patti's NYU Number 6 train graduation
scoot, buckshot actress talent like
arrow bow target supreme.
Magnolia Love's Hudson River
New Jersey Edgewater Pathmark,
discount turkey, Alpine Lace munster cheese,
fresh bread bake.

Heart Glow
No to wildcat Budweiser infatuation.
No to governor's kinky black sock
call girl addition.
No to S&M disco boys ecstacy
pill pop rialto.
No to renegade one night stands.
Bring on pinewood rock steady morals.
Bring on Vero Beach, Florida L.A. Dodgers
spring training promise.
Bring on America's early spring cameo
divine goodness.
Bring on eternal man woman breakfast nook best friends.

Heart Glow
18 wheel Kenworth semi south bound
like state of Maine bleach white geese,
iced coffee IBM typewriter immense logic,
holy Jewish sabbath prayers,
Dr. Peter's rock and roll guitar
rococo therapy.
Two Little Red Hens, Tennessee
Tuesday biscuits,
youths magic world is oyster grunge rialto.
Two-step flesh on flesh
Union Square whole grain commotion, yes1
Louisville, Kentucky white lace
marriage vows, forever!
Heart Glow, yes!

Pecan Pie Poetics

I am Pecan Pie Poetics
Brother Marc's downshift Saab hot rod,
Laura Boss' Barnes and Noble Clifton, New Jersey
super nova poetry read,
Prospect Park sweet dogwood bloom
like Jewish messiah.

I am youth cake walk Union Square
chit chat, clean cut Illinois day dreams,
Yorkville Greatest Generation
noble saunter, walk cane wisdom
thousand memories like
Madison Square Garden prize fight glory train.

I am Jackson, Mississippi rocket ready
wind storm,
oak tree house damage like black cheese piece
bishop bumble,
82nd Airborne Iraq 2 P.M. foot patrol
Sadar City keep velvet peace.

I am Evie Ivy's Sunset Park, Brooklyn
gentle heart beat, top notch poems
like ledge calico cat.
First grade girl China cut read supreme,
penmanship quiescence,
America's 18th century hand carve
furniture colonial excellence.

I am San Diego Mission Beach surf's
up hang ten cool daddy hodad,
IBM typewriter word groove like
April little league Saturday afternoon
asphalt green practice,
t-bone steak poetry cadence,
God's firecracker Richmond, Virginia
long way home.
Hot biscuits, butter melt,
Dizzy Gillespie trumpet
jazz be-bop no holds bar rhythm.

I am NYPD anti-terrorist unit,
Second Avenue subway break concrete
downtown scoot.
Clean and sober dollar in kitty
cheeseburger deluxe Gracie's Diner
sobriety's hard highway quest.

I am White House Air Force One
NATO Europe return, Founding Fathers
Constitutional genius like
Boston Harbor spring thaw,
church pew holy prayer,
Walt Whitman *Leaves of Grass* excellence,
sand castle eros.
Mike's Bayside Greek American spinach pie ethics,
God's Jewish covenant roast chicken divine, always!

Spring Time Glory

Spring Time Glory
Central Park miracle forsythia bloom,
tulip soft shoe crescendo
Earth Day like round Georgia peach,
God's honeysuckle Seder dinner
sister Roberta Briarcliff Manor bring it home
matzo spread.
Nephew Charlie tomato vine four Passover questions.

Spring Time Glory
Pope Benedict Ground Zero holy sanctify,
Pope Mobile like white Catholic angel dance,
Yankee Stadium two hour mass
communion waver house pack, seekers divine light.
Youth Union Square skateboard jubilee
like sabbath candle light.
Clemson, South Carolina green grass redemption.

Spring Time Glory
Pennsylvania primary fisticuffs
politics like pit bull Philadelphia roof top
gamble frenzy.
William Shakespeare April 23rd
mythic cherry blossom birthday
Globe Theater drama excellence,
love's strange patchouli bedmates,
a hundred Zen Buddhist promises.

Spring Time Glory
No to new age organic rice nose in air
yoga snarls.
No to Marxist University of Colorado
American put-down.
No to homeless refuse mental health medication
like broken sink faucet.
Yes to Norman, Oklahoma
cherry pie optimism.
Yes to U.S. Marines War on Terror
combat heroes.
yes to Greatest Generation mom and dad
oak tree life passion.

Spring Time Glory
Madison Avenue dogwood
new beginnings like three month old
great nephew Brandon cool bop.
Sedona, Arizona desert heal quiescence,
red sandstone immense beauty Hopi spirit valley
American wild west wildflower bloom.

Spring Time Glory
April end open Chevy highway points west
Irish Ian Denver hard cider soul quest,
Rocky Mountain crystalline air,
Mamaroneck Harbor speed boat
mooring supreme,
youths big dipper Vermont halcyon dreams,
winter clothes shed, green garden cameo heart hope,
Spring Time Glory, always!

God's Old Testament Miracles

I am God's Old Testament Miracles
Moses' desert Mount Sinai
ten commandments bring it home straight
back law,
U.S. Coast Guard Long Island Sound
small craft rescue,
Mamaroneck Harbor full moon quiescence,
hot double-dip diner coffee,
Volvo midnight Hutchison River Parkway
easy beat.

I am Passover Red Sea liberation part,
freedom time glory like black
underground railroad true grit.
Iwo Jima U.S. Marine blood heroes.
Iowa City, Iowa Memorial Day stand proud
flag wave.
Scarsdale High School march band
half-time look sharp glory,
half back break open like Snickers Bar
touchdown run.

I am Andrew's two-step Bar Mitzvah
sour pickle Torah read,
hardscrabble May Arkansas tornado alley
death like Darfur kill fields,
Sadar City Al Qaeda shoot-out.
Cream of Wheat morning on go breakfast,
sidewinder poetics like Gregory Corso
Bleecker Street wolverine howls.

I am Mexican Cinco de Mayo Corona Park
cool Dos Equis beer,
tamales, beef tacos, love America
like butterscotch immigrants.
Climate change china stack,
McDonald's one dollar sweet iced tea,
May Colorado snow squall.

SLOW RAMBLE

I am Jewish Friday night sabbath light,
sex abstinence teenagers,
root beer keg party,
no police bust youth clean cut, always.
Gasoline federal tax holiday, thirty three
cents summer save, Lake Placid
soft-shoe holiday,
Adirondack mountain cool crystalline breeze,
trinket shop jamboree.

I am Synagogue sweet wine chosen people
three thousand year rock steady desert stronghold.
May 8th rent check pay off like
Yorkville loan shark, Con Edison keep light
big time glow, cable T.V. Fox News
Indiana pine forest heartland straight shoot.
Vivande Coffee Shop counter man Bogdan
Romanian cool,
freebie lemon meringue pie,
2 A.M. hot latina woman hop sway,
America's cotton candy greatness,
Irish Peter's Swig Bar Jamison shots,
Marlboro cigarette smoke,
sleep tight light Wyoming honey bear
thousand morning hellos.

Flash Flood Saturday

Flash Flood Saturday
Madcap rain like nuclear bomb fall out
Second Avenue wet skin,
flip-flop toes,
umbrella cave in.

Flash Flood Saturday
Jones Beach cover scurry,
JFK Airport flight delay,
Cedar Rapids, Iowa river wildcat currents,
Jesus' end of world Bible grey cloud
open like Noah's Ark rain.
Animals two by two,
Manhattan taxi slow down,
western Iowa Boy Scout tornado death
knell.

Flash Flood Saturday
Jennifer's Bronx waitress can-do dream,
support welfare dad, dead-beat boyfriend,
bartender Peter Brazil lover's Jamison shots,
Swig Bar dry awning Marlboro smoke.
Yellow slicker Yorkville waists.

Flash Flood Saturday
Sally Milgrim always upbeat poetic
Hunter College professor can-do,
brandy, kahlua, milk magic potion
like Romanian gypsy.
Paradise, California forest fires senior citizen
rough breath,
Tim Russert Meet the Press giant
heart attack death,
short string longevity.

SLOW RAMBLE

Flash Flood Saturday
Father's Day tattoo big daddy's
little tykes hand in hand, blue collar American dream
homemade classroom cards,
hamburger hot dog barbecue,
cool Dos Equis beer.

Flash Flood Saturday
Highway Joe twenty-five on road beatnik ramble.
Five years Europe, Taos, New Mexico
return like poet Jack Micheleine
dry Thomkins Square Park street rain cover,
shelter like Saint Peter's holy Church,
Mamaroneck suburb homes basement flood,
Grand Central Parkway slow down.

Flash Flood Saturday
Holy faith, blueberry pie hope,
Kodak camera family album,
Woolworth's five and dime wonder,
rain torrent like Minnesota needlepoint
cushion,
great nephew Brandon crib tuck in,
aquarius five month old cool cat.
Always high ground Montana grace.
Flash Flood Saturday, tough go!

Glory Train Consciousness

Glory Train Consciousness
Rocky Mountain tree line,
summit peak like Alice in Wonderland
looking glass,
Mary M's Boulder, Colorado trail blaze,
top shelf mountain mama hike boots.

Glory Train Consciousness
Teddy Roosevelt National Park
magic creation,
God's roundhouse grace,
Sunday mooring Pentecostal church sermon.
Computer internet home school, yes.
Cameo heart optimism.

Glory Train Consciousness
No to ten Budweiser gorilla 2008
Second Avenue shouts.
No to baby boom plastic surgery hondo girls.
No to University of Maryland frat boys
down and dirty mid-term cheat.
Bring on Sunday afternoon Metropolitan Museum
Matisse impressionistic slow float.
Bring on John's street-wise NYPD homicide detective
clue gather like chicken eggs.
Bring on Charlie Chelnik's Barcelona
late night back street paella illumination.

Glory Train Consciousness
WQXR Mozart midnight
cognitive thought process like
quicksilver Union Square skate
board teenager,
Trinity Church choir
Tanglewood 9/11 God Bless America,
July Fourth Boston Pops,
George Gershwin "Summertime" grace.

Glory Train Consciousness
Pecan pie Bible read, Union Pacific
freight train deliverance.
Hunts Point Cross Bronx Expressway
grocer's haul.
Gemini sun duality like cleft foot
Iowa hog,
David Elsasser Nightingale poetry read
rainbow quiescence.

Glory Train Consciousness
Bedroom Massachusetts John Adams knowledge,
think like dust bowl twister,
J.S. Bach miracle harpsichord groove,
pinewood freedom like Roanoke, Virginia
southbound freight line.
Poets Denver dusk revolution,
eye on summer evening azure grace,
Glory Train Consciousness, always!

Apple Pie Liberty

Apple Pie Liberty
Pennsylvania pine top cabin,
late June afternoon rain drops,
miracle America, blessed like
Jesus son of God Galilee ramble.
Founding father Constitutional genius.

Apple Pie Liberty
General David Petraeus Iraq can-do
sweet military surge like old time
dollar fifty gallon gasoline pump.
Roughneck middle east Israeli muscle.

Apple Pie Liberty
No to nuclear bomb terror Iran.
No to Hamas Lebanon car bomb blood.
No to anti-war Neville Chamberlain
weak spine appeasers.
Bring on U.S. Marines Fallujah
tough brother semper fi heroics.
Bring on Coleman Hawkins saxophone
cool bop magic.
Bring on blessed American farmland patriots
red white blue grace.

Apple Pie Liberty
Billie Holiday jazz vocal supreme
like blues satin doll.
Old school poets 40 hour work week,
computer jam, late night
pork chop create.

Apple Pie Liberty
Philadelphia soul vibrations
like chitlins, sweet potato pie,
freedom's sky the limit highway 40
opportunity,
straight-back morals, girl scout
Mom's merit badge sew
Noah little league pitcher's excellence.

Apple Pie Liberty
Summer solstice quiescence,
Laura Boss' Hudson River Hondai
River Road Pathmark scoot,
Santa Cruz surf's up afternoon
catch a wave cool,
Cliff's U.S. Navy medic
Bosnia, Gulf war combat heal.
West Point computer high tech infra-red night goggles,
upstate woodland summer train,
Lady Liberty's New York Harbor
welcome arms,
Apple Pie Liberty, dig it!

Onion Peel Friday

I am Onion Peel Friday
Wyoming cowboy cap gun shoot 'em up,
Bleecker Street gelato ices,
Brooklyn Bridge Norwegian waterfall genius.

I am mid-summer redneck howl,
Erin's Greensboro, North Carolina
magnolia dream time grace,
God's barnyard bring it home covenant,
Bon Jovi Central Park hucklebuck concert.

I am youth's Massachusetts wilderness
Lake Hoosetonic canoe paddle joy,
Joan's Santa Fe New England return heal
like break wing sparrow,
Botanical Garden greenhouse geranium miracle graft.

I am Dallas, Texas long-neck Long Star beers,
July 100 degree ice cream melt heat wave,
American cheshire heart exceptionalism,
homestead like Tennessee
Smoky Mountain log cabin jubilee.

I am WPLJ-FM radio youths late night
salt tears,
black Bible read like short stack
maple syrup pancakes,
Astoria Place black cube sculpture
tattoo journal entry, Martin guitar pick
gasoline fumes rush hour like Mississippi
River log jam.

SLOW RAMBLE

I am Cornelia Street up-scale white linen
three-star café,
Sally Miligrim's Manhattan martini
Waldorf Astoria jig-saw puzzle class.
Big Dipper cameo fire heart,
Virgo half moon,
FDR Drive downtown scoot like Ohio River
summer car wheels,
Zen Buddhist Levi blue jean jacket truth,
beatnik cool daddy Greenwich Village
literary excellence,
freedom's brisk Vermont wind, yes.

Home Run Jubilee

Home Run Jubilee
Frankfort, Kentucky little league
July glory days,
Bastille French vino like Jesus
holy red blood,
Bob Feldman Quartet jazz sublime.

Home Run Jubilee
Heavy metal Ryan New York Yankee heart
Derek Jeter all star short-stop excellence,
middle of plate fast ball aluminum bat
crack,
lower east side tattoo holy New York University
cheshire hipsters.

Home Run Jubilee
Center field fence hard ball
rocket crescendo,
hot rod fans jackhammer like
Lexington Avenue high rise
union construction craft workers.

Home Run Jubilee
Bobby Murcer dies like sweet
pin-stripes Yankee Stadium angel,
hip sway mamas line Union Square like
antique Haitian dolls.
Summer rolls down Biloxi, Mississippi magnolia
green garden.

Home Run Jubilee
Classic Q radio Pink Floyd
"Dark Side of Moon" rock brilliance,
Prairie Fire poetry silk glide
Sunday night feature.
Green Magma vitamins,
red Winston carton,
late night switchblade righteous west coast howls.

SLOW RAMBLE

Home Run Jubilee
John Z's dreams 18 hole golf fandango,
Jeff body surfs Jones Beach
like salty dolphin.
Movie genius Elaine Minionis "Voice of Serenade"
moves towards mountain top Colorado film
festival.
Babies sleep in black fathers muscle arms,
strollers scoot down Varick Street
like one-horse buggies.
Home Run Jubilee always looking good!

Strawberry Happy

Strawberry Happy
Double dutch jump rope Harlem
July cool,
Richmond front veranda porch
pick-up sticks,
San Francisco Fisherman's Wharf deep soul kisses like
writer Richard Brautigan rainbow trout,
Hudson Valley Martin guitar pick.

Strawberry Happy
5 A.M. late night Seventh Avenue South
gypsy ramble,
Greenwich Village Tal Ronen
string bass crescendo,
Lincoln Center New York Philharmonic
mostly Mozart big daddy excellence.
Memphis Beale Street, cotton hand hold.

Strawberry Happy
Summer day camp yellow bus
5 P.M. dinnertime green garden return,
Tribeca money lofts like Rolex watches,
Tatersall family SUV Adirondack mountain
week-long vacation like log cabin
night breeze joy.
North Star holy pine tree constellations.

Strawberry Happy
C.W. Post sophomore
Jones Beach oil down lifeguard,
California dream like morning eucalyptus
tree fragrance, Santa Monica farmer's market magic
 avocados.
Blue grass howls, Roanoke, Virginia,
New Jessy firehouse all you can eat
spaghetti dinner.
Hopscotch Tennessee 4th graders,

schoolyard magic pick-up baseball delight.
Strawberry Happy
Mom and Dad still road trucking,
glory time Greatest Generation ethics,
God's cloverleaf heal,
Cincinnati south Ohio lazy lemonade
cumulus cloud afternoons,
full moon barbecue like John Kennedy
silver dollar, t-bone steak glory time eats.
Laid back prairie America cameo heart
poetics,
cheshire cat big tooth smile.
Strawberry Happy, dig it!

Creativity August 1st

Creativity August 1st
IBM typewriter locomotive
big wheel engine hum,
word on paper like Guttenberg Bible
cotton candy big tent Minnesota circus delight.

Creativity August 1st
Mom's stone sculpture magic marble
nudes like Renoir genius,
late night Yorkville catfish howls,
Williamsburg, Brooklyn
loft space artists like beatnik angels,
ruby red watermelon heart.

Creativity August 1st
Greenpoint paint palette
acrylic medium number 2 brush delicate
swerve.
Linda Schneider Grand Rapids, Michigan midwest
poetry eloquence.

Creativity August 1st
Austin, Texas Sixth Street pedal street
guitar country western long neck cool.
High wire computer multi-media
urban cat's meow,
Katherine's Manhattan dance silk grace,
eggs over easy apprenticeship.

Creativity August 1st
Jazz Mobile free bird jazz concerts,
James Jenning American Theater of Actors
Shakespeare supreme,
Hell's Kitchen denim muses,
Broadway Disney Lion King tourist
pack theater like small antique trinkets.
Interstate 40 Oklahoma red clay hills
mirage like Zen Buddhist whole grain vision.

Creativity August 1st
Tanglewood Boston Pops
George Gershwin cool breeze summer
quiche lorraine, California merlot wine.
New England state of Maine quilt blanket
sew in excellence.
Holy highway artistic Greenwich, Connecticut
tree arbor beauty,
Colorado Rocky Mountain cobalt blue
magic stream,
American bold 18 wheel semi long haul
poetic excellence,
Creativity August 1st, always.

Soy Bean Futures

I am Chicago commodities market soy bean
futures,
Lake Michigan lunch hour easy beat stroll,
Wrigley Field Cubs first place heroics.
Windy City broad shoulder straight whiskey shot.
Old Town hazy guitar pick.

I am Bowling Green, Kentucky Methodist church
heaven hold sermon,
Interstate 35 Madison, Wisconsin
magic highway bound.

I am Beale Street Memphis sweet midnight
kisses, blues fandago like
Delta John Lee Hooker genius.
No to cocaine weekend tattoo riffs.
No to Oyster Bay Tiffany Mercedes Benz
wife swap.
No to pot smoke mad dog poets.
Bring on America's common sense
liberty excellence.
Bring on small tykes Carl Shutz Park
playground sandbox joy.
Bring on New York State Troopers
sombrero hat rainbow integrity.

I am Golden Gate Park frisbee jubilee,
Buddhist temple meditation like
free wheel Charlie Mingus bass sanctity.
Gracie's Diner breakfast special
Mexican Billy's counter-man cool.
Rhinebeck, New York August rain squall
like Noah's Ark end of world cleanse.

I am God's rock steady sovereignty,
thousand midnight corduroy prayers.
Paul, Jeannie and Noah Sondheim's
downtown carrion grace,
Jewish sabbath candle light like
Virginia firefly.

SLOW RAMBLE

I am federal post office liberty forever
stamp, rent bill first of month bring
green cash pay-off,
four dollar a gallon gasoline stretch
family budget like Newark Star Ledger rubber band.
Atlantic coast big time drill,
bring crude oil home like Bible prodigal son.
I am Washington, D.C. Jefferson Memorial
tidal basin
Founding Fathers Constitution equality,
Brooklyn Cyclones double-play magic,
pecan pie Atlanta, Georgia southern Baptist faith,
  always!

XI
STRAWBERRY
HARMONY
2010

PETER CHELNIK - HEY GIRL - COLLECTED POEMS

Joy to the World

Joy to the World
Snickers bar hardscrabble glory train
bean stalk ethics like Compton,
California soup kitchen. Holy gang war peace
Greenwich Village poetry read delight.
Egg nog wildcat epiphany.

Joy to the World
God's rainbow covenant
Cabbage patch dolls
back closet memory,
George Washington High School
uptown basketball scrimmage.
Ludlow Street bourbon kisses.

Joy to the World
Tiffany ox engagement diamond,
Empire State Building midnight serenade.
Cats eye marble like Los Angeles
phone line psychic.
Bucks County wood burn furnace quiescence.

Joy to the World
Christmas day Jesus birth
Joseph and Mary desert manger, celestine star
magi wonder.
Heartland America Wal-Mart shop spree,
high tech iPods like
NASA shuttle gear genius.

Joy to the World
Green earth calico dawn like
side saddle Pony Express westward bound.
Kansas fallow field, bread basket
feed third world grace
Pentecostal morning prayers.
Alaska snow freeze Fairbanks ice fishing
salmon catch.
Mr. Ehrets concert choir excellence.

Joy to the World
Lentil soup rise and shine
lunch.
Leg of lamb sugarland faith like
Louisiana pecan pie.
Poetry's pine tree spirit, hot chestnut crimson delight
Nashville, Tennessee country music
slow waltz. All is well
Joy to the World, yes!

Winter Solstice

Winter Solstice
Nip and tuck short string afternoons,
5 p.m. tunnel dusk, New York City
December rain,
iced Swig barroom coffee chat,
County Derry Mark, young buck
broad laughs,
Marlboro Light street side cigarette smoke.

Winter Solstice
Navy blue pea coat bundle up
Thursday afternoon scurry home
like yellow school but Yorkville
school kids.
86th Street corner Christmas tree
outlaws, Cape May, New Jersey
wildcat three grant on highway
cash in pocket.

Winter Solstice
Minestrone soup, hot Tennessee biscuits,
upstate Hunter Mountain snow fall,
Judy Whitfield rock steady Woodstock
hipster back stream ice meditation,
Colony Club closed down, winter time hibernation.
Lovers snuggle like Alaska polar bears.
Memphis Beale Street easy beat hugs.

Winter Solstice
Chanukah lights wood mantel glow,
cinnamon hope Inauguration Day month off
like Chesapeake and Ohio Rail line,
vintage Volvo tune up.
Dradel renegade spin, dervish whirl joy,
cotton night dream wonder.
New Age licorice visions.

Winter Solstice
Devon John three year old electric train
fascination.
Metro north family Grand Central bound.
18 wheel semis New Orleans overland route.
Buttermilk pancake optimism 2008 close out,
God's primrose grace.
Robert Frost Ripton, Vermont stone fence,
velvet jubilee celebrate like
hot mince pie delight.

Winter Solstice
Dr. Peter's East 71st Street down home keep
it simple cure,
Jones Beach singular Atlantic beauty,
Beethoven sonata like
White Plains Jewish Community Center
patchwork faith, prayer book ethics.
Cobalt blue renaissance,
Winter Solstice yes!

Flannel Prayers

Flannel Prayers
God's sugar cane sanctity,
Handel's Messiah magic
like Union Pacific freight train,
Greenwich Village morning
touch sky vigil,
winter freeze iced box poetics.

Flannel Prayers
One dollar lettuce head corner 86th Street
big cat rialto,
tape measure barroom conversations,
prize fight afternoons
school teachers Budweiser huddle
Friday week-end like tape measure home run.

Flannel Prayers
Synagogue sidewinder grace,
eternal light cranberry sauce ethics
Hunter College semester finish.
Sally Milgrim rainbow retirement, American heroine.
New Rochelle chicken pot pie Saturday
night hi-jinks 1959.

Flannel Prayers
Rosary bead Jesus faith like
rock steady Saint Monica Catholic priest
Dan Isaac English Lit big cat
educate.
16 year old doorstep kisses, Rolling Stones desire.

Flannel prayers
2008 rag tag Manhattan hipsters,
Metro sexual pretty boys stove pie
denim jive,
cut squash Macintosh apple quiescence
Ice storm Pennsylvania to Maine
electricity dead pan out, kerosene lamps on overtime.

Flannel Prayers
Zen Buddhist incense meditation
downtown M15 bus late night carrion
ramble, brown bag Beatnik aesthetics
Episcopal church pew redemption
holy home-made brownies
Kwanza bring it home salvation,
night pillow flannel prayers always!

Candy Cane December Dawn

I am Candy Cane December Dawn
radiator up high like Nutcracker
elegant ballet dancers,
Plymouth Rock Miles Standish
stark winter death,
Manhattan icebox freeze.

I am Chicago O'Hare Airport 48 hour
flight back up, Christmas gift open like
Florida navel orange,
upstate New York dairy farm early
morning cattle milk,
New Orleans hot baguette, chicory
coffee.

I am Harley Davidson leather outlaw rider,
Hunter Mountain downhill ski delight,
Bette's Polish Masbeth midnight
mass,
fish communion
eastern European laughs.

I am Hannukah candle light burn
potato latkas, pot roast
small trinkets dradel Las Vegas wheel spin.
Kwanza African American proud faith like
Bob Marley rastafarian dreadlocks.

I am Brazilian Dora's Toyota Prius back
road scoot,
St. Louis soup kitchen ham
candied yams, string bean casserole.
Mormom Tabernacle Choir like
Salt Lake City angelic glow.

I am flannel shirt poetics,
WQXR Vivaldi like Jesus humble
down home birth. Mary and Joseph
wood manger holy grace.
Pointsetta plants ruby red flower delight.

I am new year table top promise,
iced coffee typewriter jag,
Scotch plaid blanket night sleep,
prayers like telephone line
black crows, velvet faith, dig it!

Sassafras New Year

Sassafras New Year
Brooklyn sidewinder
2009 leap frog notions like top notch poetics
honey bear hibernate slow motion
Manhattan freeze.
Divine Central Park boat house hot chocolate.

Sassafras New Year
January hide and seek jack frost alliteration.
Glamour girl retreads Madison Avenue huddle,
poets howl like San Francisco North Beach
angels 1961.
Medication vials line bathroom
shelf, like kewpie dolls. Hats and hooter FM radio
midnight hop scotch.
Marijuana rockabilly hipster haze.
Peppermint metaphors like north star quiescence.

Sassafras New Year
Morning New Testament bible read,
86th Street toothed smiles,
youth like Harlem junkies 1972,
Rockefeller Center Christmas tree
holy glory train celebration.
Cinnamon apple bake joy.

Sassafras New Year
Patchwork quilt eternal optimism.
blueberry smoothie morning start up
like Volvo turn key ignite.
Number 4 subway line Fulton Street
bound like hungry wildcat.

Sassafras New Year
59th Birthday end of month like corned beef
and cabbage Viande Diner Thursday chow down.
America's blessed prairie grace,
Hudson River New Jersey bound
rialto.
Teamster dock unload sweat grind excellence.

Sassafras New Year
Hiking boot, cotton layers, knit watchman's hat
cold Ohio stark breeze,
protect freedom like
Paul Revere midnight ride,
John Adams Massachusetts dignity.

Sassafras New Year
Eye on rainbow horizon
sky silver like steel kitchen
knife,
cheerful Jackson Heights greetings,
tandoori chicken nirvana
cotton sheet halcyon hope, dig it.

Thursday Morning Create

Thursday Morning Create
Sunshine like Coney Island ferris wheel
leap frog cool like
kaleidoscope poetic cadence
Navaho Indian peace pipe rialto.
Pow-wow indigo grace.

Thursday Morning Create
Reading glasses wide angel chain saw
alliteration,
Hebrew prayers along Mediterranean magic
beaches,
Thomas Edison cornerstone logic
grey sparrow January magic migration.

Thursday Morning Create
Fordham University radio new breed folk music,
Greyhound bus points west like thunder road
Bruce Springsteen music delight.
Hitch hike highway Key West quest
end of road like last cool be-bop
miracle poem.

Thursday Morning Create
Fish cakes pasta horizon eye
like U.S. Marine Afghanistan sniper,
cotton candy IBM typewriter
carbon ribbon jubilee,
baby boom generation laced boot aesthetics,
clean and sober iced coffee,
West Palm Beach rainbow vibration
Atlantic Ocean sea breeze.

Thursday Morning Create
Andrew Wyeth paint palette,
winter pigeons like glory train
patriots,
Snickers bar sweet optimism
J.S. Bach quarter tone prayers,
Brooklyn soup kitchen feed homeless
charity rialto.

Thursday Morning Create
Broad shoulder construction honchos,
hot tea danish, American
engineer genius,
clarity like cats eye marble, slide rule blueprint
high rise steam fitter can do.
Highway pine tree vibration,
New Orleans street car serendipity
thousand poems in fingertip hands, yes.

Flat Out Heart

I am flat out heart
Biloxi, Mississippi warm January
breeze,
hobby horse delight
Mom's painting passion like
banana cake jubilee.

I am Los Angeles 90 degree surf's up
heat spell,
Phoenix, Arizona five alarm chicken wings,
Mexico Cuervo Gold tequila shots
south Texas open sky pick-up truck
can-do,
friends holy red checkercloth rialto.

I am Melbourne, Florida senior citizens sketch class,
greatest generation Buick wisdom,
1930's depression memory cool
big band Benny Goodman swing excellence.

I am three quilt big apple six degree
sunshine caresses,
Jewish sabbath four thirty
candle light,
Israel's F-16 protect and defend
homeland,
Gaza Strip Arab hate yarn twist.

I am classy Charleston, South Carolina
shrimp dinner,
DeeAnne Gorman Dixie velvet jazz voice
moonshine mythic NASCAR
red neck Daytona 500, Dale Ernhardt
drive, speed demon.
Hot window ledge pecan pie.

I am corduroy emotion,
New Balance sneakers sugarland
howls,
romance like Virginia Beach
syncopated hold hands beach walk 1969.
Mobile, Alabama hot biscuits,
salt air Gulf breeze,
fried chicken cuisine like
Lincoln Town Car SUV.

I am fuzzy bear compassion,
Temple Shari Tefela righteous
soup kitchen,
rice and beans boogy down Bronx
compassion
the Lord's interstate Maryland route 95
southbound glory.
America's Founding Father's
goodness,
Liberty's ruby red
cash and carry quiescence,
love's rodeo soulmate, always!

Camomile Tea Tuesday Night

Camomile Tea Tuesday Night
Grace Slick Jefferson Airplane flat
out groove,
toddlers dream red roses
corduroy teddy bears.
America's economy staggers like
vodka drunk.

Camomile Tea Tuesday Night
Episcopal church pews full like
black jack deck,
aces wild.
Yesterday big apple blizzard
white lace wedding gown
school cancel like
February rent check.

Camomile Tea Tuesday Night
Swig barroom loud Irish howls,
Tribeca 4-star sushi,
Jeff skis Hunter Mountain like
silver wildcat,
Viande Diner waitress Bette
rock steady, dreams sweet Toronto
three honey bear kids with
fiance Sylvester.

Camomile Tea Tuesday Night
Joan Carney places acrylic paint
on glass like 21st century Georgia O'Keefe
Santa Fe holy mama lion fierce,
touch sky like western punk rock saint.

Camomile Tea Tuesday Night
Youth eros heart throb,
forty year Zen meditation,
Sunday clock moves hour forward
like humble south Jersey poet.
Wyoming cattle hand,
short order baby boom
sugarland dream.

Camomile Tea Tuesday Night
41 cents sunflower postage
stamp,
five dollar Abraham Lincoln
pocket fold, up-beat top spin, back yard snowball fight.
Winter's long down parka reach
Bangor, Maine to Lake Tahoe,
fire hearts bring it home
optimism like Founding Fathers
Declaration of Independence,
highway providence, southbound.
Ham on rye, mustard hope,
Camomile Tea Tuesday Night, yes!

Flannel Peace of Mind

I am flannel peace of mind,
Thursday night March slumber,
two comforter Manhattan jubilee.
High school junior milk shake
and burger date,
butterscotch late winter miracle
sun.

I am dawn holy prayers, cobble road
kick stone,
sirrus Woodstock smoke clouds,
hearts on fire like
Tennessee barn burn,
west side baby boom women holy sanctity,
yoga class bring it home delight.

I am Kama Sutra buy back
George Washington Bridge
New Jessy bound, car rent,
dreams like vinyl record stack
Manhattanville College fertile ground
seed plant 1972,
Northern Westchester Gods
holy ground, wait on spring
like pregnant honeybee mom.

I am Santa Barbara County magic
chablis, surf's up like Las Vegas aces wild,
Dr. Romano's high class soft hand
dental skill,
five dollar Third Avenue french
cologne,
Franciscan monks spirit compassion,
the Lord's paisley bible stewards.

I am cut red roses
Myrna's Kendal Miami sign of taurus
straight back neon common sense,
Aspen, Colorado powder ski wonderland.
Bedroom french kisses like
Brazil magic orchids.

I am Doro's Cobble Hill Brooklyn ethics
brother Marc's Suzuki motorcycle
upstate high speed tear up
back road like two fried eggs
side of crisp bacon.
Sabbath faith like denim plumber's pants.
Pennsylvania horizon. American dream, always!

Full Moon Women

Full Moon Women
Calico cheshire smiles,
Mississippi southern charm like
chocolate shake,
late winter marriage vows,
horizon love like antique
patchwork quilt,
computer graphic halcyon magic.

Full Moon Women
March carrion desire,
crabcake Baltimore harbor cake kisses,
brown bag Budweiser delight,
first miracle child on way
like crystaline stork.

Full Moon Women
head over heels romance,
love dove hand hold
like Romeo and Juliet back
seat Chevy smooch.
California dream love time,
sophomore high school first kiss,
Manhattan island cameo magic flesh.

Full Moon Women
Baby boom warrior ladies,
blonde hair cougars like
take charge Marine first lieutenant,
breast feed memory Nashville country twang, 1981.
Bring home bacon blue collar husband,
Cleveland Clinic Florida women surgeons
Australian Vicki's law supreme logic,
thousand night prayers corduroy family
mythic red white blue freedom country.

Full Moon Women
Soccer moms carpool rialto,
ballet lessons, math tutor
like young Albert Einstein
math frazzle.
Homework Cross Westchester Expressway
open highway.

Full Moon Women
Rent bill paid like clock work,
electricity magic Fox News Cable,
Sister Roberta and Jerry's 41 year
old stand together marriage.
America's holy land female poets late night
computer riffs,
cognitive clarity Austin Sixth Street
pedal steel guitarist excellence
Bonnie Raitt bring in home cool.

Full Moon Women
New York Liberty women basketball,
Madison Square Garden el supreme,
Smith College spring time dreams,
stand by man Sedona, Arizona New Age fandango,
midnight caresses equality's
honeybee rialto.
Full Moon Women dig it!

Sweet Sunshine

Sweet Sunshine
Greenwich Village late afternoon
sunlight golden glow,
painter's palette alive like
Colorado prairie fire,
Joanne Pagano Weber's
big apple art excellence.

Sweet Sunshine
Noon time Manhattan Crosby Street ramble
Union Square hipster hand out like
red robins,
Spring Equinox magic kaleidoscope
renaissance.

Sweet Sunshine
Heart beat on heart beat
cotton sheets twenty year
marriage rock steady rialto,
family like northern Vermont
stone cabin.

Sweet Sunshine
No DUI roadblock rain afternoon hassle.
No stock market rock and roll tumble.
No sub prime mortgage fracture.
Bring on holy Jesuit priests.
Bring on flannel poets,
rainbow craft like Indiana humble grace.
Bring on God's early morning dawn
calico prayers.

Sweet Sunshine
North Carolina spring break
60 degree salt air,
cameo grace, Mom's sculpture
hammer and chisel excellence,
Long Island City
artist loft open house.

Sweet Sunshine
Hobo Joe's Myrtle Beach groove
Manhattan bound like
Canadian geese spring return,
thousand pinewood stories,
59th bedrock birthday
always on American road.

Sweet Sunshine
Little Rock, Arkansas
afternoon light like hot fudge sundae,
grand piano rialto,
flower blouse jubilee,
spring glory time promise,
down parka shed like ripe artichoke.
Sweet Sunshine, yes!

Early Spring Celebrate

Early Spring Celebrate
Norman, Oklahoma ice storm
power out like cut clothes line
bone chill, Interstate 40 car wreck
dreams on hold like grade school boiler
break down.

Early Spring Celebrate
Spring rears head like yellow
Prospect Park forcythias,
grey holy sparrows, Virginia Beach
rainbow Tuesday afternoon down
home chocolate fudge glee.

Early Spring Celebrate
No to Wall Street insider trading.
No to get slick, job loss unemploy fracture.
No to identity theft computer swindle.
Yes to Founding Fathers fierce raw
bone individualism.
Yes to freight train capitalism
like Minneapolis small time bakery shop chain.
Yes to God's ethics like Moses
Mount Sinai lightening covenant.

Early Spring Celebrate
Valley Forge winter hibernate over
April dream, revolution's liberty victory,
like strawberry shortcake delight
Yorktown British fleet surrender.

Early Spring Celebrate
Juliette's African American's Ivy League bound
Dalton School senior thesis excellence.
Washington, D.C. freedom time
educate choice,
Saint Joseph's parochial school
text book memory,
study habits like Dutchess County
red brick monastery.

Early Spring Celebrate
Iced coffee paint palette Greenwich Village
Horatio Street afternoons,
stage coach aesthetics,
19th century Missouri Territories westward bound,
snow melt Fargo, North Dakota
Red River sand bag heroics.
Brooklyn College volunteers
fill empty food pantries like
cats eye marble bag collection.

Early Spring Celebrate
Ryan Pickering Rhinebeck two step
dream, sidewinder eros,
heavy metal Metallica buy back
easy beat.
Hundred calico notions,
Americas leather belt notch
down parka shed,
David Elsasser west side poetry
workshop jubilee.

Early Spring Celebrate
Gemini moon Atlantic Ocean joy,
Manhattan 10th Avenue easy breeze,
Woodstock deer herd food quest.
Winter over like five alarm buffalo wing chow down.
Fresh notions along Gulf Coast,
Florida panhandle cotton shirt warmth,
March basketball madness,
final four like clean stripe sheets,
hundred cherry pie dreams.
Early Spring Celebrate, always!

Saturday Morning Pancakes

I am Saturday Morning Pancakes
Butter melt hot righteous
Vermont syrup
April cool breeze like southern Ohio
wood barn hay stack.
Needle point optimism
Ford pick-up truck Michigan Saturday morning.

I am Adirondack trail bike
flannel shirt broad shoulders notions
Rand McNalley map highway rialto.
God's white light miracles
ridgeline morning coffee.

I am American heartland little league
mud practice,
wood bat excellence,
Dad's hand on uniform shoulder
eggs over easy wisdom.
Noah's high school curve
ball supreme, Yankee Opening Day
brand new stadium deluxe mythic beauty.

I am Thomas Jefferson
Declaration of Independence liberty
calico cat freedom.
Maple tree buds Central Park
cameo heart quiescence.
UNC Chapel Hill, North Carolina
mint julep southern morning.

I am hilltop atonement
Jewish Sabbath, red wine hold prayer
Rabbi like 50 year oak tree,
salt tears telephone love affair
over like schooner
life raft abandon.
Three-card monte rainbow hand hold.

I am rough and ready hombre
Albuquerque five alarm chili notions,
Saturday eros Carbondale, Illinois
green garden beauty
paprika hugs like hot apple pie
vanilla ice cream scoop.
Magic carpet east coast line.

I am Atlantic City turkish taffy
Mohawk Indian fire spirit
Cape May ocean salt quiescence
like gin rummy game,
self-reliance pick self up
thousand times, Pine Barrens straight back spirit,
on road like Jack Kerouac westward
holy jam, yes!

Prairie Love

Prairie Love
Kansas sunflower
down home jubilee,
ginger bread cottage, antique iron wood burn stove
hereford cows miracle
spring pasture fence in.
April morning halcyon kisses,
long skirt swirl, denim
Levi jacket.

Prairie Love
Youths upbeat strawberry promise
wishing well aesthetics,
typewriter rides like
Chervolet dreams,
Gods Sunday church go
hands together, prayers
sanctity like hot oven biscuits.

Prairie Love
Homestead desire like lake skiff
Midwest rock solid big sky values
April spring planting, oak grove beauty,
garden tulips rainbow bloom.
Caresses like honey bear hugs,
vinyl record collection
rare Rolling Stone Magazines.

Prairie Love
Constitutional midwest freedom
highway drag strip rialto,
pecan pie late evening
flesh on flesh
forever passion like 747 jet stream
California bound.

Prairie Love
Early spring thaw, sunlight
like antique prism,
needle point optimism,
man and woman together like
oil and vinegar tomato lettuce salad.
Hickory honest solitude,
National Public Radio
late night be-bop jazz.

Prairie Love
Red checker cloth kitchen coffee conversation.
Cameo faith, wedding band rock steady long haul
patchwork quilt evening warmth
brownies milk
America's infinite easy breeze eros
like corn field excellence,
holy cinnamon conversation
crescent moon magic delight, dig it!

Iced Green Tea Ecstacy

I am Iced Green Tea Ecstacy,
April noon time Columbia University
jazz radio,
New Jersey telephone redondo
Cynthia Toronto hip swing
good buddy friendship,
halfway home like
cross-country Greyhound bus.
Manhattan east bound Interstate 80.

I am Jewish Friday night prayers
miracle candle light,
Creators bullet train excellence
honey comb glory,
Washington, D.C. tidal basin
cherry blossom delight like
wet Atlantic Ocean kisses
Mamaroneck Harbor salt breeze
Rhodes 19 wood haul easy rhythm.

I am springtime grace like
apple pie cool milk
Polish waitress Bette gemini toothed
smile,
mud planting time northern California
eucalyptus delight,
new world like Haight Ashbury
hippie tribe rainbow optimism 1967.

I am mom and dad's back beat
common sense ethics,
Lexus fender bender repair,
127th Street Continental Auto
Body Shop excellence,
Passover seder like down home hoe down
brother Marc's Brooklyn fire always.

I am Palm Springs afternoon dry heat,
ceiling fans like Swiss clocks, oversized rubber bands,
midtown Manhattan Saint Patrick's Cathedral
Cardinal Dohlen
pine tree midwest good vibrations.
Atlantic breeze like chocolate
iced cream cone,
Hope's flannel 59 year quiescence, yes!

Feeling Good

Feeling Good
Paisley somersault spiritual practice
afternoon late April rain like lady's
alabaster skin
tea ceremony Manhattanville College
dorm, Moira's cherry pie
vibration 1972.

Feeling Good
Fourth grade long division
Chattanooga Interstate southbound
18 wheel semi freedom roll.
Vanilla soy milk
denim renegade typewriter ride,
Bud Lite slow motion kick back heels
Golden Gate Park robin red breast, jubilee.
Rock solid hoola-hoop metaphors.

Feeling Good
Rainbow optimism like
Mikey Mineloa Long Island Toyota scoot.
Key ring jangle like silver wind chimes
ice coffee ridgeline rialto, gun power grey horizon
God's singular Biloxi, Mississippi wonder.
Lionel Hampton sweet vibrophone birthday.

Feeling Good
Umbrella kisses, 4 PM America's
exceptionalism, climb granite mountain
Oregon Mountain trail blaze, lace hike boots.
Exxon gasoline fill up,
Omaha, Nebraska west bound holy prairie rialto.
Volvo kitten hum solitude,
Charles Mingus acoustic bass supreme.
Evening prayers, U.S. Navy Seals
rough and ready Somali pirates mission accomplished.
Acrylic on canvas Stockbridge artists.

Feeling Good
upstate New York tulip bloom,
kick can down country road
thousand Earth Day hossanahs
work shirt dream like maple
tree bloom,
Jones Beach easy breeze spring delight,
whipped cream hot chocolate, golden honeycomb
  kisses,
Feeling Good, always!

May Wonderland

May Wonderland
Yellow tulip metaphor serenity
Jesus' antique tea cup redemption
patchwork quilt poetics like
baby boom lower Broadway Birkenstock
shuffle,
love bead joy,
Zen meditation Brooklyn morning quiescence.

May Wonderland
Green Georgia pastures,
southern ladies easy beat honey suckle
delight like cool iced mint tea.
59 year old on road fandango
Interstate 40 Amarillo, Texas panhandle
morning country radio pedal steel guitar.

May Wonderland
Fern Filner's San Francisco drum circle magic,
sunshine Thursday afternoon
like patchouli oil caresses,
Tai Chi yoga earth bound rhythm,
firm yoga pad, sandalwood incense
Vermont body excellence,
balance like Spring Equinox raw egg.

May Wonderland
Shoulder to shoulder
poetry tutorial Carolyn Stoloff
8th Street Greenwich Village hard drive.
Youths eternal, optimism
like big dipper, north star
Woodstock maple tree beauty,
Love's Converse sneaker crescendo.

May Wonderland
Brooks Brothers bow tie shake and bake, spiff up
like Fifth Avenue fat cat,
steamers broiled lobster, hot date.
Cowboy aesthetics, six shooter like
Lips Magazine poem publish,
evening pillow top prayers
faiths apple pie, eight cylinder Chevy truck power,
May Wonderland, dig it!

Strawberry Harmony

Strawberry Harmony
Catalina Island soft shoe
Santa Ana breeze,
skateboard hydroglyphics,
Amazing Grace Episcopal church pew
holy stain glass morning light.
Nancy Brandt's actor's excellence
radical Living Theater quicksilver
fantasia.

Strawberry Harmony
Cellist Jay Shulman's upstate Claverack
garden plant,
three hundred thousand mile Volkswagen Jetta
still humming,
Sunday faith like Vermont maple
syrup pour,
72 degree cumulus cloud Harrison, New York
Mom and Dad down home American common sense.

Strawberry Harmony
Myrna's Miami Christian grace,
heart like green Iowa corn.
Interstate 80 Denver bound
subterranean sleep layover,
God's Jewish synagogue Torah scroll.
Spring bloom like Jesus
lilac bloom sacrifice.

Strawberry Harmony
Stock Market up swing
Colorado camp fire smoke,
Rocky Mountain summit,
recession end like Sixth Avenue water pipe break
  repair.
American dream alive like
Greatest Generation suburban
tract house glory train.
Top notch cotton sleeve kids public education.
Patriots lock and load stand fast.

Strawberry Harmony
Classic Q rock and roll late night
instant decaf jubilee,
Big Apple quiet like computer unplug,
windless West 79th Street boat basin river mooring,
purple dawn salvation, dreams like Mr. Softee ice cream
optimism like South Carolina
needle point quiescence.
Enterpreneur's red clay hard drive
create jobs like neighborhood pigeons.
Strawberry Harmony, yes!

Home Run Crack

Home Run Crack
New York Mets David Wright
left field bases loaded fence clear
hoe run, hot dog jubilee,
grade school green grass Citi Field
wonder,
America's century old magic past time.

Home Run Crack
Noah's little league pitch excellence,
Central Park May strike out magic fastball.
Double play bring it home,
A-1 oil baseball mitt,
aluminum bat like New York Philharmonic
conductors baton.

Home Run Crack
Summer right field dreams,
Varick Street nephew Charlie
Saturday afternoon rite of cotton
uniform passage.
Moms dads wood stands cool out
like salt and pepper shaker kitchen
table aesthetics.

Home Run Crack
Short stop fielding error. Manager forgives
like street corner cop.
runs batted in Little League clean up batter
Williamsport, Pennsylvania World Series.
Curve ball cottonwood back yard
whiffle ball Dad's 20th Century
bond,
White House T-Ball supreme like
first grade read skills.

Home Run Crack
Columbia University Lions
Ivy League come back baby
break even season,
Atlantic sea breeze Baker Field weave
glory days like New York Yankees
Mickey Mantle homer,
generation's rainbow memory, yes!

Always Upbeat

Always Upbeat
St. Louis cartwheel Budweiser
poets,
America blessed like Six Flags
ferris wheel.
Touch sun vibration,
Number 30 tan block,
Santa Monica Beach surf's up salvation.

Always Upbeat
Humboldt County metaphor
jubilee,
Lake Erie trim sail faith,
thousand 2009 honey bee salvations.
Vermont peppermint kisses.

Always Upbeat
Springfield, Missouri home school kids,
cherry pie excellence,
youth like ginger bread long way home,
16 year old Scarsdale High School
driver's permit,
McDonald's big mac burger run,
Shakespeare kaleidoscope genius,
bring home Hamlet like southbound
18 wheel Kenworth semi.

Always Upbeat
Late night Grateful Dead riffs,
cross country spring time June hoots,
garden plant like Brooklyn green thumb
renaissance.
Magnolia born again Christians,
Taconic Parkway Chatham, New York
bound,
Madison, Wisconsin State Street cool ramble.
Yes to liberty's denim wide arm embrace.

Always Upbeat
David Elsasser, Su Polo magic Saturn
poetry read,
Ford Mustang excellence like Sony
wide screen television,
Zen meditation, sandalwood incense burn
smiles like Little League coach
cobalt blue affirmation,
flannel Carbondale, Illinois deep laughs.

Always Upbeat
Granola hope, half shell clams
like rare 47th Street diamonds
Lotto pick six winners,
U.S. Marines Semper Fi leatherneck
heroes,
keep peace like county sheriff.
Mamaroneck High School young buck grace,
cotton sheet morning wake up alarm clock.
Always Upbeat, yes!

Kaleidoscope Wonder

Kaleidoscope Wonder
Nebraska prairie half moon delight,
dreams like Steely Dan lyric brilliance
Walt Whitman metaphor green arboretum
excellence.
Love's senior history class eros.
Big Apple Circus trapeze skill.

Kaleidoscope Wonder
God's miracle providence
Interstate 80 Chicago bound,
windy city Old Town folk guitar
quiescence.
Hyde Park tree lined tudor homes
flapjacks bacon breakfast supreme.
July fourth East River fire works gotham excite.

Kaleidescope Wonder
Poetry Slam Bowery Poetry Club
get down, rock and roll language riffs,
Houston Street 1 A.M. scuffle home.
Bob Feldman tenor saxophone cool brother,
always hip sideman
Allen Ginsberg, beat deluxe
Jack Micheline.
Rye Playland kewpie doll know down grand prize,
Nancy's Episcopal Trinity Church communion affirmation.

Kaleidoscope Wonder
Savannah, Georgia sunrise like red ruby,
southern easy beat
eggs and butter grits
hedonism half shell
bronze flesh candy cane youth.
Antique wedding band patchouli dreams.

Kaleidoscope Wonder
Massachusetts Shaker Village,
oak tree discipline,
John Deer field plow,
Richmond, Virginia Tuesday afternoon
kisses,
Jesus' pinewood grace,
Lenox Hill Hospital emergency room salvation
yellow taxi FDR Drive Bangladesh
cool blue wisdom.

Kaleidoscope Wonder
Mozart tears, Tribeca Hudson River heartbreak
like cats eye marble, mamba snake.
Pick self off hard sidewalk
again and again.
Cherry pie freedom awe,
glory train Greenwich Village howls
notions like strawberry shortcake,
Kaleidoscope Wonder dig it!

Wednesday Morning Sunshine

Wednesday Morning Sunshine
Whole wheat pancakes rialto
butter melt maple syrup serenade.
Sperry top sider dry out
rain gone like FDR Drive traffic snarl,
God's ice coffee blessing.

Wednesday Morning Sunshine
Chicago Grant Park miracle green loop
Tylenol bottle pills,
pick pocket grace,
Manhattan number 6 subway line Fulton
Street bound.

Wednesday Morning Sunshine
Blue work shirt jubilee,
Intrepid Hudson River museum
U.S. Navy World War Two
liberty quest,
10th Avenue homeless panhandle
glory train Manhattan
June dawn like pink bouquet.

Wednesday Morning Sunshine
Flag Day red white blue shiny
city on hill American heroics,
Amanda's salutorian eighth grade
gifted children hard grind,
Washington Heights rainbow genius,
Stuyvesant High School bound
like Joseph Brodsky
Moscow Pulitzer Prize glory crystal poem.

Wednesday Morning Sunshine
No to 9.4 unemployment rate voo doo.
No to capitalism musket assault.
No to Williamsburg, Brooklyn morning
heroin jones.
Bring on God's tortoise shell prayers.
Bring on entrepreneurs
twelve hour days expand business
like back yard Connecticut garden.
Bring on poetry pinewood craft.

Wednesday Morning Sunshine
New Jersey tulip bulb plant,
garden work gloves,
tomato vine joy like
California late night phone calls,
peppermint beginnings, always!

Midnight Sidewalk Grace

Midnight Sidewalk Grace
Lamp post crescendo Second Avenue
crystalline air,
God's solitude like
crescent moon Hebrew letters,
carnival slow saunter.

Midnight Sidewalk Grace
Wednesday night Jaimison Whiskey fracture
cheeseburger Viande Diner like
Athens, Greece back street
heart open chakra.
Lazy south Georgia Swanee River
poems like yellow taxi scoot.
Thousand paisley questions.

Midnight Sidewalk Grace
Stiletto heels New York University girls
wolf packs like Marxist Collective,
ragtime homeless cigarette
panhandle,
Gotham macadam crack hard times.

Midnight Sidewalk Grace
Bronx hard muscle tattoo boys,
magazine shack ice blue Orbit gum.
Zig Zag roll paper redondo, glass hashish pipes
chicken and lentil Bombay, India
late night dinner
Newsweek Magazine Obama White House
hard drive.

Midnight Sidewalk Grace
M-15 downtown bus, 45 year old grey Navy veteran
bottle blonds wait on wire bench
like Zen Buddhist monks.
John Z, WFAN Radio sports
allegro, dreams fantasy
baseball computer trade,
mussels marinara,
wild west Big Apple streets late 1970's.

Midnight Sidewalk Grace
Poetry craft ike magic turquoise muse
Summer Solstice 1:45 stealth bomber season change
Vagrants double dutch Fifth Avenue
bench carrion dream,
NYPD keep peace 86th Street slow
motion hero cruise,
northwest wind quiet God's oneness,
Midnight Sidewalk Grace, yes!

Friday Night Straight and Narrow

Friday Night Straight and Narrow
Twelve midnight rag-tag curfew,
high school juniors stay at
gingerbread home, public television watch
mythic monopoly game,
gin rummy righteous delight.
Home made apple pie
telephone call romance.

Friday Night Straight and Narrow
Canvas stretch downtown Greenpoint
Brooklyn quintessential create.
Dahlia Lite FM soft pop love songs
clean cut denim dreams,
prepare Saturday morning soccer game,
help little brother math lexicon,
late June abstinence, morals.

Friday Night Straight and Narrow
No to backwoods Budweiser,
Absolut Vodka bottle wildcat weekend escape.
No to marijuana destroy mind fracture.
No to cobra sexing it up.
Yes to pinewood morals like
Tracy's elegant William and Mary College
straight back book crack.
Yes to hour long first date film discussion.
Yes to cheeseburger carrion sobriety.
Yes to Jane N's George Washington U April afternoon
touch D.C. sky, friendship.

Friday Night Straight and Narrow
High grass Purchase, New York
aesthetic explore,
Melissa P's photography pearl string,
tweed jacket quest,
Oregon dreams like poets red tulip
devotion,
Vermont big dipper miracle
Mike and Ann Cefola's telescope gaze.

Friday Night Straight and Narrow
Red Volkswagen innocence,
Cape Code lobster feast bound.
Inspiration like dollar in twelve step
kitty, the Lord's heal.
Christine's Virginia Beach hand hold,
blonde hair low tide rialto.

Friday Night Straight and Narrow
No to Scarsdale Open House parties
mad dog drunks, morning shotgun hangover.
No to frat boys blue room sexual
revolution neck and pet.
No to hit and run flat tire love.

Friday Night Straight and Narrow
Holy white lace marriage vows like
monarch butterfly Isleboro, Maine cameo heart
meadow,
flannel shirt fidelity crystalline values
Friday Night Straight and Narrow, always!

Kentucky Yarn Cats Cradle

I am Kentucky Yarn Cats Cradle,
July morning prayers like
Mississippi River grace,
God's Wyoming fresh air quiescence,
niece Amy's 36th year ring a levio
birthday.

I am cobalt blue sky redemption
Madison, Wisconsin State Street down
home midwest smiles,
Lexington Avenue midnight garbage hauler
ballet grace,
Patricia's sassy
poetics like Bloomingdale's
Memorial Day Weekend sale.

I am Ernest Hemingway grace under
pressure,
Paris, France writers craft.
Teenage skateboard holy fandango,
black dudes dread lock bring
it home.
St. Albans Queens Rasta cool out.

I am toddlers first cheshire cat steps,
Gerber's baby food carrots,
apple sauce delight,
mozart's summer afternoon
holy jubilee.
Bob Feldman tenor saxophone
Lisle Ellis acoustic bass
be-bop excellence.

I am Santa Cruz, California whole
grain cow down,
surf's up Half Moon Bay
sunset delight,
Nightingale 13th Street
Poetry groove,
classy like Canal Street
engagement band.

I am door women Carmen's Bronx street wise
savvy, redemption like
number four train Yankee Stadium bound
Afternoon rain Sally Milgrim telephone calls
fire lady
quicksilver taxi mama.
July fourth rib eye barbeque,
Independence Day sanctity,
Lexington and Concord
Boston Tea Party rebel.

I am God's home made apple pie grace,
straight shooter justice,
NYPD keep Gotham peace,
mid-summer's noble midnight hellos.
Tony and Ecuadorian John Gracie
diner late night overnight cool.
Mr. Mohammed's curry and rice, on sly Johnny
　Walker Red
Bronx Islamic self discipline,
12 hour magazine hard work shift,
new moon beginnings, dig it.

August Joy

August Joy
Linda Schneider's Grand Rapids, Michigan
apple orchard grace,
red magic cardinals like
firebrand poets,
God's rainbow sugarland salvation
back corner Columbus, Ohio French
kisses.

August Joy
Midnight halcyon prayers,
Yellowstone National Park
Old Faithful like
U.S. Constitution,
Philadelphia rock steady
Liberty Bell
summer Manhattan jobs, cash
in pocket, new Levi's plaid work shirts,
six inch stiletto heels.

August Joy
Friday afternoon Yorkville
cumulus clouds, Scott's bartender
cool bop Cuervo Gold touch sky.
Holy spirit South Carolina
Charleston Harbor cool breeze,
Wall Street Journal like eggs over easy
bacon home fries.
Jesus' judgment day promised land rialto.

August Joy
83 degrees low humidity
Long Beach Joan Deitrich
subway big apple day trip adventure.
Second Avenue senior citizens
quiet smiles,
Vietnam Vets low rider Marlboro smoke
Zen Buddhist wind chimes like
Beethoven sonata,
America's blessed Montana big sky
wonder.

August Joy
Spencer's Duke University freshman
bound desire, clean cut college kids
starched shirt khaki play it cool.
Muslim holy mosque evening prayers
like Baghdad freedom train slow motion
peace of mind,
Scarsdale Library summer grade school
kids reading passion.
Cotton sleeve clairvoyant librarian.

August Joy
Pre-season football workout like
fudge sundae hand hold first date.
New Age cinnamon candle
crystal devotion.
San Diego Harbor sail boat regatta,
down home strawberry vibrations,
August Joy, yes!

Red Rose Poetics

Red Rose Poetics
Pistil stamen metaphor
fandango,
wood trellis like
New York Times crossword puzzle,
internet poem publish
big sky Idaho cumulus cloud e-mal.

Red Rose Poetics
IBM maple syrup Sunday afternoon
carbon ribbon ride,
Sequoia National Park
Redwood brilliance.
Holy microphone stand hi-jinx,
cameo heart fire sidewinder performance.

Red Rose Poetics
Rosary bead Saint Monica's Church
Sunday mass,
Moira O'Gray's Chatham, New York
green garden grace.
Taconic Parkway night time scoot.
Green valley similes like word
economy, cool daddy Exxon gasoline
fill up.

Red Rose Poetics
God's rose petal beatnik jazz
Mission Distinct San Francisco
Thursday evening finger snap
howls,
Christine Graf's fourth floor
Manhattan long stem green rose
workshops,
tooth smile easy does it
critique like calico cat
morning milk breakfast.

Red Rose Poetics
Boston book publish bull eyes
dart toss,
Pennsylvania Poconos
fresh air like peppermint
candy canes,
high top Converse sneaker
Union Square slow float,
journal pad Starbucks cafe
latte lower Broadway revelation.

Red Rose Poetics
Ezra Pound hard apple core poetics,
bring it home,
concrete images like Vancouver, Canada
tattoo youth,
Snicker bar faith,
Ford Explorer Interstate 95
Savannah bound, Baby Boom highway butterscotch
   dream 1969
Red Rose Poetics, always!

Green Valley Harmony

Green Valley Harmony
Queen Anne lace miracle delight,
pine cones like Christmas ornaments,
the Lord's bee hive super nova grace,
late August varieties of sunlight,
touch sky like rock and roll angels.

Green Valley Harmony
Camp fire ember light,
lovers like cool blue trout
stream, currents.
Knapsack ball park hot dogs,
cool Budweisers,
amber garden dreams.

Green Valley Harmony
Catskill Mountain denim jeans
vibrations,
tabby cat content,
purple ridgeline groove,
workboots toss aside,
mountain woman long skirt hike up
like yellow corn husk.
Love's cherry pie bond.

Green Valley Harmony
No to muscle car city smog.
No to pot smoke aesthetic brain warp.
No to welfare check empty pockets
10 per cent unemployment.
Yes to San Antonio, Texas library card.
Yes to Henry David Thoreau
Walden Pond wilderness beauty.
Yes to rainbow halcyon aesthetics.

Green Valley Harmony
Sandalwood incense pine tree
groove,
Catholic prayers like rosary bead
maple tree beauty,
apple pick Fishkill, New York
Gala apple down home crunch.

Green Valley Harmony
Red blood boysenberry pine tree trim,
flesh on flesh like honey bear eros,
righteous peace of mind,
Saturday afternoon denim delight, yes.

Found Penny Good Luck

I am Found Penny Good Luck
Heaps up like Aqueduct Raceway
long shot,
Financial Center hot dog stand like
U.S. Army chow line
grade school principal Jackson Hole, Wyoming
crystalline air.

I am Found Penny Good Luck
Second grader Davis School fresh shoes
first day. American holy map,
clean chalk board like
New Hampshire beaver dam,
day dream window crescendo
mathematics cool easy flow.

I am Found Penny Good Luck
Mo's Lotto scratch off
like big apple Catholic litany,
West Berlin love letter 1978
pine tree prayers
Adirondack Mountains temperature drop,
canvas stretch like Asbury Park
salt water taffy.

I am Found Penny Good Luck
Conestoga wagon westward quest,
Winchester rifle like Stephen Foster banjo,
Nebraska red clay dust.
1849 strike it rich gold rush,
holy nugget jubilee,
love's joy Jesus wagon wheel faith.

I am Found Penny Good Luck
Family bridge game three spades bid,
pool hall hustle like leather chick
highway ramble,
bootleg New Orleans French Quarter poetry,
clean and sober late night Yorkville
kisses,
Fillmore East Alice in Chains
rock and roll excellence.

I am Found Penny Good Luck
Guggenheim Museum Frank Lloyd Wright
architect brilliance
Cub Scout campfire grace like angels soul
morning September corn flake breakfast
crossing guard ballet grace, always!

Word Harvest

Word Harvest
Vermont gold tree leaf redondo,
tomato garden like Spaudling
rubber balls,
chapbook Hoboken, New Jersey excellence,
singular rainbow expression,
beatnik howls Carmine Street
string bass daddy-o cool,
cut cherry pie.

Word Harvest
Yes to Indiana corn field
September beauty,
Baptist Sunday morning knit sweater prayers.
Highway ethics like Connecticut
hill roll metaphors,
thousand prize fight come-backs.
Metal rake, long wood handle hoe.

Word Harvest
Austin, Texas poetry read jam,
tumbleweed guitar pick,
white hat cowboy cadence,
wild west fire hearts,
God's break neck grace.

Word Harvest
Self-reliance like eagle scout,
Capital Hill blue steel
Republican Democrat 21st century rumble,
George Washington American glory train.

Word Harvest
Bring on freedom corduroy similes.
Bring on Manhattan subway underground
Daily News gestalt.
Bring on vinyl record Greenwich Village
bourbon shot buy-back,
Small's Cafe miracle jazz poetics.
Bring on canvas cover hands work gloves.

Word Harvest
Miami's Kendal section hispanic
cool down,
Cuban espresso morning breakfast delight,
Laura Voogles August poetry slam
new breed language rialto,
rice and beans Atlantic Ocean
magic sea breeze quatrain.

Word Harvest
Key West end of world sunset
like red Georgia O'Keefe flower,
William Carlos Williams red
wheelbarrow poetry excellence,
new age cameo heart,
patchouli oil beach jubilee,
oatmeal optimism
word processor palm tree glee,
Word Harvest, always!

New Jerusalem Love

New Jerusalem Love
Catskill Mountain late September
fire leaves,
North Caldwell, New Jersey
deer pack,
Greek Jimmy's Viande Diner
river run Second Avenue work place equality.
75 degree lazy day Monday calico
afternoon.

New Jerusalem Love
Three holy hour e-mail
hunt and peck computer excellence,
Chesapeake Bay sail regatta beauty
Annapolis, Maryland Christian Radio
midnight nightwatch.
Autumn equinox libra sun chill out
holy American promised land rialto.

New Jerusalem Love
Lexington, Kentucky 35 year
rock steady marriage.
Hot oatmeal mornings like
Deborah's garden kale harvest,
maple tree poetics,
Sara Liebling New Hampshire
chestnut brown hair
Disney World Publishing can do.

New Jerusalem Love
William Blake honeycomb angels,
wildcat revelation,
marriage for keeps Appalachian Trail
mystic wonder,
Bear Mountain tent pitch like
harvest home warmth.

New Jerusalem Love
French kisses, early morning
snuggle, pajama leg twine,
flower Vermont breasts,
wood burn campfire quiescence.
Camomile tea greet day
like Johnny Appleseed delight.

New Jerusalem Love
Yellow daisy eros,
God's pinewood ethics like
Jewish sabbath prayer,
synagogue Friday night
candle light,
table talk cherry pies,
cool evening milk delight,
early October fire hearts,
Atlantic sea breeze heal, dig it!

Ten Commandment Rock Steady

Ten Commandment Rock Steady
Judeo Christian Mahabe Desert
west bound dusk heal,
God's Plymouth Rock America discover
like Jonathan Edwards Sunday sermon,
Barre, Vermont granite quarry blue
collar union mine excellence.

God's Mount Sinai Moses
Stone tablets bread loaf,
Thou shalt not kill, steal or
covet. Honor thy parent always.
Henry Hudson 400 year
Hudson River discover, Lord New York harbor covenant
ethics like Pennsylvania Amish
wood carriage,
September hot biscuit simplicity.

No to cardboard crumble atheist.
No to call girl heart fracture
like Bedford Hills Women's
Correctional Facility.
No to crack ladies eight ball trick.
No to domestic violence Bronx, New York
knife wield.
No to black and blue evil delirium.

Ten Commandment Rock Steady
William Blake angels, San Diego grace,
Saint Joseph's Church incense
like teen age Sunday school morals,
college bound halcyon dream.

No to gold calf false idol turn back.
No to Saturday midnight one evening
hit and run sex.
No to maple syrup lies like left over
diner pancakes.
Bring on autumn equinox holy faith.
Bring on early morning New York Times.
Bring on denim straight back prayers.

Yorkville infant pinewood cradle
Scotch plaid blanket serendipity,
Mount Rushmore patriots
mountain top jack hammer craft,
Larchmont, New York Manor Park
gazebo moss rock 18 year old freedom dream.
Ten Commandment Rock Steady, yes!

Wilderness Faith

I am Wilderness Faith
Red October maple leaf wonder,
East River Wednesday morning
cumulus cloud jubilee like
fluff white marshmallows.
Wall Street 200 point Dow Jones
racquet ball rebound,
Merrill Lynch Dora investments
like Fort Know gold bullion.

I am Wilderness Faith
Camden, Maine
transcendental harbor
easy beat,
Shaker Village wooden furniture
magic like eight year old's Legos,
midnight aries full moon Manhattan
rain,
pillow cotton dream like
West Virginia hammer dulcimer,
hot corn bread morning breakfast.

I am Wilderness Faith
Bob Feldman Jazz Band Lutheran Church
Sunday delight,
Hells Kitchen bop, flannel shirt
red plaid hope, New York Post atonement
Plymouth Rock born again holy spirit,
lace work boot Central Park soul hike.
Metropolitan Museum rooftop
magic cafe,
orange leaf autumn beauty like
Matisse paint joy.

I am Wilderness Faith
Dave Brinks New Orleans
white beans and rice,
red wine bring it home poetry read.
Big Muddy Delta quiescence,
Dixieland jazz rainbow cool,
Baptist wood pew prayers
Joy to the World hymn sing,
gospel Lafayette, Louisiana
repentance.
I am Wilderness Faith always!

Apple Pick Jubilee

Apple Pick Jubilee
Rhinebeck orchard October
blue sky grace,
Macintosh holy Lake George
Montreal cool breeze canoe camp out.
God's Mohawk Indian papoose small
tyke breast feed.

Apple Pick Jubilee
Washington, D.C. Thomas Jefferson
patriots California wine afternoon
dream,
Tennessee electric power lines,
John Mayall British blues excellence 1970
hot cream of wheat breakfast morning begin.
Dad's honeycomb business ethics,
Mom's hammer and chisel sculpture
artist inspiration.

Apple Pick Jubilee
Belfast Terry bartender arm tattoo
easy Jaimison pour,
New York Yankee Alex Rodriguez
third base sublime talent,
playoff games like pork chop,
baked potato, apple sauce
Monday night checkercloth family dinner.

Apple Pick Jubilee
Corduroy love like Chevrolet truck
Des Moines, Iowa city limits
drag race.
Rock Hill, South Carolina catfish dinner,
Budweiser red neck dream.
Two comforter Manhattan digital glow
late nights like lap top highway genius
Charles Bukowski Los Angeles create
typewriter paper excite.
Bushel wood basket magic.

Apple Pick Jubilee
Rainbow love, flesh on flesh
Ivory soap shower rub down,
God's marriage vows like ten commandment covenant,
New York Mayors debate like meatball spaghetti chow down
Channel One local hijinks
freedom's corn flake Emily Dickinson
Amherst, Massachusetts autumn joy,
thousand wood fence Greenwich, Connecticut dreams
blueberry smoothie.
Apple Pick Jubilee, always!

October Sky Create

October Sky Create
East River NYPD boat anchor,
cumulus clouds like puff oats cereal,
lambskin dreams like fifth grader
ten p.m. easy beat,
lanyard notions Illinois hillside
Coors Light delight.

October Sky Create
Albuquerque hot air balloon magic
festival,
chess piece computer advance,
spiral notebook journal like
Massachusetts birch tree revelation
Puritan new world morals
Ten Commandment God's holy law.

October Sky Create
Brattleboro, Vermont fire leaves
transform like Zen meditation retreat
cameo hearts cheshire love
like Join Mitchell
rose trellis, 1970.
Lower forty metaphor
pine cabin American basic faith.

October Sky Create
Beethoven sonata WQXR New York
classical music jubilee,
New Mexico concrete poetry image highway
90 miles an hour outback speedway,
Zen Buddhist morning wind chimes,
Oklahoma City grace
glory train sandalwood incense, Laura Boss
  editor's excellence.

October Sky Create
Bob Dylan touch Santa Monica Beach
sky, merlot wine sanctity,
rainbow similes, cadence like
Jack Micheline San Francisco
Fisherman's Wharf be-bop glow
denim coat button sew,
Boy Scout merit badge heartland
achievement.

October Sky Create
Denver, Colorado city limits
Ian Sarsfield barroom hoots,
light up like Gregory Corso Kettle of Fish
Cuervo Gold shots,
IBM typewriter like sister Roberta's
charm bracelet gold jangle,
teenage shoot crescent moon, Mustang convertible
back roads Westchester Count joy.
Word on paper quiescence.
October Sky Create, dig it!

Pumpkin Pie Notions

I am Pumpkin Pie Notions
Tennessee white lightning
silk smooth October Athens, Georgia
carrion afternoon
Amtrack quick shot southbound
chevron flight, rainbow moist kisses
Allman Brothers laid back riffs like
hot fudge sundae.
Haystack Bible revelation.

I am Baton Rouge, Louisiana State
University homecoming,
jambalaya, fried chicken delight
cayenne pepper poetics,
black gospel Pentecostal choir
always bring it home hallelujahs.
holy sugar harvest.

I am Texas panhandle ribeye steak
Interstate 40 New Mexico bound
red Volvo incandescence,
free range metaphors like barn yard
calf birthing,
wild mustang plains jubilee
cowboy big sky aesthetics.

I am Salt Lake City Mormon
clean cut ramble,
Logan mountainside holy revelation
like westward dream
Reno, Nevada Golden Nugget
gamble quest, neon 24 hour
silver dollar buy-back lust,
black jack pay off like
Lake Tahoe pine tree delight.

I am Haight Ashbury San Francisco
beat poet renaissance,
Lawrence Ferlinghetti City Lights
Book Store gold literary nugget,
jazz joint Miles Davis cool bop
Blackhawk Cafe 1956
Allen Ginsberg Howl revolution
highway American easy glide
October Pumpkin Pie Notions yes!

www.ingramcontent.com/pod-product-compliance
Lightning Source LLC
Chambersburg PA
CBHW050241170426
43202CB00015B/2868